RAMAH AT 60

RAMAH AT 60

Impact and Innovation

רָמָה בַּת שִׁשִּׁים הַשְׁפָּעָה וְחַדְשָׁנוּת

Edited by

MITCHELL COHEN

and

JEFFREY S. KRESS

NATIONAL RAMAH COMMISSION, INC.

OF THE JEWISH THEOLOGICAL SEMINARY

COVER PHOTOS: *Top left,* Camp Ramah in California, circa 1955.
Bottom, Camp Ramah in Wisconsin, 2007.

BOOK AND COVER DESIGN BY JONATHAN KREMER

COMPOSITION BY MILES B. COHEN

PRINTING AND BINDING IN THE UNITED STATES OF AMERICA BY G&H SOHO, INC.

ISBN-13: 978-0-87334-150-9

Contents

Impact: Ramah in the Lives of Campers, Staff, and Alumni

Innovation: Expanding Programs to Meet Emerging Needs and Interests

IN MEMORIAM

REFLECTIONS

The publication of

Ramah at 60: Impact and Innovation

has been made possible by the generous support of

Mildred Blaine Gershen in memory of

ALVIN E. GERSHEN, *z"l*

a long-time Ramah leader,

to whom this volume is dedicated.

We are grateful to

AB and PHYLLIS FLATT

for their generosity in sponsoring the

Ramah: Onward from 60

conference and celebration.

DEDICATION

Alvin E. Gershen, z"l (1926–1989)

"Patience, perseverance, and planning" was one of my father's favorite phrases. Looking back at advice he gave, each of these three concepts was part of the counsel he offered. One of the most important aspects he stressed was not just what happened today, but how what happened will affect the future. He lauded the past and recognized the present, but he knew that to linger too long in either was not prudent.

There was nothing more important to my father than family. Even though he passed away more than twenty years ago, his dedication to his family is one of the strongest memories we have of him — the opportunities he gave each of us and his drive to provide a complete Jewish foundation. My sisters and I understand these gifts quite well. Of greater relevance for Jewish continuity, all of his twenty-three grandchildren have been provided opportunities and the inclusive Jewish foundation he considered so fundamental.

He would be delighted with the growth and accomplishments of his family. He was so pleased with each of us. I can still remember going to meetings with my father where he would delight in telling stories about my sisters. The look on his face and the joy in his voice were infectious. Each of us can imagine listening to him talk about his twenty-three grandchildren. He would have loved the fact that his grandchildren are confident individuals who have utilized the opportunities they were given and have developed strong Jewish identities.

Twenty-three grandchildren, with a fifteen-year span in age, would have given my father a lot of new stories to tell. The grandchildren attend college in Louisiana, Wisconsin, Michigan, Massachusetts, and New York. They have made trips to Israel, Europe, and Central and South America with Jewish educational groups. These ventures would have given him new things to discuss every day. He would have shared with the world each elementary school grade, reveled in every high school activity, and taken pride in every collegiate achievement.

Our father would have loved the fact that all of his grandchildren attended Ramah camps and Israel programs and that many served on staff. He loved Camp Ramah and loved the opportunities it gave to all those involved. It wasn't just the campers and staff who got something out of their summers.

It was the parents as well. Just spending time listening to his children gave my father joy; imagining the pleasure he would have derived listening to his grandchildren's stories can only make all of us smile.

It would be appropriate to say that even though he never attended camp as either a staff member or a camper, my father had "Ramah friends" — lots of them. He was a Ramah parent, a National Ramah Commission and Poconos board member, and served as the president of Camp Ramah in the Poconos. Those experiences gave him Ramah friends; they made him a Ramahnik.

His service to the Ramah Camping Movement is why dedicating a book about Camp Ramah in his memory is especially fitting. Ramah is as much a part of our lives today as it was a part of his life. Ramah was about providing opportunities *and* a strong Jewish foundation, and both were important to my father.

Twenty years ago, in the foreword to *The Ramah Experience,* my father gave his advice about how best to confront and overcome the issues that he believed affected the Ramah movement. As always, his advice reflected an understanding of the past but focused on the future.

> These are the challenges for the next forty years. They will be met and met successfully just so long as we approach these problems collectively — the dedicated lay leader, the dedicated educator, the dedicated rabbi, and the dedicated administrator. . . . We shall meet these challenges as we work together for the continued success of Ramah.

Looking at the Ramah Camping Movement over the last twenty years through the eyes of his grandchildren, it seems that the challenges he identified have indeed been met and met successfully. "A dream does not die if it bloomed once in a soul" is carved on my father's headstone. The next twenty years will continue to be as successful as the last twenty as Ramah continues to focus collectively on the goals that must be accomplished.

As the movement enters its seventh decade, it is easy to appreciate Ramah's glorious history and celebrated alumni. Our father would have been proud to have his family continue to underwrite this important history of an integral part of the Conservative Movement.

JONATHAN S. GERSHEN, *Esq., son of Alvin E. Gershen, z"l, represents a proud Ramah family that includes thirty-seven Ramahniks who have been involved with the Ramah Camping Movement since 1960:*

Dr. Reva Gershen Lowy and William J. Lowy, Esq.; Dr. Ruth S. Gershen and Rabbi Hillel D. Gold; Eta M. Gershen, Esq. and Steven B. Cohen; Elana L. Gershen, Esq. and Rabbi Joshua S. Finkelstein; Deborah G. Gennello and Dominic Gennello; Ilene Parish Gershen and Jonathan S. Gershen, Esq.; Jenna, Adina, and Matthew Lowy; Tziporah, Tamar, Avraham, Merav, Akiva, and Elisheva Gold; Micah, Ethan, Avi, and Talia Cohen; Sarah, Eli, and Rebecca Finkelstein; Arieh, Michael, Ezra, and Jared Gennello; Alexander, Adam, and Danielle Gershen

Alvin E. Gershen, *z"l*

Photo courtesy of Papier Photographic

The Gershen Family, 2008

PREFACE

About This Book

THIS BOOK CONTINUES THE PRACTICE of sharing what we can learn from the Ramah experience. Our editorial goal is to cast a wide net in defining "we" and "learn" as used in the previous sentence. As such, this book is comprised of four sections: highlights of the Ramah sixtieth-anniversary celebration, chapters authored by researchers and observers of Ramah, tributes in memoriam, and alumni reflections.

"Ramah: Onward from 60," the first section of this book, captures highlights of the Ramah sixtieth-anniversary conference and celebration held in October 2007. Included in this section are excerpts from "We Need More Ramah," the keynote speech given by JTS Chancellor Arnold Eisen, along with excerpts from "Investing in Ramah: Our Extraordinary Past and Dreams for the Future," a panel discussion of Ramah funders, lay leaders, and parents, some of whom are also Ramah staff or camper alumni.

The second section of this book, "Learning from Ramah," consists of chapters written by a variety of professionals using a range of methods, including structured empirical and theoretical research, as well as reports of reflective practice. "Learning from Ramah" is divided thematically into three sections that address: (1) what we can learn from Ramah's leadership and history, (2) the impact of the Ramah experience on various segments of the community, and (3) programmatic elements that have emerged at Ramah in the past decade.

Ramah's sixth decade has been marked not only by exciting growth and innovation but also by loss. In the third section, "In Memoriam," we remember a number of key leaders who helped shape Ramah, most of whom passed away during the last ten years. Although this list, of course, is incomplete, we thank those friends and family members who spent significant time writing these tributes.

The fourth section, "Reflections," contains anecdotes and recollections written by Ramah alumni, including some whose names are likely to be familiar to many readers. These reflections allow a glimpse of the role that Ramah played in the lives of these individuals. They trace, in the words of the alumni themselves, the pathway of their development through the (sometimes, many) years after their time at camp. When we announced publicly through our regular email updates that we were accepting such reflections, we were overwhelmed with the response and the sheer power of the Ramah experience for so many people across our camping movement and across generations. We couldn't possibly publish everything we received.

Submissions were edited for clarity and length by Morton M. Steinberg, the immediate past president of the National Ramah Commission, who also provided an introduction to the "Reflections" section. We are grateful to Mort for putting so many hours into the editing of this section of the book and for his guidance and support throughout the entire process of celebrating sixty years of Ramah. The support and encouragement of both Mort and Dr. Charles T. Mann, the current National Ramah president, has been crucial to the success of this project.

This book represents the collected work of authors from a wide variety of backgrounds who share a passion for Camp Ramah. Each author comes to this project with his or her own unique voice and style. Although we made an effort—particularly in the "Learning from Ramah" section—to maintain a consistent tone throughout the book, we also wanted to preserve the flavor of the original contributions. To achieve this goal, we retained certain stylistic elements that varied among the original contributions, such as the use of Hebrew language, translations, and specialized terms (such as *z"l*). Submissions of work to this book were received over an extended period of time, and therefore, references to the time frame of events and milestones vary.

There are many transliterated words in this volume, and we strived for consistency. For aesthetic reasons, we chose to italicize only the first appearance of a transliterated Hebrew word in each piece.

We want to acknowledge the expertise and high degree of professionalism of our copyediting, typesetting, and advisory team, Leslie Rubin and Rabbi Miles B. Cohen. They provided us with invaluable guidance at all stages of this project.

Finally, we thank Nancy Scheff, NRC's communications director, who is the person most responsible for the publication of this book. Nancy's great talent for writing, organizing, communicating with close to 100 contributors, and keeping us all on track has been indispensible. Nancy not only made this project happen—she also added extraordinary professionalism to every aspect of the celebration of Ramah at 60 and publication of this book.

RABBI MITCHELL COHEN AND **DR. JEFFREY S. KRESS,** *Editors*

MITCHELL COHEN AND **JEFFREY S. KRESS**

Looking Back, Moving Forward

1. RABBI MITCHELL COHEN

THE CALL I RECEIVED FROM DR. SHELDON DORPH, then director of the National Ramah Commission (NRC), in the spring of 1989 changed my life profoundly. I was working as a litigator in a New York City law firm while also attending rabbinical school, contemplating some combination of law and rabbinic employment upon ordination from The Jewish Theological Seminary (JTS) the following year. "Mitch, do you know about the Camp Ramah up in Canada, near Toronto?" Shelly asked. "Their director, Judy Markose, is leaving that position after five years, and I thought you might be interested."

In truth, this question should not have come as too much of a shock. During my junior year in college at Hebrew University, Sam Fraint, Glenn Karonsky, Rob Saposh, and others convinced me, after a wonderful ten-year relationship with Cejwin camps in New York, to begin attending Ramah, given its thriving communities of motivated Jewish youth and extraordinary role models for learning. "If you really aspire to be a leader in the Jewish world, you must go to Ramah in the summer," they would say.

My first summer in 1979 as *rosh tefillah* in Ojai, California, led to six more fantastic summers as a *rosh edah* and the summer assistant director, even as I was attending law school, rabbinical school, spending two additional years in Israel, beginning employment, and meeting and marrying my wife, Cari. Throughout the 1980s, Cari and I became committed Ramahniks in every sense of the term, even though we had never attended as campers. (Now, of course, we are proud Ramah parents, with all three of our children—Talia, Danit, and Noam—completely committed to Ramah Canada, Tichon Ramah Yerushalayim (TRY), Seminar, and all their Ramah friendships.)

RABBI MITCHELL COHEN *is the director of the National Ramah Commission. After working in law as a corporate litigator for five years, he served as director of Camp Ramah in Canada for eleven years and as founding principal of the Solomon Schechter High School of Westchester for three years. He also worked at Camp Ramah in California from 1979 to 1988.*

Rooming in law school with Steve Goldstein certainly had its impact. His almost irrational passion for Ramah was contagious—he would return summer after summer as the Ramah Berkshires waterfront director, eventually founded its alumni association, and served as the president of its board of directors.

At Ojai, I found the leadership experiences incredibly satisfying. The thought of spending a career in this field was exciting and was fueled by consistent encouragement from Alvin Mars, Elliot Dorff, Robin and Gil Graff, and Etan and Debbie Milgrom, among others.

As I have heard hundreds of times from young Ramah leaders, there is simply nothing as satisfying as molding young lives, contributing to the Jewish and personal growth of children and teens, and bringing others closer to a deep and rewarding relationship to Judaism. All of this, and much more, takes place each summer at Ramah camps throughout the world.

I accepted Shelly Dorph's invitation to interview for the director position at Camp Ramah in Canada and subsequently spent eleven years in that role. Among the highlights of my career at Canada Ramah, I gained particular satisfaction helping the camp establish its Tikvah Program, rebuild and expand an aging physical plant, begin to create a committee infrastructure for capital fund-raising, revamp training for junior counselors and other staff, and continue to ascend in importance as a partner to Conservative synagogues throughout the region.

Lay support was crucial. My dear friend Ab Flatt served as the camp president for my first seven years. Together with subsequent presidents Stan Freedman and Sheldon Disenhouse, I enjoyed wonderful relationships with leaders who were passionate about the mission of Ramah, knew how to support the camp, how to lead the board, and who never let personal issues get in the way of excellent leadership. Most significantly, I was extremely fortunate to run the camp with four incredible partners, whose talent and dedication made the camp better and who touched the lives of thousands of campers and staff with warmth and caring: Dennis Maister as business manager, Debbie Spiegel as assistant director, Gloria Silverman, *z"l,* as board liaison and consultant in so many ways, and Howard Black, the summer assistant director, who would take time from his law practice each summer to come to camp. Running camp was always challenging, but the fun and the satisfaction that we shared far outweighed any difficulties.

After eleven years at Ramah Canada, I was intrigued by the challenge of creating and leading a new Solomon Schechter high school in Westchester County, New York. I gained deep insight into the world of formal education through my three years as the principal. Eventually, however, I returned to

Ramah as the national director in 2003, recommitting myself to the unique combination of informal Jewish education and camping called Ramah, which I believe continues to have a more significant impact on nine thousand campers and staff annually than any other experience for our youth.

National Perspective

For a camp director and upper school principal, the goals of the positions were reasonably clear—certainly not simple, or easily achievable, but clear. Enroll participants, hire the best staff possible, and run a safe and fiscally-responsible educational program.

When I began as the director of National Ramah, I quickly learned that no such definition existed for my new role. On the one hand, Ramah camps in the recent era have achieved a high degree of independence, with mostly strong and autonomous boards of directors and professionals responsible for all aspects of camp operations. National Ramah movement-wide programs and support can add tremendous value to an individual camp's program and operation but are not always considered essential to basic functioning. On the other hand, I continue to find that some of our most important work focuses on keeping Ramah camps deeply connected through policy and new programs, the sharing of best practices, and the convening of leadership training on many levels. And, of course, the NRC is there for all our camps when difficulties arise, as has been evident numerous times over the past seven years.

The similarities among the seven overnight Ramah camps are astounding, by far overshadowing the differences. As I travel to each camp every summer, I marvel at the shared culture, traditions, and attitudes of the participants. Whether in Ojai, Clayton, or Wingdale, in Utterson or Palmer, in Conover or Lake Como, Ramah camps are characterized by warm, caring staff members nurturing eager campers who are willing to grow and learn from their counselors.

Additionally, each of our three Ramah day camps continues to play an important role as a vehicle for education, as well as a feeder for our overnight camps. The successful growth of the day camps in Philadelphia and Chicago strengthens our Ramah camps in the Poconos and Wisconsin. The unique, hybrid model of Nyack continues to thrive as a community for over one thousand young people each summer, combining a day camp for young children (a strong feeder for Ramah Berkshires) with an overnight camp and leadership training experience for hundreds of young adult staff.

I am often asked which Ramah camp "has the best food," or "uses the most Hebrew," or "has the best sports program," and indeed significant differences exist. We work best when this "competition" in excellence raises levels throughout the movement. As we celebrate sixty years of camping excellence and build an even stronger network of Ramah camps and programs for the future, we must continue to innovate and develop, taking the best that each camp has to offer, and helping to ensure that such excellence becomes system-wide, whether it be in fiscal practices or educational growth, recreational activities, or strong leadership.

Recent Trends and Accomplishments

During the first decade of the twenty-first century, Ramah has experienced great challenges, as well as unparalleled success. In the early part of the decade, the 9/11 terrorist attacks and the subsequent economic downturn, coming soon after the bust of the dot-com boom, created great challenges for enrollment. Most of our camps experienced some decline, but by mid-decade there was a significant increase. By 2008, over nine thousand campers and staff were participating in a Ramah summer program, the highest number in history. The current recession has hit many families and communities quite hard, but significant increases in scholarship fund-raising helped Ramah maintain its registration numbers. Nevertheless, camp affordability remains a great concern.

Of significant note is the ascent of the influence of the Foundation for Jewish Camp (FJC). Following his tenure as lay president of Camp Ramah in New England, proud Ramah father Jerry Silverman ("the best Jewish experience that my kids have ever had, and they have had them all!") became the FJC leader and took FJC to new heights. Recruiting large givers from the Ramah movement, from other camping organizations, and from the larger Jewish community, FJC has been able to leverage major funding for program grants and, most significantly, incentive awards to attract new families to Jewish camping.

In summer 2009, for example, FJC provided Ramah camps with over $200,000 in funding for new campers. The success of FJC fund-raising in recent years has challenged Ramah leadership, both national and regional, to consider the increased opportunities for fund-raising on a movement-wide basis. There are strong indications that more of our leaders than ever before are ready for these cooperative efforts and that a coordinated approach with major funders and foundations will inure to the benefit of all Ramah camps and programs.

Harold Grinspoon from Springfield, Massachusetts, a well-known Jewish philanthropist and friend of Camp Ramah in New England, created a division of his charitable foundation specifically supporting Jewish camps. Through matching grant programs, board development, and professional mentoring, the initiatives of the Grinspoon Institute for Jewish Philanthropy have helped Ramah camps raise millions of dollars for new capital projects and organizational improvements and are helping our boards and professionals to see fund-raising as more essential than ever to the health and future of Ramah. At a 2007 meeting of the Ramah directors, Harold implored us to "stop being so scared to ask for money. You people are geniuses at running great camps and inspiring Jews, but you have to have more self-esteem about fund-raising!"

In the last few years, the NRC has been able to secure major new funding for the strengthening of our camps. The Avi Chai Foundation, for example, has awarded the NRC a major grant for increasing the use of Hebrew language at Ramah camps, and the Legacy Heritage Foundation is funding innovative Israel education. The Jewish National Fund has funded staff training programs that bring Ramah counselors to Israel for Negev-based service projects, and the Jewish Funders Network has funded an NRC initiative to train our teen campers in youth philanthropy. The Weinberg Foundation provided a grant to enable children with special needs from poorer families to attend our Tikvah programs. Various individuals have provided funding to connect our young adult leadership with the leaders from Masorti youth programs in Buenos Aires, Berlin, Ukraine, and Israel. Most notably, a generous gift from Miriam and Mort Steinberg has helped us endow these efforts.

The NRC has piloted many other initiatives in recent years, not necessarily dependent upon major funding, but aimed at providing more leadership training, connectedness among Ramah camps and Ramah alumni, and positive messaging about the Ramah brand among Conservative Jews and North American Jewry in general. Our online development has included a vastly expanded program bank, Hebrew-language scripts for drama productions, resource materials for camp fund-raising, the extremely popular Ramah marriages website (www.ramahmarriages.org), and the Ramah College Network for high school or college students seeking other Ramahniks on university campuses. The NRC has provided follow-up programming for *shelihim* after they return to Israel to capture the enthusiasm generated for Jewish life of our Israeli staff, and it is piloting new programs to connect Ramah graduates on North American campuses and in major cities.

All these initiatives require staff time, and the NRC staff continues to grow. In addition to the hiring of student or young alumni interns each year, the NRC designated Amy Skopp Cooper as the national assistant director. In addition to her work directing the Nyack Day Camp, Amy now leads many National Ramah initiatives, working with lay leaders, donors, directors, staff, and others. Having Amy as a partner in the directing of all these programs has been indispensible to our growth, as her talent and energy brings excellence to all these projects.

Parallel to these NRC efforts, our camps have developed more sophisticated methods for seeking support from camp alumni and regional donors and foundations. While some of our camps have seen more success in fund-raising than others in recent years, all Ramah camps have demonstrated increased professionalism in development and alumni relations and show great promise for growth.

Toward the Future

Will these trends last? Some believe that Jewish camping, currently a hot topic in the first decade of the twenty-first century, will peak as a communal priority in the coming years. Others see a more optimistic future, especially for Ramah. To continue to thrive and grow as we face the future, we must focus on the following three areas: strengthening, expanding, and extending—strengthening our existing programs while maintaining our high standards, expanding the number of campers involved in Ramah programs, and extending Ramah and Ramah-like experiences to every season of the year.

Strengthening existing programs while maintaining high standards. From its inception, Ramah has maintained an elite profile, simultaneously creating great pride as well as controversy. Flying in the face of consumer fads and business trends in North American summer camping, Ramah maintains that length of session matters greatly—that the longer a child stays in camp, the more powerful the experience. Additionally, Ramah camps continue to require Jewish study year-round, provide formal, as well as informal education at camp, stress Hebrew language, hire a significant number of Israeli shelihim, and require staff, as well as campers, to study at camp. Ramah camps continue to emphasize a well-rounded camp program, where all campers learn outdoor skills and sports, as well as music, dance, theater, and the fine arts. Ramah camps strive to consistently improve in all of these areas, and successful advances are usually adopted throughout the movement through excellent collegiality and sharing on many levels. In addition to the excellent rapport among Ramah directors, assistant directors, and business managers, this sharing is the result of the establishment of new networks of professional collaboration among Ramah's education directors, development directors, and special needs directors, as well as multiple movement-wide staff training programs annually among camp staff at JTS, in Israel, and in various venues throughout North America.

Our partnership with JTS, Ramah's parent organization, continues to grow and thrive, especially through the William Davidson Graduate School of Jewish Education. With the strong support of JTS, the NRC helps each of the Ramah camps maintain high standards, usually in concert with committed board members from the camp committees.

Of course, Ramah achieves camping excellence not only as an institution of Jewish education. Every camp works hard to maintain high standards in sports, the arts, outdoor education, staff training, business practices, health and safety, and lay leadership development. Our camps thrive when they advance year after year in each of these areas, all of which must be maintained and strengthened individually and movement-wide.

Expanding the number of campers involved in Ramah programs. At Ramah's sixtieth anniversary celebration in 2007, JTS Chancellor Arnold Eisen stated:

> We need Ramah more. We can do more with Ramah and, therefore, we need more Ramah, more camps, more campers, more exposure, more hours, more students, more leaders, more *mitzvot,* more study, and more prayer that's enlivened by the wholeness of self that comes about only in a camp setting.

In summer 2010, Ramah opens its first specialty camp, Ramah Outdoor Adventure, under the leadership of Rabbi Eliav Bock, with generous funding from the Jim Joseph Foundation in partnership with FJC. Focusing on campers from Colorado, Texas, and throughout the southwest, but also accepting applicants from all parts of North America, Ramah Outdoor Adventure is Ramah's first truly rustic, environmentally-focused camp, providing our youth with extraordinary character-building experiences, while maintaining core Ramah values. This experiment with specialty camping, and with outdoor adventure in particular, will prove extremely instructive as we consider other avenues of growth in future years.

At present, other ventures for Ramah expansion being considered include the possibility of another Ramah California campus in the San Francisco Bay area, as well as possible new Ramah day camp programs in various cities. Some of our camps have started new programs in special needs education, building upon our forty-year excellence with our Tikvah programs. Most recently, Darom, California, and Poconos have started family camp programs for families with children with special needs. Berkshires established its Breira B'Ramah inclusion program. Wisconsin, California, and New England continue to expand opportunities for young adults in their inspiring Tikvah vocational programs.

Ramah Programs in Israel has expanded greatly in this decade under the leadership of Dr. Joe Freedman. After a few years of low enrollment in our Ramah Israel Seminar during the years of the *intifada,* Ramah became the only teen program in the Jewish world to surpass its own years of record enrollment. Seminar now attracts well over 250 Ramah teen graduates of Ramah camps each summer and continues to experiment with new and exciting supplemental programs. Together with TRY and USY High, our academic high school programs in Israel, our Ramah Israel Institute (RII), serving over a thousand Israel travelers (school and synagogue groups, children and adults) each year, and our Ramah Israel Day Camp in Jerusalem, more people than ever are enjoying a Ramah experience in Israel.

Extending Ramah and Ramah-like experiences to every season of the year. Should Ramah continue to primarily be the address for Jewish youth during the summer only? Or should Ramah also forge new partnerships with our synagogues, schools, and communities, extending the lessons of Ramah informal education, the talent of Ramah staff, the strength of Ramah's organizational excellence, and the positive associations with the Ramah brand into the fall, winter, and spring seasons? This question, currently the subject of intense strategic thinking on a regional and national level, will have important implications for the future of the Ramah Camping Movement, the focus of the NRC, and perhaps the future success of the Conservative Movement in North America. As Ramah grows and the Conservative Movement contracts, Ramah can potentially play a more significant role with our youth and families. Defining that role is currently a crucial challenge and an exciting one.

As Ramah faces the beginning of a new decade and marches on toward the seventieth anniversary of what is widely considered to be one of the most successful programs in Jewish education, these and many other challenges will continue to require unprecedented levels of Ramah movement-wide collaboration and cooperation. In the end, however, nothing will ever become more important than that which has characterized Ramah from its inception—creating summer communities where children, teens, and young adults can comfortably and joyously grow as people and grow as Jews, forging relationships with others that sustain them throughout their lives. This is the essence of the Ramah experience. We are proud of our first sixty years, and we look to the future with great optimism and excitement as we continue our sacred work.

* * *

THE RAMAH CAMPING MOVEMENT is indebted to innumerable people for their roles in bringing us through the first six decades of Ramah history. Lay leaders, donors, camp professionals, summer staff members, camp families, and Conservative Movement partners have supported Ramah with great dedication. Having JTS as our parent organization has been invaluable. Throughout his tenure, Ismar Schorsch, the chancellor emeritus of JTS, was committed to the mission of Ramah and maintained close working relationships with the NRC leaders, inspiring us with his insight and vision. We are thrilled to continue this wonderful relationship with Chancellor Arnold Eisen, who spends a significant amount of time visiting Ramah camps and thinking about our future. He consistently cites Ramah as one of the most important experiences for our youth, encouraging all of us who lead Ramah to strive for even greater excellence. Michael Greenbaum, vice chancellor and chief operating officer of JTS, is the long-time secretary of the NRC. He is a true mentor and partner to me and the NRC leadership, providing us with critical guidance and support.

When the idea arose to create a new book for Ramah's sixtieth anniversary, I approached Jeff Kress, who became my partner and co-editor for this entire project and devoted countless hours to helping ensure that this book achieved excellence. Representing the best of the collaboration between Ramah and JTS, Jeff always brought his sense of academic integrity to this project and continues to be a wonderful colleague.

Lastly, as we continue through the seventh decade of the history of Ramah, we must thank Shelly Dorph, National Ramah director from 1989 to 2003. Shelly's passion and vision for Ramah laid so much of the groundwork that continues to propel us into the future.

2. DR. JEFFREY S. KRESS

I CAN TRACE MY JEWISH DEVELOPMENT by the summer overnight camps I attended. I started at a camp named after a Native American tribe. I don't remember much about the camp except for the Friday night ritual gathering at which the camp director, wearing only a loincloth and an elaborate feathered headdress, would chant incomprehensibly while stomping around and praying loudly to the god of fire. The god of fire (in the guise of a counselor hiding in a tree, as I later realized) would respond by sending a burning coal into the gas-soaked pile of kindling and branches in the middle of our circle, igniting a soaring bonfire. It made quite an impression on my bunk of eight-year-olds; we thought twice before misbehaving. It also made me glad that Judaism has not maintained a tradition of loincloths.

JEFFREY S. KRESS, *Ph.D., is an associate professor of Jewish Education and a senior research assistant at the William Davidson Graduate School of Jewish Education of The Jewish Theological Seminary. He also coordinates the school's concentration in Informal and Communal Jewish Education. Dr. Kress was recently appointed as the chair of the Network for Research in Jewish Education. He attended Ramah Berkshires in 1984 and from 1986 to 1989 and participated in the Ramah Israel Seminar in 1985.*

I then spent several summers at a non-denominational Zionist camp, followed by a few summers at an Orthodox, politically right-leaning, Zionist camp. By my freshman year in high school (an Orthodox day school) I was, perhaps understandably, quite confused! I tried Ramah Berkshires at the suggestion of a close friend in high school. It would be a mistake to describe this decision as motivated by some deep connection to—or desire to explore—the Conservative Movement. At the time, what I knew about the Conservative Movement could be summarized by four words: *not Orthodox, not Reform.* I tried Ramah because as a student in an Orthodox day high school from a nominally Conservative family, I was looking for a more relaxed summer, religiously speaking. For me, it took some time for the Ramah experience *to take,* as it were. Starting Ramah at the age of fourteen in the oldest *edah* posed some social challenges. I felt like a newcomer to Ramah. It seemed like some of my bunkmates had been attending Ramah from birth. Actually, some of my bunkmates—being "staff brats"—*had* attended Ramah from birth (or before, though I am not sure if in utero experiences count). There was a lot of shared history—at least the type of "history" that results from years of confabulated memories—at the camp that was very much alive in the minds of my fellow campers: "Remember when Matt and Sarah [names changed to protect the innocent and also because, frankly, I cannot remember the real names of the people in question] messed up their lines in the Bogrim play?" or "Our swim instructor is so much better this year! Remember last year . . . ?"

It took a few years—a trip to Israel, working on *tzevet mayim*—for there to be enough history for me to have something about which I could reminisce along with the Ramah lifers. It still surprises me sometimes that Ramah has become a part of my life now.

Despite my late start and my initial ignorance of Conservative Judaism, Ramah came to be a very meaningful place for me. To me, Ramah's impact was augmented by my experience at college. Socially, there was overlap between my "camp friends" and my "college friends," many of whom attended one of the Ramah camps as youth, and several of whom spent summers with me at Berkshires during our college years. Regardless of which of the camps my friends attended, Ramah experiences provided a common shorthand that was important in making connections in a new, large, diverse setting such as college. Also, through Ramah and my campus Hillel, I learned that there were Conservative (and Reform and Reconstructionist and non-denominational) Jews who took their Judaism *very* seriously and were deeply engaged in the Jewish tradition (though the traditions in which they were engaged looked very different from one another). I learned to think in terms of *differently* Jewish, not *more* or *less* Jewish. Though the term would not become a buzzword for several years, I came to appreciate Jewish pluralism. And, I started to learn that Conservative Judaism could be defined by what it *is* and not by what it *is not*.

Ramah also had a very personal impact on my life in a way that is easy to observe. I spent part of my winter break during my junior year in college at the lovely Homowack Hotel in the Catskills as part of the Weinstein Staff Development Program. It was there that I met my wife, Adena Lebeau, who was at the time a Ramah Wisconsin staff member (yes, we are a Berkshires-Wisconsin intermarriage, or perhaps a Wisconsin-Berkshires intermarriage; in either case we have successfully come to terms with this). Other elements of impact are less visible. One of my first "teaching" experiences, for example, was at the *agam* and I have occasionally thought that (almost) everything I know about Jewish education I learned on the Ramah waterfront:

• The importance of attending to the social and emotional elements of learning along with a focus on "content"—I knew that I was teaching much more than proper backstroke form.

• The impact an educator could have even when not formally teaching and the need to create structures to foster meaningful educator-learner relationships.

• That with appropriate motivation, students are willing (happy, actually) to take part in even repetitive tasks that might otherwise seem "boring" (even treading water can be fun!).

• That complex outcomes can be accomplished when broken down into small and simple steps and that everyone can make progress toward those outcomes.

The fact that I was teaching swimming and canoeing is hardly relevant. Standing in front of a class at JTS or in front of a group of professionals at a professional development seminar, I believe there is a certain line that I can trace to the Ramah experience—in particular, the confidence to speak in front of a group. That first experience of standing on stage and leading the entire camp in song or cheer is somewhere below the surface.

My Ramah experience also blurred the distinction in my mind between learning and "fun." The campers I worked with were developing as people and as Jews, but aside from the *kittot,* this was achieved through relationships and experiences, not lesson plans. As a Jewish educational researcher, I am interested in a related blurring, that of so-called *formal* and *informal* education. Further, I have come to appreciate Ramah not only as a place where learning happens but also as a setting from which we—Jewish educational researchers and practitioners—can learn. Over the years, Ramah has contributed broadly to Jewish educational theory, research, and practice. It has done so both through formal research and through serving as a testing ground for new ideas and as an inspiration for many Jewish educators. I am glad to be a part of Ramah's sixtieth-anniversary celebration and am honored to work together with Ramah's professional and lay leaders. I know that Ramah will continue to be a *mofet* (exemplar).

I conclude with a few words of acknowledgment. I have learned much from my collaboration with my co-editor, Rabbi Mitch Cohen, who brought his passion for Ramah and his thoughtful and caring leadership to this project. Mort Steinberg's work with the Reflections helped make that section a reality. It has been an honor to work together with Ramah's professional and lay leaders on this book, on Ramah's sixtieth-anniversary conference and celebration, and on other projects. I echo Mitch Cohen's acknowledgement of these individuals. In particular, Nancy Scheff was the engine that kept this project moving, providing the needed boost and momentum, as well as substantive input that greatly enhanced the product. When I first came to JTS, Chancellor Ismar Schorsch (now Chancellor Emeritus) designated me a member of the National Ramah Commission, and Dr. Aryeh Davidson (former dean) further encouraged my involvement with Ramah. My work has been further supported by Chancellor Arnold Eisen, Dr. Steve Brown (former dean), and Dean Barry Holtz. My colleagues at the Davidson School and the Department of Jewish Education at JTS have been influential in my thinking and research. Co-teaching with Cheryl Magen taught me much about the world of Ramah and Jewish camping. My thanks to Dr. Maurice Elias for all of his ongoing support and guidance. Finally, I thank my wife and fellow Ramahnik, Adena Lebeau, and my children, Ezra and Kira, for all of their love and support.

Ramah: Onward from 60

MITCHELL COHEN

Celebrating Ramah at 60

As the year 2007 approached, the National Ramah professional leadership team gathered to discuss how to celebrate the sixtieth anniversary of the Ramah Camping Movement, which began in Wisconsin in 1947. I sat in my office with our senior leadership: Amy Skopp Cooper, our national assistant director; Jeff Goodman, our national business manager; and Nancy Scheff, our communications director. Along with Mort Steinberg, the immediate past president of the National Ramah Commission (NRC), and Jeff Kress, assistant professor of Jewish Education and a senior research assistant at the William Davidson Graduate School of Jewish Education of The Jewish Theological Seminary (JTS), these outstanding leaders helped develop the vision for this celebration that is finally coming to a conclusion with the publication of this volume.

In October of 2007, National Ramah hosted "Ramah: Onward from 60," a conference and celebration at JTS that was attended by more than 400 people. In addition to a keynote speech by the new JTS chancellor, Arnold Eisen, the day included a panel discussion on the impact of Ramah, featuring Ramah lay leaders Ab Flatt and Julie Beren Platt and philanthropist Harold Grinspoon; Jerry Silverman, then president of the Foundation for Jewish Camping; John Ruskay, the president and chief executive officer of UJA–Federation of New York; and Peter Geffen, founder of Kivunim and the Heschel School in New York City. Excerpts from Chancellor Eisen's keynote speech and the panel discussion are included in this volume. The conference also included breakout sessions led by Howard Blas, Steve Brown, Margaret Danishefsky, Joe Freedman, Michael Greenbaum, Ariela Keysar, Jeff Kress, Joe Reimer, Shuly Rubin Schwartz, and Yaara Shteinhart-Moghadam, many

RABBI MITCHELL COHEN *is the director of the National Ramah Commission. After working in law as a corporate litigator for five years, he served as director of Camp Ramah in Canada for eleven years and as founding principal of the Solomon Schechter High School of Westchester for three years. He also worked at Camp Ramah in California from 1979 to 1988.*

of whom have authored chapters in this volume. Of course, there was Israeli dancing and Jewish music throughout the celebration.

In the evening, everyone watched the premiere of a new short documentary, *Transforming Lives: Ramah at 60,* an excellent presentation that captured the feelings of Ramahniks across the generations. We thank Charles Wantman, president of Audio Vistas, who generously donated many hours of his professional services to the production of *Transforming Lives.* Amy Skopp Cooper was instrumental in creating the vision for this project and in the planning of the entire conference and celebration.

We are grateful to the many speakers, participants, and discussion leaders who brought their expertise and passion to the Ramah sixtieth-anniversary conference and celebration. National Ramah was fortunate to have a terrific group to organize this event. Nancy Scheff supervised all aspects of our communications. Orlie Prince, the conference coordinator, masterfully handled registration and logistics, in conjunction with Eileen Kern, the NRC bookkeeper. Our marketing and communications assistant, Michael Edelstein, was instrumental in the implementation of all aspects of event production. Scott Topal, a longtime Ramah Nyack staff member, helped to create a terrific multimedia presentation. Jeff Goodman oversaw all event planning and made certain that no detail was overlooked. He coordinated the efforts of the National Ramah team, which included Judy Greene, Steven Gross, Shoshana Holzberg-Pill, and Shana Zionts, as well as a group of energetic student volunteers.

Finally, I want to thank my wonderful friends, Ab and Phyllis Flatt of Toronto, for their financial support of all the events celebrating Ramah's sixtieth anniversary. Ab and Phyllis are longtime supporters of Camp Ramah in Canada, as well as Ramah camping throughout the world.

ARNOLD EISEN

We Need More Ramah

KEYNOTE SPEECH

"Ramah: Onward from 60" Conference and Celebration
The Jewish Theological Seminary, October 14, 2007
Excerpted and edited by Rabbi Mitchell Cohen, National Ramah Director

IT'S BEEN SIXTY DAYS SINCE, thanks to Mitch, I had my first intensive exposure as chancellor to the wonders of Ramah—the wonders of Ramah that first came into being sixty years ago. Mitch Cohen and I were driving up to Palmer after a visit to Nyack, and we were almost prevented from arriving in time for Shabbat because of a defective windshield wiper on the rental car. I know that since the opening of Ramah Wisconsin and the subsequent expansion from one camp to two and then to many camps, that things along the way were, of course, almost prevented by obstacles far more serious than that windshield wiper.

But here we all are, sixty years later, to celebrate one of the finest accomplishments of The Jewish Theological Seminary and of the Conservative Movement, and I think it's fair to say, objectively, wearing my hat as a scholar of American Judaism, that Ramah is one of the finest accomplishments of American Judaism as a whole. I'm honored to be part of this occasion. In true Ramah fashion, going back to the founding principles, we are not here just to have a good time, but to learn something, to reflect on what we've done so as to prepare another generation of American Jews for informed and intelligent participation in Jewish life.

I am very happy to be able to devote time working on Ramah's growth, as I think Ramah is absolutely essential to the core mission of JTS. I'm doubly

ARNOLD EISEN, *Ph.D., one of the world's foremost experts on American Judaism, is the seventh chancellor of The Jewish Theological Seminary. Since his inauguration in 2007, Chancellor Eisen has met with world leaders, engaged in prominent interdenominational and interfaith dialogues, and championed a transformation in the education of the next generation of Conservative leadership. Before coming to JTS, Chancellor Eisen was the Koshland Professor of Jewish Culture and Religion at Stanford University. Chancellor Eisen received his Ph.D. in the History of Jewish Thought from Hebrew University.*

pleased that while I missed out on Ramah when I had the chance to be a camper, I get to make up for lost time by joining the senior staff now as chancellor. This, as is the case for every other Jewish endeavor, starts with Torah. So let's begin by looking at where we are in the Torah's cycle: the transition from *Noaḥ* to *Lech Lecha,* which is the transition from creation to covenant, from the children of Adam to the children of Israel, from God's partnership with all humanity to the particular set of responsibilities and possibilities opened up to Jewish human beings through the covenant with Abraham while retaining those that we have as human beings as a whole by the covenant with Noah.

Why does the God of all humanity choose to benefit all humanity by means of a small portion of humanity—the children of Israel, which is the Jews? The key, I think, comes when you look at the end of chapter eight, right before the blessing for Noah and his children, which reminds us that as long as creation endures, God recognizes seed time and harvest, cold and heat, summer and winter, day and night.

So land, space, and time are going to be specially apportioned here to a people specially gifted with God's presence and God's laws, and this people can produce a kind of society, a kind of a life with a capital *L* that, as Deuteronomy chapter four puts it, is going to cause the nations of the world to say, "how wise and understanding are the People of Israel; I wish we could have laws like they have, I wish we could enjoy God's presence as they do." I say all this because I think it's directly relevant to the educational mission that we have as Jews and certainly that we have at Camp Ramah.

We have to create human beings who are capable, by virtue of the agency they have, the wisdom they accumulate, the experiences they have, and the education they're given, to make use of God-given talents including mind, heart, soul, and body; to make use of knowledge gained through science and through historic experience; to make use of the capacity for distance and objectivity, as well as the capacity for relationship and love; to make use of all of this, to exercise responsibility for God's creatures and for the world in such a way that we can become successful partners of God.

If I think that this is Ramah's mission, then based on this I want camp to foster Jewish human beings. I want to foster Jewish human beings gifted with the sense of responsibility, agency, and partnership. I want to make them feel at home in the world, including the natural world. I want them to be confident of their individual talents, but aware that fulfilling themselves using these talents comes only when joined in partnership with the talents of others. I want them to take pride in the uniqueness of the Jewish way in the world, and I want them to be respectful of all the other children of Noah, determined to work with them, no matter how complex, to fulfill the charge laid upon us all by the covenant with Noah.

One needs community to make plausible—and to make coherent and compelling—the claims that Jewish tradition offers. I have to gather together a community united by a time and space that are mine, surrounded by images and architecture that reflect my values and not somebody else's, before I can be persuaded that my tradition is worth carrying on. I hope you see where I'm going with this.

The need for a new kind of Jewish community in the modern world is the fundamental reason why I think the strengthening and the creation of more Ramah summer camps is not only a clear and present opportunity, the single best opportunity we have, but is a necessity, an absolute necessity for Jewish survival. Therefore, this is essential to the core mission of JTS, as JTS is dedicated to living fully in the modern world while at the same time being fully immersed in and authentic to our tradition.

Judaism cannot thrive in the modern period if we begin from a perspective of individualism without the creation of Jewish times and spaces. At Ramah, for once, Jewishness is essential to who an individual Jew is and not peripheral; for once, time and space are ours and not somebody else's, and we don't have to struggle to create a Jewish space in the midst of a larger Gentile space; for once, we don't have to try to find an hour or two for Jewish time amidst the larger time, but we have seven days a week, twenty-four hours a day, in a situation that is ours, where we can build community. Camps do this better than any other opportunity we have. Day schools are second best. They are also indispensable, but camps and day schools together are indispensable if we are going to get Jews to regard Jewishness as central to who they are, now that the Jewish communities of the past—where Jewishness was taken for granted—no longer exist.

When I look at Ramah, I think of the precious opportunity it gives us to transmit content and meaning and substance to life, to Torah, in a Jewish environment. Along with the ability to control time and space, camp provides a Jewish language, as well as a Jewish calendar to enact what we might call the grammar of Jewish everyday existence. Ramah combines this with the advantages of summer and of outdoors, when young people feel vitality coursing through them, where Jewishness is equated with life in a very natural way. Our campers and staff form new relationships, and see themselves grow in the wholeness of being a Jew, perhaps here to a larger extent than anywhere else. The person playing sports is integrated with the person inside the study hall, or creating art, creating a whole person united with the person at prayer.

I think Jewish summer camps are an absolutely indispensable resource for all American Jews right now because nowhere else do we have the opportunity to create communities and to fill them with Jewish meaning.

We need Ramah more. We can do more with Ramah and, therefore, we need more Ramah, more camps, more campers, more exposure, more hours, more students, more leaders, more *mitzvot,* more study, and more prayer that's enlivened by the wholeness of self that comes about only in a camp setting. We need communities wherever we are. We need them in our day schools. We need them in our afternoon schools. We need them in our synagogues. We need them in our secular organizations. But for goodness sake, we can never find them as ready-made or as easily constructed as we can find them in camp.

Similarly, we need Jewish meaning wherever we can place it. We need revitalization. We need reinterpretation. We need a kind of Judaism that's going to speak to my eighteen-year-old son and my twenty-one-year-old daughter, but also a Judaism that speaks to me in my fifties now. We need a kind of Judaism at Ramah, right now in 2007, that's going to foster leaders of this community in 2030 and 2040 and, God willing, 2050. So we need to imbue a kind of authenticity, a kind of comfort in this tradition, a kind of depth to this tradition which gives people the ability to innovate and to change—confident that when they innovate and when they change, they are carrying on what they were given instead of disrupting it and leaving it behind for something new.

I'm proud that I get to lead JTS at this time, when we're all thinking about how we can take Ramah forward for another sixty years of growth. I'm proud that I can stand here today, when we have nothing to fear from history, making sure that Jewish young people are not taught to safely guard their Jewishness in a pocket, keeping it locked and hidden away lest it be tarnished or disrupted or destroyed by what they encounter in the larger world. No, on the contrary, at Ramah we teach them to be confident that their Jewishness, that this Torah that they're given, this covenant which they are the heirs to, is strong enough, durable enough, flexible enough—it has withstood 3,000 years of transformation—that it can take anything the modern world is going throw at it. There is no new idea that they are going to study in their science class or their history class or their bible class of which they need to be afraid.

Ramah stands for a kind of possibility for wholeness when young people need that sense of wholeness most, when they're most fearful of the world, most insecure about their own abilities, and most afraid that their physical prowess is not going to be sufficient for what life has to throw at them. So this is a vision of education of Ramah, a vision of sport, as well as prayer, of the arts, as well as study, a vision of six days of the week that leads to Shabbat in a way they do not for many of us living in the larger world.

I think I have good reason to be optimistic about the future of our movement, and I know I have good reason to be even more optimistic about the future of Ramah.

My colleague Shuly Rubin Schwartz closes her article from twenty years ago on the early years of Ramah's history with this thought: "Ramah, as early as its initial six years, played a major role in restoring to the Conservative movement faith in its future."[1] If there is a need for such a restoration of confidence today, I think Ramah is well placed, uniquely well placed to provide it. This is my vision then: Jewish human beings raised in pride of who they are, confident in their unique talents, aware of their responsibility to join with others, Jewish and Gentile, to steward the world and improve the lot of their fellow human beings. The Jewish part of each self is not squeezed at Ramah by the human, or set off at a distance from it, but expansively reaches into every aspect of mind, heart, soul, and body.

I want to have more and more campers at more and more Ramahs who are involved with learning, who are attached to their community and their people, who are skilled at human relationships, who are practiced in the mitzvot. I want to have more and more human beings at Ramah who understand the gift that they have been given, the ability to develop answers for themselves to the eternal questions of why the Jews, why Judaism, how to live Torah, how to partner with God. And to do all of this inside of the Jewish time and space, of wholeness and of joy that are not easily available elsewhere. I want a Ramahnik at home in nature, at home in themselves, proud of who they are, at home and in love with the language of the Jewish people and the grammar of Jewish community.

Abraham had to leave his father behind and set out in a whole new direction in order to get the covenant. Finklestein, Davis, Ettenberg, et al., had some existing undertakings on which to build. But they, too, had to risk a new direction in order to get the unique Ramah model off the ground. We are luckier on both counts. This generation of Jews has so much going for it, so much already in place, and the Ramah model is a good one in need of another injection of energy, of thinking, and of support. We have a wealth of experience on our side. We have the Torah on our side and we have one another. May we inaugurate another sixty years of creativity and growth which will take us all the way to the ripe old age of 120 and beyond. Thank you very much.

Responses to Questions from the Audience

THE SUCCESS OF SYNAGOGUE SCHOOLS is very dependent on the success of partnership with Ramah because we can accomplish in an informal educational setting far more than one can accomplish in the afternoon and weekend setting;

I think the sum total of the product, the holistic nature of living Jewishly twenty-four hours a day, seven days a week, is a far more powerful element of the experience than any particular thing we put into it. Ralph Simon said a long time ago that Ramah will put a child in a total Jewish environment and enable him to live the ideal Jewish life from the time he gets up until he goes to bed.

WHAT IMPRESSES AMERICAN JEWS more than anything else when they go to Israel, time after time, is that they are overwhelmed by the public Jewish time and space, by the sense that you're just Jewish there. They can't get over it. Similarly, I think what the Ramah experience has to offer is the sense of the naturalness of Jewishness, the totality of Jewishness, the release from the hyphenated character of Jewish identity that all of us carry with us all the time. Now the trick is going to be to enable Ramah camper graduates to leave the hyphenated life with as much harmony as possible as we all try to do out here in the real world. But it seems to me, this is the quintessential meaning of Ramah: this sense of wholeness.

TO THE DEGREE THAT AMERICAN JEWS feel connected to Israel, feel at home when they visit Israel, that is a function of their feeling of connection to the Hebrew language. And yet we Americans, we're provincial linguistically. We get by in a way the rest of the world doesn't have to, because English is the world language right now. All the more reason why, at Ramah, when we have the chance at a total Jewish time and space, when we can accustom Jewish young people to the language and grammar of Jewish living, when we know that Hebrew is possible in the situation emerging, that we not give up on Hebrew. The Jewish people right now cannot afford to give up on Hebrew language. We have all sorts of new technology literally coming online over the last few years for making language live in new ways for people. I'm hoping that Ramah can take advantage of that new technology to make Hebrew again a living force in American Jewish life.

Note

[1] Shuly Rubin Schwartz, "Camp Ramah: The Early Years, 1947–1952," *Conservative Judaism* 40, no. 1 (Fall 1987): 38.

PANEL DISCUSSION

Investing in Ramah: Our Extraordinary Past and Dreams for the Future

"Ramah: Onward from 60" Conference and Celebration
The Jewish Theological Seminary, October 14, 2007
Excerpted and edited by Rabbi Mitchell Cohen, National Ramah Director

MODERATORS

Mitchell Cohen, *National Ramah Director*
Amy Skopp Cooper, *National Ramah Assistant Director*

PANELISTS

Ab Flatt, *Past President, Camp Ramah in Canada*
Peter Geffen, *Founder, The Abraham Joshua Heschel School; Founder and Director, Kivunim — The Institute of Experiential Learning for Israel and World Jewish Communities Studies*
Harold Grinspoon, *Founder, Harold Grinspoon Foundation*
Julie Beren Platt, *Board Chair, Camp Ramah in California*
John Ruskay, *Executive Vice President and CEO, UJA-Federation of New York*
Jerry Silverman, *President, Foundation for Jewish Camping*

AMY COOPER: [Introductory remarks in Hebrew] Panelists, this is an audience of passionate Ramah supporters steeped in our rich history and deeply committed to our future. We've asked each of you to respond from your own perspective, reflecting upon your own Ramah experience as a parent, camper, funder, or some combination of these roles. What would you say is the strongest case that Ramah can make to encourage others, including foundations and Federations, to invest in Ramah?

MITCH COHEN: Julie Beren Platt, our first speaker, is the president of Camp Ramah in California. Julie lives in Los Angeles, and she's been chairing the board of directors for the last couple of years, having previously served as their development chair. She's a member of the board of directors of the Ziegler

School of Rabbinic Studies, the executive committee of the Federation of Greater Los Angeles, and the executive committee of Sinai Temple. It has been a pleasure working with Julie, whose passion for Ramah comes both from her own upbringing, as well as her role as a Ramah parent.

JULIE BEREN PLATT: As Mitch just mentioned, I come to this with a perspective of the past, and I work every day for the future of Camp Ramah. I want to respond to today's topic in two ways, one on an emotional and philosophical level and one on a much more practical level. For me personally, a Jewish girl from Wichita, Kansas, the only Jewish girl in my senior high school class of 700 and one of just seven members of my Hebrew school class—thankfully for me the other six were boys—Camp Ramah was transformative. It inspired me to a life of observance and of communal service. Equally and interestingly, my five day-school-educated Jewish children from Los Angeles have had the same experience at Camp Ramah. It is for them the most positive Jewish experience of their lives.

My great aspirations for Camp Ramah in California are driven by my own family's Ramah experiences and by my passions, shared completely by every member of my board, to strive for a better and better and better experience for our campers. Steven Cohen, research professor of Jewish social policy at HUC–JIR, and Keysar and Kosmin's *"Eight Up"* study confirm that Jewish camps have proven to exert lasting long-term influence on young adult Jewish identities, influencing our young adults to grow and to make good adult choices and, by extension, we grow Jewish leaders, both lay and professional.

Now, for the practical side. Since it is clear what a Ramah camper must experience, where it will hopefully lead in their personal choices and hopefully in their community involvement, we have to work to not only make access as easy as possible, but as well be as competitive as possible. Steven Cohen's study of the L.A. camping community led us to two very significant findings. Jewish camping is more cost-sensitive, and we are clearly competing with the secular camps. The great news is that the word is out. The success of Jewish camping is a nationally recognized imperative. Our L.A. Federation has joined with all the area Jewish camps and provided significant incentive funding. But frankly, it would never have organized or capitalized so quickly were it not for the leadership and partnership of Jerry Silverman and the Foundation for Jewish Camping. In addition, we have to respond to the competition of secular camps, both specialized and not. We have to raise significant endowment and capital funds to build the best facilities and to provide the best programming. We have to offer high-level sports, drama, arts, music, outdoor experiences, as well as—and even more importantly—impactful *tefillot* and Jewish educational experiences. The challenge is great but not unattainable. We have to be the best we can be at everything — a very tall order. The results have and will continue to follow.

AMY COOPER: Jerry Silverman is the current president of the Foundation for Jewish Camping. Under his leadership and with the enormous support and vision of its founders, Robert and Elisa Bildner and current chair, our very own Skip Vichness, we extend our enormous gratitude for the work you are doing on our behalf: advocacy, leadership training, and helping to raise millions of dollars for camper scholarships. Jerry is a Ramahnik. He is the former president of Camp Ramah in New England. His wife, Erica, works for Ramah New England, and they also have five children who have all attended Ramah camps and programs. In Jerry's own words, "Our kids have had all the best Jewish experiences, but Ramah is the program that created their deepest love for Shabbat, for *ivrit,* for Jewish identity, and the most wonderful lifetime friendships." We are honored that Jerry is with us today.

JERRY SILVERMAN: Thank you, Amy, and thank you, Julie, very much for your kind words. As a parent, a former lay chair of Ramah New England and now as president of the Foundation for Jewish Camping, I would present the case like this: it's about passion, and it's about having the ability to bring the story of camp and paint a picture to the community and to funders. Let me give you an example at the risk of alienating my daughter. As a parent, I have a memory of dropping off my daughter Alison at Camp Ramah Palmer, leaving her there not knowing a soul as we had just moved from California to New England, and I was feeling absolutely sick to my stomach as I was never a camper, and I dropped her off at this place where we had no clue what it was really about. Four weeks later, picking her up and driving to her bunk and seeing her literally glued in a massive hug with twelve girls, crying, not wanting to leave and listening to them talking about writing, visiting, and coming back in eleven months, it was literally almost impossible to peel her away. The drive home was incredible. My name changed, by the way, that summer. When she left for camp I was Daddy. In the car, I was Abba. And that has stuck from that point on. Camp leaders must always ask what are the big bold initiatives that you want funders to invest in that will really make a difference in realizing the vision of the camp. Investors today will invest significantly in projects that will have the opportunity to create significant outcomes. The Grinspoon Institute and their foundation have proven this with their program. It's about thinking big and bold and having a vision.

This past Shabbat we were at the University of Maryland for parents' weekend. We went to Hillel to the KOACH service, the Conservative service.

A rabbinical student from JTS was there, who was a *rosh edah* at Wisconsin this summer and refers to David Soloff of Camp Ramah in Wisconsin as the *mashiaḥ*. The president of KOACH is a woman from Ramah Ojai. The vice president of the Jewish student union is from Ramah Palmer. One of the Israel advocacy organization leaders is from Darom. Ramah graduates are leaders on college campuses today. Frame the discussion using and painting real life scenarios. The strongest case is the type of community that we're all graduating, and how they are energizing the community around them. But we have to give it context in how it falls into the future of the next sixty years of Ramah. Thank you.

AMY COOPER: Harold Grinspoon is a great friend of Ramah, Jewish camps, and Jewish educational institutions. The Grinspoon Institute of Jewish Philanthropy has enhanced the vibrancy of Jewish life in western Massachusetts and beyond and has provided mentoring and training for Jewish camps, day schools, retreat centers, and other institutions to help them become more effective organizations. Harold's genius is that with his investment of $5 million to Jewish camping over the last few years and the establishment of various incentive-matching programs, he has been able to leverage over $25 million for Jewish camps. With deep gratitude, it is my pleasure to introduce Harold Grinspoon.

HAROLD GRINSPOON: My journey, as Jerry Silverman said a few minutes ago, all started with Camp Ramah. My visit to Camp Ramah this summer was an amazing, beautiful experience. As you probably know, the buzzword today in the Jewish world is "camping." And it's so exciting to be out here in that world. It's amazing—but maybe I'm jumping ahead of my story. So, a number of years ago I went to Camp Ramah, and I saw a nice camp that wanted a few dollars. I gave them a few dollars, and I walked away. And then through persistence on Jerry's part, who invited me back over and over again, and finally one day it dawned on me as an entrepreneur: I'm proud of where I invest my money, and Jewish camping was a place to put some money.

What do wealthy people do with their money? We Jews have a high rate of assimilation, so I figured maybe we should help Jewish camps, so we started this Grinspoon Institute for Jewish Philanthropy. We have sixty-five non-paying clients—all the Ramah camps and others that we help with board development, to help them feel really good about themselves and about asking other people to support Jewish camping, since Jewish camping is essential.

MITCH COHEN: Thank you, Harold. Ab Flatt has served on the Camp Ramah in Canada committee for decades and in 1990 when I became director of Camp

Ramah in Canada, he took over as president and served in that role for seven years. Ab's leadership was absolutely fantastic. He was my mentor, my friend, and my colleague, and I am so happy that my friendship with Ab and his wife, Phyllis, continues to be strong. Anyone who knows Ab knows that Ramah is his passion. He brings that passion everywhere he goes, and together with Phyllis and her brother Harold Wolfe, they continue to give generously to Camp Ramah. Ab, it is my pleasure now to introduce you to everybody here today.

AB FLATT: Why did we decide to send our four children to Camp Ramah in the summer? Attending day school, practicing the wonderful traditions of our religion in our home, as well as feeling part of a community, all played a role in this decision. At Camp Ramah you live being Jewish twenty-four hours a day, seven days a week. "Camp is different!" It has a *ruaḥ*—a spirit—a feeling that is so very hard to explain unless one experiences it firsthand. One of our sons expressed it this way, "I can walk into a synagogue anywhere in the world and feel comfortable because of my experience and summers spent at Camp Ramah." We have been blessed with fourteen grandchildren, and so far everyone of camp age has gone and is now going to Camp Ramah in Canada. I am so delighted that their parents, former Ramahniks, have made this choice for their children. Visitors Day is a highlight for all of us each summer and has been for over thirty-five years. We look forward to many more years in the future as the little ones come of age to enjoy and benefit from what this program has to offer.

AMY COOPER: Dr. John Ruskay is the executive vice president and CEO of the UJA Federation of New York. In this post, he serves as the senior professional of the largest Federation in North America and the largest local philanthropy in the world. Among his many Jewish leadership positions, he served as vice chancellor of The Jewish Theological Seminary for eight years.

Of significant note today, I'd like to point out that John spent many of his formative years at Ramah Nyack, Poconos, and the Berkshires. In fact, in an article he wrote this summer about his childhood at Camp Ramah, he wrote: "If I had not attended Jewish summer camp in my early teens, where I was introduced to the power and intense beauty of Jewish life, Shabbat, and Jewish community, it is quite likely that I would never have been highly identified Jewishly and not likely have chosen to devote my professional career to strengthening Jewish life." We are delighted to welcome you.

JOHN RUSKAY: Thank you. It's a great pleasure to be here at this event, which has the feel of a camp reunion. And I'm honored to be on this panel with people who have done so much and continue to do so much for Jewish camping.

Ramah changed my life. I think the core of Ramah is that it provides the opportunity for people to be introduced to a total living Jewish community. For those not raised in a committed family, not raised in a committed community, it can be—as it was for me—a life-changing and transformational experience. Said differently, until you experience a Shabbat, why learn what so many educators want to teach? I think when people claim that the sole answer to the challenge of Jewish renewal is Jewish education, particularly formal, they're failing to understand that for people not raised in a committed environment and never having been exposed to the beauty and power of Jewish life, there's little motivation to learn. That's why so many of us have tried to move the community to focus on Jewish summer camps, Israel trips, and youth groups to strengthen Jewish identity.

I also want to acknowledge, certainly for me as an adolescent and then a young man in my twenties, the import of experiencing the Jewish professionals who led Ramah and demonstrated that we could create environments that could change Jewish lives. I want to acknowledge Jerry Abrams sitting right in front of me. He was the director of the camp that I first attended in 1961, Camp Ramah in Nyack. I was with you the first year it opened. And in 1964 at Berkshires. These summers changed my life. Neither camp was about facilities! As one who later served on the sports staff at Camp Ramah in the Poconos, camp was not about the sports facilities. I actually sometimes think that there is a notion that we're going to compete on facilities, we're going to compete in sports, in computer equipment; yes, we should do all of them well. But the essence of Ramah is that it introduces people to live in an inspired community, a sacred community, a society of *kedushah.* I think we can get diverted on other points. I love sports. And I love all the other specialized activities. But Ramah must primarily be about Jewish life. It's about Jewish community. It's about connecting people with purpose and meaning.

I want to urge us to keep our focus here. And in this spirit, I want to acknowledge the people who took the lead in creating Ramah, which was a gift to us because it provided entrée into a world that I would never have been exposed to; one that shaped my life both personally and professionally, and connected me with a people and a tradition that I may never have been connected to.

This is a great moment. In my view, the North American Jewish community is increasingly focused on this broad issue. In small steps, we're reaching more and more young people we may not have reached otherwise. In New York, we have created Campership, a new camper initiative to provide an incentive for 300 new campers who never had attended Jewish summer camp to do so. I want to acknowledge my colleague, Dr. Alisa Kurshan, an incredibly gifted professional, who facilitated the creation of this program. Next year, we'll provide the scholarship incentives to send 600 new campers to experience Jewish summer camp.

I think we can cascade this; let people understand that with additional investments, we can increase the numbers who have the experience that so many of us did. But let us make certain that we keep our eyes on the prize and remain focused on the core; this is about making certain that when children attend Ramah and other Jewish summer camps, the camps are inspired settings for Jewish living and learning. We want to make certain that when they go to camp, that's what they experience. Thank you.

MITCH COHEN: Thank you, John. We have something else in common now and that is that both of us had Jerry Abrams as our first camp director. Peter Geffen is currently the director of Kivunim—The Institute of Experiential Learning for Israel and World Jewish Communities Studies, a program for students graduating high school to spend a year in Israel and throughout the world. Peter is also well known as the founder of the Abraham Joshua Heschel School in New York City and as a visionary in the world of Jewish education.

I met Peter when he sent his daughter, Nessa, to Camp Ramah in Canada and agreed to come and spend time teaching our staff and inspiring all of us involved in the camp's leadership. Peter, an alumnus of Ramah in Connecticut, Glen Spey, Canada, Poconos, and Israel, has been a friend and teacher, and it's my pleasure to ask him to share his thoughts with us today.

PETER GEFFEN: Ramah taught me to be an educator, first, in the informal setting of camp itself and then within the classroom. More than this seemingly practical skill-building, however, Ramah taught me to value the field of education and ultimately to choose it as my life's work. Ramah conveyed the subtle yet commanding message that education was a center of power and influence. We never discussed Wall Street or business. Ours was a universe of ideas, some eternal and others brand new. There is little question about the Jewish part of Camp Ramah. You've heard all the evidence for it today. The broader piece may not be spoken of as much, yet I am sure that it fuels every one of us in this room. Let us go out of this conference and really turn our relationship to Ramah into something far more dynamic so as to build upon what we were given toward the creation of a future far greater than what we've experienced and what we've seen ourselves. Thank you very much.

MITCH COHEN: Thank you Peter, and many thanks to all of our panelists.

RAMAH 60 רמה

Learning from Ramah

STEVEN M. BROWN

"I Make Jews": The Role of Rabbi David Mogilner, z"l, and His Influence on Ramah

IT WAS MY FIRST SUMMER in camp, 1961. I was in Bogrim (entering eighth grade) at Ramah Poconos, and I was trying to fit in. One day, my bunkmates decided to lift the table during the phrase in *birkat hamazon* referring to "this table at which we have eaten." For some reason, Rabbi David Mogilner, who stormed over to our table in red-faced fury, chose to throw me out of the *ḥadar ochel.* He commanded me to wait for him outside. My Hebrew was good enough to have understood that much. I stood outside waiting for the next shoe to fall—maybe I would be sent home. The wait seemed interminable. All the campers and staff had already left the dining room. Finally, I saw him come out, take a seat on one of the white Adirondack chairs scattered in front of the dining room, and begin to schmooze with a few staff members. At long last he lifted his hand and beckoned me with his index finger. I think he said in Hebrew something like, "Do you know why I threw you out?" I replied in the affirmative, and he said something on the order of, "Don't let it happen again." I quickly returned to my bunk and huddled with my *madrich* who was aware of what had happened. It was at that moment that I learned the meaning of the bunk as "home haven,"[1] a term I was to learn formally years later when I entered the Mador program for counselors in training. But what I now know is that the phrase, which I thought "Mogy" had invented, was one he learned from his teacher, Joseph Schwab (Brown, 1997). As we learned from him, so he learned from his mentors and teachers. The elements of my encounter with Rabbi Mogilner are echoed again and again in tens upon tens of loving comments, reflections, and tributes sent to me as I began contemplating this retrospective tribute to my teacher and mentor.

RABBI STEVEN M. BROWN, *Ed.D., is the head of school at the Jack M. Barrack Hebrew Academy in Philadelphia and a former dean of the William Davidson Graduate School of Jewish Education of The Jewish Theological Seminary.*

As I write this chapter, my career as a Jewish educator is in its forty-third year. Not a day goes by that I do not remember something Rabbi Mogilner taught me or that I do not ask myself how he might react to what I am doing, saying, or thinking. He is alive and well in my heart and mind. When I offered to write this retrospective on his influence on Ramah and me, I asked Rabbi Mitch Cohen, National Ramah Director, to send an e-mail message requesting other people's recollections of Rabbi Mogilner's work and influence. I was overwhelmed with responses. Accordingly, I decided to allow those voices to speak in this article. My own recollections about him and how he influenced me were affirmed repeatedly by testimonies to many of the same ideas, values, and philosophy of education that I feel shaped me as a young educator and have stayed with me throughout my career. Many of the reflections on particular "Mogilnerisms" stem from a document that he used to teach his famous course at the *Mador Le'immun Madrichim* (National Counselor Training Institute).

This retrospective on Rabbi Mogilner's life and influence as a Jewish educator includes a look at his strong and powerful personality as a force in itself; his role as rabbi, teacher, and mentor to a whole generation of Ramahniks; an analysis of his educational principles and theory of educational practice; comments on the centrality of Hebrew and Israel in his work; and a summary of his educational administrative approach, drawn from respondents' accounts and his own memoranda.

Launching Mogilner

David Mogilner was a bunk counselor in Camps Massad, Sollel, and Ramah Wisconsin. He directed Ramah Wisconsin (1958–59); Ramah Poconos (1960–67, 1975); Ramah Israel Seminar (1969–70); Mador (1966–67 in the Poconos and 1971–75 in the Berkshires); and served as National Ramah Director (1968–74). He graduated from Yeshiva University in 1952 and was ordained by the Rabbinical School of The Jewish Theological Seminary (JTS) in 1957.

Respondents recall Rabbi Mogilner in vivid ways: a giant in my mind, fresh and enthusiastic, our rebbe, at once a tyrant, a father, a master teacher, and a source of inspiration to a seventeen-year-old kid; he was the professor for teaching group dynamics and education theory, as well as a camp director and a terrific rabbi. Some were quite afraid of him, especially when they were younger. Others, like Rabbi Wayne Franklin of Temple Emanu-El in Providence, Rhode Island, recall that "he was prepared not to be the most beloved person around because he was hard-driving and insistent. But he had his eye on the ball and helped everyone in his camp community learn to share the goals and reach the goals with him." Architect Daniel Alter describes him as "an intense man with wavy dark hair, olive skin, a slight paunch, dark framed glasses, and a cigarette in his hand. He would shout or yell if he felt that was required to make his point. But he was often seen smiling and his intensity was part of his charisma."

Rabbi Mogilner was a product of a different age in American education and society. Given his commitment to role modeling and being an example of the ideal person, his addiction to smoking, his often enraged temper, and his sometimes intimidating way of disciplining campers and staff probably would not be well received today. He once told us that he "decided" when he would get angry and to use anger purposefully. I wonder how much of that was a cover for his intense drive to perfect the educational environment for which he had charge and constantly to tune every aspect of it to align with his vision.

Although he enjoyed being the center of all things at camp, he could be self-effacing. Rabbi Shalom Lewis of Congregation Etz Chaim in Cobb County, Georgia, fondly recalls his 1966 Mador experiences with Mogy:

> At the morning Mador meetings in front of Mogy's house, he took one glance at our group (total of seventy-five) and could identify who was not there. It was amazing . . . no hesitation but literally a split-second glance. I recall another such meeting; for some reason none of us was sitting up close to Mogilner. He pulled off his shoes and smelled both feet as he asked, "My feet don't smell, why are you all sitting so far back?

Longtime Ramah staff member and Jewish educator, Edwin Frankel, Poconos radio station director, responded to Rabbi Mogilner's request to be interviewed on the first day of camp for later broadcast (in Hebrew, of course):

> Having lived for a year in Israel, I opened the give and take with the words *kevod harav* [Honorable Rabbi]. He immediately stopped me and demanded, *"Kera li David"* [call me David]. It was never easy to call him David, but from that moment his humility shined."

So central was Rabbi Mogilner to the spirit and culture of the camp that it is easy to understand the memory described by William Agress, a religious-school teacher at The Jewish Center in Princeton:

> I was at Ramah Poconos in 1964. The candidates for U.S. President that year were Johnson and Goldwater. So we decided to run our own candidate for President: David Mogilner. To this day more than forty years later, whenever I hear the song "Waltzing Matilda," in my mind it becomes "Launching Mogilner, launching Mogilner, *anaḥnu* launching Mogilner *hayom*."

The song went on with the words: *hu oleh ve'oleh umistovev bamarom, anaḥnu* launching Mogilner *hayom*. But William neglected to add the second verse, which I remember very well. Lest anyone think Mogilner's decisions and personality were always popular with campers, another verse was later appended: Launching

Mogilner, launching Mogilner . . . *hu yored veyored umistovev begehinnom, anaḥnu* launching Mogilner *hayom!*[2]

The approach-avoidance many felt toward Rabbi Mogilner is captured by attorney Morton M. Steinberg, the immediate past president of the National Ramah Commission, who remembers him as camp director in Wisconsin (1958–59).

> He always spoke *only* Hebrew to the campers, which distanced him from us but in retrospect was the encouragement we needed to learn the language—if you wanted to know what was going on and what was being said during announcements, you had to learn Hebrew. As a result of his demeanor and his Hebrew, we all expected that he would be very strict in his discipline if we had to encounter him directly for any misbehavior. Of course, when the time came when I had to face him directly (I was fourteen), I was not happy. . . . It occurred when about five of us were horsing around in our cabin and eventually caused the pipe to a bathroom sink to break, spurting water all over the bathroom of an adjoining cabin. This was major and the next day we were called into the director's office. He was very serious and spoke in a grave tone of voice. Of course, he spoke in Hebrew so I didn't understand a word of what he said, but one of the guys did, and he was our spokesman. And he responded repeatedly with *ken* and *lo*. Finally, it was evident that Mogilner was through talking, and we got up to leave. When we got outside, we all asked our friend what our punishment was to be—we each had to pay camp a 25-cent canteen book coupon for the repair of the pipe! I was never so relieved in my life.

Why are these incidents so seared in our memories? They are not bitter memories, but ones in which we were deeply impressed with the man's principles and standards. Was he the demanding parent, the drill sergeant, or just a man who was passionate about his vision of how things ought to be? He had a clear, articulate vision of 24/7 educational theory and practice that guided every waking moment. Perhaps this comment from attorney Lois Gimpel Shaukat helps us better understand the combination of strictness and benevolence that characterized this man:

> I learned from Rabbi Mogilner many things and for some reason the thing that stands out—and this seem peculiar to some—is that "less is more." His presence—both in stature and style was imposing—at least to me, and I'm pretty sure to other campers as well. With that imposing presence was an incredible warmth and sense of caring—a pretty atypical combination of personality traits. The way I learned from him that "less is more" is that with a glance—either approving or disapproving, a smirk or a stern eye—he conveyed a very clear message. Without saying a word, he was able to convey depths, and I used to find myself amazed at the extent to which he seemed

> to know exactly what was going on where and with whom at all times. I learned from his behavior . . . that few words and small gestures have more power than many words and big gestures.

Interestingly enough, long before cognitive research in education pointed to the power of covering less content but studying it in greater depth (less is more), Mogilner seemed to intuit this research-based finding, making it part of his own theory of practice.

Rabbi Mogilner's humility and constant role-modeling manifest themselves in small but powerful ways. Joanne Ginn Glassoff, teacher at Solomon Schechter Academy in Howell, New Jersey, and at Congregation B'nai Israel in Toms River, New Jersey, recounts her summer in Bogrim when it was her bunk's turn to wait tables.

> Somehow I was assigned to the *hanhalah* (senior staff) table. It was my first experience carrying so many dishes and doing all that is involved with meal time tasks. . . . I was in awe of the rabbinic presence and weight at the table. Rabbi Mogilner always helped me clear the table and stack so I would not be the last one into the kitchen with my dishes, as he saw I was having trouble getting the adults to finish so I could clear. I remember a kind hand and face that I could count on at each meal that week.

He also could be quite insistent about the way people treated one another in day to day encounters at camp. Cindy Goldfarb Blum, an early-intervention specialist, describes one encounter:

> As a Bogrim camper at Ramah Poconos during the summer of 1966, I developed a friendship with a slightly older boy who was a member of the kitchen staff. Typically, during meal times, he would venture out of the kitchen into the ḥadar ochel to be sure the wait staff was performing adequately. If he neared my table, we would exchange greetings. It was during one of these greetings that Mogilner overheard me refer to my friend as "kitchen boy." What a mistake that was! Swiftly, Mogy escorted me outside, chastised me for using a term that could be interpreted as referring to a person of lesser value and embarked on a lecture about social strata and respect for all individuals regardless of the role they played in a community. The incident left me in tears for more than a day. Despite the fact that I had used the term in jest, playfully flirting with this older boy, the incident had a strong impact on me. And, quite surprisingly, as a college student and in my developing professional life, it remained a constant reminder of the place in society people often find themselves and the dignity they muster to perform a contributory role. I spent a great part of my career in special education and early intervention working for a nonprofit human services agency in Head Start communities in Philadelphia. It was in these communities that Rabbi Mogilner's words constantly reverberated in my ears.

Rabbi Mogilner was a passionate, zealous, and assertive presence—always "on" and always in charge. He was mission driven, could get upset if things were done that violated his educational and religious principles, but would show that half smile, acknowledging his delight and embrace of campers and staff when pleased. Rabbi Benjy Segal, who directed the Ramah Programs in Israel, summarizes this complex man when he says:

> Perhaps I should immediately correct the impression that he was our "rebbe." He had his Hasidim [disciples], and I was one of them, but he did not play the role of *tzaddik* [righteous person]—or if he did, it was a tzaddik for an age that was cynical, sober, enlightened, doubting, an age of faith that was more determination than blindness. He did not hide his faults. He was too busy doing to worry about that. He did not pretend to be holy or particularly spiritual, and I grew to understand that refusal to reflect his self-image as an educator, one who eschewed any hint of manipulation. . . . Certainly David would not be comfortable with my sentimentality, though I can imagine him smiling because, among his other charming characteristics, he knew he was that good. I might only conclude by saying that his biggest heritage was the demonstration that education works. That simple message has supported me throughout my professional career.

The full force of Mogilner's personality, energy, and drive left lasting impressions on campers, staff, and even parents. Parting the veils of nostalgia would force us to admit that he might have tried more subtle approaches at times to make his points and still be successful in getting his message across, but then we might not have attributed so much of what we learned to his influence and overwhelming force. I do not think he acted this way to create a legacy; he just lived out his mission, passion, and vision day to day, thus leaving so many indelible impressions.

His decision to teach the Mador and his madrichim on a regular basis (two to three times per week) also should be noted. Modern management theory suggests that leaders should delegate everything possible to subordinates *except that which only they can do themselves.* Rabbi Mogilner understood well that if he were to have a profound influence on the camp culture and educational milieu, he had to work with his staff, personally, on a regular basis to help shape their thinking and work. I learned from that, and when I became head of a large Solomon Schechter day school in Philadelphia, I taught my Jewish studies faculty weekly and the entire faculty monthly. Nothing I did made more of an impact than that "teacher-student" relationship with my staff. It was a profound lesson I learned from Rabbi Mogilner. As Ramah reaches its sixtieth anniversary, the directorate ought to remember its critical role in shaping the minds and hearts of staffs and recognize the tasks that should be delegated and those that remain the prerogative of the top leader.

Ramah is My Pulpit

David Mogilner also was a rabbi and teacher of great significance for numerous campers and staff, leaving a life-long imprint on their minds, souls, and hearts. Vicky Kelman, director of family education at the Bureau of Jewish Education (BJE) of San Francisco, upon receiving the 2003 Covenant Award, wrote:

> I became a Jewish educator because a significant teacher (Rabbi David Mogilner) told me one summer, "You have the power to change the world." His words became entwined with the famous Robert Kennedy saying, "Some men see things as they are and say 'why?' I dream things that never were and say 'Why not?'" A gift of having come of age in the Sixties is the optimism that one individual can make a difference and that a group of individuals with shared goals can change the world. (Covenant Foundation, 2003)

For many respondents and for me personally, David Mogilner was in every sense a rabbi, teacher, and mentor. Unfortunately, he left us very little in the way of articles or writings, other than his camp handouts, administrative memoranda, and one article, entitled "Ramah is My Pulpit," which appeared in the Ramah fiftieth anniversary volume in which he enunciated his personal mission as rabbi and teacher:

> Immediately upon being ordained by the Seminary, I accepted an appointment as a Ramah director. My mother was upset; what could tell [*sic*] her friends when they asked about me and the pulpit I didn't accept. She found it difficult to say that I was a camp director. After all those years of study and preparation, it didn't sound like a "job for a nice Jewish rabbi." She didn't think to say I was a Jewish educator—there was no formal school building involved. She chose rather to say, "He works with youth." She really was right; Ramah was my pulpit and my constituency was young people. . . . Through the years, whenever I would speak to a group of parents about Ramah, I would define Ramah as a "Jewish, educational institution in a camp setting." I would talk about Ramah and not Camp Ramah. I was very careful about the words that I chose and I wasn't playing semantic games. Yes, the "Ramah experience" takes place in a camp setting, but the notion of Ramah as "just a camp" does injustice to it as the major force it is in Jewish life. . . . Every Ramah director is the director of a "*ḥeder* under the elms"—which provides Hebrew language studies for everyone; Jewish ideas for everyone; each according to his own level, her own background and intellectual maturity. . . . Next time they ask you, Ma, tell them what I do, tell them why I do it. Tell them I have a job that befits a "nice Jewish rabbi." Tell them I wouldn't have done it differently if I had to start over again. But, most important of all, Ma, tell them "Ramah makes Jews." (Mogilner 1997, 89, 90, 93)

Perhaps, without even knowing it, Rabbi Mogilner eliminated the overused and misunderstood dichotomy between formal and informal education.

That dichotomy has become an unhelpful canard in education. A "*ḥeder* under the elms" is a wonderful way of eliminating the false notion that educational settings or institutions are either formal schools or informal experiential places. Both have elements of informal and formal structures in order to be impactful and compelling. As we shall see later, his educational principles crossed these artificial boundaries to create a holistic approach to education that enveloped the whole person. Ironically, the "*ḥeder* under the elms" image was all too true. Although the camp reflected a Deweyian progressive philosophy, often the "formal" classes were mired in a traditionalist, frontal, very non-progressive approach. Ramah has struggled with this conundrum for years, often lessening or eliminating some of its "formal" classes. But we ought to realize that less of bad is not better. The same dynamism and creativity that goes into the rest of the program should be used to target a reconsideration of the "formal" or text study portion of the program drawing from the constructivist, personal meaning-making approach based on cognitive research on how people learn best. The "*ḥeder* under the elms" could become a place where students learn cooperatively, actively, and are able to make personal meaning from what they study.

Rabbi Elliot Dorff, Rector of the American Jewish University in Los Angeles, eloquently testifies to Rabbi Mogilner's hands-on style of leadership and the life changing role he played in campers' lives:

> It was the summer of 1958 at Camp Ramah in Wisconsin. I was 15. Every Monday night throughout the summer Rabbi Mogilner met with the Machon [the division of the oldest campers] to discuss Jewish practices and beliefs. At the first session, he started by asking how many of us kept kosher in and out of our homes. A certain number of people raised their hands. Then he asked how many of us did not keep kosher at all, and some of us raised our hands. Then he asked how many of us kept kosher at home but not out, which was my family's practice, and so I raised my hand along with others. Then he said: "It's you guys that I don't understand!" After all, we were inconsistent. Then, from week to week, beginning with concrete issues like *kashrut* and Shabbat and gradually engaging more abstract issues like revelation, prayer, and finally God, he was on the attack, effectively asking how anyone in his or her right mind could follow any of the traditional practices or believe any of the traditional beliefs. Now I recognize that was an ingenious tactic to take with teenagers, for it made us defend the tradition, rather than the other way around. Furthermore, for me, a rebel at heart . . . , this was nothing short of a revelation. Here was a rabbi, someone who had devoted his life to the Jewish tradition, and he was not only willing and able, but actually eager to ask questions that would undermine the basis of everything Jewish. More than any of the answers any of us suggested that summer, what stuck in my mind is the depth of the questions and the openness to consider and evaluate any answer. This convinced me that you did

not have to turn off your mind to be seriously Jewish, that Judaism clearly engaged your emotions, made an art of your life, and stimulated you to act morally, but it was open to deep intellectual inquiry as well. It was after that summer that I became an observant Jew. . . . David Mogilner had instilled in me the sense that my Jewish commitments were not simply a matter of habit or family tradition, but of serious and well thought-out conviction.

Rabbi Mogilner's influence was more than as a camp director or teacher. Rabbi Benjy Segal writes:

I see David as my teacher and rabbi, and I understand his influence on my life to have been immense. . . . David . . . was the first person to teach me Jewish thought, in monthly evenings [sessions] he would hold for teenagers in his home; and [he was] one of the first people to teach me Talmud (in a small group of three, all intending to go to rabbinical school). This model of personal integration of Jewish knowledge from various fields and general knowledge taken from varied disciplines was and remains for me the challenge of a decent Jewish educator. He achieved it, lived it, and demonstrated it, leaving it as a model for all who worked under him.

Paul Plotkin of Temple Beth Am in Margate, Florida, a youth director and rabbi for over thirty years recounts what he learned from Mogilner:

This is not a nine-to-five job I have. It is a lifetime calling of "Mogilner education," causing people to choose to change their behavior to a more intense Jewish life. Therefore, my life needed to be lived but always in such a way that it didn't interfere with my calling. I and my family, of course, had many needs, and we addressed them and lived them (well and fully I hope) but always 'off the clock' because when I was 'on duty' I was educating, and that was my focus. I chose this life, Mogilner framed it for me, and therefore, I was not resentful nor ever saw the job as in conflict with my needs. I always took care of them, but I learned at Mador to take care of them first and then totally dedicate myself to my "students."

Laurie Hoffman, executive director of the Center for Jewish Education of Rockland County, New York, remembers Rabbi Mogilner's teaching abilities:

[M]y teacher Rabbi David Mogilner, may he rest in peace, was by far the best teacher I have ever learned from. He integrated every aspect of teaching and learning into our [Mador] program. He was an excellent example, he made us into a group, he taught us process and used the process himself, he taught us problem solving by giving us *real* problems to solve. He was an example in total of what he taught.

Yes, he ran things like a boot camp and was very demanding. And yes, educational theory has changed considerably since then as have so many Jewish communal dynamics, but his passion for teaching and touching lives remains as an enduring legacy. Rabbi Moshe Saks adds:

> I had already decided to apply to JTS Rabbinical School, and both working for David Mogilner and getting to know him only strengthened my desire to become a Conservative rabbi. . . . Even today, I still use a Mogilner phrase when asked what I do for a living (the same question Mogilner was often asked by his mother when he was a camp director). "I make Jews," he used to say. After twenty-five years in the rabbinate, I haven't found any other phrase that so perfectly fits what we do.

Rabbi Cliff Miller, senior cataloger, Library of JTS, and rabbi of Temple Emanu-El in Bayonne, New Jersey, recalled a phrase in Rambam (Maimonides) he learned from Mogilner in a section warning about whom to appoint as a judge. Though Rambam states this concept in the negative, that is, not to appoint one who is not of the following characteristics, Rabbi Miller remembers it in the positive sense as summarizing Mogilner as teacher and rabbi to so many:

> *Ish hagun veḥakham beḥokhmat hatorah*—'a worthy man, learned in the wisdom of the Torah' (Maimonides). David Mogilner used the strength of his personality; his strong, principled, and integrated approach to education and Judaism; and his natural teaching abilities in the service of shaping and molding the hearts and minds of many who would go on to leadership positions in the Jewish community all over the world. He understood Ramah's original mission to prepare leaders for the Conservative Movement and North American Jewry. His success in achieving those goals reverberates till this day.

Da Lifnei Mi Attah Omed:[3] **Some Principles of Mogilner Education**

In a course I regularly taught in the William Davidson Graduate School of Jewish Education at JTS, "Introduction to Curriculum and Instruction," I always began the first class by asking students to review what in my opinion is the finest curriculum ever written. I divided them into groups and assigned different parts of the curriculum to each, inviting them to extrapolate or tease out the underlying educational principles that are antecedent to the particular curricular item. We then generated a list of principles and analyzed them. That curriculum, "The Counselor's Daily Routine," (see excerpts in Appendix A and related educational principles in Appendix B) was written by Rabbi Mogilner who used it as the centerpiece of his education course for the Mador Le'immun Madrichim, the National Ramah Counselor Training Institute, which he headed. He spent the entire summer unpacking its underlying conceptual and educational basis.[4] It was the first, most powerful, and still to this day, the finest course in education I have ever had. Many of the respondents to my call for reminiscences for this article concur. It is the richest, most powerful expression of the daily enactment of a truly integrated approach to formal and informal experiential learning. And though fashion may change (few of us put on *maggafayim* [overshoes] when it rains), his concern for the physical welfare of children, for example, is still very much central to any educational enterprise. A fusion of principles 17 and 20 (see Appendix B) still means that camp staff should spread out among campers during *tefillah* and "over pray" to serve as role models and encourage imitation.

Rabbi Mogilner was really the first college professor for many of my generation. We had just graduated from high school and entered the Mador program. He treated us as young adults, not older teenagers. He took Schwab's approach to inquiry methodology seriously and created an academic and curricular structure that made us think. He asked us to work backwards, to extrapolate from the givens of camp (e.g., waking up before the campers, waking them individually, looking at routine behavior as a source of understanding developmental and personal issues) the underlying educational principles that gave rise to these particular ways of enactment in everyday camp life. No wonder so many respondents credit him with such a profound influence throughout the rest of their adult lives. He was the first person to invite us to reflect somewhat objectively on our own educational experience and to teach us a way of mature thinking and acting that was transferable to parenthood, professional life, and standards of educational practice. He transmitted a theory of practice.[5] Though the "Counselors Daily Routine" looks like a cookbook, he used it simply as a starting point to engage Madorniks and counselors in thinking about a theory of educational practice that was holistic, learner centered, and transformative. He was, quite simply, the master of what we call informal education, which is better termed, educating the whole person. He translated theory into everyday tangible practice. Ruth Tomases Joffe, Ph.D., recalls:

> After a fellow Madornik was tardy to class, Rabbi Mogilner taught that when one arrives late to a class or meeting, it suggests that the person who is late values his own time above that of others. While I cannot claim to always be punctual, I make an effort to be, in part because of this view. This perspective has influenced my way of approaching human interactions in general by encouraging me to take into consideration the influence of my behavior on others.

The first summer I was a madrich, I was in charge of the youngest bunk in camp. One of my ten-year-old campers was having a very bad day and evening and was getting into fights and fisticuffs with other kids in the bunk. I actually had to wrestle him down to the ground and get on top of him to stop his outbursts. He had lost his father not too long before, and I think he was angry inside. When I tried to calm him, he just screamed back, "Why should I stop?" I replied without hesitation: "Because you are a Jew, and this is not how

Jews behave!" I felt all the tension go out of his body. He relaxed. I guess the combined weight of my body and three thousand years of Jewish tradition gave him pause. We had no further trouble with him the rest of the summer. This incident was for me the coming together of all that Mogilner taught me about the teachable moment, and the necessity of understanding the importance of daily, routine behaviors in children in order to educate them toward a given end.

Judy Dvorak Gray, director of communications for Masorti Olami, the World Council of Conservative Synagogues, details yet another example of the teachable moment, which occurred during the summer of 1962 when she and several other twelve- to thirteen-year-olds were sent to Rabbi Mogilner's house by their counselors after picking on a fellow camper:

> We sat on the rug on the floor of his home, and he stood over us, looking each one of us directly in the eye: *"Da lifnei mi attah omed!"* he boomed out. "Know before whom you stand!" he repeated. I knew who was standing before me, and I was petrified! It took me a while to realize that he was talking about God and that he was teaching us that God judges all of our actions including how we treat our fellow human beings. It was indeed a powerful lesson. By the end of the session, we were crying—not because of any punishment imposed on us, but because we realized the effect of our actions on our bunkmate. To this day, when I hear that expression, I am back on the rug in his house and trembling!

Although those of us who knew Mogilner thought most, if not all, of his ideas were his inventions, it is important to note that he was part of a cohort of pioneer Ramah directors heavily influenced by the guiding hand of Rabbi Seymour Fox, dean of the JTS Teachers Institute. In the service of Ramah, Fox drafted many JTS faculty members and other well-known educators such as Ralph W. Tyler of the Center for Advanced Study in the Behavioral Sciences and Joseph Schwab, Harper Fellow of the University of Chicago (Brown 1997). Fox, Mogilner, and the other early pioneer directors were heavily influenced by Lou Newman, who directed Ramah Wisconsin (1951–53) and later became my predecessor as head of the Melton Research Center for Jewish Education at JTS.

> His ideas were strongly influenced by those of John Dewey, and the Progressive approach to education permeated many elements of his thinking. Committed to participatory education and to a democratic environment, Newman was noted for his dual belief in respect for the individual and individual respect for the group. Most important, because he believed that camp could affect character, he wanted to create an atmosphere to build it—not only one that would teach Hebrew and provide a "good time." (Schwartz 1987)[6]

The "Counselor's Daily Routine" is a very detailed list of actions based on theory. Mogilner was a stickler for details because he believed the educative process was embedded in the myriad of daily encounters and decisions made by staff relating to campers. Professor Joe Lukinsky, *z"l*, reminds us:

> David was extremely careful about preparation. He hated sloppiness in this regard. He was famous for "Mogilner's Laws," which were actually the famous "Murphy's laws" although he may have had a few original ones, too. The one that he stressed the most was: "Whatever can go wrong, will go wrong." If you were using a film projector or slide projector, it had to be in working order and the one in charge of the program had to test it in advance and know how to work it, too. Also crucial was the matter of alternatives. What will you do if, in spite of all care, the projector does not work? What is your alternative in reserve, and it had better be good, too. No excuses."

Ultimately, it was from his behaviorist definition of education that all the myriad of details flowed: education is a process of changing people's behavior with a given goal or end in mind. Notice his important use of the word process, which implies iteration, recursiveness, and repetition. This notion of changing people's behavior based on values was reinforced daily by Mogilner. Long before the movement for outcomes-based assessment appeared that is so prevalent today, he focused his staff on an outcomes- or goals-oriented approach to educational planning. Formative and summative evaluations were not much a part of his teaching, other than to be implicitly contained in thinking through the planning and execution of an educational program.

Careful attention should be paid to the list of educational principles in Appendix B derived from the "Counselor's Daily Routine." The last six are particularly powerful metacognitive approaches to educational practice. Mogilner defined morality as the conflict between right and wrong. He taught that ethics is the conflict between opposing "rights" or forces. Thus, in many educational settings, the tension that must be negotiated is between conflicting rights, for example, attending to the needs of the group while caring about the individual. On another level, it's the conflict of allocation of scarce resources (money and personnel) in an educational setting; or about resolving the tension teachers face as to whether coverage of more material or in depth treatment of less material is the way to shape instruction.[7] Similarly, as in #17, sometimes the educational means to an end is a goal in itself. The way a madrich leads a bunk discussion on a group problem or on setting up a routine task such as daily *nikkayon* (bunk clean up) teaches a methodology of democratic problem solving in a respectful manner. Perhaps most critical to the educational enterprise is #21, that is, very few educational situations can be reduced to the application of only one principle. This is the counterweight to a cookbook approach that the "Counselor's

Daily Routine" might seem to infer. Teaching recent high school graduates in the Mador on the verge of their college years to think this way was a bold and innovative approach to shaping their theory of educational practice. Mogilner's emphasis on detail, the interrelatedness of all the parts to the educational whole made him the exemplar of holistic, integrated, and transformative educational theory and practice.

Ivri — Dabber Ivrit!

It was 1963, and I was a camper in the Machon, the oldest division in the Poconos. My wonderful counselor, Shelly Podwol (now Rabbi Shalom Podwol of Congregation Am Ehad in Park Forest, Illinois) decided our bunk would perform two songs in front of the camp at dinner one evening in the ḥadar ochel. One song was in Hebrew, the other in English. After the applause, we sat down at our tables, and Rabbi Mogilner stormed over, enraged. He said in Hebrew, of course, to us, 'Thank you very much for destroying Hebrew in camp!" Mild-mannered, sweet Shelly was stung because he meant no harm. Quietly, over the next few days he procured a translation of the English song, and we proceeded to learn it in Hebrew and perform it in the ḥadar ochel. Rabbi Mogilner was pleased. I remember the first words of the song to this day: *levanah keḥullah hibbita alai levad, beli ḥalom benafshi, beli ahuvati*—the first line of "Blue Moon." It was a time in the history of Ramah in the Poconos when the only permissible language spoken in the ḥadar ochel or in any public setting was Hebrew; no compromises, no justifications for English.

Lois Gimpel Shaukat recounts a poignant story of Mogilner's powerful commitment to speaking Hebrew at camp:

> [J]ust a few days before his sudden death, we performed [the play] "*Ish Ḥasid Haya*" [Once There Was a Hasid] as our *edah* (Bogrim) play. One of the vignettes was the story of a very large man named Gedalia. . . . I played the part of Gedalia, and . . . I needed to borrow a pair of pants from Rabbi Mogilner. I didn't exactly relish having to ask Rabbi Mogilner (in Hebrew, of course, since he would ignore you if you spoke to him in English) to borrow his pants for a play. I did ask him, . . . and of course, I had to explain to him exactly why I needed to borrow *his* pants—a delicate matter for a fourteen-year-old girl with not great Hebrew. And of course, Rabbi Mogilner in his inimitable style of few words and heavy gestures, insisted on a detailed explanation—anything to get a kid to keep speaking in Hebrew. Anyway, I borrowed the pants, stuffed them with lots of pillows, performed the play, and I returned them to him at dinner a couple days later, the day before he died. I mostly think of Rabbi Mogilner as having pants that were not easy to fill.

Mogilner's commitment to Hebrew was soulful and natural. Edwin Frankel recounts it well:

> From the very start it was clear that Hebrew, a Ramah value that I held especially dear, was truly central to him. Ramah directors at all the camps in which I worked spoke Hebrew publicly. He also spoke Hebrew in private, depending on who was around. It was fully natural, never strained, and rarely particularly sophisticated. The Hebrew he spoke was Hebrew that the campers and staff could readily understand.

David was always an accessible role model. How many of us recall the famous Mogilnerisms: *"Hasha'ah achshav, lefi she'oni shehu be'etzem she'on hamaḥaneh, hi . . ."* and *"Im kar li, kar lachem, vekar li!"*[8] William Agress reminds us that "he had a unique way of combining English and Hebrew that allowed campers to understand him and learn Hebrew at the same time. Whenever we left the ḥadar ochel [or when instructing waiters to continue their work during announcements], we were told to do it '*besheket uv-finesse.*'"[9] Rabbi Mogilner was heavily influenced by his knowledge of the approach of Camp Massad in the 1940s and inspired by his own experience at Sollel, a work-study, Hebrew-speaking camp for seventeen-year-olds with differing approaches to Zionism (Schwartz, 1987).

For Mogilner, the Hebrew language was the key to the kingdom of Jewish identity, learning, and love of the people and land of Israel.[10] It was central to the formation of a unique group culture and individual bonding with the larger group. From his earliest days as a counselor at Massad, Sollel, and Ramah Wisconsin, he was an ardent Zionist and eventually fulfilled his lifelong dream of making aliyah.

Mogilner's lifelong commitment to Israel and his personal goal of aliyah is echoed in the offering of Rabbi David Geffen, Ph.D., author of the *American Heritage Haggadah*:

> [I] met him twice—once at camp, the other [time] at a study group for Conservative professionals, not rabbis, in Judaica, at the home of the Tigays [Dr. Jeffrey and Helene] in Philly . . . we were studying material from *Yeḥezkel* [the prophet Ezekiel] . . . Chaim and Adina Potok, the Tigays, the Silbersteins, the Mogilners. . . . Jeff Tigay presented, Potok responded, the rest of us were quiet. Mogilner shouted out: "Why in the world are we studying *Yeḥezkel*? We all belong in Israel where the dry bones[11] (he said it in Hebrew) are truly alive. If we want Conservative Jewry to make an impact on Israel, you Tigays, you Potoks, you Silbersteins, you Geffens must make aliyah." A year later, Mogilner [was] dead; three years later we made aliyah.

Mogilner was very instrumental in increasing the number and quality of Israelis (the *mishlaḥat*) who were recruited to work in the Ramah camps each summer. He insisted that they be met at the airports (I assume as a gesture of hospitality and to prevent them from taking any side trips before arriving at camp!). In June 1972, he wrote in a memo to directors:

> It is my understanding that those *mishlaḥat* members who will be going to Canada and Wisconsin will be housed overnight, and all others will be picked up at the airport and taken directly to camp. Please arrange that this be done by someone more than just a driver, whose Hebrew is a bit more expansive than *ken* or *lo*. (Mogilner, June 13, 1973)

Checklists and the No Trust Assumption

Long before modern business theory and practice touted the benefits of "management by walking around," Rabbi Mogilner practiced that strategy zealously in his daily administration work at camp. Dr. Baruch Feldstern of Pardes Institute in Jerusalem testifies to Rabbi Mogilner's penchant for knowing what was going on and demanding that people think through their educational decision making:

> While I cherish my years at Ramah and greatly enjoyed the summers that I was a counselor, the role itself of being a counselor under Mogilner was not relaxing. I think I went around expecting that at any moment he might pop out from behind a tree and ask me, "What is your educational justification for the activity that you just ran?" Once it actually happened just that way. One Shabbat morning my campers had tefillot, followed by a talk or some other program in which they were totally passive, followed by lunch. After lunch they were supposed to have, say, forty-five minutes of rest time. I felt they had had more than enough inactivity already, plus I knew that they often missed out on tennis courts or sports fields because older campers beat them to it Shabbat afternoons. After half an hour I let them leave the bunk for the fields. As I was myself walking up from the bunk, Mogilner popped out from behind that ominous tree and said, "Where are your campers?" Feeling like Adam in the Garden, I told him what I had done and spelled out my rationale. He simply said, "Okay," and moved on, probably looking for another tree to hide behind. I don't think he thought that I had done something great. But I think that at worst, he may have considered what I had done as an error of judgment, and he was satisfied that I was thinking the way he wanted his counselors to think.

There is an important message in this tale of Mogy hiding behind the trees. He was not a perfectionist so much as someone insistent upon thinking through one's educational goals and objectives. He could tolerate errors of judgment but had little patience for sloppy planning or lack of thoughtfulness in making educational decisions.

Attorney Gerry Kobell, a former Poconos business manager, a long-time member of the Camp Ramah in New England executive committee, and a former officer of the National Ramah Commission (NRC), has eloquently summarized the thoughts and experience of many respondents' views of Rabbi Mogilner's administrative talents and focus:

> David Mogilner was a master teacher, who taught me, as his business manager at Camp Ramah in the Poconos for five years, from 1962 through 1966, (and as a Bogrim madrich in 1961) to find the ways and means, even in a remote setting with [a] limited budget, to enable specialists to actualize their ideas and programs to the maximum extent. The achievement of excellence was always the objective. David was also a consummate administrator, and the camp hanhalah meetings unhesitatingly tackled the myriad of programming and scheduling conflicts that taxed our limited facilities, especially on rainy days. We had schedules for *yom bruntsh* [brunch day], *yom bruntsh gashum* [rainy brunch days], *yom meyuḥad* [special days], and *yom kerikhim* [sandwich days], all with their special changes involving seven *edot*. . . . And he did it all in Hebrew and with good humor. I remember one day in late April, in my first month as business manager that he called me with what he called "good news and bad news." What was the bad news? The caretaker just quit. What was the good news? David said that he was not very good anyway! It was hardly an auspicious beginning for a new business manager entering into his senior year of college, but David was not worried. He had utmost faith in the people he had chosen for an assignment, and we all felt strongly committed to fulfill his expectation to the maximum extent possible. David also seemed to have boundless energy. Despite the late night meetings, he was the first one up to meet with the camp doctor, dining room steward, and myself to review the day and the problems that could be encountered. David did not have late mornings. He only had late evenings. . . . He was also keenly aware of the enormity of the task before us as Jewish educators. He knew that many of our campers encountered varied degrees of practice and observance at home and that the Jewish living we were teaching could not always be continued through the year. "*al na nerammeh et atzmeinu*" he would say, "we should not deceive ourselves that we would always be successful."[12]

Miles Bunder, retired Jewish educator and founder of Yashar Lachayal in Israel, comments on his experience of Rabbi Mogilner's administrative concerns:

> In 1965 I served as assistant steward in Poconos as part of a training program approved by Burt Cohen. Did it again in 1966 and in 1968 took over as steward in Camp Ramah Canada for four years. Then Palmer in 1973. . . . Rabbi Mogilner taught me the importance of serving good, wholesome food to staff and campers, and how it affected each and every day. We would meet every morning, and when we saw rain, or a particularly tough day, we would change the menu to offer a better dessert, or add some "child friendly" items to the menu. I loved Rabbi Mogilner. I considered him one of the reasons I went into Jewish education and stayed with it for forty years.

> He was the ideal director, except for one fault, which he and I joked about—he looked terrible in shorts.

Two major administrative philosophies were foundational to Rabbi Mogilner. He believed strongly in creating an administrative checklist for all educational programming and planning and using that list to insure that all the details of a plan or project were fine tuned, checkable, and thought through in advance. This made an indelible impression on Rabbi Wayne Franklin:

> I remember learning from David about making checklists for programs—learning to think through each and every detail that would be needed to prepare for an event, execute an event, and finish up after one. I still use what I learned from him. It may not be the most profound lesson he taught, but it has been very helpful. And I can tell when others don't prepare this way!!

His second major managerial belief was his "no trust assumption." Although he believed in delegation of responsibility, he also believed that it was the supervisor's sacred responsibility to assume that the tasks assigned may not be properly performed unless the supervisor checked on progress and verified compliance. Dr. Joe Freedman, director of Ramah Programs in Israel, puts it this way:

> The No Trust Assumption: don't rely on any person or thing unless you have a reason to (from experience). Sounds very cruel—like something Donald Trump would say, but it really works!

Rabbi Mogilner became the first National Ramah Director in 1968. Unfortunately, Ramah's economic health and the momentum of the founding generation was in decline and Rabbi Mogilner "reaped the whirlwind" (Brown, 1997). Similarly, the youth culture of the late sixties and early seventies became suspicious of authority and "presented the camps and their sponsoring institution (JTS) with unprecedented challenges" (Brown, 1997). Rabbi Mogilner's administrative style as National Director reflects this mode. His memoranda to camp directors preserved in the JTS Ratner Center for Conservative Judaism Archives are quite stark, commanding, top down, and no nonsense. He is focused on proper billing and collection of fees; sees himself as commander-in-chief of all the camps and head steward of upholding their fiscal and spiritual standards and quality. But that half smile is evident in his ability to poke fun at himself, such as in a memo that begins: "I am enclosing a literary selection from the *Wall Street Journal* regarding opening and closing dates of camp, mishlaḥat evaluations, Ramah printing, all past sins and future omissions." It is a cartoon of an executive sitting behind a desk piled high with papers, talking to a colleague standing alongside saying: "These memos are to remind me of those memos" (Mogilner 1972).

He worked with the camp directors as a cohort and was open to innovative approaches to deal with some of the youth culture issues such as the proposal by Poconos director, Danny Margolis (now the director of the BJE of Greater Boston), in 1974 to

> restructure the camp educationally, religiously, and programmatically (as well as administratively) in order to improve the quality of the camp's program, as well as to test a series of alternative designs for how summer camps, particularly Ramah camps, should be structured and organized.

Although open to this radical proposal, Mogilner's memo to directors reads:

> I must insist on an immediate reaction, if you have not already done so (see my memorandum to you of October 10). I think Danny's proposal will have a tremendous effect on the Ramah camps if followed in its entirety and before allowing him to go ahead, in whole or in part, I would like to hear from you." (Mogilner 1973)[13]

The financial woes of the camps and the Seminary's vulnerability resulted in numerous memos on fiscal prudence and responsibility. In one colorful memo, he wrote:

> I am writing to remind you of the need for monthly billings, even during the course of the summer, for all your camper and accounts receivable, so that you do not get caught in September with the huge account receivable sums that were outstanding at the end of last session.

He adds five colorful stickers that can be appended to different bills urging payment or noting past due status. In response, another director sent him an alternative set of stickers that his camp preferred. It's not clear whose stickers prevailed (Mogilner 1971a).

He was driven even in this national role to make people live up to what he perceived as their responsibilities and would brook no equivocation: "If you don't return immediately your comments on the general salary scale and the medical salaries sheet you will spend a lot more time sitting at the directors meetings" (Mogilner 1970).

Rabbi Mogilner's own tensions between caring about others and achieving his educational objectives in his way are evidenced by the following two examples of his administrative style and thoughts as National Ramah Director. In one memo he bemoans

> the noise level and time wasted during meetings [of Ramah directors]. Along with individual's [*sic*] senses of frustration are problems (serious problems) in our own group dynamics. I'm not a nut on sensitivity training and dynamics—certainly not in the light of what has been said around the table before about these—BUT it is incredible how often we interrupt

> each other, how often we are defensive, we go out to score points and not to raise issues or arguments, and wind up shouting and trying to get things out without any realization of where we've been, where we're trying to go, etc. We cannot afford to look forward to seven days of meeting with no agreement on these matters. I refuse to participate in sessions where one person will say "please don't interrupt, let me finish" and then go right on and interrupt someone else. I'd like your comments. (P.S. There are others who felt similarly). (Mogilner 1969)

All this from the man to whom we all looked to learn the art and practice of group dynamics with campers and how to lead a discussion with them! In his attempt to centralize authority and leadership of the camps in the national office, he writes:

> I am writing in regard to the Ongoing Ramah Policies. Now that the book is pretty much complete, I expect the procedures to be followed at every one of our camps and in all areas. I would expect that every administrator especially familiarize himself with those sections that deal with tuition procedures, guest procedures, medical procedures, fiscal procedures and administrative, maintenance and commissary procedures. I would expect records to be kept according to the procedures, inventories to be made up according to the procedures, etc., etc. *Deviation from these procedures as presented will not be acceptable without written confirmation from me.* [Italics are mine] (Mogilner 1971b)

Rabbi Mogilner's complexity as a man and an educational leader led, I believe to constant tensions within him between the *matzui* and the *ratzui*—between reality and the desirable. Perhaps this final vignette, which captures yet another side of his administrative role, for example, relating to parents, best captures that tension: Sandy Savitz Gruenberg, Judaic Studies Curriculum Coordinator and Learning Center Director of the Solomon Schechter Lower School of Westchester, writes:

> Rabbi Mogilner was frequently so cool and strict with parents. One year when I was on staff, my parents could only come up on one day, and it turned out to be Tish'ah Be'Av. When my parents entered the camp, and he saw them, he said in his firm tone, "Don't expect to get any food here today." My mother in her inimitable polite manner replied, "Rabbi Mogilner! The food we came to camp for they don't serve in the dining room." He gave his little smile and could not have been sweeter to my parents the entire visit. He was someone to me who could always learn from others and could accept people on their terms.

Mogilner was the first National Ramah Director. Clearly, he operated under the assumption that there was to be a unified, national administrative, educational, and religious policy shared by all the camps, and that indeed, JTS was in charge of the camps' educational mission and vision. I doubt the other directors were always happy with his commanding voice, but it is clear he had a coherent vision of shared mission that informed all his work and administrative strategies. We are in a very different place today with camps demanding a certain amount of independence from the central authority of JTS and the National Ramah Commission. As Ramah reached its sixtieth anniversary, the questions of what unifies the camps as a whole and where individual differences can exist and flourish without straining the meaning of what it means to be called a Camp Ramah, continues to be a crucial issue.

Baruch Dayyan Ha'emet

David Mogilner died suddenly of massive heart failure at Camp Ramah in the Poconos in 1975 when he was serving as interim director. He was forty-four years old. One could assume that given his Type-A personality, overweight frame, his moderate-to-heavy smoking, his hard-driving determination, and sometimes volatile personality that such an end was always a real possibility. How ironic that his brother was serving as camp physician and could not help him. How ironic that David created the ultimate teachable moment for the staff and campers. The loss felt by his family, Sue Schiff Mogilner (Fox)[14] and his children, Hyim, Avinoam, Shifra, Elisheva, and Eitan was incalculable. Rabbi David Seed of Adath Israel Congregation in Toronto, Ontario, captures best what many respondents who were in camp that tragic summer recall:

> I was a Madornik in [the] Poconos in the last summer of David's life. I actually remember giving a *devar torah* on the *Ashrei* with the edah that morning and seeing an ambulance drive out of camp. We later learned the news that he was gone and all of us, especially the Madorniks were devastated. We had worked so closely with him as our teacher and mentor, and now we would no longer have the opportunity to learn from him. We understood quickly that we had responsibilities to our campers to fulfill while learning to deal with our own grief. It colored the rest of our summer, but instilled in us the idea that if we were going to continue to keep his legacy alive, we would have to do so by sharing what he had taught us if not in his name then by teaching others the lessons he had given us.

David Mogilner taught us to be role models; to know before whom we stand; to make Jews, and to make a difference. He was in so many ways *ish hagun veḥacham beḥochmat hatorah.*

Appendix A

Selections from Rabbi David Mogilner's "The Counselor's Daily Routine"

I. **Wake-Up Period**
   A. Wakes up 15 minutes before campers to attend to his own needs.
   B. Wakes up campers individually.
   C. Sees that the camper is properly dressed for weather and that he changes clothes daily. (Waker-upper will advise counselor as to proper clothes for that day's weather.)
   D. Sees whether they wash and brush teeth and use the bathroom.
   E. Whenever possible encourages camper to make bed before going to services.
   F. Sees that camper leaves for services on time.
   G. One counselor leaves with the first group, second counselor stays until last camper leaves.
   H. During this period the counselor looks for:
      1. Variations in wake-up habits.
      2. Variations in personal standards of cleanliness.
      3. Relation of each youngster's behavior on awakening to behavior rest of day.
      4. Kind of interpersonal relationships practiced among campers.

II. **Helping during the Services**
   A. Sits among campers.
   B. Helps set up prayer area prior to prayer.
   C. Concerns oneself with the aesthetic appearance of the prayer area.
   D. Brings benches and prayer books during the services if necessary.
   E. Helps campers follow service.
   F. Serves as an example to the campers, here, as well as elsewhere in camp program.
   G. "Over prays" in the sense of partaking in the prayers in a "louder" tone than usual.
   H. Concerns oneself with proper replacement of used religious articles.
   I. Sees that campers get into dining hall for breakfast on time.
   J. Walks among campers on way to dining room.

III. **Meals**
   A. Arranges for one staff member to be at table before campers enter.
   B. Concerns oneself with *hamotzi* allowance.

C. Sees that campers' behavior is indicative of the fact that *hamotzi* is a prayer.
D. Sees that there is a minimum of noise and confusion at the table.
E. Sees that each camper receives a portion on first serving.
F. Encourages campers to eat.
G. Complains to *proper* authority if quantity or quality of food is deficient.
H. Deals with waiter in Hebrew unless campers can do so.
I. If there is singing or someone speaks in front of the dining hall, he makes sure his table pays attention.
J. He makes sure the dishes are passed up at the end of the meal.
K. Sees that campers are aware that *birkat hamazon* is a prayer.
L. Sees that campers have copies of *birkat hamazon* until they know it.
M. Sits at the table in such a way as to:
   1. Be physically close to as many campers as possible.
   2. Be in a position to always see the dining room control area.
N. During the meal one watches for:
   1. Routine Hebrew usage.
   2. Campers interpersonal table relationships.
   3. The manner in which a camper eats.
   4. The kind of food a camper eats.
O. The counselor realizes that he is on display:
   1. His table manners
   2. The food he eats
   3. The way he reacts to food
   4. His participation in *birkat hamazon*
P. Takes last always.
Q. Plans for non-eating "waiting periods" at the table.
R. Sees that the campers walk leisurely out of the dining room.

Appendix B

Some Principles of Education Evident in Rabbi David Mogilner's "The Counselor's Daily Routine"

1. Education may be defined as a process of behavioral change toward a given end.
2. Pre-planning of all aspects of an educational activity is essential for success.
3. Every counselor is at all times the "example" of the ideal personality.
4. The counselor acts toward individuals individually.

5. The counselor acts in areas that concern the physical (broadly defined) welfare of the camper.
6. A counselor can never attend to his or her "private business" and work with campers at the same time.
7. The physical environment helps to shape any educational experience.
8. Every educational situation has its own set of priorities and so flexibility on the counselor's part is essential for sound educational programming.
9. The counselor sees routine as a means by which a camper's personality is expressed.
   9a. The counselor views a camper's break of routine as a problem of the camper's learning to accept and deal with responsibility.
10. Counselors must be aware of the developmental tasks applicable to any given age.
11. Every educational group has its own dynamics and personality that point to the way in which that group should be educationally managed.
12. A good educational goal clearly defines the desired end-achievement in behavioral terms.
13. Good educational planning should take into consideration the following components: awareness, anticipation, atmosphere.
14. Educational methodology should always be the result of a clearly stated goal.
15. The pacing of an educational activity is crucial to its success.
16. A variety of media over time should be used to reinforce educational goals.
17. Sometimes the educational means to an end is a goal in itself—e.g., a counselor's method of allowing campers to choose how the bunk will be cleaned teaches problem-solving skills.
18. There are times when a counselor does something herself because of the values inherent therein, e.g., picking up a piece of trash along the way.
19. Educational planning may be programmable via the use of administrative checklists, but an approach to education makes sense only in terms of general principles rather than specific laws.
20. A counselor uses his or her physical proximity to children to affect the instructional situation.
21. Very few educational situations are reducible to direct application of only one principle.
22. The conflict of two principles poses an "ethical problem."

Notes

[1]The camper's bunk was to serve as a refuge or safe haven from the expectations, pressures, even the tensions of living in the camp community and participating in various activities with specialists and teachers.

[2]Launching Mogilner, launching Mogilner, we are launching Mogilner today. He goes up and up and orbits on high, we are launching Mogilner today. Launching Mogilner, launching Mogilner, we are launching Mogilner today. He goes down and down and orbits in Gehinnom (the netherworld), we are launching Mogilner today.

[3]"Know before whom you stand."

[4]Professor Lee Shulman, President, Carnegie Foundation for the Advancement of Teaching, proudly reports that David was his counselor in Wisconsin in 1953 and 1954. Shulman recounts hearing discussions among junior counselors who studied with Dr. Seymour Fox at Wisconsin, and who had a powerful influence on Mogilner: "Fox conducted a daily seminar with the junior counselors. Nearly every day we would hear them recite mysterious names like Bettelheim, Redl, Erikson, and Dewey. There was one particular text that captured our attention. We suspected that it was a dirty book because its title, *Love Is Not Enough,* could hardly have been used to describe anything else, and it was reputed to include photographs. Late one night, after the junior counselors had gone off to do whatever such elders did after they were deluded into imagining that we campers were asleep, the most intrepid of us stole onto the cabin's front porch and found the forbidden volume. *Love Is Not Enough* was a real disappointment, at least form the erotic perspective!" L. S. Shulman, "Education Theory and Ramah," in *The Ramah Experience*, ed. S. C. Ettenberg and G. Rosenfield (New York: The Jewish Theological Seminary and the National Ramah Commission, 1989), 49–56.

Interestingly, Mogilner, who studied with Fox, made the choice not to immerse counselors-in-training in theoretical literature, but to teach them how to create and implement their own theory of practice based on the work of many of these theorists. For the camp setting, I believe Mogilner's approach was more developmentally appropriate for the Mador cohort.

[5]In today's educational lingo, he really taught us how to be a real *madrich* (counselor/guide). His "Counselor's Daily Routine" lays out a wonderful way of learning to be a guide on the side, rather than a sage on the stage!

[6]Mogilner and others modified Newman's approach, but "Fox, Mogilner, Cohen, Abrams, Lukinsky, and others never abandoned them altogether." M. Brown, "It's Off to Camp We Go: Ramah, LTF, and the Seminary in the Finkelstein Era," in *Tradition Renewed: A History of the Jewish Theological Seminary*, ed. J. Wertheimer (New York: The Jewish Theological Seminary, 1997), 1:823–54.

Later it was Schwab who took the pioneer group through a reconsideration of camp staffing patterns and methods. It was Schwab who helped them develop the notion of the bunk as home haven, an unpressured retreat from the specialty areas of camping skills, sports, crafts, and the arts. It was Schwab who emphasized careful "planned education," which led Newman to propose the Mador training program, which later Mogilner inherited and developed. So as we listen to some of the voices of generations of Ramahniks who felt the spell of Mogilner's educational influence, we need to understand that he, too, had his mentors and teachers. Mogilner probably developed his anti-competition approaches from Newman's influence; see S. R. Schwartz, "Ramah Philosophy and the Newman Revolution," in *Studies in Jewish Education and Judaica in Honor of Louis Newman,* ed. Alexander M. Shapiro and Burton I. Cohen (New York: Ktav, 1984), 7–21.

[7]Attorney Jonathan Funk of San Francisco remembers the summer of 1975: "Rabbi Mogilner told our Mador group that summer, 'The world is not black and white, *kinderlakh*; it is gray.' Perhaps not the most profound of his teachings, but to a group of know-it-all teenagers, it

was a message worth learning. These words have come back to me many, many times over the years as I have confronted difficult situations, and it has given me reason to assess things from more than one perspective."

[8] "The time now, according to my watch, which is in essence the camp clock, is . . ." and: "If I am cold, you are cold—and I *am* cold" (implying the need to dress accordingly!).

[9] "Quietly and with finesse," using the English term "finesse" in the Hebrew sentence.

[10] Ruth Tomases Joffe remembers: ". . . when Rabbi Mogilner talked about his reasons for making aliyah. He told the staff that when they decided to get married, Sue told him she couldn't imagine living anywhere other than in Israel."

[11] This term is a reference to Ezekiel's vision of the dry bones in chapter 37.

[12] Mogilner often opined that if we were successful 20 percent of the time with 20 percent of our learners, we should consider that phenomenal success. We might not agree with that level of success today, but it probably gave him cause for great optimism and energy in his efforts.

[13] Mogilner's openness to innovation, change, and personal initiative was remarkable for such a disciplined and focused leader. I had the hutzpah in 1968 after taking a course in the development of liturgy with Dr. Avraham Holtz at JTS, to propose a loose-leaf siddur approach to reigniting interest in Jewish prayer in camp. On the first day of camp, all the campers received a loose-leaf book with the skeletal framework of the *matbea shel tefillah* (traditional halakhic prayer structure). Literally, it contained only the surrounding *berachot* that formed the *petiḥot* and *ḥatimot* (openings and closings) of the prayers. It included the three full paragraphs of the *shema* and the first three full paragraphs of the amidah, followed by just the ḥatimot and finally, *aleinu*. After the first day's five-minute tefillah, campers exclaimed: "We never realized that there were so many berachot in the siddur!" The rest of the summer was spent in rebuilding the siddur. A separate curriculum was created for each edah. Campers cut out the "filler" from pages printed and included in the end of the loose-leaf book; pasted the filler (e.g., *ahavah rabbah*) in the correct place on the blank page ending with the pre-printed *berachah*, e.g., *haboḥer be'ammo yisra'el be'ahavah* ("who chooses the people Israel in love") the night before it was to be introduced into the service by madrichim. They then studied it in their formal classes, added their own glosses and interpretations, pictures, dried flowers around the prayer or on the blank facing page, or added three-hole punched ancillary materials distributed by the staff. By the end of the summer, campers went home with their own personalized siddurim. This lasted several summers until it collapsed under the weight of reproduction and fatigue! I do distinctly remember Mogilner commenting when asked why he let me do this: "I have a counselor who is *meshugga ladavar* (crazy about the matter). Should I not let him do it?"

[14] Some years after David's untimely death, Sue Schiff Mogilner married David's friend, colleague, and teacher, Dr. Seymour Fox. As dean of the Teachers Institute at JTS, Fox created the Melton Research Center for Jewish Education and after making aliyah, was head of the School of Education of the Hebrew University and then became President of the Mandell Foundation. Ironically, Seymour died in Israel suddenly of heart failure on July 10, 2006. He was 77 years old.

References

Brown, M. 1997. It's off to camp we go: Ramah, LTF, and the Seminary in the Finkelstein era. In *Tradition renewed: A history of the Jewish Theological Seminary*, ed. J. Wertheimer, 1: 823–54. New York: The Jewish Theological Seminary.

Covenant Foundation. 2003. Covenant Awards Booklet.

Dorph, S. A., ed. 2000. *Ramah: Reflections at 50: Visions for a new century*. New York: National Ramah Commission.

Maimonides, Moses. *Mishneh Torah, Hilkhot Sanhedrin, perek* 3.

Mogilner, D. 1969. Unpublished memorandum. New York: Joseph and Miriam Ratner Center for the Study of Conservative Judaism.

———. 1970. Unpublished memorandum. New York: Joseph and Miriam Ratner Center for the Study of Conservative Judaism.

———. 1971a. Unpublished memorandum. New York: Joseph and Miriam Ratner Center for the Study of Conservative Judaism.

———. 1971b. Unpublished memorandum. New York: Joseph and Miriam Ratner Center for the Study of Conservative Judaism.

———. 1972. Unpublished memorandum. New York: Joseph and Miriam Ratner Center for the Study of Conservative Judaism.

———. 1973. Unpublished memorandum. New York: Joseph and Miriam Ratner Center for the Study of Conservative Judaism.

———. June 13, 1973. Unpublished memorandum. New York: Joseph and Miriam Ratner Center for the Study of Conservative Judaism.

———. 2000. Ramah is my pulpit . . . to my (or any Jewish) mother. In *Ramah: Reflections at 50: Visions for a new century*, ed. S. A. Dorph, 89–93. New York: National Ramah Commission.

Schwartz, S. R. 1984. Ramah philosophy and the Newman revolution. In *Studies in Jewish education and Judaica in honor of Louis Newman*, ed. Alexander M. Shapiro and Burton I. Cohen, 7–21. New York: Ktav.

———. 1987. Camp Ramah: The early years, 1947–1952. *Conservative Judaism* 40 (1): 12–43.

Shulman, L. S. 1989. Education theory and Ramah. In *The Ramah experience: Community and commitment*, ed. S. C. Ettenberg and G. Rosenfield, 49–56. New York: Jewish Theological Seminary and the National Ramah Commission.

PETER A. GEFFEN

Manifest Destiny: Camp Ramah Extends the Borders

WHEN ONE TRAVELS the Jewish world as I have had the privilege of doing in recent years, one is struck by the commonality (across geographic borders) and continuity (across centuries) of Jewish life. This is complimented by the (virtually) limitless ability of Jewish life to incorporate and integrate into itself an expansive array of localisms. Costume, architecture/music/art for synagogues, cuisine (to the borders of kashrut), dance, hand movements in prayer, shoes on, shoes off, calligraphy, and philosophy all lend color and flavor to Jewish life as lived from Alibaug and Cochin in India to Taroudant in Morocco and all points in between.

America, being so young and possessing no such range of native culture to engage its huge twentieth-century Jewish population, has given us something else. We have internalized the most critical aspect of the American experience, the geographic-expansionist character known in American history as Manifest Destiny—that we were made to make it from sea to sea. When one observes the American Jewish scene, one sees and feels the limitless horizons of what is and can be Jewish, drawn not only from the past but through creatively experiencing the present and anticipating the future. Throughout North America, the Jew looks very similar in costume and color from one city to the next, but American Jews have felt a "manifest destiny" to expand what it is that we do as Jews beyond the bounds of costume and cuisine. We feel empowered to develop new forms of ritual; use music in synagogues at times where before it was taboo; include Eastern meditation and Western poetry in our prayers; and create art, music, drama, and dance that we call Jewish yet

PETER A. GEFFEN *is the founder of the Abraham Joshua Heschel School in New York City and the founder and director of Kivunim—The Institute of Experiential Learning for Israel and World Jewish Communities Studies. His connection to Ramah began in 1953 at age seven at Camp Ramah in Connecticut and continued at various Ramah camps and Ramah Israel programs until 1985.*

draws its inspiration from new sources, as well as old. We create new cultural forms rather than simply place old wine in new bottles.

What empowered us to take such bold steps into new territory—creating alternative synagogue forms (e.g., *ḥavurot*); radically alternative schools; and new forms and rituals of marriage, bar and bat mitzvah, life cycle moments, and so on? I think that it was in no small measure the universe of Camp Ramah that generated a unique and powerful influence, imbuing its campers with a spirit of freedom, independence, and opportunity that fueled these Jewish communal developments of the past half century. No accounting of the creative expansion of modern American Judaism can miss the autobiographical commonality of so many of our contemporary leaders who often shared only one common training ground: Camp Ramah.

For me, Ramah taught openness and inclusiveness. When as a seven-year-old in the 1950s, I began attending Camp Ramah in Connecticut for a full two months, Ramah, like the rest of America, was insular and had a limited (although some might say, focused) agenda. Not only was the outside world virtually invisible in camp, even the broader Jewish world had a very limited serious exposure; Israel and Zionism, for example, were symbolic at best. The annual Israeli *mishlaḥat* (emissary staff) that we take for granted today had not yet been conceived. Issues of the outside world such as the raging cold war and the nuclear threat rarely were discussed. In Ramah in the Poconos, where each morning we raised the American flag (and recited the Pledge of Allegiance) *and* raised the Israeli flag (and sang *Im eshkaḥech yerushalayim* "If I Forget Thee O Jerusalem"), we never discussed why we did so or what was taking place in either of our two countries.

But following John Kennedy's election to the presidency and the opening of the 1960s, Ramah quickly became a center for discussion (and ultimately activism) of the issues of race, war, and peace; Israel and the Arab nations; poverty in America; and certainly drugs, sex, and rock and roll. This transition was neither an accident nor an imposition from the outside, but emerged as a natural outgrowth of the seeds sown in the first decade of the experiential programming at Ramah.

Ramah had prepared us to take in conflicting and diverse points of view; to understand that a big world of ideas and thought awaited us outside our narrow and self-limited universe. I could become a civil rights worker in June and return to camp in July and August; I could serve as a civilian volunteer during the Six-Day War in Israel and return to camp to advocate "land for peace" and the internationalization of Jerusalem, and I could even show the highly controversial anti-Vietnam War film *Inside North Vietnam* by Felix Greene in camp and still (albeit barely) remain within the consensus of Ramah life and leadership. I successfully had been taught that the borders were there for testing and not for restricting, however challenging this would become for the camps' senior leadership. I always was made to feel that my growing political activism made (at least some of) the Ramah directors (e.g., Don Adelman, *z"l*, and Ray Arzt) proud.

I was given my freedom at Camp Ramah. Oh, I know this may sound grandiose, but it is true. In 1953, it was commonplace for city kids to spend as much time away from "summer in the city" as possible. For a child as young as seven to spend such a large proportion of his or her life living "independently" and communally made a powerful and lasting impression on all of us. Some of us were hooked for life; others never returned, but all were deeply affected. The fact that this experience took place within a creative Jewish context was a subtle, maybe even subconscious factor that should not be minimized. It many ways, it was the subtle, certainly the informal, that produced more results than any formal instruction or learning (of which there was a quite a bit).

I grew up in Ramah. I transferred from Ramah in Connecticut to Ramah in the Poconos from ages ten to thirteen. I moved to Ramah in Canada the summer it opened (1960) when I was fourteen and fifteen and continued on there (and in Glen Spey) as waiter, water skiing instructor, bunk counselor, and *rosh edah* (division head) through the 1960s, finishing my Ramah employment in Israel through the 1970s and early 1980s. There is no experience, educational institution, or person that can come close to the influence that Ramah had on me. Many of my closest friends, teachers, and mentors come from those years as well. I would not be who I am without Ramah, and I could not possibly have accomplished my life's work without it.

What does that mean exactly, you might ask? I will start with the community of children that is Ramah. There are, of course, adults throughout the camps. But they are overwhelmingly outnumbered by children under the age of sixteen. When you watch campers walking toward the *ḥadar ochel* (dining hall) at sunset on any summer day, you can feel the power of that multitude. It is a child's world. And for most of its history, certainly since the 1960s, most of the adults in camp were once children in camp. Whereas parents may attempt to remember what it was like to be a child, counselors are too close in age to have forgotten. Hence, a unique environment of child-centeredness is created. It was in camp that I first felt the power of youth to act consequentially, exerting influence and power. In my mid-teens I became United Synagogue Youth (USY) national president because of what I had internalized at Ramah. I knew and understood what a kid could do. I learned how to listen, and I learned how to lead.

For the development of Judaism and its practice, Ramah changed the rules of the encounter. Rabbis and teachers did not lead; children led. It was not only that I learned the *nusaḥ* of davening at camp; I learned the nusaḥ of prayer settings, prayerfulness, prayer leadership, prayer participation, and prayer power. To this day, when I serve as a volunteer hazzan for high holiday services at my synagogue (Congregation B'nai Jeshurun in Manhattan) or when I conduct a bar or bat mitzvah service for family or friends, I rely upon the little boy at Camp Ramah in the Poconos who first stood before his peers and chanted a morning service. Although I learned much when sitting in the pews of my childhood synagogue, it is camp that fuels my memory of the building of competence and skill and courage to stand before my people and ". . . sing a new song to Adonai" as the psalmist says.

Camp, of course, took prayer into the woods, encountering nature in ways that the urban and even suburban synagogue could not possibly do. In this way Ramah taught that prayer could take place anywhere; led by anyone (even though girls were denied these roles in my youth, the inevitable logic of their inclusion was manifest in our experience); and be open to the inclusion of creative expressions in word, music, art, thought, and meditation that characterize much of the prayer experience of our Jewish world today.

Ramah taught me to be an educator, first in the informal setting of camp itself and then within the classroom. More than this seemingly practical skill building, however, Ramah taught me to value the field of education and to ultimately choose it as my life's work. Ramah conveyed the subtle yet powerful message that education was a center of power and influence. We never discussed Wall Street or business; ours was a universe of ideas, some eternal and others brand new. Because of my work in Camp Ramah, I was hired at Park Avenue Synagogue in New York City at the age of twenty-one and given the freedom and support to build a post-bar/bat mitzvah program that would keep its teenagers involved. I conceived the establishment of an alternative day school model in the creation of the Abraham Joshua Heschel School in New York City because my own Ramah education had empowered me to think creatively, boldly, and independently. Did my genes play a role? My family, my father, my grandfather? Yes, of course they did. But it was Ramah that fueled me; that nurtured and nourished me; and gave me direction, conviction, and resources for what I was feeling inside.

Camp was not all theology or seriousness. It was also where I learned to have fun, to play pranks, and get myself into trouble (a very good thing for a rabbi's son). It was the site of my first girlfriend and first kiss: where I learned about sex. I threw my first successful out; hit my first double, and learned to imitate Duke Snyder at the plate. Ramah taught me to swim, to row, to paddle, to sail, to water ski, to hike, to pitch a tent, to make a fire, to make a bed, to fold a towel, and to clean a toilet. Ramah taught me to share my food, my treats, my dreams. Ramah taught me to watch my mouth and restrain my fists.

At sixty, Ramah must be recognized and recognize in itself the greatness of its work and accomplishment. To the founders, Seymour and Sylvia, and to the multitudes of directors, counselors, colleagues, and peers who were the gifts that Ramah gave to me—I wish to say thank you. Words cannot express my gratitude. And I am joined by thousands whose lives were molded and changed for the good through your legacy.

MICHAEL GREENBAUM

Ramah: A Paradigm for Conservative Jews

AT A CONVENTION of the Rabbinical Assembly in the 1980s, I recall hearing Rabbi Wolfe Kelman, the executive vice president of the Rabbinical Assembly, observe that he knew of no other movement in the history of Judaism that was as negative about itself as the Conservative Movement. Indeed, even a cursory overview of the history of the movement reveals a highly self-critical group fixed more on its failures than its successes. Is it too extreme to suggest that today the movement consists largely of doubters and critics, rather than adherents who are proud, even passionate about Conservative Judaism and its critical importance to the survival of traditional Judaism? I think not.

How is it, then, that amidst this preoccupation with such negativity, one educational enterprise has managed to transcend this movement-wide obsession with all that is wrong and be characterized as a success? I speak here of the National Ramah Commission (NRC) and its panoply of seven overnight and three day camps scattered around North America and its programs in Israel. Indeed, it has been noted on many occasions that Ramah is the movement's most successful accomplishment.[1]

Notwithstanding an external environment that over the decades has challenged Ramah's mission and founding principles, the Ramah Camping Movement has managed to withstand those forces, whether external or internal, and continue to produce an identifiable product in keeping with its founders' wishes; a product that has made a meaningful contribution to the traditional Jewish community. "Notwithstanding fiscal problems, shifts in educational emphases, and unceasing efforts to adapt to the changing demography of North American Jews, Ramah remains . . . authentic, steadfast, and inspiring."[2]

Indeed, although much greater study of the Ramah experience remains to be done, a 2001 study, which itself emerged from a larger longitudinal study, convincingly shows the considerable impact of Ramah on Jewish youth who

RABBI MICHAEL B. GREENBAUM, *Ed.D., is vice chancellor and chief operating officer of The Jewish Theological Seminary, where he is also an assistant professor of Educational Administration. He currently serves as the secretary of the National Ramah Commission.*

have had a Ramah experience. The research, conducted by Ariela Keysar and Barry A. Kosmin, shows that when Ramah campers are compared to other campers, Ramah is more successful in inculcating its norms and values in its campers.

> Ramah emphasizes religious practice, the power of Jewish community and belonging, and Israel. . . . [T]he widest gap of any variable is on weekly Shabbat celebration. . . . Ramah campers clearly express a more Zionistic outlook than teenagers who attend other Jewish camps.[3]

So what is it that characterizes the Ramah program that has enabled it to transcend the otherwise ubiquitous negativity of Conservative Jews? How is it that Ramah is regarded as such a success by those familiar with it, including the vast number of Conservative Jews who are highly critical of virtually all other efforts and initiatives of the Conservative Movement? Chancellor Emeritus Ismar Schorsch has observed that:

> [T]he Seminary stands for a Judaism grounded in the soil of the Jewish State. . . . [I]t is also a Judaism that makes demands upon us as individuals. It sets boundaries and curbs appetites. Its religious discipline constantly reminds us that we do not live by bread alone. . . . [T]he Seminary stands for a Judaism that has never become fossilized, a Judaism unafraid to confront the challenges of any age. . . . In sum, the Judaism of the Seminary is an authentic yet modern, vibrant yet balanced, clear, yet multifaceted expression of an eternal religion.
>
> Our[s is a] determined quest for a genuine synthesis of the old and the new, the Jewish and the secular, the national and the emotional, the parochial and the universal.[4]

This, by extension, is also what characterizes what Ramah stands for. Whether we look at principles established with the founding of the first Camp Ramah in 1947 at Conover, Wisconsin, or at the latest mission statement adopted by the NRC in 1990, we see an enterprise characterized by a desire to inculcate in young people the values, philosophy, rituals, and practices of this Judaism.

> What comes to mind when we think about Ramah, besides camp, summer, fun, and sports is young people engaged in Jewish learning in an open and informal, yet sensitive environment, identifying as Jews, and learning to live as committed Jews in an open, pluralistic environment. Indeed, as Professor Ralph Tyler, Director Emeritus at The Center for Advanced Study in the Behavioral Sciences, and an early advisor to Ramah noted, Camp Ramah is more than a summer camp. It's a setting in which campers are responsible for planning and developing the activities in light of their group deliberations on purpose and consequence.[5]

In 1977, Jakob Petuchowski wrote that "Conservative Judaism refuses to elevate the lowest common denominator to the status of a norm, due in part, to the existence of Camps Ramah and Ramah's educational standards, which at the time, required campers to be engaged in a minimum of six hours of Hebrew school per week throughout the year."[6]

So, perhaps the success of Ramah, both in fact and in perception, can be said to be attributed to four factors, to:

- Being built on a vision that its early leaders carefully developed, nurtured, and passed along to others.
- The creation of a group of early lay leaders who understood the vision and worked to insure its realization.
- A similarly dedicated group of professional leaders, mostly Seminary students and faculty, who recognized in the program a unique way to achieve the broader educational goals of the Seminary.
- An ability to adhere to its founding vision and values, notwithstanding the external and internal pressures for change and dilution of its operating principles. In doing so it earned respect from the larger community for its ability to stand for a serious Judaism.

Regarding the first of these four factors, it is noteworthy that the title of a lengthy interview by William Novak with Rabbi Seymour Fox, is titled "Vision at the Heart."[7] In this interview Fox notes that:

> We wanted to create an educational setting where young people would be able to discover their Judaism and learn how to live it in their daily lives. We hoped this would nurture Jews who were deeply committed to their tradition and actively involved in American society.[8]

Novak adds that "Ramah emerged out of an ambitious dream, a carefully considered idea of educational possibilities."[9] Indeed, a review of the literature reveals an overwhelming preoccupation with the undertaking of an educational vision that would change the face of the North American Jewish community; perpetuate the educational and religious goals of the Seminary with its commitment to traditional Judaism; and build leadership—lay and professional—for the Conservative Movement.

But had the visionaries had only their vision, they could not have produced the outcome that they did. Indeed, without the communal lay leaders who embraced that vision and invested in it, the vision could not have taken off, let alone resulted in the enterprise that came to be known as the Ramah Camping Movement. Alvin Gershen, himself a key lay leader in the Ramah Camping Movement until his untimely death in 1989, observed that "the real success story [was] the ability of professional and lay leaders to work together with respect and dedication toward a clearly developed common goal."[10] This was also true of the key lay leaders associated with the first Ramah camp in Conover, Wisconsin.

> They were personally and emotionally involved . . . convinced of [Ramah's] value . . . for the whole Movement, that their attitude towards the Movement . . . would have been adversely affected had they not been able to involve the national leadership in [support of the] . . . project.[11]

Much of this cooperative work was done under the organizational umbrella of the NRC, which included a core group of dedicated Ramah lay leaders whose primary loyalty was to the success of Ramah in general and their camps in particular.

> Over the years the Commission worked with the camps to supervise their operations, assist in short- and long-range planning, provide consultative support in areas such as capital improvements, maintenance, and commissary, and operation of a joint insurance program for the camps. The Commission also worked closely with the Seminary to maintain educational standards.[12]

The intensity of commitment of the early lay leaders was rather unique for its time. Fox notes that "in the 1970s and 1980s, most American Jews of status and means cared mainly about Israel, hospitals, and defense organizations. Jewish education and culture ranked very low."[13]

These lay leaders gave of their love and money because they embraced the vision, and they understood the potential to be realized for the Conservative Movement and the American Jewish community. They sent their own children to the camps and spent time at their respective camps. These lay leaders replicated themselves over the years and their successors continue to be a major force in the furtherance of the Ramah mission. So when Gershen attributes the success of Ramah to the ability of everyone involved to work together, he is only partially correct. They could not and would not have been able to do what Gershen lauds had they not been motivated by the achievement of a common goal and a shared vision.

This was equally true for those who staffed the individual camps. First, the camps did not skimp on staff; making sure that the selected individuals were people skilled in the area for which they were hired, yet willing to learn and be stimulated by their staff colleagues. In time, staff emerged out of the ranks of the local camps. The camps produced staff who by virtue of an extensive camping experience already had developed their own passion for the Ramah experience. Notwithstanding their having been former campers, a great many of the professional staff were students of The Jewish Theological Seminary and quickly came to understand the connection between the educational goals of the Seminary and the mission of Ramah. Former National Director Rabbi Burton I. Cohen has written that from the outset the Seminary recruited staff for Ramah from its student body [and] provided a scholar-in-residence from its faculty.[14] Cohen also notes that "from [the summer of 1947] until the present [1989] there has been no entering class at the Seminary which did not have in it one or more alumni of Ramah."[15]

It was not just that subsequent staff members emerged from a population of campers, but Ramah, particularly in its early years, saw one of its goals as being leadership development. In an effort to maintain a high quality of staff, Ramah in its first years, limited the number of campers accepted so as to be certain that it could provide a staff that met Ramah's standards. To deal with the issue of the limited numbers of qualified staff available, it created its own leadership training program, known as Mador. Open to high school graduates only, it produced a significant number of key professionals for the Ramah system.[16]

With the Mador program, Ramah was able to continue to be highly selective in its recruitment of staff while simultaneously expanding staff, enabling it to found additional camps.[17] For a great many of these individuals, their steadfast connection with Ramah represented the charting of a new path for Jewish professionals. As Fox observed, "At Ramah they were really going out on a limb in terms of their future careers."[18]

But so great was their belief in the vision and their commitment to its success that they were willing to be pioneers in the creation and execution of Jewish camping as yet another avenue of Jewish communal service. Indeed, Ramah created the Jewish camp director as a viable occupation for rabbis and Jewish educators.

That Ramah has managed to be viewed by the great majority of Conservative Jews as a success might suggest that Ramah has neither faltered during the course of the past sixty years nor had difficult moments. On the contrary, Ramah has encountered its fair share of trials and tribulations during these past six decades. Indeed, the 1970s were a particularly difficult decade in which the camps faced significant financial challenges, along with deteriorating physical plants throughout the camping system.[19] That decade also required Ramah to confront the challenges of an emerging egalitarianism that was a development affecting the entire Conservative Movement at the time.

Throughout these past sixty years, the relevance of Ramah's mission and the nature of its program have, from time to time, come under scrutiny. For example, as the population of Conservative children in day schools increased, many questioned the need for a program of intensive Jewish learning and living over the summer. In addition, the need for and desirability of an eight-week program came under scrutiny. Today, several of the camps offer four-week sessions. Eight-week programs have been under attack for some time due to the evolution of the single parent family, the escalating cost of overnight camp, and the desire for multiple summer experiences.

For the founders and visionaries of Ramah, the place of Hebrew in the program was of paramount importance. Over the years, Hebrew has become less and less a focus of the program. To their credit, the camp leadership and the NRC leadership continue to grapple with the challenge of keeping Hebrew as a pillar of the program's educational goals. However, the founders would be very disappointed today were they to know the degree to which Hebrew has slipped from the core educational mission.[20] Following close behind the decline in the use of Hebrew in the camps is the declining commitment to formal classes. Here, too, communal pressures for a less stringent and less formal program have been felt.

And yet notwithstanding these issues, as well as others that are beyond the scope of this essay, Ramah continues to be held in high regard by those familiar with it and passionately supported by its alumni and supporters. In November 2007, Ari Magen, then sixteen years old, contacted all the campers in his *edah* from Camp Ramah in the Poconos through the online networking site Facebook to suggest that they all wear a Ramah T-shirt to school on a given day to show their "Ramah pride." In just a few short weeks, word had spread and more than one thousand high school and college-age campers, former campers, and staff members from the United States, Canada, and Israel wore a Ramah T-shirt to school on the prescribed day. Magen noted afterward "[W]e all need Ramah in our lives."[21] Were a thousand young Conservative Jews equally passionate about needing Conservative Judaism in their lives! Might not Ramah serve as a paradigm for Conservative Jewry; teaching us that we are capable of believing in ourselves as Conservative Jews and that we are capable of being .passionate about Conservative Judaism and its relevance for our times despite its critics, despite its imperfections, and despite its ups and downs?

Indeed, were we all to be equally proud and passionate about Conservative Judaism and its manifold contributions to Judaism and the Jewish community, I have no doubt that we would be a more successful group both in our own eyes and in the eyes of world Jewry.

Notes

[1] One such occasion was on November 25, 1986 when Chancellor Ismar Schorsch addressed a conference celebrating Ramah's fortieth anniversary. In *Thoughts from 3080: Selected Addresses and Writings*, 7; Alvin E. Gershen, foreword to *The Ramah Experience: Community and Commitment,* ed. Sylvia C. Ettenberg and Geraldine Rosenfield, (New York: The Jewish Theological Seminary, 1988), ix.

[2] Burton I. Cohen, "A Brief History of the Ramah Movement," *The Ramah Experience*, 16.

[3] Ariela Keysar and Barry A. Kosmin, *Camping Experience 1995–1999: The Impact of Jewish Summer Camping on the Conservative High School Seniors of the 'Four Up' Study* (New York: National Ramah Commission, 2001), 32.

[4] Ismar Schorsch, *The Seminary at 100*, ed. Nina Beth Cardin and David Wolf Silverman (New York: JTS Press, 1987), 3.

[5] Ralph W. Tyler, preface to *The Ramah Experience*, vii.

[6] Jakob Petuchowski, "Conservatism and Its Contribution to Judaism," *Judaism* 103, 26 no. 3 (Summer 1977): 355.

[7] Seymour Fox, interview by William Novak, "Vision at the Heart: Lessons from Camp Ramah on the Power of Ideas in Shaping Educational Institutions" (The Mandel Institute and the Council for Initiatives in Jewish Education, 1997).

[8] "Vision at the Heart," 10.

[9] "Vision at the Heart," 2.

[10] Cohen, "A Brief History," 11, 12; Louis Winer, *My First 89 Years* (Self-published, 1993), 20.

[11] Simon Greenberg *The Ramah Camps: Their Place in the Conservative Movement*, undated manuscript, Ratner Center, R.G. 27–2-19, Simon Greenberg File.

[12] Cohen, "A Brief History," 11, 12.

[13] "Vision at the Heart," 35, 36.

[14] Cohen, "A Brief History," 10.

[15] Ibid. This has remained true until the present day.

[16] Burt Cohen, "Louis Newman's Wisconsin Innovations and Their Effect upon the Ramah Camping Movement," in *Studies in Jewish Education and Judaica in Honor of Louis Newman*, ed. Alexander M. Shapiro and Burton I. Cohen (Ktav, 1984), 34.

[17] Chanan Alexander, "Ramah at Forty: Aspirations, Achievement, Challenges," in *The Seminary at 100,* 111.

[18] "Vision at the Heart," 43.

[19] Michael Brown, "It's Off to Camp We Go: Ramah, LTF, and the Seminary in the Finkelstein Era," in *Tradition Renewed: A History of the Jewish Theological Seminary*, 1, ed. Jack Wertheimer (New York: The Jewish Theological Seminary, 1997), 841–43; Winer, 21.

[20] Indeed Fox acknowledges that "Ramah's second failure was that, despite all our efforts, we never became a Hebrew-speaking camp." "Vision at the Heart," 40.

[21] National Ramah Commission, e-mail message to author, April 17, 2008.

ALVIN MARS

Jewish Education and Ramah: Changing Behavior in a Particular Direction

I WAS TERRIFIED. Everyone else seemed to know what was happening. They knew the rhythm of the place. They knew where things were. They knew when things happened. They knew what was expected of them. All that I knew was that I was new—and that I didn't know anything!

It was the summer of 1964, and I had come to Ramah for the first time as a *madrich bachir*, a senior counselor and also a trainee to become a future *rosh edah*. I did not fully understand the concept of an edah, let alone the role of rosh edah. *Madrich bachir* was a term I had never heard. I am not really sure that I knew what the word *bachir* meant. I had not been a camper at Ramah, although I had visited a friend there for one weekend when I was fifteen. Certainly, I had never been on staff. My summers had been spent at day camps and Boy Scout camp. But, I had decided that my life and career were to be devoted to Jewish education, and I had even applied and been accepted to a graduate program in Jewish education. And there were friends and advisors around me who said that if I really wanted to understand Jewish education, I would need to spend at least one summer at Ramah. So, there I was!

My discomfort was not just the result of being in a new place. It was also because I was in the presence of so many people who were known to me by reputation only. They were rabbis and educators and professors who seemed to know so much and whose every word carried the weight of experience, know-how, and great learning. I was afraid to open my mouth lest what I said would reveal how little I knew and the paucity of the experience I had. These were men and women who were already in their late twenties. Some were even in their thirties. A few were pulpit rabbis and others were teachers and principals. Most were married and had families. They knew children. They knew Ramah.

RABBI ALVIN MARS, *Ph.D., is the senior consultant to the president of Jewish Community Centers Association of North America (JCCA) and is adjunct professor of Jewish education at The Jewish Theological Seminary. He was the founding director of JCCA's Mandel Center for Jewish Education. He has also served as the director of Camp Ramah in California and the director of the Brandeis-Bardin Institute.*

They knew education, and they knew life. I was a twenty-one-year-old kid. It was all very intimidating.

And the most intimidating one of all was the camp director, Rabbi David Mogilner, *z"l,* my Ramah director. Simply put, he was larger than life. He seemed to be the embodiment of everything that was Ramah. He was intelligence, and he was Jewish learning. He was educational philosophy, and he was camp counseling know-how. He was the model of serious Jewish commitment, and he was the consummate Jewish educator.

I feared him, and I was in awe of him. He sat with us regularly in education classes and used the daily, weekly, and summer schedule and the counselor's daily routine as our texts. He made us think of the educational implications of everything we did, from the first moment that we woke our campers until we sang the Shema with them after lights out at night. We needed to think of how we behaved at morning *tefillot,* of how we distributed food at our tables, of how we managed the work wheel in our cabins during *nikkayon.* He taught us about the notion of home haven, of making our bunks a safe place for our kids so that that they could go out into the life of hard knocks that the camp provided, and then have a place where they could return to lick their wounds and be loved and comforted.

He even taught us one of the most important lessons we would ever learn about being a Jew in the open, accepting environment of twentieth- and now twenty-first-century America; and he did it, quite simply, by describing the vehicle that Ramah created to have campers select their daily and weekly activities. By requiring our kids to make choices between art and baseball and hiking and camping and canoeing and fencing, we were teaching them how to choose and how to live with the consequences of their choices. It was only baseball or basket weaving, just games and activities; and the specific choice was not important, but rather the process of choosing. But it was, in fact, vitally important. It was the stuff of the life of a kid while at camp. It was the kid's life. And as Mogilner taught us, in life one needed to know how to choose if one were to choose to be a Jew in a society in which it was so easy to opt out, or worse yet, just fade away because one did not bother to make a conscious choice to maintain a Jewish identity.

The educational tool that Mogilner used that was the most intimidating of all for me was his constant demand for *hatzdakah ḥinnuchit,* for educational justification. Every time you opened your mouth and suggested a program or an idea, you had to be prepared to justify it with a rational, reasonable, educational, and Jewish justification. "My God, can't I just live life and enjoy it with these kids without thinking about it and justifying it?" "No," would be his answer. What makes Ramah an educational institution is that anything and everything that happens must be open to educational justification. If you cannot justify it, you probably should not be doing it. If you are serious about being a Jewish educator, even for just this summer at camp, you *must* be prepared to think about everything you are doing, what kind of impact it is going to have on the kid, and whether or not it will be positive Jewish education.

I remember the day, the class, and the session when this remarkable man within the remarkable institution that is Ramah repeated an unremarkable definition. David spoke in Hebrew as he restated John Dewey's behaviorist definition of education as a "change in a person's behavior." And then he said that that was not enough for Ramah. Rather, at Ramah, Dewey's definition would have to be restated as a "change of a person's behavior in a particular direction." It does not seem like very much now, but those were words that gave meaning and purpose to my own life as an educator. For, it clarified for me what was one of the most important elements in the educational and institutional strength of Ramah. Ramah had a clear purpose. It understood its direction and its mission. Embedded within it were both a notion of best practices, those educational methods and programs that can touch a person and effect change, as well as a clear sense of what the direction of change should be. Its vision of the Jewish person it wanted to create was clearer than in any other place that I have ever worked.

The educational lessons I learned had an impact on every Jewish educational institution I ever headed. For me, at the beginning of my career, the Ramah experience was as broad as the Poconos camp and as deep as David Mogilner and the staff he brought together. What I consequently discovered was that my experience was replicated time and time again at Ramah camps across the country and with directors who were very different in temperament from David Mogilner. Years later, I myself was privileged to become one of those Ramah directors.

Discussing and defining what is meant by "a particular direction" is interesting in and of itself. Ramah has been the stalwart of the Conservative Movement, creating a living environment that links the notion of historical Judaism to a vibrant present. It has been the Conservative Movement's quintessential living laboratory, a laboratory for the Jewish future. It has occasioned strife and struggle as issues of great import were faced each summer at camp, often long before our scholars at The Jewish Theological Seminary and in the movement faced them.

Much has happened during these summers with youth communities tucked into a mountain valley, seemingly removed from the push and pull of everyday life, yet giving shape and texture both to the life of the individual Jew who has attended and to the larger community to which she has returned.

It is to these Jews and to this Jewish community of which we are all a part, to the stakeholders of contemporary Jewish life, to which I want to give my attention. Cast in the language of this magnificent institution that is Ramah, these stakeholders would include the following: (1) our campers, (2) our parents, (3) our staff, (4) our movement, and (5) our people, the Jewish people. And the ultimate question I want to ask is how has the direction of the lives of each stakeholder been affected by Ramah over these sixty years, and what are the qualitative differences that Ramah has made to them?

In thinking about this question, I considered the appropriate metaphor to capture the experiences, the memories, and the learning of Ramah. One morning during my personal davening as I was beginning with *pesukei dezimra,* I read the words of Genesis 22 (the *akedah,* the binding of Isaac) as I do almost every day, and I began to envision Ramah as the mountain peak experience it is, both figuratively and literally. And then a question entered my consciousness that I could not shake. How is Ramah like the akedah?

What a problematic question that is, and what uncomfortable imagery it offers for thinking about Ramah! After all, the akedah is about the binding of Isaac, and it is about a parent's willingness to sacrifice his child. Who is prepared to do that? No one I know! We all want to enhance our kids' lives. We would rather sacrifice ourselves for our kids and not the other way around. And so I would like to struggle with this problem of the akedah a bit and see how it might better help us understand those who are the stakeholders in Ramah and capture a bit of what Ramah has meant to their lives.

To do this I discuss the following five things: a television commercial, a snow bound Hebrew class, a painted stone, an educational myth, and *birkat hamazon.*

The Television Commercial

I remember being caught up in a number of commercials that were ingenious in their use of misdirection and disingenuousness. They sold different products, but more or less, they told the same story. Picture this: a teenager is packing up and ready to leave for college. You can sense his inner turmoil, a mixture of the excitement of things to come and melancholy about leaving his home and parents behind. This is a rite of passage for him, but how will his parents manage without him? There seems to be genuine sadness and concern, both for the child and for the parents. In fact, in one of the commercials, the mother does not even descend the steps to bid the youngster farewell. The implication the viewer draws from the student's expression is that he empathizes with his mother's pain at his leaving home. The conclusions of these commercials vary, but the message is always the same; the parents are happy to get rid of the youngster. In one, they dance for joy and start packing for their vacation in Hawaii. In another, it becomes obvious that the mother was unavailable to say goodbye because she was too busy measuring the child's room with plans to use the space for a master bedroom expansion.

This is certainly a redefinition of what it means for a parent to stay behind. At first, I thought that these parents could not be Jewish. It was not the way Jewish parents were supposed to behave. Whatever pleasures becoming an empty nester bring, the angst of sending your child out into the world, symbolized by going off to college, is a family rite of passage that is emblematic of change, usually irreversible change. And that is something that causes concern and insecurity for parents, not to mention for children. In the commercials, could the investment of the parents in their children have been so minimal that children were viewed as mere impediments to a more comfortable, private lifestyle?

Then I thought of the akedah, of Abraham and Isaac, and even of the two lads they left behind. "You stay here with the donkey," Abraham told them. When Abraham left his homeland, he was leaving his past. As he took Isaac off to sacrifice him, he was, in a real sense, leaving his future. These were hard decisions. There was pain between parent and child, heading off to that mountaintop. And there must have been some disgruntlement, too. How did those lads feel? After all, weren't they and their feelings discounted? Abraham and Isaac were going off to a peak experience somewhere. They might well be changed by the experience. But what would become of the lads? They would not be sharing the experience. Ultimately, they would never be able to fully comprehend what had happened, and they would be left behind in more important ways than were implied by the mere fact that they stayed in place with the donkey.

I could not see that commercial, nor contemplate this Torah story without thinking about my experiences with parents: Jewish parents, loving parents, who sent their children off to a summer at Ramah. There were those who saw it as a wonderful opportunity and believed that it was great for a child to be at camp, any camp. There were those who did not give it much thought at all. The children need to do something constructive in the summer, and Ramah sure sounds constructive. And there were those who were really concerned about Ramah and sent their children to camp with great hesitation.

When I was the director of education at Beth Sholom in Philadelphia, I was proud that we were able to send fifty-five of our students to Ramah for a summer, and that was when everyone went for an eight-week session. Fifty-five was a large number in those days, but I remember how much more difficult it was to convince the parents in my congregation to send their children to

Ramah than it was to convince the children that they should go. Usually, a charismatic teacher or youth group leader could influence the students, and of course, their friends' encouragement was the most powerful device of all in my recruitment arsenal.

The parents already were members of a Conservative synagogue, but they seemed to be afraid of the religious experiences their children would have at camp. Different from the parents in the television commercials, they seemed to sense that sending their children to a Ramah camp for a summer was more than just gaining some empty-nest intimacy. The child would certainly be returning, but would it be the same child?

The power of the Ramah experience is something that informed parents learn about very rapidly. From my years as an education director, a day school director, and a Ramah director, I remember the many conversations I had with parents. They expressed their issues differently, but the heart of their concern was whether their child would return from camp different, different from what he was now and different from them, his or her parents and their family. Some focused on whether their sons would wear *kippot,* and others struggled with their own personal refusal to make their homes kosher. These conversations really amused me because, for most, the child had not yet been to camp and could not have thought of the idea, let alone made the request. In effect, the parent was saying that I want my child to have a peak experience, but I do not want that experience to remove my child from me. I want my child to learn. I want her to grow. But I do not want her to change and thereby grow away from me.

Of course, there were those parents who were happy for their children's opportunity and regretted that they had to be left at the base of the mountain, much as the two lads were left in the akedah story.

Over the years, Ramah camps have learned how to enable our Isaacs (i.e., our children) to bring their Abrahams (i.e., their parents) along up the mountain with them for the experience. Today, there are adult accommodations for summer institutes at Ramah. There are family camps to share the rich experience among young, and not so young, alike. There are even winter *shabbatonim* at Ramah in California and Ramah Darom, packaging the Ramah Shabbat experience in a format appropriate to create inspiring, elevating adult experiences. Different from the akedah, in the Ramah of today, neither lads nor parent*s* would be left behind.

A Snowbound Hebrew Class

I was twenty-one. Rabbi David Clayman was maybe thirty-three or thirty-five. I remember the first time we met. He invited me to his office at Mount

Airy Jewish Community Center where he was rabbi. He hired me for some short-term employment.

There were some youngsters in his shul he wanted to send to Ramah, and they wanted to go. But there was an important impediment that stood in their way. Before they could be admitted, they had to pass a Hebrew admissions exam, and David Clayman was afraid that the Hebrew language program at his synagogue school had not properly prepared them. And so, he hired me to teach at his synagogue for about three hours a day over the course of the entire winter vacation from public school. That I showed up every day was no surprise. I was being paid to teach a class. But there were about half a dozen students who came daily, who trudged through the winter streets even after a major snowstorm that made the windows of our classroom appear to be encased in walls of snow and ice.

I was impressed! Not only did they learn a lot of Hebrew, but they passed the test and were admitted to camp. And the experience is one that has remained with me as a teacher for a lifetime. The students were great; they seemed to have an intense inner motivation. They wanted to go to camp. Basically, the class taught itself. I was just along for the ride, empowering these teenagers to acquire those skills that would enable them to go to camp.

I wonder if there are any of our camps that have these kinds of requirements today. Certainly, that was not the case in the California camp during the years that I directed it.

I am always impressed with any youngster who decides to attend Ramah. In the first place, going to any overnight camp or even to a different overnight camp for the first time must be a daunting prospect for a youngster. Making a decision to attend Ramah with its religious dimensions adds an overlay of the unknown for many of our campers. One has to admire their guts to make such a decision and go through with it.

We may not make the hurdles quite as high as those that the students in my winter vacation class faced; however, the hurdles are there. And, although the children do not really know what the payoff will be at the end of the course, they are prepared to accept the challenge of going to Ramah anyway.

In a real sense, these are young people who are much like Isaac in our story of the akedah. No, we are not leading them off to slaughter, God forbid! But we are asking them to go to the mountaintop, to Ramah, and we have no real way to tell them what that means. It is just an experience we want them to have, and we promise them that it will touch their souls, change their lives, and be a lot of fun, too. And all of what I have just written cannot mean anything to a youngster who still does not have the experience of going to camp. Nevertheless, they trust us, much as Isaac trusted Abraham.

The story of one of the students in my class underscores the potential that Ramah has to touch the lives of its campers: to shape them and give them added meaning and purpose. This youngster's name was Bennett Solomon, of blessed memory. When we met for the first time in that Ramah Hebrew class, he was twelve years old, not yet bar mitzvah. He was handsome, tall, and blond with a winning smile, on the threshold of adolescence.

I was there for his first summer at camp, and what happened to him was as wonderful as it was unremarkable for Ramah. He had a fabulous counselor and a great group of kids as his friends and confidents. That group remained together pretty much throughout all their years at Ramah, went to Ramah Seminar in Israel together, and returned for the National Mador, which then operated at Ramah in the Poconos in Pennsylvania. After Mador, Bennett served as a counselor and in many other educational staff capacities during the following summers.

Bennett's world became Ramah. He was in constant touch with his friends during the winter, and this was long before anyone even heard of the Internet. These bunkmates supported each other, cared about each other, and maintained their personal connections through high school, college, graduate school, and during the establishment of their families and professional lives. From that group have emerged rabbis, physicians, business people, college professors, and Jewish educators. Bennett was one of the latter. He attended Brandeis University and completed his doctorate at Harvard with a dissertation on the idea of curriculum integration in day schools. He became the headmaster of a Schechter day school in the suburbs of Boston and built a school of recognized quality. Unfortunately, his life was cut short by disease, but even in his limited years, his contribution to the Jewish people was very great.

Bennett Solomon is emblematic of the power that Ramah has to shape the lives of its campers. It challenges them to undertake a journey to its mountaintop, it exposes them to fabulous educational role models, it envelops them with a rhythm of Jewish life that is made real and intense by the shared experience of young people living in close community, and it provides them with a network of friends and experiences that lasts a lifetime. And what must not be forgotten—it does all this by connecting them to their tradition and their people and invests them with the commitment to make their own contributions to that tradition and people.

The Painted Rock

It was my second summer at Ramah, my first as a rosh edah. The painted rock refers to the last element of a major program our edah, Nitzanim, undertook over a period of a few weeks. On one special day, a *yom meyuḥad,* we constructed a program that took the entire edah on what today would be called virtual aliyah. The youngsters traveled across the lake on rowboats, or marched in lines from distant sections of the camp pretending to come to Israel from the four corners of the world, a reenactment of *kibbutz galuyyot.* They constructed a *ma'barah* (new immigrant's camp), cooked Israeli food, defended their encampment as the Army would have, had an evening campfire presenting skits from their countries of origin, and listened to a radio broadcast of the United Nations vote on the partition on Palestine of November 1947. The next day and the week that followed, they collected rocks and worked to build a map of Israel that surrounded the flagpole on the boys' campus. The map was to be made of rocks painted blue and white and set in a bed of cement that had been poured into a furrow that was dug in the shape of the map of the State of Israel.

It took a few weeks to finish the project because we were all better counselors and educators than we were builders and artisans. Digging the outline was tough and tedious, but painting the rocks was the craziest activity one could imagine. Have you ever tried to paint a rock? It's easy to do it on one side, but what happens when you have to turn it over? And we were dealing with thousands of rocks that we had gathered. What happens is that a little paint gets onto the rocks, but all the boys and girls in the edah turn blue and white themselves from head to foot. What a mess it was, but what fun! Although these may not have been the kinds of rocks Abraham collected to build his altar on Mount Moriah, these Ramah stones did, indeed, help to build an experience for our campers who touched them, painted them, and were in turn touched by them.

I smile when I think of this, and at the same time, my smile reveals a bit of melancholy because I cannot think of that activity and that summer without remembering rabbi-to-be Chuck Rheinish, of blessed memory. Chuck was tall and broad. He was a big fellow, but not one to be feared. He was a kind of a teddy bear, very soft and loving in spite of his size. He was great as a counselor in Nitzanim, the youngest division.

I do not believe that Chuck was then more than eighteen years old, but his leadership potential already was evident. I was then a wise old man of twenty-two, and I delegated the overall operation and administrative responsibility for this activity to Chuck. He was very effective, and he motivated his friends on our staff to accomplish things at a level of excellence that I have rarely seen, even in some of our finest Jewish educational institutions with the best teachers and administrators.

When I think of Chuck, I hear the voice of David Mogilner echoing in my ears, when he would say, "The real power of Ramah is that it is a place where youth is empowered to educate youth." Consequently, it becomes a place where youngsters learn from accessible role models, those who are not more than a few years older than they are themselves. And those who were the educators were learning at least as much and perhaps even more than the students.

I think it is no coincidence that so many rabbis and educators developed at Ramah. We all learned Judaica. We all had classes in education. But more important, Ramah was a living laboratory of experience, growth, and educational training that taught each of us lucky enough to be on staff how to be a parent, how to be a teacher, how to be an administrator, how to be an institutional leader, how to be a caring person, and how to be a competent human being. We learned this from each other on staff, and we were mentored, each one of us, by someone a bit more experienced, a bit more knowledgeable, and a bit more mature.

When I became a Ramah director, I quickly realized that Ramah was probably an even more valuable experience for each young person I brought to be on staff than it was for each child who came to be a camper. Teaching, after all, is the most effective tool we have for learning.

An Educational Myth

A criticism that is often leveled at the Ramah experience is that it creates a hothouse environment for Jewish life. It isn't real. It does not replicate what the child experiences in her or his family at home, and it is often very far from the experience the youngsters have in their own Conservative synagogues in the city. Ramah, therefore, is a make-believe world, one that cannot be replicated at home and when our campers try, they are destined to experience frustration and failure.

I believe that rather than being a shortcoming, this hothouse and mythical environment at Ramah is actually one of the great gifts to the Conservative Movement and to the world of Jewish education.

Sometimes myth can shape reality. Is the akedah story a myth? Even if it is, it has helped to shape the reality of who we are as Jewish people, parents and children, and how we behaved individually and collectively over the generations.

Likewise, Ramah creates Jewish educational myths built upon educational experiences provided to its campers that are rooted in a vision of, and goals for, a more vibrant Jewish future. The notion of educational myth[1] states that it is the role of the educational institution to have a vision for how the world would become. The world is not yet so. It is myth, not reality. But it is the role of the educational institution to create that world within its boundaries, as if that myth were reality. For those who have the experience, the myth will become reality, and it will inspire them to live their lives in the world according to what they have experienced. This is what Ramah has been doing so well for all the years of its existence. I even remember a time when Ramah extended that myth into a winter program called Leaders Training Fellowship (LTF), which extended the same futuristic vision of the summer into the city lives of its campers. Ramah's vision of the Jewish future, its hothouse myth, has changed the lives of tens of thousands.

Birkat Hamazon

For me, a single line that we recite in the birkat hamazon is emblematic of Ramah's contributions to the entirety of the Jewish people. The line is: *Haraḥaman hu yevarech et medinat yisra'el reishit tzemiḥat ge'ulateinu* (may the Merciful bless the State of Israel, the beginning of the flowering of our redemption). The story of how this line came to be part of our daily ritual is a Ramah story. I believe it represents the kind of Jewish educational struggle we experience as we try to make sense of the literary nuances found in the akedah story and their meaning for our lives.

It happened in the summer of 1965 at Ramah in the Poconos. David Mogilner had gathered a very large *hanhalah.* There were *rashei edot, yo'atzim* (advisers) for the edot, yo'atzim for Mador and for the madrich bachir program, as well as a collection of rabbis and professors-in-residence. As a consequence, meetings, especially those with a theoretical or philosophical agenda, were often painfully long. Sometimes it felt as though there was too much wisdom in the room.

Israel had celebrated seventeen anniversaries. It was two years before the Six-Day War, an event that would generate an upheaval in Jewish identity and Israeli consciousness. There were already those on the Ramah hanhalah who believed we must begin to introduce the notion of the contemporary State of Israel into our daily religious observance. David Mogilner had just returned from an extended stay in Israel as had others. The California camp already had added a line to its version of birkat hamazon stating: *Haraḥaman hu yevarech et medinat yisra'el veyagen aleha* (may the Merciful bless and protect the State of Israel).

The proposal was made that the same words be added to our birkat hamazon in the Poconos. What followed was a week of emotional deliberation. I remember one discussion that led to anger and tears when one rabbi claimed that the modern State of Israel was a temporal matter, and our prayers can be directed only toward that which is eternal. Benny Mushkin, a local educational director on the camp staff, suggested a compromise. His proposal was to begin the phrase with *Haraḥaman hu yevarech et medinat yisra'el* and add the modifying words from Israel's Declaration of Independence, *reishit tzemiḥat ge'ulateinu*. The compromise was adopted and added to the birkat hamazon the following Shabbat. As far as I know, it has become an accepted part of our ritual, far beyond the boundaries of a Ramah camp.

Who knows how many such discussions on a myriad of issues and concerns of the Jewish world took place at Ramah? It is reasonable to believe that the fabric of Jewish life and of the Jewish people today is woven of many threads that were spun on the wheel of Jewish living and learning experience at Camp Ramah.

So we understand that over the course of sixty years, Ramah has had a significant impact on all who have had contact with it: its campers, its staff, its movement, its parents, and its people.

My experiences at Ramah were my most formative experiences as a Jew and as an educator. Certainly, that is the case with regard to my years as director of Ramah in California. But it is especially so for the years I spent at the Poconos as a counselor, rosh edah, *yo'etz*, and professor. I learned more from David Mogilner and the camp during the few summers I spent at the Poconos than I did in four years of undergraduate work and six years of graduate work in education. I learned how to think as an educator. I learned how to think and feel as a Jew. I learned how to create experience for others, how to create a world that created a new future for them as Jews.

I am convinced that my Jewish educational vision and practice, as well as the course of my career at the University of Judaism, the Brandeis-Bardin Institute, the American Hebrew Academy, and the Mandel Center for Jewish Education of the JCCs of North America were shaped by my Ramah experiences. When all is said and done, I believe that my years as a Ramah director were among the most fulfilling and meaningful of my career. For me, working with a youngster within a Jewish educational setting that creates a total environment is the most powerful work I could ever want to do as an educator. For me, Ramah has been an unbounded blessing.

May our people be blessed with another sixty years of Ramah achievement.

Note

[1] "Educational myth" is an element of a Reconstructionist philosophy of education, a theory of education unrelated to Reconstructionist Judaism. The only connection is that the thinking of John Dewey was a significant influence in both.

JOSEPH REIMER

Leadership at Ramah: The Changing Role of the Camp Director

THE WORLD OF JEWISH CAMPING is rapidly changing. We alumni of these camps may think of them as unchanging islands of calm and repose. But nothing could be further from the truth. While we have been living our busy lives, these camps have undergone dramatic changes that call for serious investigation. What does it take in our era of globalization for Jewish camps to remain both attractive to Jewish families and effective as instruments for the transmission of Jewish culture and religious traditions?

This essay focuses on the Ramah overnight camps and particularly, on the directors of those camps. In reading the literature on Ramah, I was struck by how little focus there is on the professional camp director. I find that surprising because in recent decades in the literature on schools, there has been a great deal of focus on the school principal as a leader in that context. I learned from that literature and my own professional experience that a voluntary educational system cannot grow and develop without direction from a sustaining, stable, and forward-looking leadership—especially in times of rapid institutional change.

I argue throughout this essay that although Ramah at 60 has every reason to be proud of its Jewish educational legacy and vision, there must be a serious reckoning about how this movement can simultaneously remain faithful to its core mission *and* creatively respond to the rapidly changing world of Jewish camping. Ramah cannot afford either to jettison its basic educational principles or to rely on those principles alone as an adequate response to these changing times. Indeed, the great challenge to Ramah leaders—and particularly, its camp directors—is how to present the core Ramah principles in ways that still excite key stakeholders while also creatively reinventing many aspects

JOSEPH REIMER, *Ed.D., is the director of the Institute for Informal Jewish Education and associate professor and former director of the Hornstein Jewish Professional Leadership Program at Brandeis University. Dr. Reimer serves as lead faculty for the Executive Leadership Institute (ELI) for Jewish camp directors sponsored by the Foundation for Jewish Camp.*

of camp life so that campers, families, and community members will experience Ramah as new, inviting, and challenging.

The Changing World of Jewish Camping

In November 2004 I received a call from a man I had never met. At that time, Jerry Silverman recently had assumed the professional leadership of the Foundation for Jewish Camping. In our first conversation, he bemoaned the lack of serious leadership development for directors of Jewish camps and invited me to join him and Dr. Richard Levin, an executive coach and corporate consultant, in planning a new, cutting-edge leadership program for the directors of residential non-profit Jewish camps. Given my previous involvement with the development of informal Jewish educators, I did not hesitate to accept Jerry's invitation.

In planning for this institute for Jewish camp directors—eventually to be called the Executive Leadership Institute (ELI)—Richard Levin and I interviewed twelve senior Jewish camp executives from a variety of camping movements. As outsiders to the world of camping, we wanted to know how their world was changing and, more specifically, how the role of the camp director has changed over the past decade. Their responses did not vary significantly across movements and helped to shape our own assumptions about the professional development needs of the camp directors who became the ELI Fellows.

The world of Jewish camping in their view has been changing in these dramatic ways:

Changes in regulation. If you can remember when you or your parents could drive a large, gas-guzzling car without having to buckle up, you remember the period when camps were relatively free of external regulation. Those times are long gone. Today, whether in relation to the environment, health, or child safety, camps have become highly regulated. With regulation comes new rules, greater complexity, and administrative headaches. Camps must both buckle up and staff up to meet the new codes that define their industry today.

Changes in families. Camps always have had to market to families. Children by themselves, after all, do not choose a camp to attend. But there was a time when after choosing a suitable camp, paying the fees, and sending a child off, parents were happy to receive a periodic postcard. No longer. With instant communications come the ever-involved family members who want to know on a daily basis if their Stephanie is having a great time and their Scott has hit that long ball. Paying expensive fees, they feel entitled to know that their child is having the best possible experience each and every day. The camp staff must work much harder to meet those expectations and demands.

Changes in campers. Campers have always had childhood problems like homesickness, competition for friends, and heartbreak on the mound. But today's campers carry extra burdens that make their care that much harder. On the medical side, there is the enormous increase in medications that children take today. In the dining room, there are the mushrooming food allergies and alternative diets that must be considered. In the bunk, there are the fears and anxieties that come with less stable family lives and the greater difficulty that this generation has in mastering the social skills to get along with their bunkmates. Kids today are harder to care for, and the camp staff feels these differences because campers live at camp twenty-four hours a day.

Changes in staff. Camps have always employed a very young staff to care for children. In that way, camps are like armies—the young lead the young in the campaign to win the battle. But camps find it harder today to compete for the *right* young people to be counselors in the bunks and specialists in various activities. Counselors usually are college students who face their own pressures to earn money and advance their careers. Camps must compete with a larger world of jobs and internships to retain their best staff. And without a mature staff, you cannot run a great camp program.

Changes in the market. The lazy, hazy days of summer are a thing of the past. Summer time is now to grow, soar, and see the world. An industry of recreational possibilities has grown up to offer families with means every conceivable summer adventure. Jewish camps are one of many possible offerings and must compete to capture their share of the eligible market. Camps struggle to be attractive, and the old tricks no longer work. Every camp—similar to every private school—is under unrelenting pressure to do better and offer more, just to keep pace with the ever-changing opportunities that Jewish families want for their children.

In brief, the world of camping was once a relatively secure oasis from the pressures of the competitive world; today, competition has entered the front gate, parked on the camp lawn, and announced: I am here to stay. Camping is no longer a Mom and Pop country store, but rather, the rural extension of all one had once hoped to leave behind in the home environment. These changes may have crept in gradually, but now they affect every residential camp. Ramah is no exception.

The Changing Role of the Jewish Camp Director

Each of these major changes in the world of Jewish camping impacts the role of the camp director as the professional leader of the camp. The following is how our informants describe the primary changes in the role of the camp director over the past decade.

From leading cowboy to team leader

A history of senior staffing patterns at Ramah would reveal a clear trend: running a Jewish camp has become as complex an operation as running a day school or a Hillel foundation. Today a camp director does not run the camp directly: he or she directs a staff team that runs the camp. When I think of the direct access I had as a *rosh edah* to my camp director, I am amazed. Today my successor probably reports to an assistant director and a *yo'etz,* positions that did not exist yet at camp during the 1970s. There is also an expanded staff to manage the kitchen, infirmary, and physical plant of the camp.

Leading a larger, more complex staff requires a different set of skills than being the one person in charge. The leader must carefully build a team of senior staff members that work well together and then divide the multiple realms of responsibility among them. The director coordinates and supervises their diverse roles through the rush of the summer weeks. The leader must know when to step in and when to back off and let the team members handle the crises that arise. There is little room any more for the proverbial cowboy who rushes in to save the day. Today the need is for maintaining and updating systems that must run smoothly if this complex operation is to be managed well.

From the authority figure to boundary-negotiator with families

My wife tells the following story from the late 1950s when she and her cousin were campers at a well-known Jewish camp. Her uncle died suddenly of a heart attack one night during that summer. Her mother called the camp director to share the tragic news. In those days there were no answering machines or services. The camp director yelled at her, saying that she had no right to wake him up and that this could wait until morning.

Fortunately, that kind of arrogance is gone from camp life, for the most part. Today camp directors and senior staff recognize that family members are as much their clients as are the campers. They rely on parents to prepare their child for camp and also to communicate all the information the camp requires to take charge of the care of that child. Parents then must trust that the camp will competently care for their child.

Trust is the crux of this relationship, but these days, trust is in shorter supply. Parents are more anxious about the well-being of their child and find it harder to trust the camp authorities. They want more for their child and are never sure if that extra demand is being met. Camp authorities still must set clear boundaries but also must help parents see that their child can thrive in a camp environment many miles from home.

The camp director sets the tone for the communications between the camp and its families. He or she personally can handle only a small fraction of those communications, but often that fraction is the most delicate. Last summer one director shared with me his written communications with a mother whose teenage daughter lost a significant amount of weight over the four-week session. This mother was reasonable and could recognize the many ways the program monitors the health of the camp's teenagers. Yet her daughter had lost weight, and the tension in these communications was palpable. It takes a lot of skill for a director to communicate the required information, express real concern and empathy, and yet show that the camp did all it reasonably could to care for this girl, who despite the camp's attention managed to lose critical weight without detection. The camp director is the last resort for the parent who feels her trust was not sufficiently honored. How these tensions are resolved says a lot to families about the critical trust factor in their relationship to the camp.

From managing staff to developing staff

In most Jewish camps, the educational staff is made up of former campers who have been selected to become staff. Many camps have some form of counselor training and counselor-support systems. By the time a young adult is given responsibility as a bunk counselor or specialist, he or she is usually well-known in the camp community and presumably knows well the values and rules of the camp.

Yet these young adults are still adolescents. They may aim to be responsible counselors, but they also want to enjoy the summertime with their friends. There is a built-in tension between these two desires, and directors report that enjoyment frequently comes at the expense of responsible behavior. Rarely does a summer go by that a director does not have to send home some staff for poor judgment or for breaking camp rules. Sending home a staff member hurts each time.

Even more difficult are the cases where the staff lapse does not involve breaking the rules but indicates a lack of mature capabilities. In one camp I visited, a young adult staff member who had grown up in the camp had asked to be promoted to a new level of responsibility. The camp director was hesitant but finally agreed. As the camp season progressed, the staff member's difficulties in managing younger staff became apparent. The camp director chose to work with her, but she could not keep up, and her unit was suffering. The director knew what he had to do, but it pained him to let go a valued young woman who had grown up in the system.

Jewish camps are intimate communities, and directors are responsible to develop their young staff to become more capable and mature leaders. Yet directors often feel they are put in a position of making demands on young staff that are often not mature enough to assume the required responsibilities. They must inspire and teach, but ultimately directors must know how to balance care for the staff with the demanding needs of running a camp. That balance becomes more difficult each year.

From camp leader to community leader

Camp directors never expect to get much sleep during the summer. One does not last in this job if one cannot tolerate the brutal summer schedule and the very palpable pressures of being the person ultimately responsible for the health and welfare of hundreds of campers and staff all summer long. Most camp directors express a long sigh of relief when the camp season ends.

Tolerating these pressures always has been the hallmark of this profession. What has changed is the other nine months of the year. Whereas in the past camp directors could relax after the summer, today the job has expanded considerably for the reasons cited above, and down time has been reduced to a minimum. Because there are far more regulations to attend to, recruiting campers and staff is more difficult, and the physical plant and camp program require constant updating, the director is busy for much of the year.

As Jewish camping has come to be recognized as a powerful tool for Jewish socialization, camp directors must align their camp more closely with the larger Jewish community. For years camp people sought the proper recognition for the importance of their work. Now that this recognition is at hand, camp directors must become more articulate spokespersons for their mission. They must become community leaders as well as camp leaders.

From having boards to developing active boards

As non-profit organizations, Jewish mission camps have always operated—directly or indirectly—under the supervision of a lay board. However, the role of the lay board has evolved considerably over the past decades. Today, most Jewish camp directors — certainly at Ramah camps — cannot fulfill their professional responsibilities without close coordination with their top lay leaders. No longer is the camp board or committee, as was often true in the past, a rubber stamp for the director's authority.

Camp leaders—much like their professional peers throughout the Jewish community—are rarely prepared for the elaborate partnering required these days for developing and maintaining healthy and effective working relationships with lay leaders. Professionals tend to see themselves as the experts in their craft—in this case, running camps. Seeing yourself as the expert can make it hard to know how to share your power and authority with lay people who do not have that expertise. Yet that is exactly what this newly activated partnership calls for.

Camp directors express concern about how to manage this new relationship. They know they must have active and involved board members to successfully enter the beckoning realm of major fund-raising. Yet there is confusion about how to develop the right kind of board structure and relationships. There is uncertainty about how to be both the professional leader in charge of camp and the professional partner who consults and learns from the expertise of capable lay leaders who volunteer their time and advice on how to strategically build the camp.

From raising funds to engaging in strategic fund-raising

For many years, non-profit Jewish camps raised money from families and organizations close to the camp. Indeed many camps could never have opened their doors had there not been generous friends willing to offer the needed financial backing to purchase and ready the sites that these camps occupy.

Yet, Jewish camps are entering a new era of fund-raising that earlier camp directors would not have recognized. Due to increasing market pressure to improve facilities and programs that families want for their children, Jewish camps require a new level of financial investment that often cannot be drawn from annual revenue streams. Jewish philanthropists with a sustained interest in the future of these camps are the most likely source of this investment. And those philanthropists are not likely to invest in a camp that is not well-governed by both a competent professional staff and a lay board that exercises true oversight for the operation of the camp.

Taken together, all these changes mean that the old equations of camp leadership no longer work. A camp director can run a great educational program and have a terrific team in place to internally manage the camp operation. But if that director does not have his or her finger on the pulse of the market and the full trust of an active board that partners in developing a strategically sustainable fund-raising campaign, that camp is not likely to thrive in the decade ahead.

Ramah and the role of the professional camp leader

Given all these changes, when thinking specifically about Ramah at 60, I begin with these two questions:

1. How can a camping movement like Ramah remain true to its animating educational vision and yet successfully meet all the considerable challenges that arise from the changing world of Jewish camping?

2. How can a camping movement like Ramah develop and nurture professional camp leaders who together with their lay leaders guide their camps toward a successful future while managing all the new pressures and expectations that now define the role of the camp director?

I view these two questions as integrally linked. In the case of Ramah, educational vision and camp leadership are meant to be two sides of a single coin. The camp director is the individual who most clearly embodies the educational philosophy of Ramah. Yet given all the changes in the world of camping and in the role of the camp leader, we must ask: How can a Ramah camp director today be expected to accomplish, with professional integrity, all the accumulating demands that define his or her position? Is it not imperative for this movement to be asking itself if its traditional understanding of the role of the camp leader must be overhauled?

In looking at the recent history of Ramah, I see that this crisis in professional leadership is not a new phenomenon. At the end of *Ramah Reflections at 50: Visions for a New Century* (Dorph 2000), we find the list of all the camp directors of the Ramah camps from 1947 to 1999. What is striking to me is that from 1969 to 1999 in many of the residential camps there was a rapid turnover in professional leadership. It does not take a Harvard leadership consultant to tell us that Ramah as a movement cannot sustain its lofty educational vision if it does not get a firm handle on how to prepare, supervise, and nurture leaders who can give their camps the stable and sustaining leadership a camp requires to grow and flourish.

A look back at the history of Ramah

Although not much has been written specifically about the historical role of the Ramah camp director, we can infer from what has been written about the mission of Ramah how the early leaders of this movement viewed the role of the camp leader. I will focus in particular on the writings of the late Seymour Fox who in the late 1950s and the 1960s functioned as the leader and spokesperson for the movement.

Fox presents a rich set of ideas about the educational mission of Ramah. He explicitly claims that Ramah should not be thought of as primarily a camp, but as "an educational institution."

> The leadership of Ramah hoped to create an educational subculture that was more than a school, more than a youth movement, and more than a camp. . . . This [camp] setting was chosen because it offered more time. Ideas,

> programs and activities could be developed without the constraints of the rigorous school schedule. . . . It was favored because the educator as a role model in this setting meant something very different than the educator as a role model in the school or youth movement. Here one could observe the educator as he himself grappled with ideas, considered alternative lifestyles and succeeded or failed in these endeavors. (1989, 19–20)

Fox and his colleagues envisioned Ramah as a *vast stage* on which Jewish educators could bring to life an exciting alternative Jewish universe. They created a legacy of Ramah as a unique Jewish educational environment through which significant Jewish ideas and experiences could be presented to and impressed upon both campers and staff members. Indeed, I am one of many young Jews whose direction in life was inspired by the summers I spent at Ramah in the 1960s.

Note that Fox refers to "the educator as a role model." I do not know if he had the camp director specifically in mind, but Fox consistently thought of camp leaders as educators and role models. That model emphasizes his view—as we see below—that everything that happens at camp must be viewed through an educational prism: how will this or that administrative decision be viewed by staff and campers as reflecting the core values of the camp?

That is a powerful question, but also a limiting one. Its power comes from the vision of Ramah as an alternative Jewish universe in which all aspects of camp life are meant to reflect a sustaining Jewish vision of the good life. But it is also limiting because it fails to recognize that camps are also very much part of the ongoing mundane world in which vision is not the only value consideration that must be weighed. In this essay, I try to honor the power of Fox's traditional vision of Ramah and yet suggest an alternative perspective that recognizes that vision must be weighed against other countervailing forces that call for change and revision.

Fox: The Role of Vision at Ramah

In 1997, many years after he had left his active involvement with Ramah, Seymour Fox together with William Novak published *Vision at the Heart,* a reflective piece that included an essay called "Lessons from Camp Ramah on the Power of Ideas in Shaping an Educational Institution." This essay represents the clearest statement of how this legendary figure envisioned the Ramah mission and the tasks of leadership within this context.

"There is nothing as practical as a great idea" is the opening line and theme of this essay. Ramah's greatness lies in its big ideas. Before there were camps, there were big ideas on which to base these camps.

Ramah emerged out of an ambitious dream, a carefully considered ideal of educational possibilities. Big questions were asked: What kind of Jews, what kind of people, do we want to nurture? What ideas will guide this new camp? What happens when compelling but conflicting philosophies about the meaning and purpose of Jewish life must coexist in one institution? How can Judaism be transmitted to children and to teenagers as vital, engaging, and necessary?

Fox offers this creation myth to press his major point that what make an educational endeavor great are the ideas that it embodies. Educational institutions are not merely social arrangements that at a given moment people create to meet certain social and cultural needs. Ramah was not simply the product of the emerging Conservative Movement after the war years that required a more encompassing educational environment than its synagogue schools and youth movements could provide. These institutional imperatives, in Fox's view, were the backdrop to the opening of these camps. These camps *became* Ramah. They ascended to their intended heights when, through their leadership, they intentionally seized this historic opportunity to fashion themselves in the image of a number of compelling ideas.

Fox spells out what those compelling ideas are and lauds the unique relationship between Ramah and The Jewish Theological Seminary (JTS) that nurtured this creative process of ideas informing practice and practice informing ideas. He looks back at those formative years as defining Ramah as a movement and identifies both the core purpose and core values of this movement.

The purpose of Ramah in its largest sense is "to create an educational setting where young people will be able to discover their Judaism and learn how to live it in their daily lives . . . deeply committed to their tradition and actively involved in American society" (Fox 1997, 10).

The core values (Fox 1997, 13–17) that give definition to what it means "to live their Judaism in their daily lives" are:

- engaging with Jewish texts.
- being involved with prayer and spiritual life.
- exploring music, art, and drama as legitimate religious expressions.
- mastering Hebrew.
- becoming active and responsible citizens guided by the principles of Judaism.

Fox links each of these core values to the thinking of a particular professor at JTS. For example, he claims that Ramah's core value of prayer and spirituality was deeply influenced by the ideas of Abraham Joshua Heschel. Prayer at Ramah is not simply the practice of daily minyan supplemented by *kabbalat shabbat* at the lake. "What *tefillah* (prayer) meant at Ramah was deeply influenced by Heschel and his students, including the concept of *kavvanah* (devotional intention) and the idea of *tefillah* as an opportunity for contemplation and self-improvement" (Fox 1997, 16). As this example illustrates, Fox views these core values as derived from great ideas that elevate their meaning to a level of philosophic significance and make Ramah a compelling educational experiment.

Vision and Leadership at Ramah

When the "Lessons from Camp Ramah" essay was published, I thought Fox had captured important truths about Ramah in its first generation and had left us with much to think about the ongoing role of vision and ideas in Jewish education. However, recently I started to wonder what this essay tells us about leadership at Ramah. I believe that in Fox's view, the primary role of Ramah's professional leaders is to mediate the realms of ideas and practice and to take compelling ideas and translate them into enduring educational practices that define much of the camp program.

Support for this position can be found in a subsequent publication in which Fox is more explicit about the role of the principal in a school.

> If the principal is not encouraging, supporting and leading the school in the translation of the vision's ideas into day–to-day practice, the school will drift, its teachers will lose their focus, and students and parents will be denied the excitement of an education whose details are designed to offer them both discernment and meaning.
>
> Equally, if those responsible for administering a school are not partners to the vision and full participants in actualizing its aspirations, then the vision is likely to deteriorate into slogans, rather than being rooted in the real life of the school. The means of education are not neutral, whether they involve school discipline, a school's policy on scholarships or the job description of a new secretary. . . . The environment of a school — its 'oxygen' — is determined by the commitment of the entire staff. (Fox 2003, 270)

Fox is making two key points that are highly relevant to camp leadership as well:

1. Both children and adults in an educational system look toward the leaders to point the way and answer: Why are we here and what are we engaged in doing together? If the leaders are themselves not clear on a direction and purpose or are unable to communicate those to others, then the direction will drift, purpose will atrophy.

2. Purpose and direction — what Fox calls vision — must inform all aspects of the shared life. If the camp program (what the educational staff

is responsible for) and the camp environment (what the business staff is responsible for) do not mesh, everyone eventually will feel the gap and doubt the camp's seriousness of purpose. You cannot teach about justice in your lessons and treat your maintenance staff unfairly.

These two points taken together explain why Fox insisted that the Ramah camp director must be a Jewish educator: for that leader must both understand and embody the big ideas that *are* Ramah and translate those ideas into every aspect of camp life—from how campers are treated in the bunk to how the camp processes its sewage or contracts with its kitchen staff.

Built to Last

Several years ago I visited Camp Ramah in Wisconsin as part of a research team. I had never been to this Ramah, and what I observed was truly impressive. This visit started me thinking seriously again about Ramah as a summer camp. My research partner, Max Klau, suggested that to understand what we saw there, I needed to read a business book called *Built to Last* by James Collins and Jerry Porras (2002). Max's suggestion would prove pivotal to my own rethinking of the place of vision in today's world of Jewish camping.

Collins and Porras write about American corporations that both have lasted a long time and have outperformed their peer companies in terms of long-term earnings. These are Fortune 500 companies that have proven their enduring value over successive generations. The authors are interested in these companies as exemplars of excellence over time. Through a sophisticated research design, they investigated the characteristics that distinguish these companies from their competitors who also have lasted over time but have not succeeded to the same extent in financial terms.

What surprised me is that these authors also are interested in the role that vision plays in helping to create and sustain a highly successful company. They, like Fox, said that to understand why a single organization stands out among its peers as an exemplar of excellence over several generations, you must take into account, among other factors, the way values and purpose figure in their operating principles. But Collins and Porras have a very different take on vision than Fox had.

Whereas Fox is singularly focused on whether an educational institution is guided by a compelling vision, these authors view vision—which they carefully define—as only half the equation for success over time. In their view, what successful organizations must balance is a fidelity to enduring values and purpose, as well as an eager willingness to change anything that serves as a means to realizing those core values and purpose.

> The fundamental distinguishing characteristic of the most enduring and successful corporations is that they preserve a cherished core ideology while simultaneously stimulating progress and change in everything that is not part of their core ideology. Put another way, they distinguish their timeless core values and enduring core purpose (which should never change) from their operating principles and business strategies (which should be changing constantly in response to a changing world). . . . They understand the difference between what is truly sacred and what is not. And by being clear about what should never change, they are better able to stimulate change and progress in everything else. (Collins and Porras 2002, 220)

In their view, a vision is not simply a set of ideas that defines this organization's core values and enduring purposes. Rather,

> A good vision builds on the interplay between these two complementary yin-and-yang forces: it defines 'what we stand for and why we exist' that does not change (core ideology) and sets forth 'what we aspire to become, to achieve, to create' that will require significant change and progress to attain (the envisioned future). (Collins and Porras 2002, 221)

By focusing on this ying/yang polarity, these authors offer a key insight. As important as it is for Ramah to be clear about and true to its core ideology, it is equally vital to clarify what is *not core* and hence, what is changeable. What is required to promote enduring progress is not only fidelity to a defining ideology, but also a liberation from unspoken loyalties to particulars of the educational program and ways of doing business that are *not core* to Ramah's values and purpose.

Collins and Porras lead us to realize that if an organization like Ramah wishes to be seriously faithful to its core ideology and also be successful in today's world, its leaders must rigorously ask themselves: Are we currently best positioned to realize our core values and purposes? The likely answer will be that they are *not* best positioned because they are holding on to past arrangements that once seemed essential, but that today may function as barriers to future success. Indeed, not rigorously examining what must change will undermine the organization's fidelity to its principles because inefficient means dull the impact of those principles. Even the greatest idea will seem uninspiring if presented in ways that seem cumbersome and dated.

Who Defines the Vision of a Camp?

Following Collins and Porras, I am arguing that Ramah's leaders today face the dual task of renewing the core values and purpose of this movement *and* asking very hard questions about whether the camps are well positioned to deliver that vision-inspired program to today's changing clientele.

But who defines what the core values and purpose of a camp are? If these are to be the camp's guiding stars, were they set in the organizational firmament years ago and are they permanently set?

In Fox's view, Ramah is one of the few educational enterprises whose founders were deliberate about setting out both purpose and core values. They did so with great thought and deliberation and with a keen sense of what Ramah's unique contribution should be. In his view, their pioneering work should still be the guiding star; these are the values that make Ramah what it is. Fox cannot imagine a Ramah camp that did not take these values and purpose as fundamental. That does not mean that these values are not open to differing interpretations and expressions or that the past is the final word on core values. But Fox does not imagine that these values will go out of fashion or become irrelevant. In that sense, he views these as core and unchanging.

Collins and Porras also cite many cases in which a company's core purpose and values were established by the founding generation. But they also warn that it is very easy to confuse core values and cultural norms. Just because "we have always done it this way" does not mean that a given practice reflects a core value. To help sort out what are truly core values, they ask organizational leaders hard questions like:

- Can you imagine these core values being equally valid 100 years from now?
- Would you hold these values even if at some point they became a competitive disadvantage?
- If you were to start a new organization tomorrow, would you still build in these as the core values?

I imagine Fox would have answered each of these in the affirmative. But I am less sure that would be true for all or most Ramah leaders today. Indeed, it may be very important to be raising these kinds of questions to discover if there remains a consensus among the lay and professional leaders as to what is core and unchangeable, and what should be viewed as cultural norms that developed over time but could be changed to make Ramah a more effective modality for educating today's campers and families.

Does Ramah Have the Right People on the Bus?

Where Collins and Porras differ most dramatically from Fox is on the question of what comes first in building a successful organization. Fox identifies big ideas as the first element that forms the basis for a vision of excellence. Collins and Porras place primary emphasis on getting "the right people on the bus" and building a solid work structure and discipline that will allow those people to flourish together. In their view, the vision emerges from having the right people working together rather than the other way around.

Over the last twenty to twenty-five years, there has been a clear correlation between continuity in leadership and overall camp success on both the educational and managerial levels. At times there were periods of considerable instability at the director level at Ramah camps. In fairness, instability also has characterized the leadership of other sectors of North American Jewish education. Ramah does not stand alone in this regard, and in the past few years there has been more stable leadership in Ramah. Nevertheless, the hard questions about leadership are not limited to stability. They include what type of leadership these camps will require to grow and prosper by contemporary standards of camping excellence in today's changing world.

Getting the right people on and the wrong people off the bus is a complex matter. I am not sure that a simple formula such as "Ramah camps need to be led by Jewish educators" can guide the thinking required for preparing Ramah's future leaders today. For as Collins makes clear, there is no objective measure of who is "right" or "wrong" for a given organization. The right people are those who will fit the ethos and culture of the organization and whose work style best matches what this particular organization expects and requires of its leaders. At Ramah the question of who is right is made more complicated by the regional differences among the camps and by the differing demands that the various local boards of directors have placed on the directors whom they have a hand in selecting and evaluating. Ramah must not rely on a "one size fits all" formula for selecting and developing their camp directors.

Some Ramah directors have told me that they feel caught in a cross fire between the traditional vision of Ramah as a Jewish educational institution and the demands of local board members that they run their camps by the standards of an efficient business. I doubt that these cross pressures are a new development, but these pressures grow more acute with the changes we have described in the world of Jewish camping. Indeed, I am convinced that these cross pressures will continue to weigh heavily on the Ramah camp directors and will necessitate a rethinking of the traditional definitions of what skills will be required in the future to be a successful director of a camp.

Although I cannot answer who are the right professionals to lead the Ramah camps into their future, I can share what we have been learning through ELI about what it takes in today's changing world of Jewish camping to become a successful camp professional leader. This contribution is necessarily speculative as it is based on but one year of intensive work with our nineteen Jewish camp directors from around North America. It also is not specific to the needs of Ramah camps. Nevertheless, these observations may serve as a beginning for a much longer inquiry into who are the right leaders for the Ramah of the future.

What Skills Will Future Camp Leaders Need?

Through conversations over several years with both professional and lay leaders of Jewish residential camps, and in intensive seminars over a period of a year with nineteen Jewish camp directors from the many movements, Richard Levin and I came up with a list of five clusters of professional skills that we think are essential for successful professional camp leadership in today's changing world of camping.

Communicating a compelling story

Ramah always has prided itself on delivering this powerful message: Some camps can make all the difference for your child and family. Some camps can be transformative; Ramah camps can be Jewishly transformative.

The problem with that message today is that many Jewish venues claim to be transformative. So what makes Ramah special?

Answering that question via a compelling story is a first essential skill for a camp director. By "story" we mean a multi-media narrative that incisively tells both outsiders and insiders what makes this camp a very special place. It sums up in a few words and images what people uniquely love about this place. With color, verve, and emotion, the story illustrates what this camp contributes to people's lives—in the case of Ramah—how this camp enriches their Jewish lives.

Today's camp leader must be an authentic storyteller with great versatility. There is a story that works for recruiting new families and staff. But there are other versions for recruiting board members, building communal support, and engaging donors. This camp story has many versions but must convey a consistent message: the vision of the leadership for this camp; not only what the camp is today, but what it can become tomorrow.

This story ultimately is a love story, and the camp leader is its bard.

Managing complexity

I visited a camp leader this summer who was dealing with all of the following issues at once while also running the camp:

1. The assistant director had announced he would be leaving after the summer.

2. A seasoned professional on her staff was accused by another staff member of theft.

3. The groundskeeper was not working at the same level of consistency or effectiveness as in past years.

4. The parent organization had just appointed a new executive who had to be educated about the camp's role in that organization.

5. The chair of the camp board was urging caution in what the director would say to that new executive.

6. This director recently had given birth to a child and also was dealing with balancing home and work issues.

There was nothing particularly unusual about this situation; this was not a crisis situation. This visit brought home that today's camp leader must be a master juggler who is at ease balancing a lot of different balls in the air at once.

I contend that camp life has grown far more complex, and this trend has major implications for who can succeed today in the role of a camp leader. Camp leadership requires a high degree of face-to-face interaction with staff, families, campers, and community members. The role calls for that unusual combination of a leader who is a talented communicator but can also step back and deal with a lot of small details and pressures that could overwhelm others.

The camp directors I most admire exhibit the capacity to be totally immersed in the daily concerns of camp life while also reserving space in their brains to dream the big dream of what this camp can become. They master the complexity while never forgetting that camp is about something much larger than the details themselves.

Leading by delegating and inspiring

With complexity comes the requirement to lead by delegating and inspiring. Camps appoint a single leader, but that leader inevitably leads by building the team that shares the leadership tasks. The quality of that team tells a lot about the quality of that leader.

It is never easy sharing power and authority. Yet that is exactly what camp leaders must do today. They must invest young people with the responsibility and authority to lead units within the camp in accordance with the vision of the camp. Young people can succeed at this only when they are part of a team that cares for them, nurtures their talents, offers critical feedback, and stands behind them when the going gets tough. Camp leaders who create such teams reap the rewards of shared power and responsibility. But with talented people in short supply, camp leaders always are struggling to put together teams that will work well and last beyond a single season.

A successful camp leader today relies on a lot of different experts who in other contexts would not be working under the same roof. How the leader manages their input, inspires their commitment, and orchestrates their diverse contributions tells a lot about the health of that camp as a cohesive organization.

Educating and learning at every level

The vision of the camp guides its leaders to what they are aiming to achieve, but only their social and emotional intelligence—their capacity to learn from all levels of this business—allows them to adapt their operations to achieve a maximally successful camp organization.

The best camp leaders today are constantly educating others on the vision (core purpose and values) of this camp. But at the same time, they are constantly learning from others how best to achieve that vision. Who are those camp leaders learning from? The answer is they are learning primarily from the following key stakeholders:

- Campers and families have much to teach about the current market and the emerging needs of children and their families today.
- Educational staff members have much to teach about the daily operations—what works or does not work in the bunks, on the playing fields, around the swimming place, and in the creative spaces for the arts and spiritual practice.
- Administrative staff members have much to teach about operating the systems that allow the camp to manage the grounds, the dining hall, the infirmary, and interactions with the surrounding world.
- Board members have much to teach about the financial health of the camp, its place in the larger Jewish community, and its strategic growth possibilities.
- Rabbis and educators in the communities have much to teach about how the camp aligns with the larger movement—the synagogues and schools—that also serve this constituency.

All these stakeholders may not be aware of how much they have to teach the camp director until he opens the doors of communications with them. But having the skills to build these networks, tap the knowledge base of these stakeholders, and know how to use their knowledge to draw a map of the camp's opportunities and challenges are key leadership skills for future camp directors.

Planning and effecting change

Camps are dynamic operations. Camp leaders must have their fingers on the pulse of the camping market, on how other camps are innovating, and on what is emerging as best practice in Jewish experiential education. They must be constantly thinking: How can we make this a better camp operation—better in serving its clientele and better in realizing its core vision?

No camp director can bring about ongoing change and improvement alone. Effective change inevitably involves all the key stakeholders. The best camp leaders today do not simply envision change and seek support for their envisioned project. Rather, they reach out to others, learn from them, and use that input to plan change that will gain wider support. When people hear a compelling story for why an envisioned change is required, they are moved to support the change because it speaks to them as partners in the destiny of this camp.

A camp leader who learns to listen and collaborate with key stakeholders and knows how to make proposed changes happen with adequate financial and communal support will be able to lead her camp into a successful future.

The Future Leaders of Ramah

Although I agree with Fox that the Ramah camp director must embody the Ramah vision and know how to translate that vision into camp practices that involve all the camp's staff, I want to conclude by suggesting an expanded version of the camp director as educator. I am referring to an educator who knows not only how to embody a vision but also to ask the tough questions that Collins and Porras insist are required to successfully lead an organization in our times.

The problem with having pride and confidence in a long-standing vision is that it can generate a sense of certainty and even an unbending attachment to past truths and practices. In the case of Ramah, the pride in its Jewish educational mission can become a certainty that we know best how to run our camps, and any substantive suggestion for change can be interpreted as a retreat from the standards of Ramah. Fox's call to embody an established vision can become a defensive stance in the face of calls for adaptive change.

In this paper I am calling on Ramah's professional leaders to adopt a different stance in relation to the vision of Ramah. Rather than thinking in "either-or" terms, it is advisable to think in "both-and" terms. Instead of believing that Ramah must stick to that established vision *or else* Ramah will cease to be true to its Jewish educational principles, I suggest that leaders can be both true to the Ramah vision *and* open to investigating how best to realize that vision in our day. They can be open to the possibility that not every established educational practice is necessarily still an effective means for realizing that vision and that the director may need to adapt a learner's perspective in relation to input from key stakeholders.

I have learned from Collins and Porras that when leaders become overly confident in the established practices of their organization, they invite inevitable decline. Collins and Porras advocate a dual-mindedness in leaders that I suggest is apt for Ramah at 60. Leaders must have full confidence in the purpose and core values of their organization *and* radical uncertainty as to whether the organization is actually well-aligned to best accomplish that vision and those goals.

In the fall of 2007, the New England Patriots enjoyed unprecedented success in the regular professional football season. Their win-loss record was 16–0, and they broke a number of records for offense. Yet in the pages of the *Boston Globe,* I read that their coach, Bill Belichick, assessed his team's efforts each week in terms of where the team needed to improve. He was obsessively concerned with what did *not* go as well as it could even when the team had yet to lose a game. Belichick embodies the kind of leader that Collins and Porras admire: he is eager to ask the hard questions even in the face of a natural tendency to feel confident and coast with the team's success.

In contrast, I have been at Ramah—as well as other Jewish camps—where the director has told me privately that he does not have full confidence in his senior staff and no longer believes that key camp programs are at the quality level that he expects. It is urgent that these camp leaders ask the hard questions of what can we do to constantly improve the quality of our staff and programs. There have been some great examples of innovative leadership at Ramah in the past two decades. However, I also think there has been some coasting and complacence in the face of the admittedly very difficult task of insisting upon excellence.

There also have been recent occasions when Ramah directors were taken to task by board members for not consistently managing the camp systems at a level of business excellence. Michael Brown reports that questions of managerial accountability have existed for several decades in the Ramah system (Brown 2000). Ramah directors are consistently asked to manage the complexity of the business operation with the same dedication and skill as they manage the camp's educational programs. Their success in balancing these goals will continue to be crucial to Ramah's ongoing success.

What is required is a different understanding of what it means today that a Ramah camp director should be a Jewish educator. There remains the essential demand that Ramah camp directors live the life of a committed

Conservative Jew and be schooled in the fundamentals of contemporary Jewish educational theory and practice. But there must be the added dimension of the educator as adult learner. Ramah directors today require the humility to recognize that they probably do *not* bring all the skills and knowledge they need to run an excellent summer camp. As a result they must be on a continuous learning curve to achieve both self and organizational improvement. They can find teachers at JTS and other institutions of higher learning but also at camping conferences, management workshops, and private meetings with board members, local rabbis, and interested lay advisors. The key is to realize that to be an educator today, a camp leader must constantly be learning and growing as a Jew and a professional leader.

It has been clear for some time that there cannot and must not be any dichotomy between being a serious Jewish educator and a dedicated manager-leader. There is no room for Ramah directors to take refuge in the seriousness of their educational vision at the expense of managerial competence and leadership capacities. Camp directors, just as school principals and congregational rabbis, must be expected to have expertise on both ends of this continuum. That is asking a lot of our professional leaders; it is the mandate of all who care about Jewish camping to support these leaders in their pursuit of excellence in both educating and learning.

References

Brown, Michael. 2000. The most important venture ever undertaken by the Seminary: Ramah in its first four decades. In *Ramah reflections at 50: Visions for a new century,* ed. S. A. Dorph, 25–88. New York: National Ramah Commission.

Collins, J., and J. I. Porras. 2002. *Built to last: Successful habits of visionary companies.* New York: HarperCollins.

Dorph, S. A., ed. 2000. *Ramah reflections at 50: Visions for a new century.* New York: National Ramah Commission.

Fox, S. 1989. Ramah: A setting for Jewish education. In *The Ramah experience: Community and commitment,* ed. S. C. Ettenberg and G. Rosenfield, 19–37. New York: Jewish Theological Seminary.

Fox, S. with W. Novak. 1997. *Vision at the heart: Lessons from Camp Ramah on the power of ideas in shaping educational institutions.* Jerusalem: The Mandel Institute.

Fox, S. 2003. The art of translation. In *Visions of Jewish education,* ed. S. Fox, I. Scheffler, and D. Marom, 253–95. Cambridge: Cambridge University Press.

SHULY RUBIN SCHWARTZ

The Three Pillars of Ramah: Then and Now

RAMAH WAS A TRANSFORMATIVE EXPERIENCE for thousands of men and women fortunate enough to spend their formative years in its embrace. I count myself among those who benefited from the magic of Ramah and who sought to ensure that their own children also would be inspired by it. But as a graduate student in American Jewish history, I was determined to try and understand the nature of that magic, to contextualize the Ramah experiment, and to isolate those factors that made it unique. This interest culminated in my decision to write my master's thesis on the early years of Camp Ramah.

As I discovered then, Ramah was neither the first Jewish educational summer camp nor the largest. Earlier camps, such as Achvah, Cejwin, Modin, Yavneh, and Massad, had experimented with offering formal study, creating a Hebrew environment, fostering traditional Jewish living, promoting Zionism, and cultivating future leaders.[1] Ramah was not even the first incursion of the Conservative Movement into Jewish camping. Shortly after its founding in 1918, National Women's League had already looked into running a Jewish educational summer camp for girls. League officers wanted the next generation of Jewish girls to be better prepared than their mothers to establish Jewish homes, and they understood that a summer camp could be an ideal setting in which to model Jewish living. Women's League endorsed an existing camp, the Camp for Girls at Sylvan Lake, in return for assurances that the camp would be administered in accordance with Jewish law and that the counselors would be recommended by the League. Unfortunately, the camp functioned successfully for only one year. After a disappointing second season in 1921, Women's League withdrew its support.[2]

Ramah's uniqueness, then, did not stem from its role in pioneering the distinctive features of Jewish educational summer camping. What made Ramah work was the innovative way that it brought the aforementioned

SHULY RUBIN SCHWARTZ, *Ph.D., is the Irving Lehrman Research Associate Professor of American Jewish History and the dean of graduate and undergraduate studies at The Jewish Theological Seminary.*

elements together. At its founding, Ramah's success rested on three foundational pillars—Hebrew, Jewish living, and study—that reinforced each other to create the special Ramah ethos.

1. Hebrew

Beginning in the mid-1940s, several different stakeholders promoted summer camping as an ideal vehicle for increasing the Hebrew language competency of American Jewish children. For Jewish educators, camp offered the opportunity to maximize the number of hours a year that Jewish children who attended public school would be exposed to Hebrew and Jewish learning. Most American Jews embraced public school education as a vehicle for Americanization, and many Jewish educators shared this commitment. According to Moshe Davis, dean of the Teachers Institute of The Jewish Theological Seminary (JTS), the premise of Jewish educators

> must be that the Jewish school system is complementary to, and not competitive with, public school education. This view is . . . taken out of a deep conviction that democracy and democratic living depend on an integrated as well as upon an enlightened citizenry. . . . The best means to such social integration is a system of common public education, for the public school system is the keystone of our democratic arch.[3]

Though Davis acknowledged that Jewish day schools would provide a better Jewish education than supplementary schools, he concluded that this would never be the answer for the majority of American Jewish children. Therefore, he felt it incumbent upon American Jewish educators to devise a way for public school children to receive an intensive Hebrew language-based Jewish education. For Davis and others, Hebrew proficiency was the essential foundation for intensive Jewish learning because it is the key to studying Jewish sacred texts in the original. To realize this goal, Davis and other Jewish educators latched on to the summer months as an untapped reservoir of time that could be devoted to intensive study of Hebrew language and Judaica.[4]

In their commitment to establishing Ramah as a Hebrew-speaking camp, Jewish educators were joined by Hebraists who saw the Hebrew language not only as the key to Jewish learning but also as the soul of Jewish culture. For them, teaching and speaking Hebrew in America was an affirmation of the yearning for the realization of the Zionist dream. Finally, others endorsed the centrality of Hebrew because they looked to Ramah to cultivate a learned elite for American Jewry, and they believed Hebrew competency to be essential for such leadership.[5]

2. Study

Like the element of the Hebrew language, educators hoped that formal study of Judaica in the summer would deepen and intensify the Jewish knowledge of public school children. Beginning with the first summer (1947), classes met five times a week for one and a half hours each day. For the first few weeks, lessons were devoted to teaching the Hebrew necessary for camp living. Later in the summer, classes included stories, discussions, poems, and geography—all focused on Palestine. The curriculum also included study of Bible, Talmud, Hebrew literature, grammar, and contemporary Jewish problems. Counselors made an effort to relate the formal study of topics such as Hebrew grammar, prayer, or rabbinic attitudes toward slander, gossip, or tale-bearing to the experiences that campers had in the bunk, during religious services, and on the ball field. This dedication to moral education and character building is as essential to the Ramah ethos as the commitment to recognizing in every camp activity—including music, arts and crafts, and drama—an opportunity to reinforce the Jewish educational lessons learned in classes.[6]

In addition to seeing formal study as a way to help campers progress more rapidly in their learning, Ramah's founders also saw regular classes as one way to demonstrate their philosophical commitment to Jewish study as an essential component of a full Jewish life. To demonstrate their devotion to study, Ramah required not only campers but everyone to study—from the director to the waiters. Engaging a full-time professor-in-residence was another way to model that dedication to Jewish learning. During the first summer, the professor-in-residence, Abraham Halkin, participated in general camp programming and also held regular and frequent discussions with the counselors. Because the counselors also served as teachers during that initial summer, Halkin's support proved invaluable. According to the director of the camp, Henry Goldberg, Halkin "inspired both campers and counsellors [*sic*] and more than anything else, contributed to the raising of the morale of the latter." Overworked counselor/teachers appreciated the support and encouragement that Halkin provided.[7]

3. Jewish Living

The third component of the Ramah vision—Jewish living—reflected the desire of Jewish educators to use the summer months to model Jewish living for those who did not grow up in observant families. Creating a vibrant Jewish community for campers would also foster pride in being Jewish and comfort in living as a Jew. As Gerson D. Cohen, a staff member and life-long supporter of Ramah who later served as Chancellor of JTS, recalled, Ramah "succeeded in making us all proud and uninhibitedly Jewish in our behavior." Ramah normalized Jewish living, enabling Jews who lived in isolation from one another during the year to feel comfortable with an observant lifestyle.[8]

The main outline of Ramah living had already emerged in the first summer. The camp was strictly kosher, and Shabbat was observed. Zionism was also an essential element of Ramah's Jewish living, and knowledge and love of Palestine permeated the arts and crafts, drama, and music programs. Religious services were held every morning and Friday evenings. (Attendance at Shabbat *minḥah* was voluntary.) Campers also vied with each other to lead the Grace after Meals. As Goldberg recalled, "We aimed to plant in the hearts of the campers a feeling for prayer and a desire to pray." He noted that "at a glance one could tell that the camp was conducted under religious auspices."[9]

Though promoting a traditional Jewish lifestyle, Ramah kept the definition of "Jewish living" vague. This attitude stemmed from Chancellor Louis Finkelstein, who did not want to define Jewish living too precisely because he felt that doing so would alienate Reform and Orthodox Jews. He wanted JTS to serve as an umbrella institution for all American Jews and to train leaders for the American Jewish community as a whole.[10] Because Ramah fell under the auspices of JTS, it reflected this ethos as well. Moreover, in 1947, the leadership of the Conservative Movement had not yet fully defined Conservative Jewish living in a distinctive way. At this time, three years before the landmark *teshuvah* (rabbinic responsum) on riding to shul on Shabbat and decades before egalitarianism took hold, Conservative Judaism had yet to clarify a distinctive approach to Jewish living.

In addition to fulfilling the loftier goals of its founders, these three pillars were also designed to serve more focused ends, for American Jewry broadly and for JTS specifically. The reality and enormity of the Holocaust intensified the sense of responsibility that JTS leaders felt to produce indigenous leaders for the post-war American Jewish community. But in the 1940s, JTS was painfully aware of its inability to meet this need. The Teachers Institute was in danger of being closed due to low enrollment; JTS discontinued its freshman class because of the war, and only two students graduated in 1946.[11] JTS desperately needed to increase enrollment in its schools if it was to thrive in the post-war era and meet the growing need for Jewish leaders throughout the country. To that end, JTS established both Ramah and the year-round youth organization for teenagers, Leaders Training Fellowship (LTF), to inspire young Jews to study at JTS and then to take on Jewish leadership roles in the American Jewish community.[12] As Max Arzt explained in 1944: "To train enough rabbis to help share the burdens . . . to educate teachers, to provide for the development of scholars (who will raise future generations of rabbis and teachers), is a fundamental need of our time, and a principal obligation of the Seminary to Judaism."[13]

The growth of Ramah was part and parcel of the larger growth of organized camping in America. As American Jews became more and more acculturated to the larger society around them, they too embraced camping as a natural part of the summer experience of American Jewish children. By the 1940s, American Jews had become more receptive not only to Jewish camps, but to ones that actively fostered Jewish values and identity.[14] But the success of Ramah can be attributed not only to trends in the larger society. Its singular achievement lay first and foremost in the way in which each of its ideological pillars strengthened the other to create the exceptional environment that enabled the camp to reach its goals.

Several other factors also contributed to its enormous success. First, the establishment of Ramah grew out of the convergence of the interests and needs of lay leaders in Chicago and professionals at JTS. The yearning of Midwestern lay leaders for an intensive Jewish summer camp experience for their children matched the desire of the professional educators to provide such an experience. This led to the crucial collaboration of local lay leaders and JTS professionals that modeled the lay-professional cooperation essential to enduring institutional change.

Second, because JTS understood Ramah to be a "farm team" for its future leaders, it focused on recruiting the best students from the best communities and on hiring the most talented and dedicated adults for all of its positions—from professor-in-residence to kitchen staff. Rigorous requirements that included a minimum number of hours of formal study each week, facility with Hebrew language, and a commitment to Jewish observance, assured that only a highly selective population of campers and staff would be drawn to spend a summer at Ramah. The camp demanded a great deal from everyone in terms of study, observance, Hebrew speaking, and community building. In return, campers and staff were inspired by the mission of Ramah and felt privileged to be part of a pioneering cohort that believed it would make a difference in the future of American Jewry.

Third, in contrast to the other Jewish educational summer camps of the era, Ramah cultivated a rebellious stance vis à vis the predominant American Jewish ethos. According to Jonathan Sarna, Shlomo Shulsinger strove, through Camp Massad, to mold children to live a Hebrew-infused Jewish life. Through the Brandeis Camp Institute, Shlomo Bardin sought to transform college-age men and women into Jewish personalities.[15] The success of Ramah stemmed from its openly subversive goal of cultivating a Conservative Jewish elite that would "supplant everyday American values and behavior with authentic Jewish values and behavior but as well to change the mores of the Conservative movement."[16] The camp focused its efforts on pre-teenage youngsters and especially on teenagers, the age group most susceptible to role modeling and to rebelling against parental authority, to create a distinctive identity that would be reinforced by peers and role models. In this way, the leadership of Ramah hoped to invigorate Conservative Judaism by cultivating an elite that would be more dedicated, knowledgeable, and observant than their parents.

Finally, Ramah's success also stemmed from a sense of desperate urgency about ensuring Jewish survival. In the post-war era, Ramah's founders felt they could afford no margin of error. They believed that Conservative Judaism could not sustain itself without Ramah and that American Jewry would not be able to cultivate a rich Jewish life without Conservative Judaism. With such missionary zeal fueled by the haunting specter of failure, the founders had the motivation to fuel its success.

The Movement Today

Ramah has undergone an enormous transformation in the sixty years since its founding, growing from one camp in Wisconsin to a movement that currently serves over 6,500 campers and 1,500 college-aged staff members, both here and in Israel. Ramah has touched tens of thousands of lives over the past six decades, and during this time, American Jewry has changed dramatically in size, scope, and constituency. The community has become more secure economically and more fully integrated into American society on every level—economically, socially, culturally, demographically, and politically. At the same time, the maturation of the Zionist vision, the influence of Mordecai M. Kaplan's expansive view of Judaism as a civilization, and the influx of refugees and survivors both before and after the Holocaust, have all led to a deepening of American Jewish life. The growth of Jewish day schools and Hebrew high schools, the burgeoning of Jewish studies on college campuses, and the flourishing of artistic expressions of Judaism, including art, music, and literature have contributed to a richer Jewish life in the past thirty years. Jews also have mirrored the concerns of Americans at large as they became involved in such reform movements as feminism and civil rights. To meet the growing needs of this evolving community, Ramah has been challenged over and over again to rethink its initial mission.

For example, as the Ramah movement grew to include several summer camps, its leaders had to rethink the elitist orientation. Should the benefits of Ramah be extended to as many campers as possible, or ought it remain as exclusive as it was in its early years in order to stay focused on leadership cultivation? Religious school principals debated this very issue in 1964. In an educators' forum, seven principals whose schools sent large numbers of students to Ramah reflected on its impact. Six out of the seven praised Ramah's impact on the viability and success of their Hebrew high school programs. They were elated that returning campers infused their religious schools, junior congregations, and teen groups with new vitality. But one of these educators, Jay B. Stern of Temple Beth El in Rochester, New York, mused that:

> Jewish educators . . . have often been heard to deride Ramah successes by noting that only the best pupils get into the camps. Our schools, too, would be fabulously successful if we could limit enrollment to the top five percent of pupils who are highly motivated, of above average intelligence, and from the most positive homes. . . . One wonders, therefore, whether the camps should not accept a limited number of unmotivated and even untrained campers, especially on the upper teen age level. . . . [W]e tend to feel that a minority of such campers among the majority of carefully selected top students would be carried along with the group."[17]

Stern suggested that Ramah's wild success depended on its exclusivity, and he challenged Ramah to loosen its standards so that even the "unmotivated" could be influenced by it. Both lay and professional leaders of Ramah shared the desire to make the Ramah experience available to more and more Conservative Jewish children. The establishment of the National Ramah Commission (NRC) in 1951 provided the organizational infrastructure for realizing this goal, and the opening of several additional Ramah camps in Nyack, the Berkshires, and Palmer in the 1960s made this possible. In fact, Camp Ramah in Wingdale, New York (Ramah in the Berkshires) was the first camp acquired under a ten-year plan adopted by the NRC in 1962 that called for the acquisition of five new camps before 1972, "in order to meet the growing demand for admission." Again, the increasing interest in summer camping on the part of middle-class American Jewish families mirrored the steady rate of growth of organized camping in the United States. In 1963, more than 2,000 children attended five Ramah camps or teen seminars, "but for each child served, another, fully qualified, had to be rejected for lack of space." That Ramah had moved away from a focus on recruiting only the most motivated students is evident in its desire to meet the growing demand and offer its summer experience to all those children who wanted to attend. Tellingly, the 1963 Berkshires press release does not mention cultivating an elite Jewish leadership as the overall objective of the "Ramah program." Rather, the goal of Ramah "which has attracted large numbers of youngsters from the American Jewish community, is to help the child relate the Jewish tradition to his own life in an American community."[18]

The dreams of the national leadership of Ramah in the 1960s exceeded even this expansion. Going beyond Stern's gentle challenge, one of Ramah's long-range thinkers noted that "If we can ever establish twenty Ramah camps throughout the country, we will succeed in virtually reshaping the very nature and character of the American Jewish Community."[19]

By the 1960s, then, the national leadership of Ramah was committed to offering a Jewish educational summer experience to the masses of Conservative Jewish children. However, as Ramah has come closer to achieving this goal, it has found itself faced with new challenges. The increased number of Ramah camps, with their larger facilities, has created continuing financial pressure to fill each camp to capacity.[20] This has led to a further diminution of educational standards for acceptance, leading Ramah directors today to focus on issues such as, "what are the minimum acceptable educational policies and standards of any Ramah camp."[21]

Such concerns have led Ramah directors far afield from the goals of their predecessors. Does the original goal of fostering an elite group of leaders remain desirable, and if so, can Ramah still achieve that aim when it recruits thousands of campers each year? Even if these campers were all dedicated toward this goal, the camp leadership is faced with the impossible challenge of recruiting sufficient staff with the background, skills, and motivation necessary to realize this vision. Ironically, another factor that complicated achieving this goal is the flourishing Solomon Schechter Day School movement. More and more of the most motivated Ramah campers, who would be logical targets of elite training, come to camp with much of the background that Ramah initially was designed to provide. For these campers, "formal study, Hebrew language, and Jewish living" are not a subversive challenge to their year-round routine but rather a continuation of it. As the Ramah directors have noted with regard to the strong Hebrew language skills of day school campers, this reality is

> a double-edged sword. On the one hand, there is greater Hebrew competence. On the other hand, it becomes more difficult to associate Hebrew usage with fun at camp, as so many campers associate Hebrew language with their academic lives at school."[22]

This poses an immense challenge to the staff to find novel ways to motivate and excite their campers Jewishly. Moreover, this reality also places additional pressure on the camp to recruit staff members with the rich Hebrew and Judaic backgrounds necessary to fully engage with and challenge such campers. Finally, the increasing numbers of Conservative Jewish children in day schools has created an additional challenge for recruiting campers. The parents of these children already are paying substantial tuition for their children's Jewish education during the year. Choosing day school education for their children has led some parents to opt to use the summer months to expose their children to "real world pursuits outside the Jewish orbit."[23]

Related to these concerns are those of how to continue to engage Jewish children in their teenage years. Even those campers who are positively influenced by Ramah as youngsters often seek other venues for summer activity when they reach adolescence. Louis Newman, one of the early Ramah directors who deeply influenced the ideology of Ramah, felt strongly that Ramah must challenge its older campers with meaningful and exciting activities that tap into adolescent creativity, energy, and growing maturity.[24] Newman developed several successful ways for older campers to do this, including having them engage in meaningful work in camp and volunteer for service projects in neighboring communities. In his day, there were few competing programs to lure American Jewish teenagers, and Ramah offered a compelling alternative community for American Jewish teens. Today, the population of Ramah campers includes more preteens than teenagers, because teenagers are tempted by a myriad of other summer programs that offer them alternative ways to stretch their minds, bodies, and spirit. Opportunities for teen travel around the world abound as do service and learning programs and unpaid internships in areas of potential career interest. A myriad of pre-college programs attract students interested in strengthening their academic credentials to give them an edge in the college admissions process. What must Ramah offer to maintain its edge as the premier environment for influencing teenagers to dedicate themselves to becoming forces for change within the Conservative Movement, American Jewry, and the world? And, beyond this, how can Ramah help its teenagers transition successfully to adult leadership roles so that we might all reap the benefit of their creative thinking to help invigorate the Conservative Movement and beyond?

Today, Ramah meets this challenge in many ways by focusing its efforts on staff development. For example, the Weinstein Institute brings together younger staff members for several days in a learning and training program. This experience not only motivates them to return to camp with new energy and ideas, but it also fosters a shared sense of commitment to the goals of Ramah; and in so doing, it helps foster an elite nucleus within the Ramah system.[25]

Finally, Ramah must also accommodate the needs of a more affluent American Jewish community that is more integrated into American life than ever before. Summer camp is no longer the exotic and special treat that it was for Jewish children in the 1950s and 1960s.[26] Potential campers are lured by well-equipped summer homes and competing summer camps offering first-rate facilities in gorgeous settings that provide enrichment in the arts, sciences, and sports. Even those campers who choose to return to Ramah year after year face the new reality of an electronically connected world that inexorably has altered the camp experience. Campers who can check email regularly are no longer able to shut out their home life in order to fully immerse themselves in the camp experience. With these compelling pressures and opportunities, how can Ramah compete? How can we translate the magic of Ramah into the contemporary idiom so that it can have the same impact in the next sixty years that it had in its first sixty?

One example of innovative programming that models this translation is the Beit Midrash and Northwoods Kollel at Ramah in Wisconsin. The Beit Midrash, founded in 2000 by Josh Cahan and Aryeh Bernstein, offers intensive Talmud study

> as an alternative to standard camp classes in Judaics and Hebrew. . . . [*M*]*ishmar* . . . draws campers from all backgrounds. It has grown in popularity to the point that this summer our library could barely hold the 150 participants. The singing is intense, the *divrei torah* simple and provocative, the atmosphere one of deep connectedness to God and to each other. . . . It has fostered a kind of powerful spiritual awakening. . . . Participants have come to see camp as a place of serious intellectual and religious growth. . . . Camp has thus become an avenue for increasing the presence and the level of Torah study not only in the Northwoods but in our feeder cities as well.[27]

This is precisely what Ramah accomplished in the 1950s and early 1960s. By insisting that its campers engage in intensive Jewish study and Jewish living in a Hebrew-speaking environment, Ramah raised the level of religious school education, Jewish religious life in small communities, and Hebrew high school education. The Kollel today does not emphasize the original three pillars of Ramah in the same way. It does not, for example, stress spoken Hebrew language, and it focuses on Talmud study rather than on the study of a broad array of literary texts, including Hebrew poetry, Bible, and Israeli literature. Nevertheless, the Kollel has successfully translated the magic of Ramah's distinctiveness for a new generation. As Josh Cahan reports, the

> Kollel and Beit Midrash have also been part of a flowering of higher-level programming throughout the camp, from more serious study in regular text classes to professional-quality opportunities in the performing and visual arts. . . .
>
> Through this spiritual engagement we create the potential for these teenagers to be the foundation of engaged, spiritually connected, and thoughtful communities in college and beyond.[28]

And the influence on participants is palpable. As one expressed:

> Kollel for me meant not only a place where I could learn an incredible amount in a short period of time, but also a place where I could live, become, and grow into a more refined self through the company of peers and teachers alike. . . . The most valuable gift that the Kollel granted me was a sense that I am not alone, that there are other Jews out there who share my vision of a profoundly passionate, committed, intellectually open, and spiritually energizing Judaism.[29]

This is the same kind of leadership cultivation—the modeling of an authentic, spiritual, and learned Conservative Judaism—that Moshe Davis, Mordecai Kaplan, Sylvia Ettenberg, Henry Goldberg, Simon Greenberg, and others strove to provide through the establishment of Ramah sixty years ago. The Beit Midrash and Northwoods Kollel exemplify contemporary Ramah programming that captures the essence of the magic of Ramah for the twenty-first century.

May we nurture many other programs like it. And may we continue to be inspired by the legacy of the past sixty years to help us develop ways to transmit the magic that is Ramah to the young Jews of this new century.

Notes

[1] Jonathan D. Sarna, "The Crucial Decade in American Camping," in *A Place of Our Own: The Rise of Reform Jewish Camping: Essays Honoring the Fiftieth Anniversary of Olin-Sang-Ruby Union Institute, URJ, in Oconomowoc, Wisconsin,* ed. Michael M. Lorge and Gary P. Zola (Tuscaloosa: University of Alabama Press, 2006), 27–40; and Shuly Rubin Schwartz, "Ramah: The Early Years, 1947–52," *Conservative Judaism* 40 (Fall 1989): 17–20.

[2] "Early history" file, National Women's League Archives, New York.

[3] Moshe Davis, "The Ladder of Jewish Education," *Proceedings of the Second Annual Rabbinical Assembly Conference on Jewish Education* (December 22–23, 1947), 5.

[4] Davis, "Ladder," 7–8.

[5] Schwartz, "Ramah," 18; and Gerson D. Cohen, "Religious Education in Ramah," in *The Ramah Experience: Community and Commitment,* ed. S. C. Ettenberg and G. Rosenfeld (New York: The Jewish Theological Seminary, 1989), 40.

[6] Henry R. Goldberg, "Report on Camp Ramah, Summer 1947," 3–4 , Files of Camp Ramah in the Poconos, Philadelphia; and Neil G. Gillman, "Camp Ramah: An Idea Has Come of Age," *United Synagogue Review* (Summer 1957): 10–11.

[7] Goldberg, "Report," 17; and Gillman, "Camp Ramah," 11.

[8] Cohen, "Religious Education in Ramah," 45.

[9] Goldberg, "Report," 5–10.

[10] Michael B. Greenbaum, "The Finkelstein Era," in *Tradition Renewed: A History of The Jewish Theological Seminary,* ed. Jack Wertheimer (New York: The Jewish Theological Seminary, 1997) 1:206–7.

[11] Schwartz, "Ramah," 14.

[12] Schwartz, "Ramah," 15–16; and Michael Brown, "It's Off to Camp We Go: Ramah, LTF, and the Seminary in the Finkelstein Era," *Tradition Renewed* 1:826.

[13] "The Seminary in Expansion Program," *Proceedings of the Rabbinical Assembly: 1941–44,* (June 1944) 8:302–9.

[14] Gary P. Zola, "Jewish Camping and Its Relationship to the Organized Camping Movement in America," in *A Place of Our Own,* 3.

[15] Sarna, "Crucial Decade," 37–39.

[16] Brown, "It's Off to Camp We Go," 832.

[17] Jay B. Stern, "Camp Ramah in the Congregational School," *Synagogue School* 22 (Summer 1964): 17.

[18] Zola, "Jewish Camping," 3; and press release, Camp Ramah in the Berkshires, October 17, 1963, JTS Archives, RG 28–34–18, New York.

[19] Simon Greenberg, "The Ramah Movement: Its History and Place in the Conservative Movement," unpublished manuscript, JTS Archives, RG 28–34–20, ca. 1966–70, New York.

[20] Mitchell Cohen, "Directors' Meetings — Some Follow Up," e-mail message to Ramah directors, September 18, 2006.

[21] Ibid.

[22] Mitchell Cohen, "Update on Hebrew at Ramah Camps," from the files of Mitchell Cohen, March 2006.

[23] David Soloff, "The School," in *The Ramah Experience,* 170–71; and Mitchell Cohen, "Report on the Shapiro Fellowship Seminar," Files of Mitchell Cohen, Fall 2006.

[24] Schwartz, "Ramah," 16; and Burton I. Cohen, "Louis Newman's Wisconsin Innovations and Their Effect upon the Ramah Camping Movement," in *Studies in Jewish Education and Judaica in Honor of Louis Newman,* ed. Alexander M. Shapiro and Burton I. Cohen (New York: Ktav, 1984), 31.

[25] Mitchell Cohen, "National Ramah 2006 Weinstein Institute," e-mail report, February 13, 2006.

[26] Daniel J. Elazar, "The Changing Realities of the North American Jewish Community," in *The Ramah Experience,* 140.

[27] Joshua Cahan, "Reclaiming Piety," Files of Mitchell Cohen, ca. 2007.

[28] Cahan, "Reclaiming Piety."

[29] Sigal Samuel to Mitchell Cohen, personal communication, Files of Mitchell Cohen, August 2007.

ALAN H. SILBERMAN

Ramah as a Transformative Experience: Five Key Principles

HAVING EXPERIENCED fifty-seven years of Ramah—as a camper, a staff member, a member of a camp committee, a camp president, the first former camper to become president of the National Ramah Commission, and—most importantly—as a parent and grandparent of children who have, and are, experiencing Ramah themselves, I begin to think that I have achieved some sense of perspective. (If the strength of my feelings about that perspective is increasing in the same measure as the accuracy of my memories is decreasing, I apologize.)

We speak of Ramah as a transformational experience for those who participate as campers and as staff members. We see proof of that impact in individual decisions about lifestyle, in personal priorities, in the ongoing organized connections that exist between *bogerei Ramah* (stretching in many cases over fifty years), and in participation (if not leadership) in communal institutions. The data are before us. From my own experience and perspective, the power of the data is not in their individual entries, or even in the conclusions that the data support. To me, the power—and the power of Ramah, past, present, and future—comes from understanding the principles that are the foundation of the total of individualized experience.

Any effort to create a list of principles, even core principles, is daunting. I do not claim that my list of five principles is all-inclusive. But these principles do reflect a personal sense that has emerged over my extended experience with Ramah. These principles were at work long before I perceived them. They were

ALAN H. SILBERMAN *is a partner in the Chicago-based law firm Sonnenschein Nath & Rosenthal, LLP, and is the chair emeritus of the firm's national Antitrust, Marketing Practices, Franchising, & Distribution practice. He began attending Camp Ramah in Wisconsin as a camper shortly after the camp was established and continued his involvement as a staff member, as a member of the camp's Board of Directors, and as the president of Ramah Wisconsin. In 1992, he became the first former Ramah camper to serve as the president of the National Ramah Commission. He is currently the president of the World Council of Conservative/Masorti Synagogues and a member of the World Zionist Organization (Expanded) Executive and the Board of Governors of the Jewish Agency.*

not announced in the form of a catechism; just the opposite: the challenge presented to my generation of Ramah campers, and to those coming afterward as well, was to search out and identify the core principles on one's own and with one's peers and then follow through on the conclusions that we reached.

The first principle is the **significance of role models** in shaping the identity of adolescents and young adults: the scholar who hits home runs, the young man or woman at home with Hebrew text and musical theater, the staff member who was committed to Herzl and Martin Luther King, Jr. To be Ramah campers and spend time with these role models left us with a strong sense of obligation (and possibly one that set us apart from our non-Ramah peers): we were obligated to try to develop multiple talents, but we were also required to organize priorities—the first of which was the continuity and vitality of *am yisra'el,* in all of its diverse parts.

In my list of the principles of Ramah, the next is **Jewish knowledge and the recognition that transmission of Jewish knowledge** ***midor ledor*** **(from generation to generation)**, requires a significant degree of depth. In the fifties, Ramah stretched the knowledge of Jewish teenagers in ways we hardly could have dreamed of. We were thirteen, fourteen, or fifteen years old, and we were studying Genesis in conjunction with Babylonian creation epics. We read the words of Jeremiah and spoke of distinctions between the text and the philosophy of Socrates. We learned Jewish history and placed it in the context of Western civilization without reducing the Jewish experience to just another event on the world stage. And we were privileged to learn from teachers who were, or were on their way to becoming, the most highly distinguished educators of our time. Over the past five decades, I have seen my experience replicated over and over again, in young men and women who break new ground in bringing Jewish knowledge to multiple communities. In my view, this process resulted in the acceptance of a corollary principle: a goal of Ramah is to produce men and women who are educated and also see themselves as Jewish educators, regardless of their formal profession or source of income.

I elevate **Hebrew** to the position of the third principle. I recognize that within Ramah, this principle has had an uneven history. But my understanding, based on my own experience, is that Hebrew is, and should be, a value that enables us to transmit Jewish knowledge, a personal connection to Israel, and a sense of the unity of am yisra'el. We have made more efforts to make Hebrew co-equal in the overall camp experience and to make it the language of our official communication. Whereas early Ramah campers and staff saw the Hebrew language as a personal obligation, today, more often it is seen as an interesting option. Hebrew is the language of the Jewish people. As we go forward, we must present it in those terms.

Next in the list of core principles that inform Ramah's mission is the **significance of Jewish practice and Jewish community** in maintaining the Jewish people. It is difficult to put this as fourth; but I believe that acceptance of the first three principles—role models, Jewish knowledge and one's role as an educator, and Hebrew—leads inexorably to this next value. Jewish practice in the American setting is not uniform, but engaging with the issue and trying to make principled, informed choices is and must continue to be a constant value of the Ramah Movement. The Ramah experience has become so much more important as the existence of a true sense of Jewish community (beyond eating knishes and kishke and beyond providing financial support for Israel) became more and more precarious in the last quarter of the twentieth century. The pendulum seems to be swinging the other way today, and it is crucial that Ramah be a prime mover in that process of renewal.

Because I am identifying only five core principles out of many possibilities, it is inappropriate to refer to the fifth one as "last." In many ways, it is the most important: the sense that ***am yisra'el be'eretz yisra'el*** (or *bimdinat yisra'el,* if you wish), **is an existential principle for all Jews**. Perhaps because we were only a few years past the Shoah, and because we were in the period of exhilaration following the establishment of the State of Israel, the position of Israel as an existential issue for Jews was easier for us to grasp in the earlier years of Ramah. Today it is undeniably more complicated. Israel, in the early years of Ramah, was essential to Jewish survival—a place of refuge. Today it is no less essential, not to Jewish survival in the same sense, but to the survival of values that are identifiably Jewish, grounded in our history, our texts, and our sense of mission. That is a principle that must be shaped and reshaped on a regular basis, and just as we found ways to imprint it on the generations of the 1950s and 1960s, we must develop approaches that will impact on the camp populations of today and tomorrow.

In my own experience, all five of these core principles, and all of their subsets, are wrapped together in Ramah through an overarching super principle: the duty of an individual to grapple with the core issues of Jewish life and Jewish responsibility and the duty of every person to make choices based on knowledge and on faith. Study. Think. Choose. Understand what it means to believe in something. Understand that you are not living alone, that you are part of a total community.

Ramah was intended to have impact. It will continue to have impact. And its greatest strength has been that it has continued to create and recreate the means by which that impact can be realized. We take Jewish education, and the Jewish future, very seriously. That is the legacy that we have received from Lou Newman, *z"l,* Seymour Fox, *z"l,* and others that followed them. And we know that success calls for more than mere repetition of old models, even as it calls for retention of core principles. One need only read the outstanding work of Dr. Simcha Leibovich, reviewing the evolution of educational efforts at Ramah Wisconsin,[1] to see that Ramah continues to think long and hard about education and to understand that effective education demands evolution.

I had wonderful experiences at Ramah as a camper, as a staff member, and beyond. My wife Margaret did as well. But we know that our experience of the 1950s and early 1960s was not the experience of our children in the 1980s or of our grandchildren today. We, and Ramah, are products of the Conservative Movement: we struggle with ideas and conflicts, we confront change, and we try to understand how tension can be resolved without undermining principles. If that struggle informs the work of Ramah over the next sixty years, we will have succeeded beyond measure.

Note

[1] Simcha Leibovich, *Camp Ramah in Wisconsin: 60 Years of Educational Excellence,* English version with Carl Schrag (New York: National Ramah Commission, 2008).

SKIP VICHNESS

A Period of Growth and Increased Collaboration among the Camps and with JTS

REFLECTIONS ON BEING THE NATIONAL RAMAH PRESIDENT

OVER THE YEARS, when thinking about Ramah, I find myself using a biblical-sounding phrase. To me, "Ramah is a jealous god." My experience is that when Maḥaneh Ramah reaches out and grabs hold of people, it does so in a way that is all consuming. Once you become a "Ramahnik" you are always a Ramahnik—even if your experience at camp happened twenty, thirty, forty, or more years ago.

For me, that process began on a Sunday in December of 1977 as I found myself driving from Princeton, New Jersey to the upper west side of Manhattan. I was going to an interview at The Jewish Theological Seminary (JTS) for a position as the business manager of Camp Ramah in the Berkshires.

As I recall, the decision to go to the interview was more of a lark than a serious exploration. After all, I was already happily employed in camping at a terrific private camp (Pine Forest) by two wonderful families (the Blacks and the Halperns, who have remained dear friends and mentors throughout my career). To top it all off, I had never heard of JTS or Camp Ramah!

However, at that interview I met three amazing couples, whose commitment, passion, and concern would help to change my life. The Davidsons (Pat and Al), Schlesingers (Lisa and Jim), and Siegels (Pauline and Noel) questioned me extensively that morning as to my background, while at the same time communicating how much Ramah Berkshires could use me and the good I could do. As I was going on and on about my camping background,

SKIP VICHNESS, *Ph.D., is the managing partner of GreyPine, LLC, and the chair of the board of directors of the Foundation for Jewish Camp. He is a past president of the National Ramah Commission, a past president of the New York Section of the American Camp Association, and a past president of the Solomon Schechter Day School of Essex and Union. He has also served as business manager and associate director of Camp Ramah in the Berkshires.*

particularly the ten great summers I spent at Camp Greylock for Boys, little did I know that both the Schlesingers and Siegels had family members who knew me from those days.

Any doubts I had about taking the position at Ramah Berkshires were overcome by two events in the following days. Within a week of the first interview, I was invited to White Plains, New York, to meet with the chair of the Berkshires board, Dr. Saul Shapiro, and his wife, Miriam Klein Shapiro, *z"l*, *rosh ḥinnuch* at camp. This interview took place mostly in Miriam's kitchen and around the dinner table with their five terrific children and assorted friends.

As the evening went on, my hesitations about becoming part of this environment began to melt away. The Shapiro family gave me a vision of what Jewish institutional camping could provide a family that a private camp could not. Even though I was still single at the time, I could feel a resonance for the kind of home I hoped to create for myself someday.

Saul had been chair of the Berkshires board for quite a while and would remain so during my entire tenure at the camp. There is no doubt that without his energy, commitment, and skill, this Ramah camp would not have survived the turbulent '70s. For me, Saul was the great teacher. He provided the *dugmah* of what a great lay leader should be in his relationship with a professional. He was generous of spirit and time. He was both a protector and an instructor. There was an amazing sense of partnership that he created that made professional/lay relations a joy. Over the years that I have chaired a number of not-for-profit organizations, I have tried to follow his example in the best way I could.

And what about Miriam? She was passionate, giving, smart, and determined. She was the perfect professional who never acted as the boss's wife. She learned that to deal with me, she first had to share news of the day and family, and I learned from her what it meant to combine being the most passionate, knowledgeable, and caring person in the room. She helped to teach me what Ramah was about, while also taking the time to learn what I was about and what I was trying to accomplish. I often think back to those first years when I was trying to make significant changes in the Ramah summer culture—without Miriam's guidance, I might not have survived those early years at Ramah.

A few days after dinner at the Shapiro home, I received a phone call from Joe Kruger, *z"l*, who was a member of the Berkshires board. As the founder and director for over fifty-four years of Camp MahKeeNac, Joe was one of the great legends of private camping. Joe was a great camp director and an even greater mensch. Over a delicious breakfast at his home, he explained to me how important it was that people with a private camp background involve themselves in the not-for-profit camp world. By the time I left his home that morning I had agreed to take the job—it was impossible to say no to Joe. One of the best by-products of my Ramah experience was the chance to become friendly with Joe and Frances Kruger, *z"l*—a friendship that taught me a tremendous amount about both camping and my responsibility to the Jewish community. This wonderful opportunity to know and learn from Joe lasted until he passed away at the age of 92—still vital and insightful up to a few days before he left us.

So on February 1, 1978, I showed up to work at Camp Ramah in the Berkshires. There was a bookkeeper (Selma Leibowitz, *z"l*), a recruiter (Gershon Schwartz, *z"l*), and a maintenance director (Stanley Michelson). There was no director. National Ramah Director Burt Cohen was hiring the staff, and there were fewer than 100 children enrolled in camp. From February to the opening of camp in June was an amazing time for me. I made friends that would last a lifetime—Dr. Joel Roth, Phyllis Hofman Waldmann, and Steve Goldstein, to name just a few.

I traveled day and night throughout the New York metropolitan area to recruit campers. We opened camp in 1978 with more than 400 children. Just before camp opened, Rabbi Moshe Samber of Plainfield, New Jersey, came on board as the part-time director. In 1979 we opened with a full camp! Moshe and I had two terrific summers together.

That first summer, I reconnected with my Jewish roots and found the Ramah experience to be so much more than what camp had been in the past for me. To make sure I had someone to talk to that summer, I brought with me a boyhood friend, David Ellenson, who had become a Reform rabbi. David had a great summer and then went on to establish himself as one of the great scholars of the American Jewish community. He is currently the president of Hebrew Union College.

However, the most important event of that summer was meeting a young teacher named Ilana Arnold. Ilana, an Israeli by birth, came to camp as a teacher. It was a magical summer for us as we developed a relationship that quickly blossomed. We were married the following April in a celebration that included many of our Ramah friends. Ilana would become an important part of the Berkshires community as she worked as a teacher and then as the *mashgiḥah*, as well as being the hostess to many wonderful evenings at our camp home on Lake Ellis.

In 1980 Rabbi Jerome Abrams came to camp as the director. He was Ramah's most experienced camp leader, having previously served as the director of Ramah Wisconsin and Ramah Berkshires. Jerry had an excellent understanding of how to run a camp and what made Ramah special. Not only did he do a tremendous job of taking control of the camp and, almost instantly, making it a better place, he took the time to make me understand what it really meant to be a Ramahnik. He and his wife Leah became close friends and colleagues.

Jerry gave me the freedom to do my job while also encouraging me to grow and take on more responsibility. It was one of the best team experiences I have ever had. It taught me how a senior mentor could make the people around him feel empowered and significant. It is a lesson that I have tried to implement since leaving Ramah and one for which I owe Jerry a tremendous debt.

I spent six wonderful years at Camp Ramah in the Berkshires. Enrollment was excellent, finances were under control, and with a supportive board, we began to renovate and build up the facility. The best thing that happened was the birth of our son during the summer of 1982. Shai was born in New Milford Hospital on the Friday morning of visitors weekend. We brought him home to camp that Saturday evening at age thirty-six hours. I believe he is the youngest Ramahnik ever.

Another highlight of my time at Ramah was the chance to consult for the National Ramah Commission. Under National Director Burt Cohen, I spent two years visiting other Ramah camps and working with the lay and professional leadership of those camps to improve their business and physical plants. As I visited all the Ramah camps in North America, I began to understand the tremendous impact that Ramah was having on the greater Jewish community.

During these travels, I met an remarkable group of lay and professional leaders with whom I developed special relationships. From Sid Zweig, *z"l,* in Canada to Rabbi David Soloff in Wisconsin to a host of others, it became apparent to me that the appeal of Ramah and its impact was not unique to any one geographical area or individual camp. Working with Burt to understand the issues and personalities that existed in each camp gave me a much more nuanced way of looking at institutions.

These were fantastic years for us—the camp community, our home community of Summit, New Jersey, the warmth of Rabbi Bill and Dina Horn, and the greater JTS community, as well as a growing group of family and friends, made for years that seemed to fly by. However, for us, it became apparent that there would be a "right" time to move on from Ramah.

In 1981, I had been asked to join the board of the New York section of the American Camping Association (ACA). Two years later I became a member of the executive board, serving as the section's secretary. Attending ACA meetings opened a whole new world of relationships to me as I became friendly with some of the great camp directors of the generation. Among them was a fabulous Long Island day camp owner named Ben Appelbaum, *z"l*.

The relationship that Ilana and I had with Ben and his wife, Barbara, *z"l*, quickly grew into what would become a life-long friendship that changed our lives. In early 1983, we began talking about the possibility of the Appelbaums and Vichnesses going into business together. We would do the work, Ben and Barbara would put up the money, and we would buy a day camp together. All we had to do was find a camp that we could buy—not an easy task!

However, at the conclusion of the 1983 season, we were able to purchase Harbor Hills Day Camp in Randolph, New Jersey. So the time had come and at the end of the 1983 season, we made the announcement that we were leaving Ramah. It had been a magical six years. I left with so much more than I had come with—a wife, two children, friendships that have lasted a lifetime, and a commitment to the values of the Conservative Movement. In return for all we had received, hopefully we left Ramah Berkshires and the Ramah Camping Movement better off than we had found it.

For the next ten years we set upon the task of building our business. Harbor Hills grew quickly into one of the largest day camps in New Jersey, and with Ben we were able to purchase a number of other day camps in the New York Metropolitan area. I was able to find time to serve as president of the New York section of the American Camping Association and as president of the Solomon Schechter Day School of Essex and Union. These were wonderful lay positions and, combined with family demands and our growing business, kept us well occupied. Although many of our friends from Ramah days remained, I gave little thought or interest to Ramah. It was clear to me that it was a time that had passed in our lives.

All of this changed in 1992, when Saul Shapiro called me and asked if we could get together for lunch. Saul was entering into a second term as president of the National Ramah Commission (NRC) and in a few, well-chosen words made it clear to me that he wanted me to join the board to help him complete his vision of leadership for the movement. In thinking about this opportunity, it became clear that given all that our family owed to Saul and to the Ramah Camping Movement, this was something that I not only should take on but also that I wanted to do. And so began my second career at Ramah as a lay leader.

In the early 90s the NRC was an institution in transition. Under Saul's leadership and with a new, younger generation of camp presidents and other board members, such as Alan Silberman, Paul Schultz, Roger Fine, and others, there was a feeling that the Ramah Camping Movement increasingly must become an organization that spoke with one united voice rather than what for many years had been a collection of individual institutions, albeit under the unifying educational and religious leadership of JTS.

The steps to make Ramah more of a cohesive movement were ignited by the appointment of Rabbi Sheldon Dorph as National Ramah Director and the encouragement and active interest of Chancellor Ismar Schorsch. Throughout his tenure, the Chancellor remained an amazingly active, eloquent, and supportive leader for Ramah. Many of the positive changes that happened to Ramah for the following fifteen years can be attributed to his wisdom.

In 1994, a smooth transition of leadership of the movement took place as Alan Silberman became the president of the NRC. Alan, a lifelong Ramahnik and a past president of Ramah Wisconsin, proved to be a wise and skilled leader to whom the movement owes an enormous debt. For me, his wise counsel and friendship are among my most valued benefits of my time in service to Ramah.

Along with Alan, Shelly, and Chancellor Schorsch, one other major individual was vital to the changes that began to occur within the Ramah Camping Movement: Rabbi Michael Greenbaum, the vice chancellor of JTS. In his role, he provides wisdom and support and serves as the active JTS representative to Ramah. One of the great benefits of being a National Ramah leader was the opportunity to develop a close working relationship with Michael. During all my years at the NRC, he was my teacher and wise counsel.

In 1994, this wonderful combination of leadership and events, combined with the vision of Eric Singer, a young man from Atlanta, brought Ramah to its first opportunity for growth in over thirty years. The dream of a camp in the southern United States had been a long-standing one. Now it would finally become a reality. Although it was not an easy task, the NRC was able to confront the issues of growth and change in a way that set the tone for expansion within the movement that would last for the next decade. I am very proud to have had some small part in making this dream a reality and helping to create what has become a major institution in the North American Jewish community.

As Ramah entered the late 1990s, a major change took place in the professional leadership of the Ramah movement. Rabbi Stanley Bramnick had come to the NRC in the 1960s to serve as National Business Manager and to expand, under the leadership of his friend Rabbi Al Thaler, the Ramah Day Camp in Nyack, New York. Although the day camp was a major success, Rabbi Bramnick's primary commitment to the Ramah Camping Movement was to put the NRC on a sound financial footing. Additionally, he was a steady voice urging the other camps to place themselves on a firm financial footing.

Although his was not always a popular message, his commitment to fiscal stability on a national and local level has proven to be a major factor in Ramah's renewed growth and development over the past decade.

With Rabbi Bramnick's upcoming retirement in 1998, the decision was made to bring in an individual with wide-ranging business experience to lead the business affairs of National Ramah. With Shelly Dorph leading the search, we were able to locate a young lawyer who was looking to make a change from being a litigator to a more satisfying environment in which to work and raise a family. Jeff Goodman was a terrific addition to the Ramah scene. In his decade as National Business Manager, Jeff has become a major factor in both the smooth operation of the national office, its Israel programs, and an important resource for all of the camps.

In the spring of 1998, I was asked to take on the chairmanship of the National Ramah Commission. Following Saul Shapiro and Alan Silberman was a daunting assignment. In addition to obtaining the support of my family and partners, there were a number of factors within the Ramah movement itself that led me to take on this opportunity for leadership:

• The NRC had an outstanding professional leader who wanted to take an activist role in improving and expanding the camps. National Director Rabbi Shelly Dorph, had come to the position with a vision of making the entity more of a movement rather than just a group of individual camps. It was a vision that we shared.

• In addition to Shelly, the NRC had a group of outstanding professionals who insured that each program and effort undertaken by the national office would be of the highest quality. Jeff Goodman was quickly making his mark on our business operations. Amy Skopp Cooper had taken over Ramah Day Camp in Nyack and had made a great program even greater. And finally, the Ramah Israel programs were led in an expansive and effective way by Dr. David Breakstone.

• The JTS leadership, Chancellor Ismar Schorsch and Vice Chancellor Michael Greenbaum, were committed to the success of Ramah and to using JTS resources to insure its continued vibrancy. These two men offered a superb lay-professional opportunity that included regular meetings, constant support, and profound insight. They are two leaders of vision and integrity who kept their commitment to me and helped make the Ramah chairmanship a source of constant delight. Ramah has no better friends and supporters.

• A team of lay leaders agreed to take leadership positions with me. Alan Silberman agreed to serve as senior vice president—he was to be an active partner throughout my tenure as president. He was always willing to take on the difficult and sensitive tasks. Without Alan, my job would have been much more difficult. Another lifelong Ramahnik, Gerry Kobell, a resident of Pittsburgh and a lay leader from Ramah New England, agreed to serve as vice president for finance and operations. In Gerry's key position within the national structure, his knowledge of camp and strong sense of integrity combined to make him an important member of the team. Paul Schultz, from California, and Saul Andron, from Berkshires, agreed to serve as vice presidents for Israel. As I describe later, these two gentlemen would deal with some of the most difficult issues in the history of Ramah and they would accomplish this with sensitivity, ability, and dedication. Along with Michael Greenbaum, who served as NRC secretary, they rounded out our slate of officers.

• One other member of the NRC took on a key role. Ed Zinbarg is one of the great leaders of the Conservative Movement, with a fierce commitment to JTS and Ramah. His generosity created the Shapiro Fellowship Program, which has had a major impact by enabling JTS Rabbinical School students to work at Ramah during the summer. To my good fortune, he agreed to serve as chair of the NRC Insurance Committee. Under Ed's leadership, and with guidance from Jeff Goodman, the movement made significant changes in its insurance program that have resulted in large savings for our camps. Ramah continues to benefit greatly from its relationship with Henry Skier, who, together with his children, provides outstanding insurance coverage, as well as support and advice.

• Finally, I was fortunate to have a dedicated group of camp presidents who came to the NRC with a strong commitment to making their camps better and a willingness to work together to make Ramah more effective and better able to serve the Conservative Movement. These men and women gave an amazing amount of time to both their local camps and to the NRC. Serving as president of a Ramah camp has to be both one of the most challenging and rewarding of all lay leadership positions within the Jewish community.

All of these factors—a talented and activist professional leadership, a wonderful slate of lay colleagues, and the support of JTS and camps that for the most part, had stable and quality professional leadership, made the prospect of leading the NRC a most exciting one.

I came to the position with an agenda to achieve four goals during my term. Now, almost ten years later, it gives me a great deal of pleasure to reflect that most of them were accomplished.

1. Historically, the NRC had operated as a loose confederation of camps and a place where the needs and concerns of individual camps had been represented and protected. Often, these legitimate concerns prevented the "movement" from acting like a movement and making strategic decisions that were best for the entire Conservative Movement. Under the skillful leadership

of Saul Shapiro and Alan Silberman this began to change dramatically. The founding of Ramah Darom was a definite watershed in this change. During my tenure, we worked hard to form the NRC into a board of directors that dealt with movement-wide issues. Energized committees, active professional communication beyond the director level, and a regular bringing together of the camp presidents took us a long way down this road. Over time, Ramah has become a movement that is capable of thinking strategically about its future as a vital part of the North American Jewish community. The NRC can take a great deal of credit for this.

2. There is no better vehicle for creating large numbers of committed Conservative Jews than Ramah. When I became president, the camps were basically full. At the urging of Chancellor Schorsch, we made a commitment to encourage the camps to expand their facilities and capacities to the maximum possible. Many of the camps responded to this strategic initiative by increasing their capacity by ten percent. This, combined with the steady growth of Ramah Darom, meant that from 1997 to 2003 the enrollment of the camps grew significantly.

3. For years, the NRC had operated a day camp in Nyack, New York. Rabbi Al Thaler had created a magnificent program. Upon his retirement, the camp came under the directorship of Amy Skopp Cooper. Amy is a great asset to our movement. Having observed the Ramah Day Camp in Nyack, its impact on campers, and the number of campers that went on to Ramah overnight camping, Shelly Dorph and I became convinced that creating Ramah day camps in other locations would be a positive way of furthering Ramah's mission. Starting in 1998, Ramah day camps were opened in Chicago, Philadelphia, East Brunswick, New Jersey, and the San Francisco Bay area. As with any new project, there were growing pains, but over time the camps in Chicago and Philadelphia have succeeded and evolved into successful entry points into Ramah and the Conservative Movement for young families.

4. Over its sixty years, Ramah has developed a reputation for outstanding Judaic programming. Data shows that Ramah camps do an exceptional job of creating identity, observance, and lifelong commitment. However, as with any institution, there is always room for improvement. In the '80s and '90s, many significant changes occurred in the world of camping. Although Ramah remained on the cutting edge of Judaic programming, a number of us felt that its "camping" programs needed to be refreshed. To accomplish this, with Shelly's leadership and the support of camp presidents and directors, we made a commitment to bringing Ramah lay and professional leadership together to engage with leading practitioners from the greater world of camping. I am proud that many of my partners and friends in the private camping world have

been active and willing participants in this effort. These interchanges, both formal and informal, have led to upgraded facilities, increased programming options—particularly in the adventure area—and more dynamic and choice-oriented options for campers. Today, it is normative for all Ramah directors to learn and share from other camps in their efforts to make Ramah the very best possible camping experience for our campers.

As in every leadership experience, not everything goes as planned, and not every eventuality can be anticipated. However, our major accomplishment, watching the NRC evolve into a cohesive and efficient group, bore direct results in dealing with two difficult issues.

In the spring of 2000, the director of Ramah Programs in Israel, Dr. David Breakstone, resigned his position effective September 1, 2000. David had done a wonderful job of growing our Israel programs, and we were sorry to see him go, but he was leaving to become the head of the Department for Zionist Activity of the World Zionist Organization. We chose Dr. Joe Freedman as the new director. Joe has done an excellent job and has brought energy and vision to the position, bringing our Israel programs to an ever-higher level.

Unfortunately, within days of Joe's beginning the position, the second intifada broke out. Instead of growth, security became the primary issue. Although over 200 Ramahniks attended our Ramah Seminar in Israel in 2001, our "short-term" programs began to suffer.

By the winter of 2002, the security situation in Israel had deteriorated significantly. All of the groups that had planned to go to Israel with Ramah during the winter cancelled, and enrollment in our summer Seminar was at an all-time low. Fortunately, over the years, Ramah Programs in Israel had built up a significant cash surplus and was able to keep its doors open. However, Joe Freedman was forced to let go a number of our staff. Those were painful days as the news from Israel led to a continuous downward spiral of enrollment in Ramah's Israel programs.

As a contingency, the NRC instructed our staff to consider plans for a Seminar summer that would not include Israel! Having this discussion was painful, but it was prudent to have contingencies available. Travel to Europe and South America was discussed, as was an American Seminar to be held at the new American Hebrew Academy in Greensboro, North Carolina.

At the spring meeting of the NRC, Seminar enrollment was at its lowest point in years. At the time, the NRC was still committed to a Seminar in Israel, but a vote was taken to hold a special meeting by phone in May to make a final decision. Enrollment continued to deteriorate, as withdrawals occurred on a regular basis.

As the weeks went by, the news became worse, and the pressure on us to cancel Seminar increased. A number of national organizations, including the Union for Reform Judaism, decided to cancel their trips for the summer of 2002. The *New York Times* carried a daily litany of bad news about events in Israel, the large decrease in tourism, and the cancellation of educational missions and junior-year-in-college programs abroad.

Finally, one evening in mid-May at 8:30 p.m., a conference call was held with all the members of the NRC, our professional staff in New York, and Joe Freedman in Israel. From San Diego, Chicago, Toronto, New York, Jerusalem, and a number of other cities, people weighed in with their opinions and best judgments. It was a thoughtful discussion as lay and professional leaders alike weighed their responsibilities to our children and their families, balanced by their commitment to Israel.

By around 11 p.m. it was time to vote—as one board member observed, it was bed time on the east coast, the sun was setting on the west coast, and the sun was rising in Jerusalem. In a historic vote, the NRC decided the following:

• The NRC was committed to sending the Seminar to Israel for the summer of 2002, even if only twenty campers were willing to participate. Ultimately, there were seventy-two participants.

• We would cancel only if the Israeli authorities told us they were not allowing groups to come.

• We would inform each family that if they chose not to send their children to Israel, we would understand, and we would offer an alternative program for them. Not a single parent with a child enrolled chose to take this option for his or her child. The parents told us that if Ramah told them their children would be safe, then they were sure they would be.

The final vote was taken by roll call. In the end, the vote was unanimous. If parents did not want to send their children to Israel that summer we understood and would be supportive of their decision. However, as a movement, we were committed to standing tall and publicly demonstrating our commitment to Eretz Yisra'el and our faith in the Israeli government and our professional staff to keep our children safe.

I believe this was one of the proudest moments in the history of Ramah. For me, it was far and away my greatest and most satisfying experience as a lay leader. And the children who went on Seminar 2002 had an inspiring experience and a memory that will last for the rest of their lives.

In the fall of 1999, I was asked to come to a meeting with Shelly Dorph, Jeff Goodman, and long-time Ramah operations consultant Phyllis Hofman Waldmann to discuss Camp Ramah in New England. For several years the camp had not had stable leadership and was experiencing a steady decline in enrollment. From a financial point of view, there were serious issues as to the camp's fiscal integrity.

The camp did have a strong core of new, energized lay leadership led by the incoming president, Jerry Silverman. Shelly and I agreed that a cohesive and strategic approach was vital to the long-term success of the camp. It would have been disastrous for the Ramah Camping Movement to close this camp or to allow the camp to meander along with the problems it had been laboring under for a number of years.

At this meeting, our professional leadership made a generous and positive suggestion. With the consent of the NRC and the cooperation of the board of Ramah New England, the National Ramah office would take over the day–to-day operation of the camp for the 2000 season. This would give the New England leadership the opportunity to take a deep breath and put quality professional leadership in place for the 2001 season and beyond.

Both boards quickly endorsed this suggestion. Shelly took over the role as director of Camp Ramah in New England, and Jeff Goodman took control of their office and business operations. They served in these roles, while at the same time keeping the national agenda moving forward. It was an outstanding performance. Not only did the camp increase enrollment, but it broke even financially! Using the "time out," the board was able to hire Billy Mencow as the director, who remained for a number of years, and Joel Stavsky, an outstanding business manager who came on board in May and is still a key figure in the current success of Ramah New England.

With the support and vision of the National Ramah Commission, Shelly was given the time and support to model what a Ramah camp should be and the values that a Ramah director should hold as important. It was a most impressive performance. And although some aspects of the National Ramah agenda may have suffered during 2000–2001, there is no doubt that the ability of the NRC to respond to the problems of one of the camps in a positive way made an enormous contribution to Ramah New England and to the entire Ramah movement.

The five years I served as NRC President seemed to fly along—we accomplished a lot, and we actually had fun doing it. There was a wonderful feeling of camaraderie and shared purpose that even made handling the difficult issues a positive experience.

In the spring of 2003, Shelly announced that he would be leaving the position of National Ramah Director after completing a fall sabbatical. Shelly had done an excellent job. His activist approach to the position had changed the nature and relationship of the National Director to the local camps and their directors. His vision had energized the movement and helped ignite a growth spurt that had not occurred at Ramah for over thirty-five years.

With Shelly's announcement, the Chancellor and I quickly agreed on a choice for a new director, who was ratified by the NRC at its spring meeting. Rabbi Mitchell Cohen, a lawyer turned rabbi, turned camp director, had been the outstanding leader of Camp Ramah in Canada for eleven years. Feeling that he had fulfilled his vision there, he had moved on to be the founding principal of the Solomon Schechter High School of Westchester County, New York. However, his heart was always with Ramah, and we were able to recruit Mitch to come back to his first love—camping. After all, as I said at the beginning of this article—"Ramah is a jealous god," and no one ever leaves.

At the same time that Mitch was appointed, the NRC nominating committee proposed a slate of new officers, who would take office in the fall of 2003. Mort Steinberg, outgoing president of Ramah Wisconsin, was elected to follow me as NRC President. Mort is an outstanding leader who has been at the heart of the success of Ramah Wisconsin as camper, staff member, board member, and president for almost fifty years. He came to the position with a clear vision of Ramah and his own agenda for his term of office. I was honored to be succeeded by him.

Thus, as I left my "job" in the fall of 2003, the NRC had a wonderful face for the future—young and dynamic professional leadership in Mitch Cohen, Jeff Goodman, and Amy Skopp Cooper; a committed and visionary group of camp presidents; and a talented national lay leadership. This team heralded nothing but better days ahead for the entire Ramah community.

For me, I know that all good things must come to an end, but what a fabulous five years I had as the "leader" of Ramah!

MITCHELL COHEN

The Impact of Camp Ramah on the Attitudes and Practices of Conservative Jewish College Students

Adapted from the foreword to Research Findings on the Impact of Camp Ramah: A Companion Study to the 2004 "Eight Up" Report, *a report for the National Ramah Commission, Inc. of The Jewish Theological Seminary, by Ariela Keysar and Barry A. Kosmin, 2004.*

THE NETWORK OF RAMAH CAMPS throughout North America (now serving over 6,500 campers and over 1,800 university-aged staff members) has been described as the "crown jewel" of the Conservative Movement, the most effective setting for inspiring Jewish identity and commitment to Jewish communal life and Israel. Ismar Schorsch, chancellor emeritus of The Jewish Theological Seminary, wrote: "I am firmly convinced that in terms of social import, in terms of lives affected, Ramah is the most important venture ever undertaken by the Seminary" ("An Emerging Vision of Ramah," in *The Ramah Experience,* 1989).

Research studies written by Sheldon Dorph in 1976 ("A Model for Jewish Education in America"), Seymour Fox and William Novak in 1997 ("Vision at the Heart: Lessons from Camp Ramah on the Power of Ideas in Shaping Educational Institutions"), and Steven M. Cohen in 1998 ("Camp Ramah and Adult Jewish Identity: Long Term Influences"), and others all credit Ramah as having an incredibly powerful, positive impact on the development of Jewish identity.

Recent Research on the Influence of Ramah on Campers and Staff

I am pleased to summarize the findings of recent research on the impact of Ramah camping on the Jewish practices and attitudes of Conservative Jewish youth. Every now and then a research project is undertaken that attempts to

RABBI MITCHELL COHEN *is the director of the National Ramah Commission. After working in law as a corporate litigator for five years, he served as director of Camp Ramah in Canada for eleven years and as founding principal of the Solomon Schechter High School of Westchester for three years. He also worked at Camp Ramah in California from 1979 to 1988.*

quantify the influence of Jewish summer camping. While those of us deeply involved in camping instinctively know that these experiences are among the most powerful for developing Jewish identity, as well as for building self-esteem and moral character, quantitative analyses can add important perspective and provide a context from which to draw significant conclusions and develop policy implications for the future.

In a general study of the Conservative Movement published in 2004, Ariela Keysar and Barry Kosmin reported on their research of the attitudes and practices of college students who grew up in the Conservative Movement (*"Eight Up"—The College Years: The Jewish Engagement of Young Adults Raised in Conservative Synagogues, 1995–2003,* A Project of The Jewish Theological Seminary's Ratner Center for the Study of Conservative Judaism, Dr. Jack Wertheimer, Director). This project was funded by the Avi Chai Foundation, and the report is available online at http://www.jtsa.edu/Documents/pagedocs/fourup/eight_up.pdf.

Keysar and Kosmin first interviewed over 1,400 students who had recently become bar/bat mitzvah from a cross-section of Conservative synagogues in the mid-1990s. In 1999, they followed up and interviewed these same young people, who were then in high school. The researchers published their findings in *"Four Up"—The High School Years, 1995–1999.* In the 2004 *"Eight Up"* study, Keysar and Kosmin report on their findings for this same group of young people, most of whom by then were twenty-one-years old and university seniors.

Keysar and Kosmin were able to contact one thousand of the students they had surveyed both eight and four years earlier. Their research is therefore quite unique as a longitudinal study, one that finds trends in attitudes and changes in patterns of behavior over time, based upon the influence of various factors, such as high schools attended, Israel experiences, and youth group and camp experiences.

Companion Report Looking at the Impact of Camp Ramah

In their companion report to the 2004 *"Eight Up"* study, Keysar and Kosmin break down the raw data based upon Jewish camping experiences. Their analysis of this data, particularly the information about the impact of working as a staff member at a Ramah camp, is overwhelmingly positive. Keysar and Kosmin's complete companion report is available online at http://campramah.org/news/keysar_kosmin_2004_research_findings.pdf.

As shown in the companion report to the *"Four Up"* study, students who attended Ramah as campers were more observant of Jewish ritual, more positive about Jewish and Zionist identity, more inclined to date and marry

Jews, and more active in Jewish life on campus. When the research was further refined in 2004 to test the practices and attitudes of Ramah campers who went on to work as staff members at Ramah (or in some cases, other Jewish camps), the results were even more impressive. The following are highlights of the companion report to the 2004 *"Eight Up"* study.

- **Synagogue Attendance.** Two-fifths (40%) of Ramah-trained counselors attend synagogue at least once a week, compared to just 11% of the *"Eight Up"* cohort overall and only 5% of those with no Jewish camping experience.
- **Jewish Marriage.** Over three-quarters (78%) of Ramah-trained counselors state that it is "very important" to them to marry a Jew, in contrast to just 52% of respondents overall and 39% of those with no Jewish camping experience.
- **Kashrut.** Only 17% of students with no Jewish camping experience and 29% of students overall state that they observe Kashrut outside the home. The figure jumps to 71% for Ramah-trained counselors.
- **Jewish Education as a Career.** Over one-third (40%) of Ramah-trained counselors state that they can see themselves becoming Jewish educators, nearly twice as many as the 22% of the overall *"Eight Up"* cohort and four times as many as the 10% of students with no Jewish camping experience.
- **Jewish Studies Courses.** While in college, Ramah-trained counselors are twice as likely as students with no Jewish camping experience to take a Jewish studies course, 63% compared to 31%.
- **Israel Advocacy on Campus.** Ramah-trained counselors are almost three times as likely to be engaged in Israel advocacy on campus (42%) as college students with no Jewish camping experience (15%).
- **Observing Shabbat.** Over a third of those with no Jewish camping experience (35%) say that they never do anything special on Friday night or Saturday to celebrate Shabbat. In contrast, *none* of the Ramah-trained counselors made this statement, and over a third of them (38%) *always* do something special to observe Shabbat, such as attend synagogue or a Friday night dinner. Further, a total of 60% of Ramah-trained counselors usually or always do something to celebrate Shabbat, compared to only 32% of other camps' counselors.
- **Dating Practices.** Overall, only 18% of the *"Eight Up"* cohort states that they date only Jews, compared to almost half (47%) of Ramah-trained counselors. Ramah-trained counselors are almost five times as likely as students with no Jewish camping experience to say that they date only Jews (47% compared to 10%).

A Living Environment

The Ramah summer camp setting, in which campers and staff members live and eat together, study and pray together, play ball and learn theater arts together, and water ski and go mountain climbing together, influences young people in numerous ways on many levels. Ramah focuses on the development of each young person's self esteem, to the extent that every member of a Ramah camp is valued for who he or she is. Ramah camps, through their integrated systems of formal and informal Jewish educational experiences, inspire young people to become more committed to Judaism as a culture, a religion, and a way of life. Ramah camps, through their hiring of Israeli staff members, Zionist programming, and their networks of programs for North Americans to spend time in Israel, encourage a deep connection between each Ramah participant and the State of Israel.

The Crucial "University Years"

Perhaps most significantly, Ramah camps retain over 75% of their camper populations as members of the staff. When young Jewish adults ages seventeen to twenty-two spend their summers at our camps, they graduate from their university years with a greater love for Jewish life, a stronger connection to Israel, and more powerful leadership skills that can help with all of life's challenges.

"The Power of Ramah"

Keysar and Kosmin make it clear that it is difficult to know whether the Ramah figures cited previously are so high because more committed Jewish families send their children to Ramah, or whether the impact of the Ramah experience itself is the major factor. Their anecdotal evidence, however, indicates that many young people did report that their camping experience had a major impact upon their positive Jewish development. When asked, "What do you think is the most important thing that helped shape your Jewish identity?" a number of respondents chose Jewish camping. In the words of one student:

> Camp Ramah helped me shape my Jewish identity more. Being involved in a two-month Judaism experience immersed with Judaism really placed me in a constantly Jewish environment. It taught me to enjoy the best parts of Judaism and see how special it is to have a spiritual aspect to life.

Another respondent said

> [M]y Jewish summer camp experience probably had the greatest influence on me than any other single experience. Camp Ramah simply incorporates *all* aspects of Judaism: social values, religious values, spirituality, charity,

> education. . . . Thus, one becomes part of a very complete setting of Judaism, and in this way, one can find what unifies Judaism in all these categories.

In the words of Keysar and Kosmin:

> We have demonstrated with an array of statistics, tables and charts that Jewish summer camping is an important experience in the lives of many young people and that it is associated with an increase in Jewish involvement during the college years. *College students who participated in Jewish summer camps, either as campers or as counselors at Camp Ramah or any other Jewish summer camps, are by far more engaged Jewishly than those who never attended a Jewish summer camp* [emphasis added]. These findings with regard to the Jewish college students . . . ages 18–26 replicate those in the study of Jewish summer camps by Sales and Saxe (2004).
>
> However, we go one step further. We have identified the *crème de la crème* among camp counselors. All the data presented here point to one remarkable group of young Jewish men and women, namely, those who attended Camp Ramah and later became counselors, either at Ramah or another Jewish summer camp. These Ramah-trained counselors lead the way and are far ahead of others in various markers of strong Jewish identity, intense Jewish practice and commitment to Judaism. Ramah-trained counselors are undoubtedly the elite of the elite.

From this body of research, we once again have an affirmation that among the many positive experiences that our young people might have, Ramah camping is among the most effective means of ensuring a high level of commitment to Jewish life and positive Jewish and Zionist identity.

ARIELA KEYSAR, *Ph.D., a demographer, is an associate research professor in public policy and law and the associate director of the Institute for the Study of Secularism in Society and Culture at Trinity College in Hartford, Connecticut. She is a principal investigator of the American Religious Identification Survey 2008. Dr. Keysar was the study director of the American Jewish Identity Survey 2001 and the associate director of the landmark Longitudinal Study of American and Canadian Conservative Youth 1995–2003.*

BARRY A. KOSMIN, *Ph.D., a sociologist, is research professor in public policy and law and the director of the Institute for the Study of Secularism in Society and Culture at Trinity College in Hartford, Connecticut. He has directed many large national social surveys and opinion polls in the United States, Europe, and Africa including the Council of Jewish Federations (CJF) 1990 National Jewish Population Survey and the American Religious Identification Survey series 1990–2008. He is the author of more than twenty books and research monographs and more than fifty scholarly articles in the fields of sociology, politics, philanthropy, and policy research.*

JEFFREY S. KRESS

Campus and Camp: A Study of College-Age Ramah Staff

CAMP RAMAH WAS DESCRIBED by the former chancellor of The Jewish Theological Seminary (JTS), Dr. Ismar Schorsch, as "in terms of the number of lives affected . . . the most important venture ever undertaken by the Seminary" (Schorsch 1989, 185). By and large, the "lives affected" have tended to be thought of as those of the campers who attend Ramah programs. For example, whereas many of the discussions in the volume *The Ramah Experience: Community and Commitment* use the general term "youth" to describe the population served, in the preface, the noted educator Ralph Tyler states that Ramah "is a setting in which campers are responsible for planning and developing their activities in light of their group deliberations on purposes and consequences, guided but not directed by adult personnel" (1989, vii). Although the extent to which campers engage in this deliberative planning process is debatable, few today would refer to the personnel with the most direct camper contact as "adults."

In fact, recent trends in developmental theory emphasize the age range of the staff members with the most direct camper contact as a period of "emerging adulthood" (Arnett 2004). Arnett, a leading theorist and researcher in this area, describes the span from roughly the age of eighteen through the mid-twenties as a transitional period of identity exploration.

In many segments of American society, including those from which many Ramah staff members emerge, this period of being "on hold" is far more frequently the norm than having one's career and life trajectory fixed (or at least relatively set) upon graduation from college at age twenty-one. College

JEFFREY S. KRESS, *Ph.D., is an associate professor of Jewish Education and a senior research assistant at the William Davidson Graduate School of Jewish Education of The Jewish Theological Seminary. He also coordinates the school's concentration in Informal and Communal Jewish Education. Dr. Kress was recently appointed as the chair of the Network for Research in Jewish Education. He attended Ramah Berkshires in 1984 and from 1986 to 1989 and participated in the Ramah Israel Seminar in 1985.*

itself, as described by Arnett, has shifted away from a focus on vocational preparation to become one vehicle for exploring different possibilities for one's identities, for example, as one's search for a major (and switching between majors) comes to be related to the question of one's goals and competencies. Early employment experiences, too, are coming to be seen by emerging adults as temporary waypoints on the journey to one's final destination, rather than strategic steps toward a predetermined goal. Alongside this understanding of the college years and beyond as a context for identity exploration has come a heightened appreciation of the potential of experiences in this period to have an impact on one's Jewish identity. More attention has been given to the college years as a crucial time span for the forging of a strong Jewish identity (e.g., Keysar and Kosmin 2004a; Yares, Elias, and Kress 2000).

Perhaps due to such trends, a growing appreciation is emerging that "[s]taff are essential members of the camp community who need to be considered as a target audience in their own right." (Sales and Saxe 2004, 33). The bulk of staff members—at least those with the most direct contact with campers—sit at the intersection of the two important identity-exploring contexts discussed above: they come from college to be employed at camp. This points to the potential of staff experiences in one's college years to be particularly important to one's developmental pathway. Moreover, work by Kosmin and Keysar as part of their groundbreaking longitudinal studies (Kosmin and Keysar 2000; Keysar and Kosmin 2004a) indicates that the sub-sample of participants in their research that attended Camp Ramah are, in their college years, "more observant of Jewish ritual, more positive about Jewish and Zionist identity, more inclined to date and marry Jews, and more active in Jewish life on campus" (Keysar and Kosmin 2004b, 6). Such results were intriguing and, as they were based on a relatively small sample in a study not focusing specifically on issues related to the camp experience, provided the impetus and interest for the current study, the purpose of which is to provide an in-depth portrait of Ramah college-aged staff members.

Methods and Respondents

The survey upon which this report is based was developed by the author, with significant input from a variety of sources (including the National Ramah director, the directors of the various Ramah overnight camps, and several Ramah staff members). Efforts were made to create a form that could be completed in fifteen to twenty minutes. To streamline distribution, a Web-based survey was created. An e-mail message from the National Ramah director was forwarded by the various camp directors to their staff (often accompanied by a note from the camp director as well). This note, as well as a note from the author, invited participants to complete the survey, stressed the voluntary nature of the project, and ensured confidentiality of participation and results. The Web link to the survey was included in the note from the National Ramah director. Periodic reminders were sent by the camp director and by the author. The survey consisted primarily of Likert-type rating scales indicating agreement or disagreement with the statements provided. However, for several points, participants were asked to fill in possible "other" responses aside from the choices provided. Also, two "essay" questions were included, one regarding the impact of Ramah and one regarding Jewish behavior in college.

The survey was posted from December 2004–January 2005. This span of time was chosen to (a) allow for first-year students to have completed one full semester and (b) provide an opportunity to complete the survey either during a vacation span or during the course of the semester (with the belief that some participants would prefer to do one or the other). This means that respondents in the "second-year student" cohort had been about to enter their second year of college during the summer of 2004 (the summer from which this sample was drawn) and were mid-way through their second year of college when completing the survey. The population of Ramah college-age staff is approximately 1,000 (M. Cohen, personal communication), and 408 respondents were included in this sample.

Throughout this report, the numbers in the figures indicate percentages of those responding to a particular item. When statistical analyses were performed, significant findings are reported along with brief statistical information. When possible, responses from the current sample are juxtaposed with a relevant comparison group. Detailed information about this comparison group of Conservative Jewish respondents was reported by Kosmin and Keysar (Kosmin and Keysar 2000; Keysar and Kosmin 2004a).[1]

Participants represented each of the seven overnight Ramah camps plus the Nyack day camp. With the exception of Ramah in the Poconos, which was underrepresented, the camps reflect roughly an equal share of the respondents. The respondents were overwhelmingly bunk staff, perhaps reflecting the proportionately large numbers of such staff at camp, particularly for college-age staff. The vast majority had not worked at a non-Ramah overnight camp.

A quarter of the respondents had not been campers at the Ramah camp at which they worked, 18% had never attended a Ramah camp as a camper, and 45% had attended their current camp for six or more years. The impact of this distribution (with sizable numbers never having attended as campers or having attended for many years as campers) on the life of staff members should be explored further. How are new staff members "socialized" into the camp routine? What is the social experience of new staff members as compared to staff who were campers?

There were more female respondents than male (55.7% and 44.3%, respectively), and the largest percentage of respondents (approximately 41%) were raised in the Northeast. The average age of respondents was nineteen years at the time of completing this survey. The percentage of respondents decreased with each successive year in college. Both genders were proportionately represented in each year.

On the Job: Working at Ramah

Because relatively little is known about Ramah college-age staff, we begin by reporting basic findings regarding how staff members think about their work, what draws them to work at Ramah, or alternatively, what pressures them to consider leaving.

By and large, respondents seem to agree with the educational mission of the camp, sensing not only the potential for them to be an influence on their campers, but also the potential for their own growth. Large majorities of respondents agreed that Jewish education (86%) and developing a connection to Israel (90%) should be part of a camper's experience (female respondents showing more agreement than males with the latter statement).[2]

Overall, respondents acknowledged their impact on campers' Jewish lives (93% agreeing[3] that "at camp, I have an impact on how my campers develop Jewishly") and even more so on their campers' social and emotional development (98% agreeing). Analyses were conducted to compare the responses of bunk and educational staff (including counselors, junior counselors, *rashei edah,* and teachers) with those of specialists (sports and aquatic staffs and other specialists). The former group reported more agreement regarding their Jewish impact on campers than the latter group. Female respondents also indicated stronger agreement regarding their Jewish impact on campers. The groups did not differ in their assessment of their social and emotional impact. Also, those who had been campers at Ramah did not differ from those who had not been in terms of their perceptions of their impact on campers.

Respondents generally agreed (78%) that they themselves should be involved in Jewish learning over the summer (with female respondents agreeing more than males). Fewer respondents (45%) agreed that someone in their position must speak Hebrew competently. Interestingly, no differences were found in the importance of staff learning or of Hebrew competence based on position (bunk/educational staff vs. specialists) or whether one had or had not been a Ramah camper.

Considerations for attending Ramah

Respondents were asked to indicate the importance of various factors in their decision to work at camp the previous summer. Also, they were given the opportunity to insert other reasons aside from those options provided. Figure 1 shows the percentage of respondents reporting that each option was "very important." As demonstrated by these findings, the socio-affective elements (including issues of Jewish community) dominate the decision to come to work at camp.

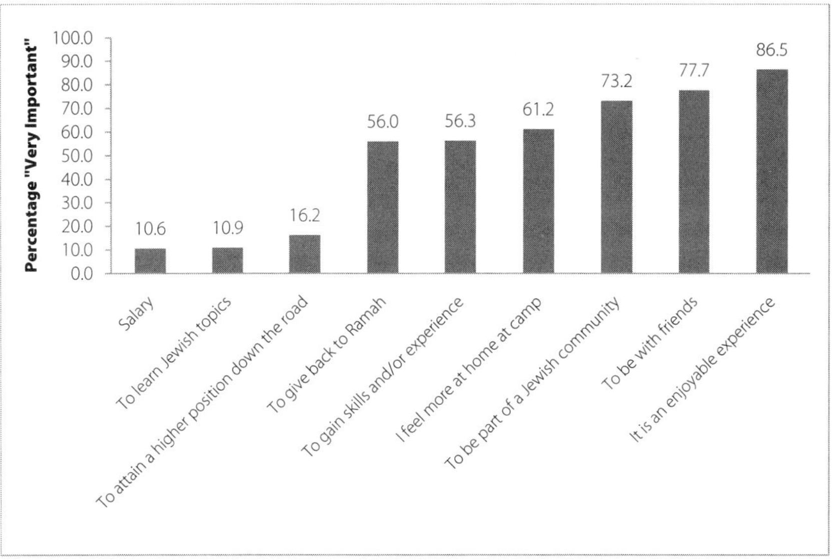

Figure 1. Reasons for coming to camp

Respondents also were asked to insert other reasons that were important in terms of their considerations for attending Ramah during summer 2004. Responses were categorized by similarity of theme. The two most commonly endorsed categories were, in order of decreasing frequency:

1. A desire to give the campers positive experiences, learning, and so on, or simply to be with the campers. A representative response is "We owe it to the kids to provide them an education and experience that will guide them in their lives as Jews and members of the human race. Therefore, I work with campers at Camp Ramah. I don't do it for the director, my *rosh,* or even myself. I do it for the campers."

2. Positive feelings about camp, for example, "Because it is the best place in the world and I would never trade my experiences at camp for anything else in the world."

Respondents also were asked if they had strongly considered not coming to work at Ramah, and 31 percent indicated that they had. The percentage of respondents that considered not attending Ramah was related to one's year in college. Notably, there is a sizable jump in the numbers of those who considered not attending between those who were first-year students *prior* to summer 2004 and those who were second-year students (as shown in fig. 2).[4] For those who were third-year students prior to summer 2004, the numbers that considered not attending decline somewhat, possibly because some of those less committed to returning have already "dropped out."

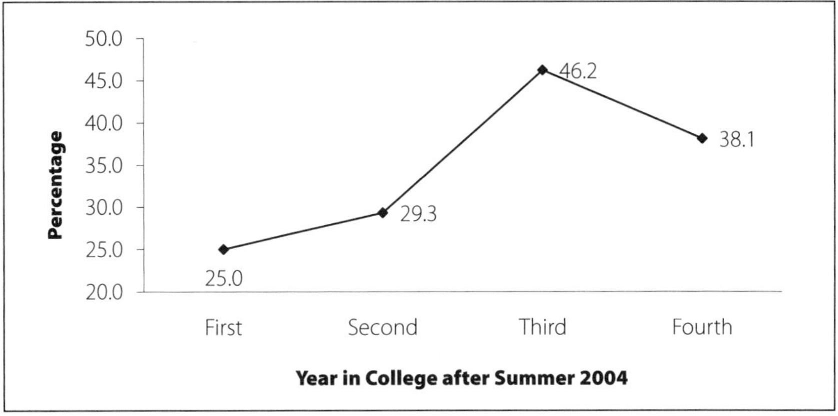

Figure 2. Respondents who considered not attending, by year in college

Respondents who considered not attending were asked to indicate the importance of various reasons in their consideration and to insert other reasons. Figure 3 shows the percentage of respondents that reported that each factor was "very important." It appears that career concerns are of crucial importance here.

Ramah and Judaism: A Staff Apart

Jewish education is a raison d'être of Camp Ramah, and college-age staff members are the front-line foot soldiers of this effort. What do the data tell us about the Jewish lives of Ramah college-aged staff? On a variety of Jewish indexes, it appears that the "norm" for college-age Ramah staff differs from the overall sample reported by Keysar and Kosmin (2004a), and is consistent with their findings of high levels of Jewish engagement among Ramah participants (Keysar and Kosmin 2004b). It is important to keep in mind that a study of this nature does not imply causality; that is, it cannot be discerned from this study whether or not working at Ramah caused these

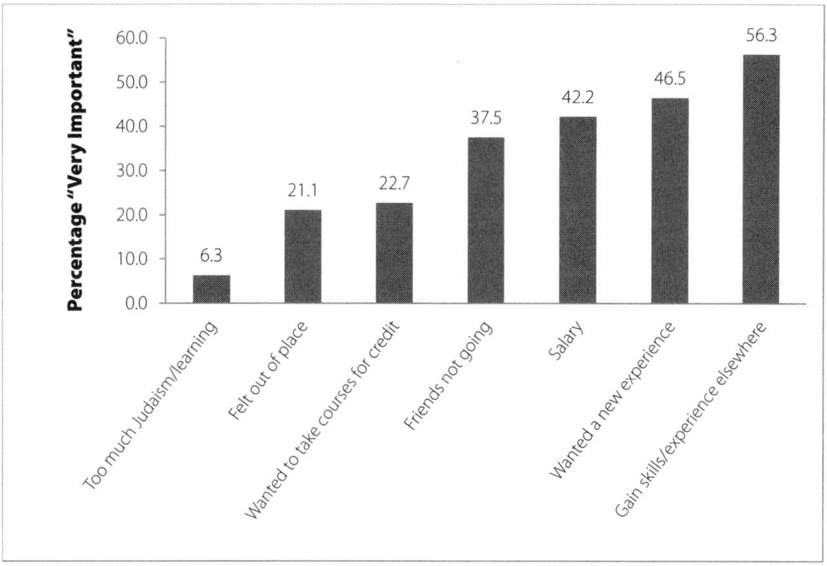

Figure 3. Reasons for considering not attending

high levels of Jewish engagement. Even so, the idea that the staff of Ramah looks different from the general population is a significant observation.

Involvement of Jewish students on campus

Respondents reported high levels of involvement with Hillel or Jewish student unions, particularly with regard to religious (80.7%) and social (78.3%) activities. Although these survey responses do not tell us the extent of the involvement, it is notable that 42.2 percent of respondents reported involvement in leadership activities at Hillel or Jewish student unions. Almost 90% of respondents were involved in at least one aspect of Hillel or a Jewish student union. Although not a perfect comparison, 68% of *Eight Up* respondents reported that they "belonged" to Hillel (Keysar and Kosmin 2004a, 11).

Responses were split regarding joining kosher meal plans. More than half of respondents reported either joining such a plan or that they would join if it were offered, whereas 46% said they had not joined such a plan. Interestingly, approximately a quarter of the respondents reported that they had wanted to join a kosher meal plan, but that such a plan was not offered at their school.

More than half of the respondents reported that they had taken at least one Jewish studies course, and close to a quarter were either majoring or minoring in Jewish studies. In comparison, 7% of the *Eight Up* respondents reported that they were Jewish studies majors, with 63% reporting that they had taken no Jewish studies courses (Keysar and Kosmin 2004a, 13). Approximately 10%

of the current respondents "placed out" of their college language requirement with their knowledge of Hebrew, and almost half of the respondents had taken at least one Hebrew language course. In terms of Jewish cultural involvement on campus, "reading Jewish-themed literature" was the most common activity, whereas "attending Jewish music concerts" was the activity least frequently engaged in.

Jewish ritual involvement

The majority of respondents came from Conservative Jewish backgrounds and considered their religious observance to be about the same as their parents. However, about one-third considered themselves to be more observant than their parents (compared with 13% of *Eight Up;* Keysar and Kosmin 2004a, 32), and 12% considered themselves to be less observant than their parents (compared to 46% of *Eight Up;* Keysar and Kosmin 2004a, 32). More than three-quarters of the respondents grew up in homes that had separate dishes for meat and milk. More than 50% either would only eat in a kosher restaurant or would not order meat that is not certified kosher. Respondents to the *Eight Up* survey were asked a similar question, "Do you eat meat and milk when you go out?" Although the comparison with the current data is not perfect, 28% of those respondents indicated that they did not order meat and milk (Keysar and Kosmin 2004a, 31).

Approximately 47% of respondents reported attending services more than twice a month, and 71% reported attending at least once a month (in comparison, 25% of the *Eight Up* sample attend at least once a month; Keysar and Kosmin 2004a, 30). More than 40% of respondents either did not ride in a motor vehicle on Shabbat or tried to limit their riding, and approximately 38% either did not write on Shabbat or tried to limit their writing. Nearly all respondents reported attending Passover seders, lighting Hanukkah candles, and fasting on Yom Kippur "yearly" while in college (97%, 94%, and 93%, respectively), and more than three-quarters reported eating at least one meal in a sukkah. In comparison, *Eight Up* respondents were asked about fasting on Yom Kippur (though they were given different response options), and 78% indicated that they did (Keysar and Kosmin 2004a, 31).

Jewish leadership aspirations

As shown in figure 4, more than three-quarters of respondents reported considering volunteer or lay leadership. Notable numbers reported considering careers in Jewish education and in Jewish communal service. Smaller percentages reported considering careers as rabbis or cantors. Although these results indicate only "considerations," and it is unlikely all of these will materialize into actual careers in these areas, it is clear that many respondents can envision for themselves a future that includes professional or lay involvement in the Jewish community.

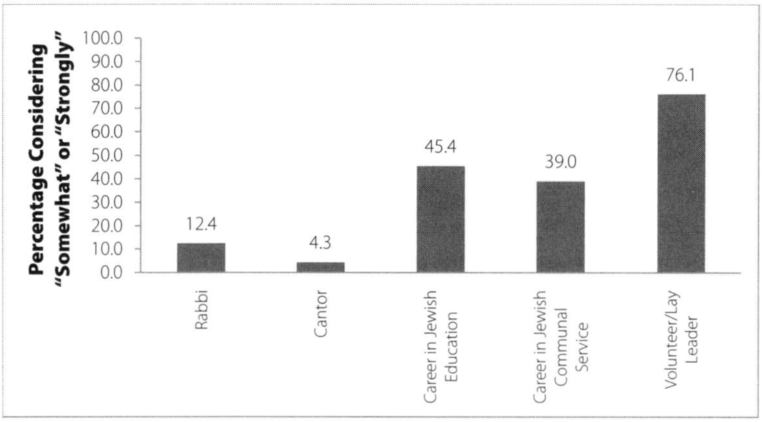

Figure 4. Jewish career and lay aspirations

Results in this section can be compared, albeit imperfectly, with responses from *Eight Up* in which participants were asked "Do you see yourself becoming . . ." various Jewish roles. In that study, 53% respond affirmatively for "Volunteer activist for Jewish institution," 26% for "Professional in Jewish institution," 21% for "Jewish educator," and 13% for "Lay leader of a synagogue" (Keysar and Kosmin 2004a, 22).

Jewish educational background

Almost half of respondents attended Jewish day school for eight years or more of elementary school, and more than 66% attended such a school for at least one year. Approximately 29% reported attending Jewish day school for four years of high school (and approximately 47% of the current sample attended post-bar/bat mitzvah religious school for four or more years). Finding comparisons for data regarding percentage of the population engaged in particular forms of education is difficult. However, in Kosmin and Keysar's previous work (Kosmin and Keysar, 2000), only 9% of respondents were in day school in 1995 (seventh to ninth grades) and 3% in eleventh to twelfth grades in 1999 (Kosmin and Keysar 2000, 25). In the same study, approximately 5% were included in the Jewish day school category, indicating those "who had attended a Jewish day school during their high school years" (Kosmin and Keysar 2000, 37). Again, although the comparison measures are not exact, the current sample does seem to represent higher levels of day school attendance.

For example, 29% of the current sample attended Jewish day high school for four years. Approximately 27% of the *Four Up* sample graduated from Hebrew high school after attending for four years (Kosmin and Keysar 2000, 37). Although graduation rates of the current sample are not known, approximately 47% of the current sample attended post-bar/bat mitzvah religious school for four or more years.

It is also interesting to consider these results and their implications for staffing and staff development at Ramah. For example, although almost half of the respondents attended Jewish day elementary school for at least eight years, and approximately a quarter attended *both* four years of Jewish day high school and eight or more years of Jewish day elementary school, a third of respondents had no day school education at all (elementary or high school). In planning staff learning opportunities in Judaica and Hebrew language, care must be taken to account for such a wide range of formal Jewish educational background. Interestingly, specialists were more likely to have attended Jewish day high school than bunk/educational staff (no difference was found for the likelihood of attendance at Jewish day elementary school), whereas bunk/educational staff were more likely than specialists to have attended post-bar/bat mitzvah religious school. Finally, close to 85% of respondents were involved in some form of youth group (mostly USY) while in high school.

Jewish social connections

Overwhelmingly, respondents reported having Jewish friends. Close to three-quarters of respondents reported that most of their friends were Jewish (compared to 28% of *Eight Up* respondents; Keysar and Kosmin 2004a, 35). Over 93% reported that at least half of their friends were Jewish (compared to 53% in *Eight Up;* Keysar and Kosmin 2004a, 35). Respondents also generally agreed that they look at the entire Jewish world as their extended family (81%) and that they relate to Jews more easily than to non-Jews (84%).

Approximately 70% of respondents reported that they prefer to date only Jews (a rate that appears higher than that for the *Eight Up* sample),[5] and 93% indicated that it is "very important" for them to marry someone who is Jewish (compared to 51% in *Eight Up,* Keysar and Kosmin 2004a, 36). Finally, more than 90% of respondents (compared to 55% of *Eight Up,* Keysar and Kosmin 2004a, 27) reported that being Jewish was "very important" in their lives, and almost all considered it at least somewhat important (similar, but still higher than the 90% of *Eight Up* respondents who endorsed this; Keysar and Kosmin 2004a, 27). Although the comparison is not exact, 18% of *Eight Up* respondents reported that they "date only Jews" (Keysar and Kosmin 2004a, 37; the current study phrased this in terms of preference).

Connections to Israel

Respondents overwhelmingly considered Israel to be "very important" to them (81%, compared to 66% of *Eight Up* respondents; Keysar and Kosmin 2004a, 17). Close to 90% of respondents had been to Israel (compared to 60% of *Eight Up* respondents; Keysar and Kosmin 2004a, 18). Of these, 46% had been there three or more times (primarily, the longest visits were in the two-week to two-month range). Ramah Seminar was the Israel experience most frequently attended by participants, with almost a third having participated in that trip. More than half spent, or planned to spend, a semester in Israel during college.

Of the survey respondents, 40% were at least "considering somewhat" making aliyah, and 12% were considering it strongly. Two-thirds of respondents were at least "considering somewhat" living in Israel for a period of time (not permanently), and more than a quarter were considering it strongly. Although these numbers merely indicate "consideration," and it is of course unlikely that all who consider actually will follow through, this does indicate that many participants desired to be connected with Israel in a significant way.

The Perceived Impact of Ramah

Although the direct impact of the Ramah experience cannot be ascertained from a study of this sort, it is possible to explore the opinions held by respondents regarding the nature of the impact of Ramah. Respondents overwhelming agreed that Ramah has had a major impact on their lives in general (close to 92% agreeing or strongly agreeing that "My life would be completely different if I had never gone to Ramah), and specifically, in terms of their Jewish practice (over 88% agreeing or strongly agreeing that "Ramah has had a significant impact on my Jewish practice"). Not surprisingly, respondents who had been campers at Ramah reported stronger agreement regarding general and Jewish impact. Also, female respondents reported greater impact Jewishly than did male respondents.

The reported friendship networks of respondents contain many fellow Ramahniks. Approximately 40% of respondents reported that at least half of their friends are Ramahniks. The Ramah social network appears to extend to college as well, with more than a third of respondents reporting that at least "some" of their friends at college were also Ramahniks, and fewer than a quarter reporting that they had no Ramahniks among their college friends. Again, not surprisingly, those who were not Ramah campers reported fewer friends who were Ramahniks. Interestingly, the differences in the percentage of friends at college that were Ramahniks between those who had and had not been to Ramah as campers approached, but did not achieve, significance. There were no gender or staff position (bunk/education vs. specialist) differences in friendship patterns.

Ramah's impact: In their own words

Respondents were asked to describe, in their own words, the impact, if any, that Ramah has had on them. Close to three-quarters of the participants provided a response to this item. The major categories (those encompassing at least 20% of the respondents to this item; not including the "Other" category) are discussed here in order of decreasing frequency, and sample responses are given.

1. Jewish impact: This broad category includes discussion of the impact on one's Jewish life ranging from the very general ("It impacted on me Jewishly.") to the very specific (for example, deciding to begin a new Jewish observance, such as "I became kosher because of camp."). Responses in this category had to do with learning about Judaism, developing a Jewish identity, and positive feelings toward Judaism.

> I attended Jewish schools for my entire childhood. While I had learned about Judaism, Ramah exposed me to a living Judaism that I could never have imagined. It ignited in me a passion about Judaism and education that I have carried with me in everything I do.

> Camp Ramah has had more of an impact on me than any other single thing I have ever done in my life. It has influenced me to become shomer Shabbat, to eat kosher, and to strongly consider making aliyah. Through Ramah, I met role models that encouraged me to [pursue Jewish studies in college].

> Ramah has let me find my own Judaism rather than just accept my parents' Judaism. While I am at home at my parents' synagogue, I consider it my parents' community. Camp Ramah is my Jewish community. At camp I learned about Judaism, and I learned to make it my own.

2. Friendships: This category was applied when a respondent mentioned the importance of Ramah in the development of friends or relationships.

> Some of my greatest and most valuable friendships I have made through Ramah, and I only wish to continue my involvement with Ramah in the future.

> The friends I have at Ramah are my best friends and have been for many years.

3. Personal growth: Responses in this category had to do with the impact of Ramah on one's general identity (other than Jewish identity, which is coded into the "Jewish Impact" category), well-being, adjustment, self-confidence, or social-emotional competence; leading one to learn about one's self, or helping one develop a sense of morals and ethics.

> Ramah has truly created the person I am today, as a strong individual with a very clear sense of morality.

> It has made me a more outgoing, take charge type of person. I have become more of a leader in my community and am more comfortable speaking in front of groups.

> Ramah also helped me "come out of my shell" because I was very shy my first year, got the lead in the play, and gained the confidence to sing and speak in front of a crowd.

Discussion

The present report is meant as a descriptive overview. Although it may be tempting to read causality into the current data and to say that attendance at Ramah is responsible for any observed outcomes, such conclusions should not be inferred. For such information, the reader is referred to studies of the impact of the Ramah experience (e.g., Cohen 1999; Keysar and Kosmin 2004b). Further, because the total population of potential participants in this survey is not known, the percentage represented by this sample cannot be specified (though we can assume it is somewhere in the range of 40%). The current methodology does not allow the comparison of respondents and non-respondents. This means that we do not know how well the self-selecting group represents the population as a whole. There is, of course, reason to believe that this sample represents a portion of the staff with more positive attitudes and connections to camp. After all, they have agreed to complete a lengthy survey online. Therefore, care should be taken in drawing inferences about the college-age staff as a whole. To validate and extend the current findings, future studies should be conducted using more sophisticated methods that would allow for better understanding the representativeness of the sample, to create an on-going database, and even to track staff members over time.

So, if causality cannot be inferred and if this sample may not be representative, then what can we learn from this study? The process of research, even in the face of questions of generalizability, can result in a description of the possible, what *may be,* or *could be,* as opposed to what *will be* (Schofield 2002). That is, even without extending the data to non-respondents, it is safe to say that in coming to work at Camp Ramah, staff members encounter an environment that they are unlikely to encounter in college or in other work settings. This environment contains a sizable portion of individuals of the same age-cohort who share a commitment to Judaism and to their work as agents of Jewish socialization.

Noted sociologist Peter L. Berger (1967), in discussing the importance of maintaining (on an individual and a societal level) structures of meaning in life, claims that "[t]he world is built up in the consciousness of the individual by conversation with significant others (such as parents, teachers, 'peers'). The world is maintained as subjective reality by the same sort of conversation, be it with the same or with new significant others" (16–17). Such social validation provides a "plausibility structure" that allows for the maintenance of a meaningful worldview. It is not simply that others model beliefs for us, but that external realities make our beliefs plausible. The challenge, writes Berger (1967, 127), is that "secularization has resulted in the widespread collapse of the plausibility of traditional religious definitions of reality."

In a similar vein, but coming from a different theoretical standpoint, psychologists (e.g., Markus and Nurius 1986) speak of the importance of "possible selves," or a sense of the opportunities and pathways that one's own identity can take. Maintaining the possibility of a particular future self can be motivating; seeing an identity outcome as implausible can be stultifying (e.g., if I think that "me as a triathlete" is possible, I can work toward this goal; if I think that "me as a triathlete" is not in my range of possibilities, motivation to achieve the outcome is dampened).

College-age staff are at an "age of *possibilities,* when hopes flourish, when people have an unparalleled opportunity to transform their lives" (Arnett 2004, 8). Berger's analysis, along with the discussion of "possible selves," implies that not all *possibilities* exert the same influence; possibilities differ in their plausibility. That Ramah can add a layer of positive experiences and memories to Jewish engagement is only part of the story. Ramah adds to the list of plausible possibilities the potential for sustained Jewish engagement. There are data to suggest that Ramah staff are acutely aware that such engagement is not the norm on campus; that their engagement is in a sense "counter-cultural." In data from this project not reported here, respondents were asked to describe the most important thing they do as a Jew on campus. Along with the expected themes (e.g., attend Hillel and services), many respondents expressed the importance of representing Judaism—and specifically, Israel—in a positive light. The following responses are representative:

> I answer my non-Jewish friends when they ask about different things I do. I am one of the only Jews they know and am the only religious Jew most of them know and so I feel that I represent Judaism for them and want to do it well.

> At college, the most important things that I do as a Jew are try and educate and open closed minds to new ideas and thoughts to show them that the Jewish people aren't as bad as is depicted in the media.

> Being president of the local Israel Alliance on campus because I have the opportunity to affect students of all walks of life and present Israel accurately and in a positive light.

It is possible to read such responses as reactions against a prevailing social structure and worldview that calls into question the plausibility of perceived possibilities. Given this, it is not surprising that Hillel activities or other opportunities, as one participant puts it in responding to the above question, to "surround myself with Jews" are attractive as they resurrect the possibilities for a Jewish future.

Though this study deals with camp staff, this line of thinking could be extended to campers as well. Campers also are exposed to Jewish relationships and forms of Jewish engagement that they may perceive or experience differently than in the past. For these campers, as with staff members, Ramah may serve to make ongoing engagement with Judaism a part of a plausible Jewish future.

Notes

[1] Throughout this report, Keysar and Kosmin 2004a will be referred to as *Eight Up* and Kosmin and Keysar 2000 as *Four Up*.

[2] All reported inferential analyses are significant to at least $p < .05$. Complete statistical information is available from the author. However, statistical comparisons between the current sample and the Kosmin and Keysar samples are not possible at this time. All comparisons between these groups are reported only as trends.

[3] Agreeing includes responses of "agree" and "strongly agree" unless otherwise indicated.

[4] Recall that those in the "third-year" cohort, which shows the jump in percent considering not attending, were actually second year students at the time they considered not attending.

[5] The comparison is not exact, 18% of *Eight-Up* respondents reported that they "date only Jews" while the current study phrased this in terms of preference. However, 41% of the *Eight-Up* respondents reported that they prefer to date Jews but will also date non-Jews (compared to 25% here; wording was the same), and 35% report that they do not care if their date is Jewish (compared to 3% here; wording was the same).

References

Arnett, J. J. 2004. *Emerging adulthood: The winding road from the late teens through the twenties.* Oxford: Oxford University Press.

Berger, P. L. 1967. *The sacred canopy: Elements of a sociological theory of religion.* New York: Anchor Books.

Cohen, S. M. 2000. Camp Ramah and adult Jewish identity. In *Ramah, Reflections at 50: Visions for a new century,* ed. S. A. Dorph, 95–129. New York: National Ramah Commission.

Ettenberg, S. C. and G. Rosenfield, eds. 1989. *The Ramah experience: Community and commitment.* New York: Jewish Theological Seminary.

Keysar, A., and B. A. Kosmin. 2004a. *"Eight up": The college years.* New York: Ratner Center for the Study of Conservative Judaism.

———. 2004b. *Research findings on the impact of Camp Ramah.* New York: National Ramah Commission.

Kosmin, B. A., and A. Keysar. 2000. *"Four up": The high-school years, 1995–1999.* New York: Ratner Center for the Study of Conservative Judaism.

Markus, H., and P. Nurius. 1986. Possible selves. *American Psychologist,* 41 (9): 954–69.

Sales, A. L., and L. Saxe. 2004. *"How goodly are thy tents": Summer camps as Jewish socializing experiences.* Hanover: Brandeis University Press in association with the Avi Chai Foundation, published by University Press of New England.

Schofield, J. W. 2002. Increasing the generalizability of qualitative research. In *The qualitative researcher's companion,* ed. A. M. Huberman and M. B. Miles, 171–203. Thousand Oaks, CA: Sage.

Schorsch, I. 1989. An emerging vision of Ramah. In *The Ramah experience: Community and commitment,* ed. S. C. Ettenberg and G. Rosenfield, 185–93. New York: Jewish Theological Seminary.

Tyler, R. 1989. Preface to *The Ramah experience: Community and commitment,* ed. S. C. Ettenberg and G. Rosenfield, vii. New York: The Jewish Theological Seminary.

Yares, A., M. Elias, and J. Kress. 2000. Jewish identity on campus: Research and recommendations for the college years. *Journal of Jewish Education* 65 (3): 41–48.

JEFFREY S. KRESS AND **MICHAEL BEN-AVIE**

Social Climate at Ramah: Relationships and Motivation

Introduction: The Broad Scope of Developmental Goals at Ramah

MANY AUTHORS HAVE DESCRIBED the broad nature of the goals and effects of Jewish summer camping. For example, Sales and Saxe (2004), discussing Jewish summer camping in general, describe camp as a "socializing agent." Writing specifically about the Ramah Camping Movement, Seymour Fox (1989, 16) uses the terms "cognitive," "affective," and "interpersonal" to describe the scope of Ramah's vision and reach. The founding of Ramah was premised on a broad definition of Jewish engagement:

> Ramah was unique, and hopefully remains so, in its attention to the development of religious sensibility. While many of the activities that comprise the "religious life" of camp did not perhaps differ from that obtained in other camps, they were driven by two considerations not always evident in other settings—religious as a world view which is important to the development of individual personality at least in a measure equal to the functions it serves as an instrument of group solidarity; and the religious tradition of Judaism as a code of private and public behavior of extraordinary ethical sensitivity. (Ackerman 1999, 50)

Although one may disagree with Ackerman's comment about Ramah's continued *uniqueness* in this regard, few would argue with this conceptualization of

JEFFREY S. KRESS, *Ph.D., is an associate professor of Jewish Education and a senior research assistant at the William Davidson Graduate School of Jewish Education of The Jewish Theological Seminary. He also coordinates the school's concentration in Informal and Communal Jewish Education. Dr. Kress was recently appointed as the chair of the Network for Research in Jewish Education. He attended Ramah Berkshires in 1984 and from 1986 to 1989 and participated in the Ramah Israel Seminar in 1985.*

MICHAEL BEN-AVIE, *Ph.D., is an educational researcher and academic psychologist at the Yale Child Study Center, performing post-doctoral research in child neuropsychiatric disorders. He has co-edited six books with colleagues at the center on promoting the learning and development of youth. In 2005, he was accepted for inclusion in the federal government's Registry of Outcome Evaluators.*

the outcomes of the camp experience. Ramah is described, through a Jewish lens, as a developmental setting that impacts on campers' self-perception and behaviors in ways that include, but go beyond, ritual involvement.

Ramah's mission statement includes language that describes "a caring, encouraging approach to personal growth and individual religious experience which interact to form Jewish identity" and "a religious commitment to social justice and the ecological welfare of our world."[1] There is an indication that this holistic view of intertwined Jewish and general developmental outcomes is not just "from the top" but is also held by the campers themselves. For example, responding to a question about the mission of Ramah, a sixteen-year-old counselor-in-training wrote:[2]

> You would like me to write that Ramah is, to me, just about Judaism. However, it is really about understanding yourself, not only as a Jew but as a person. The purpose of Camp Ramah is to allow campers and staff to experience a close sense of community while developing skills and maturing as individuals.

Furthermore, staff members report their strong belief about their impact on the social and emotional lives of their campers (Kress, this volume). In fact, language such as this, without the religious references (though perhaps with "spiritual" language), also can be found in the discussion of the goals and outcomes within the secular camping movement. For example, the American Camp Association points to the ability of camp to help teach "powerful lessons in community, character-building, skill-development, and healthy living."[3]

Social Climate: A Key Element in Effective Developmental Settings

How do educational-developmental settings go about achieving such developmental outcomes? Although the answer to this question is quite broad, one important line of research focuses on "social climate," (e.g., Dalton, Elias, and Wandersman 2001) or the way in which participants in a setting experience the quality of relationships and interactions in the setting. Such perceptions are seen not only as descriptive of the setting but also as indicators of the norms and expectations experienced by participants in a setting, the "way things are here," so to speak. The activities of participants in the setting and the norms of a setting are seen as existing in dynamic interaction; behaviors create norms, and norms create behaviors.

Social climate is related to the actual norms and regularities of interactions in a setting, or what is often referred to as the "culture" of the organization. Seymour Sarason (1971, 12), a pioneer in this area, writes:

> In many situations it is likely that one can predict an individual's behavior far better on the basis of knowledge of the social structure and his position in it than one can on the basis of his personal dynamics.
>
> All that I am saying at this point is that when we say a setting is "organized," or that cultures differ from each other, we mean, among other things, that there is a distinct structure or pattern that, so to speak, governs roles and interrelationships within that setting. What is implied, in addition, is that structure antedates any one individual and will continue in the absence of the individual. It may well be that it is precisely because one cannot *see* structure in the same way that one sees an individual that we have trouble grasping and acting in terms of its existence.

A unique ecological system is created in every educational setting due to the dynamics in the relationships among the parents, staff members, administrators, students, and other members of the community. The climate of an educational setting is created through consistency in everyday interactions. Every setting has its own distinctive social climate. However, perceptions may not be consistent among all subgroups within a setting; that is, some participants may have a more or less favorable view than others (Dalton, Elias, and Wandersman 2001).

Social climate issues have been a focus of researchers examining the "developmental assets" of settings that promote positive growth and development (Benson 2003). These researchers stress the importance of interactions between the developing person and the educational-developmental settings in which he or she participates, describing factors that contribute to positive development that can be found not only within the individual (such as coping and conflict resolution skills) but also on the environmental level. These factors include (Eccles and Gootman 2002, 90–91):

- physical and psychological safety
- appropriate structure
- supportive relationships
- opportunities to belong
- positive social norms
- support for efficacy and mattering
- opportunities for skill building
- integration of family, school, and community efforts

These elements have been developed by Kress and Reimer (2009, 349–50) to apply to Jewish informal educational settings as five principles:

• Positive developmental-educational settings are marked by safety, personal respect, and clear boundaries.

• Positive developmental-educational settings are marked by warm, caring relationships among all members of the community.

• Youth, and particularly adolescents, benefit most from settings in which they have a substantial voice in helping to shape the setting and can fill meaningful roles that contribute to its functioning.

• Multiple entry points into ritual practice and the study of texts facilitate the ability of youth to engage with the tradition.

• Quality developmental-educational settings are marked by planful attention to the affective experiences of the participants and the deep integration of "learning" and "feeling."

Given the focus of Camp Ramah on positive developmental outcomes, it is important to examine the participants' perceptions of the social climate of camp. How do campers describe the developmental (Jewish and general) impact of Ramah? How do campers experience relationships with peers and staff? Where do they find support? In what way do they perceive their own self-growth at camp? What activities motivate them? How do these issues extend to Jewish growth in camp? To address these issues, the authors conducted a survey of 525 rising sixth- to eighth-grade campers[4] in two Ramah camps.

Ramah: Caring Relationships and Positive Development Are the Norm

The data in table 1 show that overall, respondents feel at home in camp and have many friends there. Further, they report strong relationships with staff members and feeling comfortable turning to them in times of difficulty. More than just keepers of order, staff members are seen by many campers as agents of growth and development. There are significant differences between subgroups, however, with regard to certain clusters of these variables. Girls voice stronger agreement than boys[5] to clusters of items having to do with:

• Camp as a place to experience friendship and exercise talents. (E.g., "As a result of attending this camp, I have discovered new abilities and gifts that I have," and "I have made some very good friends at this camp.")

• Seeking staff support and guidance. (E.g., "When I am having personal problems because of something going on at this camp, I find an adult and I ask for help.")

• Perceptions of staff intervention with regard to behavioral issues. (E.g., "There is at least one bunk counselor or other staff member at this camp who will approach me if he or she is concerned about my behavior.")

• The role of staff in fostering general positive development. (E.g., "My bunk counselors and other staff members push me to accomplish more than I had ever thought possible.")[6]

Table 1. Relationships and Development

STATEMENTS	PERCENT "AGREEING"[7]
I have made some very good friends at this camp.	96
This camp is a place where I am among friends.	91
Most bunk counselors and other staff members care whether I am a good person.	87
If I have some type of crisis during my time at this camp, I know that there is an adult here who will help me.	87
There is at least one bunk counselor or other staff member at this camp who will approach me if he or she is concerned about my behavior.	86
At this camp, there is at least one adult I can trust to act in my best interests if I confide in him or her about something that concerns me.	84
This camp feels like a place I can call "my own" (for example, a place where I can really be myself, a place where I am comfortable).	82
At this camp, I am encouraged to share (talk about or use) my talents and ideas.	77
When things go wrong, I tell at least one adult about it.	68
As a result of attending this camp, I have discovered new abilities and gifts that I have.	66
When I am having personal problems because of something going on at this camp, I find an adult and I ask for help.	63
When I am in trouble, I continue to ask one or more persons older than me for help until the problem is solved.	58
When I am having personal problems because of something that is not related to camp, I find an adult and I ask for help.	53
My bunk counselors and other staff members push me to accomplish more than I had ever thought possible.	51
My bunk counselors and other staff members are helping me to become a better thinker (e.g., helping me become a person who is able to figure out problems and puzzles).	50
My bunk counselors and other staff members are helping me to become a more creative person.	50
When I am making a decision about my future, I seek advice from an adult at this camp.	43
I feel lonely a lot of the time at camp.	12
At least one of my bunk counselors or other staff member has told me that he or she does not think I'll ever make anything of myself.	7

As the data in table 2 show, campers recognize the importance of Ramah staff in shaping their growth as Jews and many attribute connections to Israel and to the Conservative Movement to their attendance at camp. Of course, the future intentions—Jewish or otherwise—of a middle school student are not to be taken as indicators of future realities; there is no more than a very weak connection assumed between these intentions and actual adult behavioral manifestations. Rather, these data should be understood as current indicators of the connection seen by campers between their experiences and their sense of who they are and who they might become. Interestingly, although campers acknowledge the role of staff in motivating their growth, fewer agree that they seek advice from staff when making important life decisions, Jewish or otherwise. Moreover, campers are significantly less likely to seek advice from staff about Jewish matters than they are about general future decisions. Girls voice more agreement than boys for groups of items representing the perceived impact of the camp and staff on campers' Jewish growth (e.g., the item "My bunk counselors and other staff members are helping me become a more knowledgeable Jew").

Table 2. Perceived Jewish Impact

STATEMENTS	PERCENT "AGREEING"
At this camp, all of the people who teach *yahadut kittah/shi'ur* (Jewish Studies class) make sure that I understand what is being taught.	76
One of the reasons why I like being a camper at this camp is because I am among Jews here.	71
There is at least one adult at this camp who inspires me to learn more about Judaism.	71
My bunk counselors and other staff members are helping me become a more knowledgeable Jew.	70
Attending this camp has given me a fairly clear idea of how I want to lead a Jewish life as an adult.	62
As a result of attending this camp, I am more likely to support Israel publicly among youth my age.	62
Because I go to this camp, I feel more connected to the Conservative Movement within Judaism.	61
When I have to solve challenges in my daily life, I am able to apply teachings from Judaism that I have learned at camp.	40
I seek advice when making a decision about my future from a Jewish adult at this camp because I want a Jewish perspective.	28

Motivation, Challenge, and Interest in Camp Activities

Positive educational-developmental settings engage participants' interests and provide motivation and challenge. Table 3 relates to elements of such engagement. Overall, girls were more engaged than boys in camp activities. Looking at individual categories of activities, girls were more engaged than boys in all activities except sports (boys were more engaged) and *yahadut* and *ivrit* classes (no gender differences).

Finding structured "formal" educational experiences on the bottom of the list of activities to which campers look forward will come as no surprise to most readers, though the extent of this lack of enthusiasm may be alarming. However, a large number of campers do seem to find their yahadut classes interesting and challenging. So, although it may be a stretch to expect middle-

Table 3. Elements of Engagement

STATEMENTS	PERCENT "AGREEING"
I look forward to when it is time for me to engage in . . .	
ḥugim	91
pe'ulot erev	77
pe'ulot tzerif	75
sports	75
swimming	73
Shabbat	69
camp-wide activities (for example, zimriyyah, plays)	67
yom meyuḥad	57
rikkud, shirah	45
Yahadut (Jewish studies kittah/shi'ur)	33
Ivrit (Hebrew kittah/shi'ur)	27
What's going on both challenges me and really interests me in my . . .	
ḥugim	70
sports	61
swimming	53
camp-wide activities (for example, zimkudiyyah, plays)	53
Shabbat	51
pe'ulot erev	50
pe'ulot tzerif	46
Yahadut (Jewish studies kittah/shi'ur)	45
yom meyuḥad	39
rikkud, shirah	38
Ivrit (Hebrew kittah/shi'ur)	35

school students to "look forward" to classes, and although there is certainly room for improvement in perceived interest and challenge for yahadut, Ramah educators can be heartened by data suggesting that it is possible to interest and challenge campers, even in the face of their questionable levels of motivation. Yahadut classes, which are more topical and oriented toward discussion and activity, fare better overall than do Hebrew language classes. Interestingly, both lists are topped by *ḥugim,* which are "elective" activities in which campers pursue their interests in sports, arts, and so on. That these activities would be the most engaging is not surprising and is consistent with the literature on positive educational-developmental settings suggesting the importance of participants' abilities to shape their own settings.

As shown in table 4, although campers may see *tefillot* as an opportunity to learn, to use Kress and Reimer's language (2009, 350), they do not experience them as opportunities for "deep integration of 'learning' and 'feeling.'" Although respondents do report finding it significantly more important to participate actively in tefillot at camp than they report looking forward to attending services in their home synagogues, only around one-third of the respondents claim to find tefillot to be emotionally stirring or say they are challenged and interested in tefillot at camp. Notably, the degree of "challenge and interest" in tefillot at camp does not significantly differ from that reported for the home synagogues. Finally, campers seem to be split in the degree to which they see staff members as role models for prayer, with 45 percent viewing them positively in this regard.

Table 4. Perceptions of Tefillah at Ramah

STATEMENTS	PERCENT "AGREEING"
The services at this camp are run in a way that allows me to learn how to pray.	55
Watching the adults at this camp pray makes me think that praying is very important.	45
Actively participating in tefillot (religious services) at this camp is important to me.	44
Tefillot (religious services) at this camp stir my emotions in a positive way.	38
When I am not at camp, I look forward to attending religious services at my home synagogue.	33
What's going on both challenges me and really interests me in the religious services at camp.	32
What's going on both challenges me and really interests me in the religious services at my home synagogue.	28

The Importance of Camper Choice and Empowerment

The current data show that Ramah campers, by and large, are motivated by, interested in, and challenged by many camp activities. Consequently, these activities hold enormous developmental potential. In fact, campers report the impact of Ramah on who they are Jewishly and generally. The exception to this appears to be in the more "formal" offerings of camp—classes and tefillot. While such findings are predictable, it is possible to glean some recommendations from the data. In particular, the most motivating, interesting, and challenging aspects of camp are the ḥugim. Ḥugim are electives but not optional; everyone is involved with a ḥug, but campers choose their preferences for an activity on which they will focus throughout an extended period, if not the entire summer. One lesson here relates to choice and motivation. As discussed by noted developmental psychologist David Elkind:[8]

> Camp activities are created to meet the needs, interests, and abilities of the children. In addition, children have choices as to the activities in which they will participate. Some may prefer swimming to hiking while others may prefer spending much of their time participating in crafts. Because children have a choice and can choose the activity they prefer, it gives them the opportunity to express themselves and is a form of play. And because the camp respects their personal tastes and aptitudes, they admire and respect their counselors (for the most part) and as a result learn a great deal about themselves and others.

Elkind's comments link choice with personal aptitudes and opportunities for skill development. Educators often struggle to make educational experiences "meaningful" to the learners. Connecting experiences with the interests and skills valued by participants and allowing participants to improve their skills and build their sense of self with regard to these competencies is the essence of making education meaningful. Might we think of the application of these themes to classes and tefillah? Ramah staff can, for example, consider how to integrate student interests and growth areas into the accepted structure of prayer. Might those interested in music, for example, be involved in playing their instruments as part of the service or composing/playing new tunes based on the siddur? Might this, or activities like it, become a project on which campers can work over the course of the summer and then present to his or her peers? Might older campers be involved in facilitating such "innovative" tefillot for younger campers? The importance of choice is consistent with the literature reviewed earlier that described meaningful youth input into the workings of an organization as a key element of creating positive developmental settings, and that can challenge Ramah leadership and staff to consider how youth can become more empowered in shaping the activities in which they participate;

perhaps—particularly in the older *edot*—playing a role on the committees that plan activities.

Relationships among Campers: An Opportunity for Camp Improvement

In general, camp is seen as a safe and welcoming place where friendships thrive. However, it is important to keep in mind that not all participants in an educational setting experience that setting in the same way. A sizable minority of respondents report the presence of cliques at camp (table 5), and more than a quarter of respondents agree that they have been, in some way, bullied at camp. The fact that a smaller percentage sees bullying as a serious problem may indicate either a limited amount of bullying (the bullying has not reached "serious" levels) or, more disturbingly, the sense among a small number of campers that some bullying is part of the norm (i.e., it is not a "problem"). Not surprisingly, those who report having been bullied are disproportionately represented among those who believe that bullying is a serious problem at camp. Those agreeing that they have been bullied over the summer are more likely to be boys, and those who are in their first year at camp express more agreement that they have been bullied than those in their second or third years (treated as a combined group).[9]

Table 5. Challenges in Interpersonal Relationships

STATEMENTS	PERCENT "AGREEING"
In general, bunk counselors stop campers from verbally or physically bullying other campers.	78
At this camp, if some other kids are going to do something harmful, I tell someone who can help.	64
I remain silent if my camp friends are going to do something harmful.	60
If a camper is being bullied or mistreated at this camp, another camper will usually stand up for him or her.	59
When I am worried about a friend, I feel comfortable talking to a counselor or another adult about my worry.	57
When I do something kind for another camper, a bunk counselor or other staff member usually praises me for doing so.	54
There are many groups of friends (cliques) here that exclude other campers.	38
During this summer, another camper has bullied me.	26
Bullying is a serious problem at this camp.	16
When another camper is being made fun of in a humiliating way, I join in the laughter.	8

Though this survey did not aim to define bullying or to obtain an incidence level (i.e., for those who did agree that they were bullied over the course of the summer, we have no idea about the frequency of this occurrence or the specific nature of the behaviors involved), clearly Ramah educators should continue to address this issue. Current approaches to bullying-prevention (e.g., Olweus 1993) take a systemic approach, with all community members taking responsibility not only for refraining from bullying but also for stopping such behavior when it occurs. The current data suggest that Ramah camps can intensify their attempts to foster a sense of *kol yisra'el arevim zeh bazeh* (the responsibility of all Jews for one another's well-being). Slightly fewer than two-thirds of respondents report that campers will stand up for a mistreated peer, and similar numbers report talking to staff when they have a concern about a peer. Although campers do not generally report joining in with bullying behavior, the majority report remaining silent when friends are doing something harmful. And whereas staff members are seen as making efforts to squelch bullying behaviors, they are less often seen shaping behavior using praise.

Overall, campers perceive Ramah to be a warm and welcoming place where they can feel "at home" among friends in a supportive and caring atmosphere. Although many in the camping world might take this as a given, the importance of the social and emotional elements of the experience should not be underplayed. Educational theorists and researchers have described caring relationships as fundamental building blocks for all learning (e.g., Noddings 1992), and at camp, where the intensity of relationships is magnified, the quality of interactions are paramount.

There are, however, areas in which camp staff can improve. Even within overwhelmingly positive trends, the data point to individuals who are socially isolated or even bullied. As noted, it is important to take a systemic, community-based approach to this complex issue in which responsibility for stopping the problem rests with each member of the community. The role of the "bystanders" to help stop bullying must be further developed, along with a sense of communal responsibility for the collective well-being of the entire community. Camp staff also must be more attentive to the existence of cliques, particularly as these might extend over the course of many years in settings such as summer camp. This issue is very challenging as camps value the creation of strong, lasting friendships, with "camp friends" taking an exalted role among campers' relationships. However, staff and campers must work to achieve "close-knit" without "exclusive."

Community-building does not happen automatically; it cannot be decreed, determined by posted rules, or achieved through a few ice-breakers.

It is a complex matter that requires constant monitoring and development on a variety of levels. The findings that we report suggest that staff must become more proactive in acknowledging positive behaviors and in fostering communication with campers around their interpersonal concerns for themselves or their peers. Such routines for communication are best not created in crisis situations. The bunk "sit-down" when there is an infraction of social rules should not be the primary venue for developing positive communication. Rather, positive communication should emerge from established habits and rituals of dialogue among members of the camp community. Campers should have input into the setting of behavioral expectations, and staff should process with their groups the extent to which progress was made on achieving these, focusing on situations that have challenged campers' efforts and the ways this was, or could be, addressed.

Not all members of the camp community, or any community, enter into social interactions on equal footing. New campers, not familiar with written or unwritten camp traditions, can be assigned buddies to help "show them the ropes." Older campers can team with younger campers as mentors. Further, relationship building requires skills in "emotional intelligence" (Goleman 1995), and campers will come to camp exhibiting differences in their competencies in these areas. Some campers have difficulty, for example, reading the social cues needed to join a group or enter into a game. Some may have difficulties with self-control or express themselves in idiosyncratic ways. As part of the current project, data were collected addressing campers' perception of their emotional intelligence. Though these are not reported here, there are indicators pointing toward the overlap of perceived problems with bullying and poorer self-rated social and emotional skills. A systemic approach would neither blame these campers for social difficulties at camp, nor put the onus for changing the situation on them. However, camp staff must be prepared to both promote the social and emotional growth of all of their campers and identify and address those exhibiting particular deficits and work with all campers on how to live together in a caring community with others regardless of their social and emotional skills.

Conclusions: Intentionality in Developmental Programs

Bialeschki, Schmid, and Tilley (2006)[10] conducted a multi-site-intervention research project related to camp improvement and, reflecting on their findings, acknowledge that "none of these thoughts are revolutionary in and of themselves." This is the case with the present study. What is new is the glimpse of the campers that was gleaned from observing the *intensity* with which they agreed or disagreed with items. Ramah is well known for the strong relationships that campers tend to form among themselves. The intensity of the campers' responses to the items that deal with relationships revealed that we cannot always assume that campers naturally have the skill set and competence to maintain healthy relationships with peers and adults. In fact, Ramah's emphasis on the group goes against the grain of American society—and perhaps, this is the point. Whereas American society emphasizes individualism and fluidity of group affiliation, Ramah stands for promoting a sustained group cohesion. The current research empirically validates what we had known up until now only through personal stories: those of us who remember our Ramah days with great fondness realize that Ramah served as the template for the relationships that we have formed since then. And if we understand the structure of Ramah's magic, then we are able to promote it intentionally at Ramah and in other Jewish educational settings.

The current research also provides educators with the analytical tools to figure out what to do when there is a sense of unease because relationships are not forming among the campers as expected. Responses to this sense of unease have included the way that Ramah deals aggressively with issues of "climate," both in peer-to-peer programming (bunk activities on self image, respect for others, making camp a welcoming place for all, etc.) and through intensive staff training (leadership training on a camp and national level, staff week programs devoted specifically to the problem of bullying, identifying specific procedures for staff and campers to safely report bullying so that it can be addressed early before too much harm is caused, etc.).

It is important to realize, though, that even the most basic recommendations can be very difficult to achieve. Bialeschki, Schmid, and Tilley's experience with a data-driven camp improvement process illustrates the challenges posed by even mundane findings. These authors suggest that ongoing commitment to change poses a particular challenge as good intentions must be translated into even the most minute aspects of the organization. Improving the social climate of a camp—or any other important area—requires constant monitoring. Among their recommendations are to:

• Focus on mission with intentional effort. Doing things that bear little relationship to your mission pulls energy away from improvements that could positively connect to your goals. Why do you do what you do in camp?

• Be deliberate in strengthening camp activities. Revise activity lesson plans to address skill development on a daily level. Are your campers fully challenged?

• Strengthen programming/scheduling to take advantage of every opportunity. For example, change arrival day procedures to foster community and emotional safety or alter the daily schedule to allow time for staff and campers to "hang out" with the intention of building strong positive relationships.

• Review staff patterns. Schedule more staff to supervise free time with the intention of addressing safety and relationships goals.

• Emphasize camper planning. Implement new efforts around meaningful camper involvement in planning evening programs, cabin activities, and free-time activities. Offer campers opportunities to participate in camper councils and meetings with the directors and administrative staff.

• Build staff training to model the values core to your mission. Train staff in how to facilitate/process activities that encourage camper leadership and planning, how to listen in ways that promote emotional safety, and how to have meaningful conversations with children.

• Address facility concerns. Make improvements by painting buildings and bathrooms (with camper input) and paying attention to lighting concerns. In most cases, the dollar impact is minimal when compared to the effect (Bialeschki, Schmid, and Tilley, 2006).

The concept of "developmental intentionality" (Walker et al. 2005) has been introduced as a guiding framework for structuring positive youth developmental settings. Developmental intentionality refers to (a) attention to positive developmental outcomes in all aspects of the functioning of an organization—from the broad visioning to the specific implementation of programs; (b) a collaborative process in which youth are involved in shaping their own environments; and (c) a match between the needs and talents of youth and the offerings of the setting. Although intentionality can be planned in advance, there is a component that is reactive to realities as they emerge in the life of the setting and the experience of the participants. Walker et al. (2005, 403) liken this to improvisational jazz in which there might be a general framework for action but in which those involved are encouraged to follow their own instincts while still maintaining a sense of the overall structure of the piece. Intentionality in camp programming must be planful, the vision must be clear, and camp structures and procedures must be thoughtfully examined to consider their impact on positive youth development. Intentionality also must be fluid, with ongoing opportunities for all involved to reflect on progress and challenges and make corrections as the summer moves ahead.

Intentionality also implies focus; the intensity of improvement efforts makes it difficult to focus on too many initiatives or goals at once.[11] Meaningful, lasting change requires sustained attention on a narrow set of goals across many camp venues. For example, intentionality calls upon Ramah leadership to consider the nature of staff training and learning. Although there are many topics to cover during staff orientation and throughout the summer, a smorgasbord of topics is not conducive to the type of impact one would want to have on staff. Just as we expect campers to engage in ongoing ḥugim to work on valued skills and would not expect much of an outcome from a one-shot exposure to, say, swimming class, staff members need a forum for ongoing self-reflection and support to address the complex social challenges brought by campers.

Intentionality also addresses the organizational-structural aspects of Ramah. How might campers play meaningful roles in committees for their edot, planning and implementing activities or tefillot? How might *kittot* be organized as electives to be selected, and what role do campers have in structuring these? How are bunk-staff, or even campers, involved in decision making on a camp-wide level with regard to issues that may impact on relationships within the camp? What particular needs do subgroups of campers have (for example, boys seem to be less motivated by camp activities and more subject to interpersonal difficulties compared to girls) and how can these best be met?

The answers to questions like these are complex and have broad ramifications for a camp. The current data suggest that, in general, Ramah brings a strong positive social climate that addresses the developmental needs of the campers. The structures and policies are in place to make this happen, the result of the wonderful efforts of generations of Ramah leadership. The challenge is to bring these strengths to help shine a light on those corners that still pose "climate" challenges.

Notes

[1] http://www.campramah.org/pdf/nrc_mission_statement.pdf.

[2] http://www.campramah.org/experiences/Ramah_Mission.html.

[3] http://www.acacamps.org/about/profile.php.

[4] More girls responded to this survey than did boys (59% and 41%, respectively). Approximately half of the respondents reported attending a Jewish day school in the past year, and 41% attended supplemental school. Close to half (49%) report participation in a Jewish youth group, and a slightly lower percent (45%) have visited Israel. Respondents have spent an average of three years at camp, with some, probably the children of staff members, reporting much longer attendance (up to fourteen years). Jewishly, half come from homes in which separate plates are used for meat and dairy. The largest percentage (47%) of respondents report that they attend services weekly.

[5] All reported inferential analyses are significant to at least $p < .05$ unless otherwise noted. Complete statistical information is available from the authors.

[6] It is important to note that here and in all analyses such as this, a statistical difference does not mean that any group is "low" or "high" on a particular scale, only that the differences in the responses between the groups are not due to chance.

[7] All respondents indicating "Agree" or "Strongly Agree" to a particular item are considered within the reported "Percent 'Agreeing.'"

[8] http://www.acacamps.org/campmag/0701elkind.php.

[9] Although there was a trend to report more bullying for the first years than for attendance at camp for four or more years, this did not achieve statistical significance.

[10] http://www.acacamps.org/campmag/0609kids.php.

[11] See Joseph Reimer (in this volume) for similar recommendations regarding issues of "vision" for Ramah leadership.

References

Ackerman, W. I. 1999. Becoming Ramah. In *Ramah reflections at 50: Vision for a new century,* ed. S. A. Dorph, 3–24. New York: National Ramah Commission.

Benson, P. L. 2003. Developmental assets and asset-building community: Conceptual and empirical foundations. In *Developmental assets and asset-building communities: Implications for research, policy, and practice,* ed. R. M. Lerner and P. L. Benson, 19–46. New York: Kluwer.

Bialeschki, M. D., M. Schmid, and J. Tilley. 2006. The role of supportive relationships. *Camping Magazine,* http://www.acacamps.org/campmag/0609kids.php.

Dalton, J. H., M. J. Elias, and A. Wandersman. 2001. *Community psychology: Linking individuals and communities.* Stamford, CT: Wadsworth/Thomson Learning.

Eccles, J. S., and J. A. Gootman. 2002. *Community programs to promote youth development.* Washington, DC: National Academy Press.

Fox, S. 1989. Ramah: A setting for Jewish education. In *The Ramah experience: Community and commitment,* ed. S. C. Ettenberg and G. Rosenfield, 19–37. New York: The Jewish Theological Seminary and the National Ramah Commission.

Goleman, D. 1995. *Emotional intelligence.* New York: Bantam.

Kress, J. S., and J. Reimer. 2009. Shabbatonim as experiential education in the North American community day high school. In *Jewish schools, Jewish communities: A reconsideration,* ed. A. Pomson and H. Deitcher, 341–60. Oxford: Littman Library of Jewish Civilization.

Noddings, Nel. 1992. *The challenge to care in schools: An alternative approach to education.* New York: Teachers College Press.

Olweus, D. 1993. *Bullying at school.* Oxford: Blackwell.

Sales, A. L., and L. Saxe. 2004. *"How goodly are thy tents": Summer camps as Jewish socializing experiences.* Hanover: Brandeis University Press in association with the Avi Chai Foundation, published by University Press of New England.

Sarason, S. S. 1971. *The culture of schools and the problem of change.* Boston: Allyn and Bacon.

Walker, J., M. Marczak, D. Blyth, and L. Borden. 2005. Designing youth development programs: Toward a theory of developmental intentionality. In *Organized activities as contexts of development: Extracurricular activities, after-school and community programs,* ed. J. L. Mahoney, R. W. Larson, and J. S. Eccles, 399–418. Mahwah, NJ: Lawrence Erlbaum.

ZACHARY LASKER

The Education of Ramah Counselors: Madrichim as Educators and Learners

As campers, Samantha Platt and Michael Auerbach were full of energy, soaking up everything Camp Ramah offered. Michael was from Denver and loved singing and sports; Samantha, from Los Angeles, enjoyed theater and art. They both valued their friends and Shabbat. When the year arrived for them to join the staff, they applied to participate in the Ramah counselor leadership training program. In their first year as counselors, they were placed in a unit that I supervised, and I watched with pride as they developed valuable skills in problem solving, promoting Jewish education, public speaking, team work, and program design and assessment. In that summer, Samantha and Michael exceeded my expectations, impacting the lives of their campers, building positive relationships with fellow staff members, and asserting themselves as leaders.

Six years later I was a guest at Samantha and Michael's wedding, their relationship having been kindled at Camp Ramah. We all remain committed to the Jewish community where we serve as leaders. We all have grown, too. Samantha served two summers as a *rosh edah,* earned her Master's in education, and now teaches general studies at a Jewish day school. Michael stayed involved with Jewish life as an undergraduate at the University of Pennsylvania and is now in law school. After assuming my position as the assistant director at Camp Ramah in California, I continued to support and guide Samantha and Michael while settling into my career as a Jewish educator. Samantha and Michael could sense their growth during their summers as counselors, but were unaware that the same skills acquired then would be put to use in graduate school and as they began their family.

ZACHARY LASKER, *Ed.D., is the camp director of Camp Ramah in California. He holds a Masters in Education from the American Jewish University and completed doctoral studies in Education Leadership at the University of California, Los Angeles. His research examined the ways that Ramah counselors are trained, managed, and evaluated to serve as educators and role models for core Jewish values of the Conservative Movement.*

During the summer, teenagers and young adults like Samantha and Michael are presented with a plethora of options—summer school, jobs in the retail industry, internships, travel programs, and more. The decision to work as a counselor at Camp Ramah is a choice that yields compelling benefits to the individual and also strengthens the Jewish community and its leadership.

From their first day of training, Ramah counselors face the daunting responsibility of providing a summer experience for children that must be safe, fun, educational, and transformative. Parents send their children to Camp Ramah with the hope that they will grow in positive ways. Sometimes parents have a hard time letting go, whereas other times, children have a hard time being let go. After the children arrive at camp, a staff of counselors, specialty instructors, and administrators work hard to engage campers in a program that will be life altering.

In the Ramah environment, a great deal of responsibility is placed in the hands of counselors, often as young as eighteen, who serve *in loco parentis,* and who must draw on the same types of skills possessed by highly experienced parents, social workers, nurses, rabbis, cantors, and teachers so that campers return to their families and communities transformed into stronger individuals than they were before the start of the summer. The counselors themselves are another target population for Ramah administrators interested not only in the needs of the paying campers, but also in growing Jewishly literate young adults committed to the values of Conservative Judaism and prepared to impart those values to the next generation. Literature, research, and anecdotal evidence point to two goals that Ramah camps strive for, as well as the methods to ensure their attainment. The first goal is to train staff to serve as Jewish role models, caregivers, and educators for their campers. The second goal is to prepare these teenagers and young adults for a lifelong commitment to the development of Jewish youth, to education, and to continuity as a professional, volunteer, and/or parent.

Camp Ramah as an Agency of Jewish Education

Jewish residential camps serve as laboratories where young people live according to Jewish values independent from their parents' direct influence. According to ethnographic research, most Jewish camps have a focused mission rooted in Jewish education and fall short of success when the main focus of the program is on secular values and activities (Sales and Saxe 2004). Jewish camps are part of a framework of education known as "informal Jewish education" (Chazan 2002, 7). Often juxtaposed against the formal education that takes place in schools, Chazan defines informal Jewish education in the following manner:

> Informal Jewish education is aimed at the personal growth of Jews of all ages. It happens through the individual's actively experiencing a diversity of Jewish moments and values that are regarded as worthwhile. It works by creating venues, by developing a total educational culture, and by co-opting the social context. It is based on a curriculum of Jewish values and experiences that is presented in a dynamic and flexible manner. As an activity, it does not call for any one venue but may happen in a variety of settings. It evokes pleasurable feelings and memories. (15)

As an agent of informal Jewish education, Camp Ramah has a responsibility toward socialization and education. Reimer explains that the socializing experiences of informal Jewish education should aim "to have participants identify as Jews and enjoy the presence of other Jews . . ." (Reimer 2007, 5). This single goal is important but only half of the equation. Agencies also must focus on education, which Cremin defines as "the deliberate, systematic and sustained effort to transmit, evoke or acquire knowledge, attitudes, values, skills or sensibilities as well as any outcomes of that effort" (Cremin 1977, viii). Educationally, then, the goals of Sabbath observance at Ramah are not restricted to campers enjoying a nice communal experience, but also that they understand the ritual practices of the weekly holiday and commit themselves to future observance.

Camp Ramah is classified as an institution of informal Jewish education because of its commitment to inspire Jewish devotion in its constituents. Sales and Saxe explain, "The education theory of summer camping is . . . if children come to associate Jewish life with sweetness—the smell of pine trees, the closeness of friends, laughter in the bunk—what they practice and learn at camp will remain with them for a lifetime" (2004, 55). Therefore, camp educators take campers on a hike that emphasizes the Jewish value of *bal tashḥit* (not destroying natural resources) with the hope that their love for camp and communal living will transfer to a sense of obligation and interest in nature as Jewish environmentalists.

At Camp Ramah, counselors are expected to educate and socialize campers with a focus on the core values of Conservative Judaism. In the field of Jewish camping, Ramah camps are in fact distinguished by their serious commitment to informal Jewish education (Keysar and Kosmin 2004; Sales and Saxe 2002, 2004). The mission statement of Ramah declares its aim to

> create educating communities in which people learn to live committed Jewish lives, embodying the ideals of Conservative Judaism. Out of such communities, Ramah continues to "raise up" committed volunteer and professional leadership for the Conservative Movement and contemporary Jewry. (Dorph 2000, 336)

The mission then outlines specific Jewish values and practices including Jewish text and laws, prayer, Hebrew literacy, ritual observance, Zionism, and *tikkun olam* (social justice).

Ramah educators labor over the construction of objectives and the use of methods to infuse a knowledge of these values and practices into daily activities. Each camp differs slightly in the exact structure of the day, but all allot time for focused learning of the Hebrew language, various Jewish topics, and elements of Zionism with specialty instructors. Lessons are conducted with the same serious intent held by a classroom instructor, yet the room itself is without walls and next to a tree or lake (Sales and Saxe 2004). Throughout the day, counselors also are expected to use skills as Jewish educators when they approach *tefillot,* bunk activities, evening programming, and various other programs throughout the summer. Creativity and focus are vital attributes as camp professionals work hard to blend the natural resources and recreational activities with Jewish content so that learning is engaging and fun.

Research conducted by Dr. Ariela Keysar and Dr. Barry Kosmin between 1999 and 2004 demonstrates that Ramah camps successfully impart values through staff members to campers. Starting in the late 1990s, Drs. Keysar and Kosmin selected a cohort of 1,400 students about to become bar/bat mitzvah from various Conservative synagogues in North America, whose development into Jewish adulthood would be tracked. A follow-up study was conducted with these students in 2001 and 2004. Findings in 2001 indicated that individuals who attend Camp Ramah were ". . . more observant of Jewish ritual, more positive about Jewish and Zionist identity, more inclined to date and marry Jews, and more active in Jewish life on [college] campus" (Cohen 2004, 6; and this volume). By 2004, some of these individuals had spent at least one year as a camp counselor, and the findings on their commitment to Jewish values were even more encouraging. Indeed, placing Jewish young adults in the role of caregiver and educator for a younger generation not only strengthens the Jewish identity of the campers, but of the staff as well.

The Counselor: A Job Description

> "A good counselor is one who can show campers the meaning of their actions, choices, and mistakes, and who can relate them as a group, and as individuals, to the total camp happenings." (Ott 1946, 15)

At the core of the successful operation of Camp Ramah and entrusted with the health, safety, and growth of children, stands a young adult, usually between the ages of seventeen and twenty. Each summer, scores of counselors are hired to work with campers to ensure a safe, fun experience. In his study of college-age staff at Camp Ramah, Jeffrey Kress (2005 and this volume) identifies a variety of factors that are considered when a young adult decides to work at Camp Ramah, including the opportunity to be part of a Jewish community, spend time with friends, gain skills and/or experience, give back to Ramah, and so forth. When asked to identify the factors that are very important, 87 percent responded "it is an enjoyable experience," making it the most common motivating factor, whereas 73 percent responded "to be part of a Jewish community," and 56 percent "to gain skills and/or experience." Although camp directors adhere to a mission of training their counselors to be Jewish educators and role models, the counselors themselves do not always enter the working environment with the primary focus on these same goals.

At its most basic level, the job description for a counselor requires him or her to facilitate wake-up and bedtime procedures, monitor for proper hygiene, create and organize age-appropriate activities, and ensure camper safety, well-being, and happiness while at camp. To succeed, counselors must develop sharp skills in listening, observation, and problem solving (LaFave and Loughran 2001; Sales and Saxe 2004). Balancing their desire to be "a friend" and the expectation that they assume a more adult role like a parent or a teacher, counselors exert tremendous influence and often can transform a camper's summer into a positive and memorable experience or into an unfortunate emotional scab on the knee of childhood. Why are they so impactful? Simply stated, campers put their counselors on a pedestal that no "real adult" could ever reach.

> The camp counselor with a magnetic personality stands at the heart of the camp experience. Campers look up to, and often idolize, their counselors. Counselors have 'high status,' and their influence comes from both their words and their actions. They help shape the camp environment, create the social atmosphere that embraces campers, and provide examples of what campers can become in a few short years. What is so powerful about counselors' influence is that it is not limited to any single area or sphere of activity. Counselors provide guidance and modeling on questions as diverse as relationships, sports, . . . and how to dance. (Zeldin 2006, 89)

Being a counselor requires young adults to blend skills in parenting, teaching, and cheerleading. Counselors learn these skills quickly, contributing much to the summer program, and gaining from their experience on staff.

At Camp Ramah, the bunk counselor also is expected to educate and model according to the core values of Conservative Judaism. At Jewish residential summer camps, young adults not only check for brushed teeth, comfort the homesick, and cheer campers on during basketball games, but also might be called on to model Jewish values, use Hebrew vocabulary, lead prayers, and incorporate Jewish themes into their activities. To succeed, counselors must see themselves as Jewish educators and role models, committed to raising active, engaged Jews (Zeldin 2006). Therefore, these counselors themselves must be Jewishly literate with skills as educators that emphasize being active and participatory (Chazan 2002). This is a tremendous expectation. A Jewish exclamation states *dayyenu* (it would have been enough). To ask a young adult to care for their own needs—dayyenu! To ask a young adult to care for the needs of younger children—dayyenu! Ramah pushes further and requires young adults to care for the daily needs of younger children *and* to provide them with a Jewish education.

Educating Counselors: Developmental Issues

To fully understand the importance of the seventeen- to twenty-year-old cabin counselor population in the mission of Jewish summer camps, it is important to account for their developmental characteristics. Young adults in this age bracket often are referred to as "emerging adults." They use work as a genuine means to explore their identities, seeking to clarify their own values and career trajectory (Arnett 2004). Camp administrators must become familiar with their characteristics and commit to building on them in order to design a strong training program that supports their personal and professional development.

In their handbook, *Camp is for the Camper* (2000), Coutellier and Henchey apply well-known psychological milestones to advice for camp administrators regarding camp staff. Specifically, they explain that the seventeen- to twenty-year-old age range coincides with a shift in young adults, who reach a stage in their lives when they are ready to reach outside of themselves to lead and care for others in the world. Physically, they are sexually mature, focused on body image, and desirous of the adrenaline rush that comes from a feeling of accomplishment. Socially, they are prepared for independence beyond their immediate family and friends, searching for adult leadership roles, and ready to make and keep commitments. Emotionally, young adults seek respect, multiple involvements, and opportunities to make a positive impact on the world. Intellectually, they want to make occupational choices, express their opinions, develop marketable skills, solve problems, and expand their experiences. These characteristics make them ideal candidates for training in leadership and in the arts of caring for and educating others. However, because they are accepting this responsibility for the first time, room must be provided for trial and error, and scaffolding must be built to provide plenty of support. When properly supported, their characteristics also lead to their own identity formation as future leaders in the Jewish community.

Counselors: Educators for Campers

When Ramah directors and unit heads approach counselor training, they teach how to provide a fun, safe, Jewish educational experience for campers. Most professionals enter their field after a period of academic or technical training and with some work experience already under their belts. This is typically not the case for Ramah counselors entering their first summer as practitioners in youth education and development. Great responsibility is put on the counselors' shoulders, yet they have not obtained an academic degree nor have they attended a vocational school in preparation for their work. Therefore, the task of training counselors falls on the directors and unit heads of each camp in order to ensure campers are the recipients of outstanding care and a sound Jewish education during the summer. Proper training not only provides counselors with the tools they require if they want to succeed, but also motivates them to want to succeed. Fortunately, the American Camp Association, a community of camp professionals who have joined together to share knowledge and experience and to ensure the quality of camp programs, requires accredited camps to provide training to their staff members and holds each camp accountable to fill this requirement. The following are a few key types of training, supported by literature, which Ramah camps have adopted to ensure excellent staff:

Counselor-in-Training (C.I.T.) Programs. The most thorough form of staff training is a counselor-in-training program, such as the Mador Young Leadership Program at Camp Ramah in California. This opportunity provides first-year counselors interested in transitioning from camper to staff member with a period of training of eight weeks in length, ten hours a week. Participants attend workshops in leadership, communication, program design and evaluation, discipline, youth development, and Judaica. Experienced professionals also mentor them. This type of C.I.T. program has been found to elevate young people from camper to counselor and provide skills in activity areas, as well as in group living and successful personality development. Specifically, one researcher found that counselors who participated in a C.I.T. program were evaluated more highly in their: (1) attitude and understanding of camp philosophy, (2) possession and utilization of outdoor skills, (3) ability to adjust to situations in a resourceful manner, (4) ability to organize and plan camp programs, and (5) initiative and dependability in conducting programs and carrying out job responsibilities (House 1976, 29).

Staff Training Week. The American Camp Association (*Accreditation standards for camp programs and services* 1998) requires a minimum six-day training program for staff at accredited residential camps. In general, Ramah camps use the staff training week to acclimate the counselor to the Ramah setting, introduce them to summer colleagues, provide skills in youth development, discuss camp policy, facilitate some quantity of program planning, and provide instruction in Jewish content and education (Sales and Saxe 2004).

Parallel Training Workshops. Ramah camps continue to provide staff development while camp is in session so that counselors can evaluate and improve their skill set in action. Some camps require staff to participate in a *beit midrash* program, learning skills in Jewish text and liturgy. Others create workshops for counselors to advance their skills in youth development, leadership, Judaic studies, Hebrew language, and a variety of other areas.

Camp administrators hope that these opportunities, when utilized, enable them to produce young adults prepared to embrace their duties as educators.

To succeed, counselors who are seventeen to twenty years in age must be taught a mixture of pedagogic skills in experiential education, as well as the content they are charged to cover, while also inspired to try hard and work toward the Ramah mission. Based on his study of thirty-seven camps and ninety-seven outdoor education programs, Dr. Randall Grayson (2001), a psychologist who specializes in applying social, developmental, and organizational psychology to help camps better serve campers and staff, advises that good counselor training addresses knowledge, attitude, and behavior. In this context, *knowledge* is the actual content; a good counselor understands the skills or values he or she is trying to instill in his or her campers. A positive *attitude* indicates that the counselor's heart is appropriately focused and that he or she values the content to be imparted. *Behavior* encompasses the steps counselors must take to execute the skills or model the values of the camp in an educational manner. Pedagogic behavioral techniques might include games, races, simulations, art projects, acting, or any number of other recreational activities that can be used to teach skills. Here we think back to the characteristics of seventeen- to twenty-year-olds and are reminded that they are interested both in leadership roles and expressing their opinions. If they perceive a conflict between their own agenda and that of the camp, they will quickly lose focus. If there is alignment between their agenda and that of the camp, then successful education is quite conceivable.

Solid counselor education also leaves room for the staff member to experiment with trial and error. In a theoretical article on the training of C.I.T.s, Virginia Thompson (2000) underlines the importance of giving the young counselor opportunities to "1) *Do:* Lead the activity; 2) *Reflect:* Think about the results. What went right and what could be improved? 3) *Apply:* Lead the activity again applying what was learned the first time." Providing counselors

"A New Adventure in Summer Camping"

CAMP RAMAH

Operated by the New England Region

UNITED SYNAGOGUE OF AMERICA

In cooperation with the

TEACHERS INSTITUTE, JEWISH THEOLOGICAL SEMINARY OF AMERICA

Are You Getting the Most Out of Summer Camping for Your Son and Daughter?

"RAMAH" OFFERS THE PRIVILEGE OF A NEW AND THRILLING EXPERIENCE TO THOSE SELECTED!

"RAMAH" AIMS to bring out and develop the leadership qualities of boys and girls. Our purpose is to give them the finest physical facilities available, the best of food, the most outstanding staff possible and – most important of all – a wholesome positive approach to their religious heritage; a sense of pride in their people; a feeling of "at-home-ness" as secure American Jews.

TO THIS END, the program provides constructive recreational and educational opportunities in a wholesome and meaningful environment, under ideal summer camping conditions. The religious approach of Conservative Judaism pervades the spirit of the camp.

ADD TO THIS, the warm comforting comradeship of staff and campers who understand and love each other. Add further a spirit that, in the Jewish tradition, points a way of life, that makes happier boys and girls. Yes, it's an intangible spirit that will grow through the years – that makes firm lasting friendships and warm happy days. That is "RAMAH"; that is the "heights" to which we lift your boy and girl.

LEADERSHIP DOES IT – sympathetic, inspirational, vigorous leadership, in the presence of sheltering forests, the smell of flowers and pine, near murmuring brooks, and with fleecy white clouds overhead, racing across Maine's blue skies. Happiness, safety, and health, mingled with the joy of achievement, are among the aims of "RAMAH." The boys and girls find here the guidance and inspiration so important to them in their formative years.

"RAMAH" IS A GLORIOUS DEPARTURE FROM THE USUAL CAMPING EXPERIENCE!

"Ramah" is the Acme of Summer Living!

Maine Promotional flyer, 1948

ב

Wisconsin
RIGHT: c. 1950
BELOW: 2005

Rockies
2007

Israel Programs
TOP: Seminar, 2007
ABOVE LEFT: TRY, 2006
ABOVE RIGHT: Gluck dedication, 1994
LEFT: Jerusalem Day Camp, 2007

Nyack 1961

Chicago 2006

Philadelphia 2006

Nyack
2007

Summer 1947

Report on Camp Ramah in Wisconsin

by Henry R. Goldberg, Director

To evaluate the accomplishments of Camp Ramah, it is essential that we fully understand its philosophy and objectives. These were outlined to the Director by Dr. Moshe Davis on behalf of the Teachers Institute of the Jewish Theological Seminary and the Camp Committee as follows: Aware of the fact that the Conservative Movement should and must draw its future leaders from its own ranks, Camp Ramah should serve as a laboratory for preparing a select group of boys and girls for leadership in the American-Jewish community. . . .

Since we were interested in training leaders, the underlying thought was to bring out and develop those qualities in our boys and girls which would best prepare them for leadership. Hence, creative self expression was to be stressed throughout the program. The program, in order to make possible the development of the full personality of the camper, was to be all embracing and to include athletic, cultural, and purely formal educational activities. . . .

To what extent did we succeed in implementing the objectives of Camp Ramah? The writer believes that all who have had ample time to observe the camp in action and who were objective in their judgment would agree that despite the many handicaps under which we labored, we achieved many of the goals that we set up for ourselves. The enthusiasm for the camp on the part of the campers and their parents was beyond expectation. . . .

Darom
RIGHT: Dedication, 1997
BELOW: 2007

National Ramah Commission, 1959

New England
LEFT: 2005
BELOW: 1979

Connecticut
Chaim Potok, c. 1960

ח

Canada
RIGHT: 1960
BELOW: 2004

Ramah directorate, 1985

National Ramah Executive Committee, 1998

California
RIGHT: 2004
BELOW: c. 1967

Ramah directorate, 2007

Berkshires

ABOVE: 1977

RIGHT: 2006

NATIONAL RAMAH

of the United Synagogue of America operates the Ramah camps, a department

[illegible]
Past President
Louis Winer
President
M. Bernard [illegible]
Executive Director

October 16, 1963

Dear Friend:

Another camp has been added to the Ramah network! The new camp, Ramah in New York, is located in the beautiful Berkshire hills, some 80 miles from New York City.

For the past three seasons, we have been operating a camp at Nyack, New York, in order to meet pressing requests for increased service. We believe that our new camp will enable us to render far better service to your congregation.

Located in the thickly wooded Berkshire hills, the 200 acre property, formerly operated as Kee Wah Camps, is situated in Dutchess County on route 55, north of Wingdale, New York. The camp is complete, with three waterfronts on mile-long Lake Ellis, airy bunks with toilets and showers, more than adequate play areas (including concrete tennis courts, baseball diamonds, basket-ball courts, handball courts, volley ball courts, bowling alleys and a 9 hole golf course), a beautifully appointed dining hall, a first-rate infirmary and spacious grounds. This camp was selected after a Commission committee investigated more than 20 properties and sites. The photographs on the inside pages will help you see why we selected this camp.

Very shortly the director of the camp will be writing your congregation about ways in which children can be enrolled.

Meanwhile, please advise us immediately of your estimate of the number of places required for your congregations. You should start planning now to encourage your better students to attend our newest camp.

We look forward to your continued cooperation and help as Ramah continues to grow.

Sincerely yours,

Louis Winer

Louis Winer
President

Glen Spey
1971

Poconos
LEFT: c. 1965
BELOW: 2006

Ukraine
Camp Yachad, 2005

Founder
Professor Solomon Schechter

Honorary Presidents
Doctor Elias L. Solomon
Louis J. Moss

Honorary Vice-Presidents
Professor Louis Ginzberg
Sol Mutterperl

The United Synagogue of America

5080 BROADWAY, NEW YORK 27, N. Y.
Telephone Riverside 9-1000

Executive Director
Rabbi Albert I. Gordon

OFFICERS

President
Samuel Rothstein
Brooklyn

Vice-Presidents
[illegible]
Philadelphia

Hon. Emanuel Greenberg
Brooklyn

Hon. H. P. Kopplemann
Hartford

Benjamin Platt
Los Angeles

[illegible]
Chicago

Michael A. Stavitsky
Newark

Recording Secretary
[illegible]
Brooklyn

Treasurer
[illegible]
Pittsburgh

Financial Secretary
Benjamin Markowe
Brooklyn

Chairman of Finance Committee
[illegible]
New York

*

Educational Director
Dr. Abraham E. Millgram

Director of Youth Activities
[illegible]

Director, Department of Music
Cantor David J. Putterman

April 14, 1948

Dear Rabbi:

One camp is an experiment; two camps - a movement. We know that you will be as pleased to learn as we are pleased to announce the establishment of our second Hebrew camp. The new project will be called Camp Ramah in New England, and it is located on Long Lake in the heart of Southern Maine.

Camp Ramah in New England, like its model in Chicago, is sponsored by the New England region of United Synagogue in cooperation with the Teachers' Institute. Mr. Henry R. Goldberg, National Director of the Leadership Training Fellowship and Director of Camp Ramah in Wisconsin will also supervise the new project. We hope that you will read carefully the attached memorandum prepared by him and that you will act upon it without delay.

We feel certain that you will share our enthusiasm in this new development and that you will lend every effort to advance our work.

Sincerely yours,

Albert I. Gordon

Moshe Davis

1948 BIENNIAL CONVENTION

Thursday, May 13 to Monday, May 17 • Stevens Hotel, Chicago, Ill.

with this opportunity to practice their skills, immediately learn from their mistakes, and adjust their techniques keeps them motivated to succeed.

In Jewish residential camping, the biggest challenge facing staff trainers does not lie in providing pedagogical techniques, but in preparing a team of counselors who are themselves Jewishly literate. Michael Zeldin, a leader in the field of Jewish education and faculty member at Hebrew Union College, advocates for Jewish learning on the staff level for counselors "to have an impact on their Jewish development, and from the fact that they are the primary Jewish educators of the campers. The depth and breadth of campers' Jewish learning is a function of how well educated counselors are" (2006, 105). Ramah camps often benefit from counselors who were once Ramah campers and who come armed with a Jewish education from day school or supplemental school and the college campus. Still, not all counselors are prepared or willing to lead prayers, use Hebrew language, and incorporate biblical and rabbinic texts into activities. When the counselors are at camp for the week of staff training, most camp administrators feel pressured to address basic safety and policy concerns, often at the expense of strengthening Jewish literacy in staff. Judaica—the content of the Jewish educational program—is often placed lower on the to-do list during staff training (Sales and Saxe 2004). An eye (and ear) toward camper safety is key to Ramah remaining open, but the Jewish mission falls to the side if the counselors are unable to provide content through the activities they lead.

The optimists in the field align with Grayson (2001) and argue that instilling a positive attitude in a counselor to "pull out all the stops" and reach toward the Ramah mission will motivate counselors to acquire the content knowledge and pedagogic skills they need to succeed. Zeldin (2006), recognizing the teenage/young adult's desire to succeed, explains that a powerful motivator for adults is the challenge of accomplishing a task. Therefore, if Jewish learning is a necessary step to the educational work expected of them, they will approach their work with a strong motivation to learn. Building on counselors' desires to succeed, coupled with their often undying loyalty to Ramah, directors and unit heads have a solid chance of engaging counselors in education workshops and eliciting a strong effort from them.

Fortunately, camp administrators need not carry the weight by themselves of providing their staff with the Jewish education required to educate campers. Ramah counselors have attended either a private Jewish day school that offers a secular and Jewish education or a supplemental program that meets in the afternoon, evening, or weekend. Furthermore, once in college, counselors have access to academic courses in Jewish studies and Hebrew language. According to Kress (2005), two-thirds of Ramah counselors attended a supplemental Jewish school post-bar mitzvah or a Jewish day school in the elementary years, and one-third attended during the high school years. Once in college, half take courses in Hebrew language (or place out entirely), half take courses in Jewish studies, and 90 percent are involved in some manner with Hillel or a Jewish student union. Furthermore, once in college, half of counselors intend to study abroad in Israel for at least one semester, and roughly 90 percent have visited Israel at least once. Urging, or even requiring, counselors to take advantage of the off-season Jewish educational experiences will relieve camp administrators of the lonely task of educating counselors in Jewish content.

Counselors: Educators as Learners

At the same time that teenagers and young adults are being trained to counsel and educate their campers, their own skills and values are being formed. Quite simply, in the Ramah environment, the counselor is a camper in the eyes of the administrators who are invested in growing future professionals, parents, and lay leaders for the Jewish community. Once they have passed through the ranks as campers into staff positions, counselors continue to describe camp as their Jewish home. They can identify ways that Ramah continues to help them grow as young adults. One counselor shares: "Being a first-year counselor changed me. I took all my energy and channeled it into the right places. I felt so happy with the work I was doing and the impact I made on kids, whether through planning a program or leading a cheer." Another counselor stated, "I really felt like I matured through the training program. This summer was a real growth experience for me. I faced many challenges and acquired new skills." Indeed, some counselors are consciously aware of their continued development once on staff and recognize the ways in which their future direction is impacted through their work.

From a secular standpoint, research has shown that counselors can identify many positive outcomes of their employment at camp. In a study conducted by a team of researchers for the Association of Independent Camps to understand counselors' perceptions about the camp staff experience as expressed in their own words, a group of counselors revealed several positive personal and professional outcomes from their summer work: relationship-building with other staff members and campers, appreciation of diversity, interpersonal skills, leadership and responsibility, role modeling/mentoring, development of technical skills, personal growth, administrative skills, and skills in teamwork (Bialeschki, Henderson, and Dahowski 1998). Although a small percentage of counselors will enter into professional careers in the Jewish community, many will not. Fortunately, the benefits of work at Camp Ramah will serve these young adults as they navigate their course through life and settle into a variety of communities as professional or lay leaders.

Beyond general skills in youth development and teamwork, Jewish camps are committed to imparting Jewish skills and values to their staff members that stay with them past the summer experience. Keysar and Kosmin (2004) and Kress (2005) uncover a higher percentage of commitment to Jewish values in young adults who work at Camp Ramah than in those who either only attended as campers or never attended at all. This is seen in the way these counselors lead their adult lives during the off-season, as reviewed in other chapters in this volume. Although it is not fully clear from the statistical data whether Jewish camps attract counselors who come to the job with these values already, or whether Jewish camps ingrain these values in their counselors, many testimonials from counselors demonstrate that camp motivates the counselor to connect with Conservative Jewish values.

Fostering Counselor Growth

To ensure that counselors are growing throughout their summer experience, Ramah directors must provide a thoughtful structure of supervision and support. Healthy organizations implement a system for employee supervision that ensures productivity and holds the management team accountable for success. Jewish camps should be no different. In fact, the emerging counselor-educator is particularly in need of close and trusting supervision in this first job with high stakes. Supervision must ensure that campers receive proper care *and* that counselors are growing on both personal and professional levels. Thompson explains, "Directors of successful programs remember that counselors-in-training are teens, not adults; they are still practicing many skills. Providing a safe environment for teens to practice and receive feedback supports their growth" (Thompson 2000). In Ramah camps, counselors work in a unit by grade level and report directly to a unit head. These unit heads must be sure to observe the counselors in action and provide positive and constructive feedback from which the counselors can learn and grow on a regular basis. Unit heads must also conduct regular staff meetings, perhaps daily, during which a variety of issues are addressed ranging from the needs of certain individual campers to the plan of action for the evening activity. Facilitating this good communication enables staff to be well informed, set up to succeed, and reminds the unit head that young counselors are new to professional work as Jewish educators and role models and that they need close supervision.

Ramah camps will benefit greatly from taking the positive business approach of employee empowerment. In their book *Reframing Organizations,* professors Lee Bolman and Terrence Deal (2003) speak to the importance of attending to the needs of an organization's human resources. Three of their teachings particularly stand out as applicable for counselor supervision and support. The first is their discussion of Douglas McGregor's "Theory X and Theory Y" view of employee attitudes. Whereas Theory X presupposes that employees are lazy, lack ambition, and are resistant to change, Theory Y suggests that a strong management team will manipulate the working environment so that employee goals can be realized through contributions to the organization. In the case of camp, supervisors must be careful to avoid adopting the negative attitude that counselors are lazy teenagers who are in camp just to relax and have fun with their friends. Instead, they must realize the interests of their counselors and incorporate them in the job. If counselors are interested in athletics, for example, supervisors should urge them to teach teamwork, physical fitness, and Hebrew language through a cabin relay race with Hebrew terms.

Camp administrators must treat their counselors as an investment worthy of constant care and attention, which is a second recommendation supported by Bolman and Deal who state, "The human resource-oriented organization also recognizes that learning must occur on the job as well as in the classroom" (142). As noted, many camps try hard to provide much of the staff training during the week before the campers arrive; however, they also must ensure that learning occurs throughout the summer season so that counselors can constantly evaluate and enhance their skills. An alternate model was developed by the directors of Camp Ramah in Wisconsin who designed a community internship program, allowing counselors work experience in a variety of non-camp related fields, as well as on staff at Ramah. Counselors participate as interns in various fields (e.g., law, medicine, business) while engaging in Jewish learning and then move to camp for the second part of the summer. This is a great example of investing in staff, and Ramah directors should continue to think creatively. (Similar programs exist at other Ramah camps.)

The third lesson for camp supervisors from Bolman and Deal focuses on the importance of empowering employees. Camp administrators who are truly committed to raising counselors invested in Jewish camps and the larger Jewish community must empower them to take initiative and adopt leadership roles within the organization. To do this includes "making information available . . . encouraging autonomy and participation, redesigning work, fostering teams, promoting egalitarianism, and giving work meaning" (143). Most seventeen- to twenty-year-old counselors who take on work as summer camp counselors come armed with enthusiasm and ideas about how to create an awesome summer experience. Supervisors must empower these counselors to be effective by taking into account Bolman and Deal's suggestions. Giving counselors space to bring forward their own ideas as educators enables them to feel proud of their own work. For example, the Ramah camps in Nyack, Wisconsin, and California run a grant program aimed at funding original, Jewish programming ideas of their summer staff. Involving them in managing the community also will prepare them for future leadership roles in the Jewish community as adults. This, too, is seen at Camp Ramah in California, where counselors can sit on "pre-summer committees," examining an area of camp in need of improvement and designing solutions.

Camp administrators also must focus on retention so that Ramah counselors return from one summer to the next while still in college. Based on their findings, Keysar and Kosmin (2004) conclude that staff retention during the college years is key to a counselor's identity formation. "It creates an alternative membership peer culture to that found on the campus. It provides a second and sometimes primary reference group that offers alternative values and social standards to which they can aspire as Jews" (38). To retain their staff during the college years, Ramah directors must develop methods of communication to stay in touch with their staff in the off season, package camp employment opportunities in a manner competitive to other summer employment opportunities (internships, money makers, etc.), provide new challenges for the staff during the summer experience, and in general, make the staff feel invested in the community. When retention is successfully accomplished, Jewish summer camps will be able to affect the Jewish identity of their counselors for the benefit of the Jewish community.

The Chicken or the Egg

The research on Camp Ramah and the broader field of Jewish camping indicates that the impact of the counselor on the camper and the camp on the counselor are positive, but requires more support. The views expressed by experts in the industry outline a number of important factors for Ramah directors to take into account, but must be formally tested. This helps to determine the precise areas of counselor training that require the most attention, as well as the methods for trainers to employ. The findings from the two main studies referenced certainly demonstrate that individuals who work as counselors at Camp Ramah have stronger connections to Jewish values and skills than those who do not. However, it is still unclear as to the exact degree to which the summer camp shapes this identity. Although there are individual testimonials attributing strong identity to summer employment at camp, this area of research would benefit from a study that tracks a cohort of counselors from one summer to the next, assessing their skills and values immediately before and after the season.

Conclusion

Jewish residential summer camps are a haven for educators, as they are filled with children and young adults excited and eager to meet new people and grow their skills and values. Camp Ramah in particular keeps education at the heart of its mission, in the hope of raising future leaders for the Jewish community. The primary educator in the Ramah environment is a young adult aged seventeen to twenty years old. To succeed in educating campers, counselors require proper training in the areas of youth development, experiential pedagogy, and Jewish content. When successfully trained and properly supervised, these counselors can make a lifelong impact on their campers. Further, when successfully trained and supervised, the counselors themselves grow a set of skills and values that prepares them for a lifetime commitment to Jewish living as professionals, participants, parents, and/or lay leaders.

References

Accreditation standards for camp programs and services. 1998. Martinsville, IN: American Camp Association.

Arnett, J. J. 2004. *Emerging adulthood : The winding road from the late teens through the twenties.* New York: Oxford University Press.

Bialeschki, M. D., K. A. Henderson, and K. Dahowski. 1998. Camp gives staff a world of good. *Camping Magazine* 71 (4): 27–31.

Bolman, L. G., and T. E. Deal. 2003. *Reframing organizations: Artistry, choice, and leadership.* San Francisco: Jossey-Bass.

Chazan, B. 2002. The philosophy of informal Jewish education, http://www.infed.org/informaljewisheducation/informal_jewish_education.htm (accessed December 2002).

Cohen, M. 2004. *Research findings on the impact of Camp Ramah.* New York: Jewish Theological Seminary.

Coutellier, C., and K. Henchey. 2000. *Camp is for the camper: A counselor's guide to youth development.* Martinsville, IN: American Camping Association.

Cremin, L. A. 1977. *Traditions of American education.* New York: Basic Books.

Dorph, S. A. 2000. *Ramah reflections at 50: Visions for a new century.* New York: National Ramah Commission.

Grayson, R. 2001. Staff training best practices. *Camping Magazine* 74 (6): 40.

House, K. L. 1976. *A comparison in effectiveness of camp counselors who have participated in a counselor-in-training program with camp counselors who have not.* Eugene, OR: University of Oregon.

Keysar, A., and B. Kosmin. 2001. *The camping experience 1995–1999: The impact of Jewish summer camping on the Conservative high school seniors of the "Four up" study.* New York: National Ramah Commission.

———. 2004. *Research findings on the impact of Camp Ramah.* New York: National Ramah Commission.

Kress, J. S. 2005. *Campus and camp: A descriptive report of college-age staff at Camp Ramah.* New York: Jewish Theological Seminary.

LaFave, R., and S. B. Loughran. 2001. Training camp counselors as leaders: Course helps counselors earn college credit. *Camping Magazine* 74 (2): 36–39.

Ott, E. F. 1946. *So you want to be a camp counselor.* New York: Associated Press.

Reimer, J. 2007. Beyond more Jews doing Jewish: Clarifying the goals of informal Jewish education. *Journal of Jewish Education* 73 (1): 5–23.

Sales, A. L., and L. Saxe. 2002. *Limud by the lake: Fulfilling the educational potential of Jewish summer camps.* New York: Avi Chai Foundation, CMJS.

———. 2004. *"How goodly are thy tents": Summer camps as Jewish socializing experiences.* Hanover, NH: University Press of New England.

Thompson, V. 2000. CITs are campers in transition. *Camping Magazine* 73, no. 4 (July–August), http://www.acacamps.org/members/knowledge/leadership/cm/007CIT.php.

Zeldin, M. 2006. Making the magic in Reform Jewish summer camp. In *A place of our own: The rise of Reform Jewish camping,* ed. M. M. Lorge and G. P. Zola, 85–116. Tuscaloosa: University of Alabama Press.

NANCY B. SCHEFF

Romance at Ramah: Six Decades of Ramah Marriages

THE RAMAH LEADERSHIP has always known that there are hundreds of married couples who met at Ramah. For years, individual Ramah camps have reached out to couples who met at camp. One of the walls in the *ḥadar ochel* at Camp Ramah in the Berkshires is covered with plaques inscribed with the names of the couples who met at camp. Similarly, Ramah Poconos has a *gazebo zugot* (couples gazebo). Convinced of the commonalities of the emotions and factors that lead to Ramah marriages, the leadership of the National Ramah Commission (NRC) began the first national outreach effort in the spring of 2005 to document the stories of these Ramah couples. We created a website at www.ramahmarriages.org and sent e-mail messages requesting that couples register and "spread the word" to other Ramah couples. At that time, we had no idea how much interest this project would generate.

As of this writing, 312 couples have registered on the Ramah marriages website. Although we believe that these 312 couples represent only a small fraction of the total number of Ramah marriages, the fact that so many couples have registered indicates the strong interest in this project as a movement-wide effort. The Ramah marriages webpage on the NRC website receives by far the most hits of any page on the site. As we conducted our e-mail publicity for the Ramah sixtieth anniversary celebration in 2007, we were amazed to see how many couples registered after each wave of publicity. This national project has supported the alumni outreach efforts of the individual camps. In fact, many alumni first reconnect with Ramah by registering on the Ramah marriages website; after a couple registers, the National Ramah office forwards alumni contact information to the couple's home camp(s).

The Ramah marriages project has captured the attention of Ramah alumni and staff across all camps and Ramah programs. We are fascinated by

NANCY B. SCHEFF *is the communications director of the National Ramah Commission and the public relations director of Ramah Day Camp in Nyack.*

how excited people become when they talk about Ramah marriages, and by how much they enjoy reading these stories. Why is it that the Ramah marriages project has become such a hot topic within the Ramah Camping Movement? We believe that the excitement is generated by a sense that these marriages represent an important contribution to the future of the Jewish people. Jewish camping is known to be one of the most powerful means of strengthening Jewish identity.[1] Further, researchers have documented the effect of Ramah's approach to informal Jewish education on the Jewish practices and attitudes of Conservative Jewish youth.[2] Given that Jewish marriage is viewed as one of the most important indicators of Jewish continuity, the large number of marriages that have grown out of shared Ramah experiences is additional evidence of the impact of the Ramah Camping Movement on generations to come.

An Overview of Ramah Couples

Couples have met at all of the Ramah overnight camps; they have met at Ramah Israel programs, at National Ramah staff training programs, and at alumni reunions. Marriage partners who met through Ramah friends or connections write to us, requesting to be included as a Ramah couple, even though they technically did not meet at a Ramah program. Ramah marriages have taken place in every decade following the establishment of Camp Ramah in 1947. The following table lists the number of marriages reported in each of these decades.

Marriages reported, by decades

DECADE MARRIED	NUMBER OF COUPLES REGISTERED ON RAMAH MARRIAGES WEBSITE
1950s	15
1960s	36
1970s	54
1980s	53
1990s	74
2000s	80
Total	**312**

Of the 301 couples who reported how many years the spouses spent at Ramah as campers or staff members, there were 159 couples in which at least one spouse had been at a Ramah camp for ten or more years and sixty-seven couples in which both spouses spent ten or more years at Ramah. Of the 301 couples who reported how the spouses met, 187 met when both were on staff, with an average of 4.3 years from the year they met until the year they married. Eighty-three couples met when both were campers, with an average of 10.9 years from the time they met to the time they married; and twenty-eight first met when one was a camper and one was on staff, with an average 7.5 years from the year they met until the year they married.

Shared Values and Jewish Identity

Many Ramah couples speak of the importance of the values the spouses share and of the role of shared values in creating a strong foundation for marriage. Jeffrey Tigay got to know his wife, Helene Zubkoff Tigay, at Ramah Poconos in 1963 after they had briefly met as students at The Jewish Theological Seminary (JTS). He writes, "the shared values that brought us [to Ramah] enabled our relationship to blossom much more rapidly than would have been possible in a different environment. It is one of the many things for which we are eternally grateful to Camp Ramah." The Tigays were married in 1965.

Jonathan Kremer and Ellen Helfman Kremer first met on Israel Seminar in 1970, then lost touch until meeting again years later. Jonathan writes, "Ramah in Wisconsin, Ontario, the Berkshires, and on Seminar gave me a love for Shabbat, Israeli dancing, and the best [that] Conservative Judaism has to offer. I knew that I wanted to live Ramah 24/7. When I re-met [Ellen] while Israeli dancing at MIT, shared values and experience led to love and marriage." The Kremers have been married since 1980.

Not only do couples describe the shared values that brought them to Ramah, but they also describe the influence of Ramah on shaping their Jewish identities. Richard Gavatin met his future wife, Linda Spitzer Gavatin, on Israel Seminar "in the magical summer of 1968," when they were both fifteen. Richard writes that his Ramah summer played a critical role in determining his sense of self as a Jew:

> There were two kids from Sweden. I was one of them. I met the girl who became my wife then. . . . How important for my sense of belonging was Camp Ramah? Immeasurable. No words can adequately describe the role of that summer in my commitment to Judaism. It was the turning point for me and without that summer at Camp Ramah, I would most likely have gone the way most young European Jews go: into assimilation. . . . Thanks to Camp Ramah I survived as a Jewish person!

David Cutler met Rachel Fish at Ramah New England. They were married in 2004 and write:

> Ramah helped shape both of our Jewish identities and solidified our relationships to Judaism. The Ramah experience fostered an environment of

> Jewish learning, questioning, growth, and love of Zionism, all of which play a major role in our lives as individuals and as a married couple. [We are] confident that our Ramah "upbringing" will influence our lives for years to come.

Shari Berman Kalter and Noah Kalter met at Ramah Day Camp in Nyack in 1998. Shari writes about experiencing Judaism with Noah at Ramah and the impact that Ramah has had on her life:

> Camp gave us a chance to be together in a unique Jewish environment and have an amazing summer at the same time.... Camp Ramah was/is a large Jewish influence in my life and meeting my husband and my friends there only adds to that amazing camp experience.

Another common theme of Ramah marriage stories is that couples developed strong friendships as a basis for their connections prior to developing romantic relationships. Guy Alberga and Beverley Moskovic Alberga met as staff members at Camp Ramah in Canada in 1981 but did not marry until a decade later. Guy writes:

> Bev and I became good friends while teaching swimming together over two wonderful summers. While we never dated at camp, when we finally decided to get together we had so much in common through our experience at Ramah and knew so many of the same people that we never had to struggle through that awkward first date. In fact, it was more like old friends rekindling a friendship. Our Ramah experience brought us closer together.

Jami Datnow Rosenthal and Adam Rosenthal first met at Ramah California in 1988 when they were nine years old. They write that they were long-time friends and pen pals, "and had crushes on each other off and on. . . . Years later, when we were in college, we returned to camp as Tikvah (now Amitzim) counselors, fell in love, and have not been apart since."

Jeff Blum and Cindy Goldfarb Blum of Camp Ramah in the Poconos tell a similar story. They met in 1966 and were married in 1975. They write:

> The camp environment fostered natural and comfortable friendships across genders. This allowed us to become friends first—then, many years later—lovers, all within the context of Jewish values, living as respectful and moral people. Our relationship is built on this foundation and has sustained us for over thirty years of marriage. Not only as best friends to each other, we have retained our camp friends and other Ramahniks as the people we feel most connected to in our lives.

Of course, it doesn't necessarily take a decade for friendships to lead to marriage. Vanessa Ivey and Jonathan Stein met at Camp Ramah Darom in 2002 and were married in 2006. According to Vanessa:

> I became friends with Jonathan (a year older) because his younger sister was going to be a camper in my edah. . . . Our friendship grew once the campers arrived because Jonathan came to see his sister a lot. The first Shabbat evening, he asked me to spend some time with him. We sat at the campfire circle and talked all night. From there, our friendship grew into dating.

Ramah Couples in Israel

At Ramah, Israel programming and the presence of the *mishlaḥat* are designed to encourage Zionism and strengthen campers' and staff members' connections to Israel. Twenty-five of the couples registered on the Ramah marriages website now live in Israel. Jonathan Rimon (formerly David Milgram) and Wendy Wolman Rimon write, "Our summers in Ramah provided our shared foundation of Jewish values and planted the Zionist seeds." They met as staff children at Ramah Poconos in 1961. Jonathan's family made aliyah in 1971, and Wendy made aliyah in 1974; the couple was married in 1975.

Josh Kulp and Julie Zuckerman began dating in Israel during the summer of 1995 when they were both group leaders for Ramah Seminar. They write:

> We had led fairly parallel Ramah and USY "careers" until then, both serving as *rashei edah* at our respective camps (New England—Julie; Poconos and then, Canada—Josh). We spent a lot of time together during the staff Shabbaton before Seminar and went out on our first official date on that *motza'ei Shabbat.* By the time Seminar officially started, we were already an item, and despite being in different *ḥativot* [groups], we managed to see plenty of each other. The campers only found out in the last week or so. We got engaged a few months later, and we've been living happily in Israel ever since!

Jewish Continuity and the Multi-Generational Ramah Family

The positive impact that Ramah has had on Jewish continuity and future generations of Jews is another universal theme of Ramah marriage stories. Michael Katz and Betsy Dolgin Katz met as staff members at Ramah Wisconsin in 1960. They, too, speak of the powerful effect that Ramah had on the Jewish life of their family:

> In camp we shared our love of Judaism and of children. We imagined together the kind of life we wanted to lead. . . . Jewish living, Jewish learning, and Israel remain an important part of our life and that of our children up until today.

We have received many stories from those who consider themselves to be "true Ramah families" with two generations—and in some cases, three generations—of Ramahniks attending multiple Ramah camps. Stanley Platek and Celia Silverstein Platek met at Camp Ramah in Connecticut in 1954 and married in 1957. Celia writes,

> We were staff members in Ramah Connecticut, Poconos, Nyack, and Berkshires for eighteen consecutive years. All of our children went to Ramah from infancy until they were staff members themselves. Now our grandchildren go to Ramah Berkshires. We are truly a Ramah family.

Happiness shines through the words of Ramah couples who send their own children to Ramah. Larry Pepper and Dana Yugend-Pepper met at Ramah Wisconsin in 1974 and were married in 1983. Larry writes that he and Dana

> had our favorite spots around camp where we would walk and talk. There was a tree on Nivonim hill that had a hollowed-out spot in it where we used to leave love notes for each other. . . . Now, going back to camp as parents, and seeing our daughter so happy there, where we were so happy, is very powerful.

Jon Gutstein and Susan Mack Gutstein also met at Ramah Wisconsin. They were friends throughout high school and college and married in 1992, sixteen years after they first met. Susan writes:

> Ramah has always held a special place in our hearts and the fact that we can say that we originally met there makes it even more special. We have two kids who have been going to Ramah Day Camp, and now my son is in his first summer at Ramah in Wisconsin. Hopefully, next summer my daughter will enjoy her first summer there. Another very special fact is that my son is now a third-generation camper at Ramah in Wisconsin, as my dad went there as a camper the first year the camp started.

Some of the more recently married Ramah couples, looking toward the future, eagerly anticipate the time for their own children to go to Ramah. Jeffrey Arnowitz and Tamar Brendzel Arnowitz met at Ramah Berkshires in 1995 and wed in 1999. They write, "The ideals and values that brought us to Ramah provided a great starting point for a marriage that lives with those same values. We love Ramah and can't wait to send our children." Like Jeffrey and Tamar, Matthew Seltzer and Stacy Lipschutz Seltzer, who met at Ramah Poconos in 2002, want to continue the Ramah tradition for their families:

> The Ramah community fostered our relationship by allowing us to discover just how many core values we share and opened our eyes to what our lives together could create. We could not have met at a more magical place than Ramah, and we look forward to sending our future children to this wonderful place.

Engagements, Weddings, and *Sheva Berachot*

Several of the most touching Ramah marriage stories are from Ramahniks who became engaged "on location" at their Ramah camps. Eric Weinstein and Sarah Klagsbrun met as staff members at Ramah Berkshires in 1987 but did not begin dating until years later. Six months after their first official date, they went to an alumni event at camp. Eric reports that on that day:

> [W]e were engaged at camp. . . . I asked my old waterfront buddy, Mark Neustadt, to park a boat with the ring in it by "the rock" across the lake. I nervously swam out with Sarah, we got into the boat, and I returned home with my fiancée.

Michael Small and Sheila Berk Small met at Ramah Wisconsin in 1985 and became engaged there in 1988:

> Being at camp let us discover that we had similar values, interests, and a love for Jewish life. . . . Three years after we met, we became engaged on the *mirpeset* [porch] of the *sifriyyah* [library], looking at the stars reflected on the mirror-smooth surface of Lake Buckatabon.

Numerous couples describe with delight the Ramah *ruaḥ* (spirit) that was present at their weddings and tell of the numerous Ramah alumni who attended their weddings as officiants, guests, and members of the wedding party. When reading these stories, one can imagine the Ramah feel of these weddings, as well as the emotional connection that Ramah couples have with Ramah. Jennie Goldress and Andrew Eisenberger, who attended Ramah Berkshires and were married in 1996, write, "We sang *Rad hayom* at the end of our wedding with all of our camp friends linked arm in arm."

Jonas Goldberg and Chelly Gilgore Goldberg, who spent their summers at Camp Ramah in the Poconos, were married in 1963. They report, "We even made a 'deal' with David Mogilner, *z"l,* that we would move our wedding date up to the beginning of June in order to spend the summer of 1963 at camp. David [Mogilner] and Alex Shapiro, *z"l,* were two of the rabbis under our *ḥuppah.*"

Alan Kaell and Diana Schachter Kaell met while they were on Israel Seminar in 1970 and then worked as counselors at Ramah Wisconsin during the summer of 1972. They were married in 1975 by Rabbi Burton Cohen, who had been the director of Ramah Wisconsin when they were counselors. And Jami and Adam Rosenthal of Ramah California describe how "Rabbi Reuven Taff, whom we have known for years from Ramah (he was *rosh musikah*), officiated at our wedding and there were many fellow Ramahniks there to celebrate with us."

Although hundreds of marriages are listed on the Ramah website, to date the list includes only two weddings that actually took place at a Ramah camp. In 1957, Moshe Tutnauer and Margie Weingarden Tutnauer were married at Ramah Wisconsin. They report that:

> Jerry Abrams, [Wisconsin] Ramah director, was our *mesadder kiddushin* [officiant]. . . . Our wedding was followed by the closing banquet/wedding dinner attended by 500 campers and 200 staff. The singing and dancing in the *ḥadar ochel* were not to be believed!

More than three decades later, in 2001, Daniel and Ronna Mink were married at Camp Ramah in Canada. This description of their wedding, told in the third person, paints a vivid picture of the setting in the woods of Muskoka in Ontario:

> They had a shtetl-like wedding in the woods, where the groom harvested young maple saplings for *ḥuppah* poles and used his great-grandfather's *tallit* as a canopy. . . . The bride hand-lettered two traditionally composed *ketubbot* (just in case of breakage) on clay tablets and fired them in a kiln. She also hand-built two clay wine goblets (to be placed on the table) and glazed them with the words *dodi li*. . . . [The] glass that was broken was the light bulb from the woodshop, wrapped in a beautiful piece of silk. More than a dozen [members of the] *mishlaḥat* [joined in] on the way to the woods site, and staff members sang Israeli songs as everyone rejoiced.

Although only a small number of weddings have actually taken place at camp, there are numerous couples who have celebrated an *ofruf* or sheva berachot at camp. For couples with late summer weddings, Ramah was the ideal place for an ofruf. Bruce Bromberg Seltzer and Deborah Bromberg Seltzer, New England Ramahniks, "got married at the end of August [1995], our wedding date set so we could spend that summer at camp. . . . We had an ofruf at camp and got married the weekend after camp ended." David Krohn and Risa Rosenbaum Krohn believe that they were fated to meet in 1971 at Ramah Glen Spey after their original summer plans fell through. David reports:

> We had made plans separately to be [on] staff at Palmer. When Palmer closed [for one summer] that year, we were both arbitrarily assigned to Glen Spey. (Who believes in "arbitrary"? We both believe it was the hand of God directing us to each other.) We met staff week and decided within two weeks that we would marry. We attended Palmer together the following year where I had my *ofruf* the last Shabbat of the camp year.

And, of course, there are those Ramah couples who visit camp right after getting married. Ralph Dalin and Hedy Loeb Dalin met at Ramah California in 1965 at the age of twelve and were married in 1972. They write, "On the

Shabbat following our wedding, we celebrated sheva berachot back at Ramah in Ojai." Around the same time, Leora Weinstein Isaacs and Ron Isaacs met as counselors at Camp Ramah in Glen Spey, and they celebrated sheva berachot there after their 1971 wedding.

"Double and Triple" Ramah Marriage Families

Ivan Marcus and Judy Lefkowitz Marcus met at Camp Ramah in Connecticut and are one of several multi-generational Ramah families registered on the website in which both parents and children are in Ramah marriages. Judy, a long-time Ramah Berkshires board member, has worked at the Ramah camps in Connecticut, Berkshires, Glen Spey, and Poconos. She writes with great pride:

> How wonderful to be claimed by more than one Ramah! Ivan and I spent our camping years at Connecticut where we were in the same edah but went out with others. We started going out together in Nyack the year it opened in 1961 and continued to see each other in Connecticut in 1962 before getting married in 1964. . . . All four of our children went to Nyack and Berkshires. Two of our children met . . . their spouses at Berkshires. Yuval, our oldest, met his wife Liz at one of the Berkshires Alumni Labor Day Weekends. They have three children, two of whom have already attended Nyack.

There are at least two other families that can claim three Ramah marriages. Wendy Wish Rosenthal, a staff member at Ramah California for more than thirty-five years, first met her husband Allan Rosenthal in 1965. They married in 1973. They are the parents of Adam Rosenthal (Jamie Datnow), whose story appears earlier in this chapter. In addition, Wendy and Allan's son Jeremy met his wife, Gwen Shelden, in 1998 when they were both *rashei edah* at Ramah California. Hal Spevack and his wife, Harriet Greenfader Spevack, met at Camp Ramah in the Berkshires in 1966. After getting married, they worked as staff members at Ramah Nyack, where their son Daniel was a camper at the same time as his future wife, Liz Arnold Spevack. Daniel and Liz, following in Hal and Harriet's footsteps, fell in love at Ramah Berkshires; they were married in 1996. In addition, Hal's cousin, Judy Spevack Marpet, met her husband, Mark Marpet, at Ramah Nyack.

The list of multi-generational Ramah marriages is a lengthy one. Norman Beitner and Ruth Lipnik Beitner met at Camp Ramah in Canada and got married in 1977; their son, Aaron, met his future wife, Marci Orman, at Ramah Canada in 1995. Steven Glazer met his wife, Andrea Soff Glazer, at Ramah Connecticut in 1962. After a two-day honeymoon in 1965, the Glazers spent the summer on staff at Camp Ramah in New England, where three decades later, their son, Ari, met his wife, Stephanie Goldberg Glazer. Ari leads off his own Ramah marriage story with the words, "I am a second-generation Ramah marriage."

Shira Milgrom and David Elcott met as staff members at Camp Ramah in California and married in 1973. According to Shira, "We shared the values of Camp Ramah about what Jewish life can be—and gave that to our children who also experienced Camp Ramah and other similar Jewish experiences. In fact, Yaron met his wife, Miriam [Sheinbein], at Camp Ramah and married exactly thirty years later."

Conclusion

We hope that this chapter inspires readers to visit www.ramahmarriages.org to enjoy the wonderful stories of Ramah couples throughout the world and to encourage other Ramah couples to register. The number of campers and staff members in the Ramah Camping Movement continues to grow annually, so it is certain that there will be many more Ramah marriages in the future.

As we enter the next decade and prepare for the opening of Ramah in the Rockies, we are reminded that each camp has its very own "first Ramah marriage." There is only one such marriage clearly documented on our website, from Camp Ramah Darom. Jason Cathcart and Vicki Sykes Cathcart met at Ramah Darom when the camp first opened in 1997 and were married in 2000. Jason and Vicki write, "We are both happy that Ramah decided to open a camp in the South. We will always be known as Darom's first married couple. We are grateful for the friendships, knowledge, and support Ramah has given us over the past years."

We look forward to posting many more Ramah marriages on our website in the years to come.

Notes

[1] A. L. Sales and L. Saxe, *"How Goodly Are Thy Tents": Summer Camps as Jewish Socializing Experiences* (Hanover, NH: Brandeis University Press, 2003).

[2] A. Keysar and B. Kosmin, *The Camping Experience 1995–1999: The Impact of Jewish Summer Camping on the Conservative High School Seniors of the "Four Up" Study* (New York: National Ramah Commission, 2001).

YAARA SHTEINHART-MOGHADAM AND **JEFFREY S. KRESS**

The Ramah Experience and the Religious Attitudes and Behaviors of Sheliḥim

Introduction

EACH SUMMER, without ever boarding an airplane, thousands of North American youth spend their summers living and working with Israelis. Ramah camps, along with many other Jewish educational summer camps, welcome a cadre of *sheliḥim* to their communities each summer. *Sheliḥut,* as explained by the Jewish Agency Web site, is considered to be collaboration between the state of Israel and American Jewry.

> The Israeli *shaliaḥ* is in fact an Israeli "ambassador." With activities and educational aids that he or she brings from Israel, such as posters, music, photographs, stories, and games, the shaliaḥ creates an Israeli atmosphere at camp and inspires the campers' love for Israel. . . . [I]n this environment, the campers and staff learn about life in Israel and its current culture and see the shaliaḥ as the face of Israel.[1]

The sheliḥim are invited to camp to serve as representatives of Israel to global Jewish communities and to be a cultural link between the two. The shaliaḥ's agenda includes education about Israel and Zionism. Sheliḥim bring to camp Hebrew language and a representation of an Israeli way of life. Their customs and personal life narratives are seen as connecting the campers to Israel in everyday *pe'ulot* at camp.

YAARA SHTEINHART-MOGHADAM *is a doctoral candidate at the William Davidson Graduate School of Jewish Education of The Jewish Theological Seminary. Her dissertation examines how Jewish museums conceptualize, promote, and conduct programs for students in Jewish schools.*

JEFFREY S. KRESS, *Ph.D., is an associate professor of Jewish Education and a senior research assistant at the William Davidson Graduate School of Jewish Education of The Jewish Theological Seminary. He also coordinates the school's concentration in Informal and Communal Jewish Education. Dr. Kress was recently appointed as the chair of the Network for Research in Jewish Education. He attended Ramah Berkshires in 1984 and from 1986 to 1989 and participated in the Ramah Israel Seminar in 1985.*

Being a shaliaḥ who represents Israel abroad is considered a prestigious and sought-after position by many Israelis. It is offered as an honor to soldiers and veterans and opens a path to hold other official and governmental positions in the future. Sheliḥim come from a wide spectrum of Israeli society—from a variety of socioeconomic and religious backgrounds. They are chosen based on previous experience as youth leaders or as educational staff in the army and by their professional background in various arts and sports. Approximately one thousand sheliḥim undergo training by the Jewish Agency, during which sheliḥim from all affiliations are gathered for orientation about life at camp and are assigned to the specific camp they will attend. The sheliḥim attend sessions about North American culture, Jewish life in North America, general information for expectations of camp life, and educational tools. Those who will attend Ramah camps also experience a "Conservative-style" Shabbat. For some sheliḥim, this is the first time they celebrate and observe Shabbat; for others, this experience of Shabbat is quite different from their previous traditions.

Prior to arrival at camp, the sheliḥim are assigned to be either educational/specialty staff or counselors. Educational/specialty staff members teach music, arts, drama, folk dance, sports, photography, camping, Hebrew, aquatics, and more. Counselors are assigned to a bunk and live with campers; many educational/specialty staff live with campers as well.

Whereas the cultural *mifgash* (encounter) of sheliḥut is usually thought of in terms of its impact on campers at the participating camps, the sheliḥim themselves are encountering, perhaps for the first time or for a first extended experience, the everyday cultural life of North America (or at least the cultural experiences brought to camp by the particular segment of the population that populates Ramah camps). More directly to the point of this chapter, this also might be the shaliaḥ's initial encounter with Conservative Judaism and with Jewish traditions and expressions that are the norm at Ramah camps and in many North American Jewish communities but are far less common in Israel.

Previous studies of sheliḥim in North American summer camps point toward the possibility that new religious traditions may be highly salient to this group. For example, Ezrachi finds that "Israelis indicate that they were willing to open up the question of their own Jewish identity. They are open to the possibility that there might be flaws in the Israeli approach to Judaism and that the camp experience could be a positive learning opportunity" (1994, 218).

However, Bram and Neria (2003) report less openness on the part of sheliḥim to seeing the camp experience as a vehicle for religious change. Though most of their respondents reported that their Zionist identity became stronger and that they came to see American Jewry in a different light, these

Israelis felt that they came mainly to give rather than to receive. The sheliḥim saw themselves as representing the nation of Israel and not Judaism. They did not view the experience as an encounter between a variety of Jewish streams but rather as an encounter between Israelis and Americans. Most of the sheliḥim in the Bram and Neria study did not recognize the experience as an influence on their Jewish identity.

In the current study, we look in more detail at the question of the Judaic encounter and ask further about the carryover of the experience upon the return home to Israel. Preliminary interviews were conducted with five sheliḥim in Israel. Responses, along with input from Ramah leadership, were used to create a Hebrew-language survey consisting of Likert-type scales and free response items. The interviews and the survey focused on the respondents' backgrounds (particular Jewish backgrounds), the parameters of their sheliḥut, and their perceptions of their religious experiences at camp. The survey was posted online and distributed to sheliḥim who attended Ramah during the summer of 2007. In addition, at one camp, a staff member distributed paper versions of the survey to sheliḥim there and returned these for analysis. The first author also visited a Ramah camp to speak with and observe the sheliḥim there. Finally, notes submitted by sheliḥim to the National Ramah director are included to help illustrate current findings.

Findings

Participants' backgrounds

Eighty sheliḥim, ranging in age from twenty to fifty-six years old (mean age = twenty-four years old) completed this survey. Approximately two-thirds of the respondents were female, and respondents were divided fairly evenly between those who had finished high school and those who graduated or are currently enrolled in college. Sheliḥim from each of the overnight Ramah camps (excluding Canada) and the Nyack day camp responded; however, Ramah Wisconsin was disproportionately represented (a staff member there took the initiative to collect paper copies from the sheliḥim).

Respondents report being motivated for their sheliḥut by their love for education and youth guidance, the opportunity to spend the summer abroad, a wish to represent Israel, a desire to understand and deepen the relations between Israelis and American Jewry, and the opportunity to practice and advance their English language skills. More sheliḥim were assigned to Ramah than those who specifically chose Ramah as the site for their sheliḥut (approximately 60% and 40%, respectively). We asked those in the latter group about the reasons they chose a camp affiliated with the Conservative Movement.

Some responded that they saw the movement as a middle ground between Orthodox and Reform Judaism, observant but not too much so, a place that an Israeli Jew who is *ḥilloni* will feel comfortable and at the same time learn about and be exposed to a new community.

The sample was fairly evenly split between those for whom the current sheliḥut was their first at Ramah and those who had been sheliḥim at Ramah previously. (It is not known if the respondents did a prior sheliḥut at a different camp.) Members of the latter group have served as sheliḥim at Ramah, on average, three to four times previously. Those who returned to Ramah report doing so primarily because they enjoyed the experience, not necessarily to become more involved in the Ramah organization.

Jewish identification

Studying the issue of sheliḥim and the Conservative Movement presented an immediate challenge of nomenclature that itself may be emblematic of the challenges to be discussed in this chapter. The official designation of the Conservative Movement in Israel is the Masorati Movement. The word *masorati,* however, means traditional, so asking about one's background as masorati creates ambiguity in a language without capital letters at the beginning of words. Does claiming to be masorati mean that one is Conservative (that is, that one affiliates with the Conservative Movement) or that one is from a traditional background (perhaps Orthodox)?[2] Many Israelis use the latter meaning of the term. To try to add consistency to the process, we used the term *conservativi* in Hebrew to refer to the Conservative Movement and masorati to refer to a traditional background.[3] Though definitions of these terms were not provided to respondents, it was assumed that presenting both masorati and conservativi as mutually exclusive response options would prompt for the desired meanings of these terms. Nonetheless, responses regarding denominational affiliation must be understood as potentially ambiguous.

Slightly more than half of the respondents grew up in homes they considered to be *dati,* whereas one-quarter report coming from masorati homes. Smaller numbers come from ḥilloni (13%), Conservative (5%), or other or mixed families of origin. Currently, slightly fewer than half identify as dati, slightly fewer than one-quarter as masorati, and the rest as ḥilloni (16%), Conservative (11%), and other or mixed denomination. Of the nine respondents who currently consider themselves conservativi, five report growing up in dati homes, two in Conservative homes, and two in masorati homes.

Overall, respondents report high levels of ritual participation including saying Kiddush (80%) and eating Shabbat meals (86%) weekly. Sixty percent of female respondents report lighting candles each Shabbat, and close to half of all respondents (45%) attend synagogue weekly on Shabbat. Additional Jewish ritual behavior is summarized in the following table.

Ritual Practices of Sheliḥim

RITUAL BEHAVIOR	PERCENT "YES"
Synagogue on Rosh Hashanah	79
Synagogue on Yom Kippur	88
Synagogue on Passover	61
Separate dairy and meat in the home	86
Separate dairy and meat outside the home	77

Encountering a Different Judaism

As shown in fig. 1, it appears that many sheliḥim had little knowledge of the Conservative Movement prior to their sheliḥut.[4] Only one-quarter of respondents had ever attended a Conservative synagogue prior to their sheliḥut, and their attendance was for the most part only occasional.

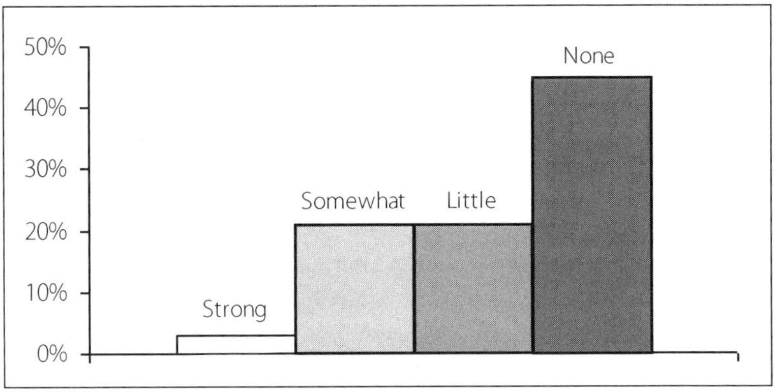

Figure 1. Knowledge of Conservative Movement Prior to Camp

For Israelis who are ḥilloni, this lack of familiarity with the Conservative Movement is part of a larger trend of limited knowledge of Judaism. Some report feeling generally rejected by Israeli Orthodoxy and feeling like outsiders with regard to Jewish ritual. For these Jews, the ritual experience of camp was particularly salient; Ramah holds the potential to serve as a welcoming and educating community demonstrating a different reality. As one shaliaḥ reports, "Camp Ramah opened us to Judaism; in Israel they viewed us as heretics, and here people welcome us and explain . . . it's like 'Judaism for beginners' for us." Many sheliḥim use the term "community" when they speak about camp. They relate to it as a community of learners, "my Jewish community," and describe the feeling of a large, welcoming environment.

Respondents were asked to report those rituals at camp that most surprised them. Mixed seating during *tefillot* was most frequently cited, generally as a positive experience, though some sheliḥim report it was strange at first and for some it was a shock that took time to become accustomed to. In the words of one shaliaḥ, "I survived, and even more than that, I enjoyed it!" Some sheliḥim commented that mixed tefillot contributed to the feeling of a warm community, as voiced by this respondent, "Mixed tefillot were strange at first, but I learned to love the togetherness."

Participation of women in prayers and ritual—receiving *aliyot,* wearing *kippot* and *tallit* and *tefilllin*—were new to all but the few Conservative-affiliated sheliḥim and seemed to be more controversial in the eyes of the respondents. Responses ranged from begrudging acceptance to embracing an empowering and wonderful new tradition. "The fact that women are treated as equals made me so happy. . . . I would love to see this liberalism in Israel."

Most of our sheliḥim indicated songs and *zemirot* to be positive traditions they encountered. The notion of joyous Jewish practice impressed them, and they report it as an exciting, pleasurable experience that brings people closer to each other and to Judaism. The most repeated response to the question of the shaliaḥ's perceptions of the religious impact of the Ramah experience had to do with opening their eyes to new and varied Jewish lifestyles.

> The encounter with the camp community along with its religious values, openness, and tolerance opened a window into a new, fascinating world for which I have the fullest respect. I hope that this world will grow bigger and affect more Jewish people from Israel and the Diaspora.

They report developing a tolerant view of the other Jewish streams beside their own. The sheliḥim report that the time spent at camp made them appreciate and respect the Conservative Movement that some came to see as their new community, "Today my friends and my Jewish community are Ramah graduates; they understand the world that I am deeply connected to."

Secular sheliḥim were opened to the possibility of leading a religious life at some point in the future. A considerable number of sheliḥim report an increase of their Jewish awareness as compared to before camp. This awareness is frequently described as being part of the Jewish people. Some of the secular sheliḥim came to see religion as more than a set of restrictive rules that was handed down to them because they found a religious Jewish community of which they truly feel a part. Orthodox respondents, on the other hand, tended to have more difficulty with the new *minhagim,* and some felt the need to protect their past convictions.

Respondents comment that they experienced many personal spiritual peaks during camp, such as this shaliaḥ who read Torah for the first time in many years: "I felt much excitement while reading the Torah. My voice was shaking. It was the most powerful religious experience I have had since my bar mitzvah. I'm excited now even as we talk."

Encountering other denominations and schools of thought and being exposed to the Conservative Movement's ideas and values at camp can lead to self-exploration of prior Jewish engagement, whether or not there was such self-exploration before camp. "Being at camp made me ask myself, 'Who am I?' and 'What is my religious path?' I had to learn new things in order to decide which way to turn."

Quotations such as these demonstrate the potential for the Ramah experience to be a catalyst for Jewish growth beyond the summer, with the communal nature of the experience serving as a catalyst. Sheliḥim describe feeling more connected to Judaism. "I'm ḥillonit, and I find egalitarianism a wonderful thing. Communal life at camp made me feel at home, surrounded by my family members. . . . I was a different person when I returned home—more Jewish than when I arrived."

The challenge of carryover

There is great potential for the Ramah experience to not only introduce sheliḥim to new Jewish expressions, but also to impact their Jewish engagement and that of their families upon their return home, particularly for those sheliḥim who return multiple times. One long-time shaliaḥ who attended camp with his family wrote:

> [E]ach summer, when we went to camp, the kids loved the Conservative *nusaḥ* for *tefillah* and the communal nature with boys and girls together. When we returned home to Israel, it was difficult for the kids to join in the Yemenite nusaḥ [of our synagogue]. But when we got home after services, we did *birkat hamazon* in the Conservative style and also *havdalah*—which is something that captured the kids' hearts—in the flavor of camp. . . . Now, my kids are in America. I am happy that both of them put on tefillin each morning (I don't put on tefillin!), and every *erev shabbat* and Shabbat morning they go to synagogue with love. The nusaḥ fits them and reminds them of Ramah. . . . I have no doubt that the window that opened for them at Ramah helps them today more than ever to connect to their Jewish roots when they are far from home.

Independently, one of this shaliaḥ's sons wrote:

> The Conservative form was new to me in every way; till then I could never understand what I was saying in prayers, let's face it, no one really does . . . I didn't even know how to start telling my friends back home how fun it is

to do the *Adon Olam* in "Rock around the Clock" style, they would never understand, you just had to be there to believe it. . . . [Ramah] taught us the beauty and joy in the Conservative form, in such a stylish way. Even the way we dressed up every Shabbat was new to me; I felt like I was going to my bar-mitzvah every week all over again.

Practices which seemed foreign before the summer may now be accepted (e.g., "Seating men and women together at shul was something that I never experienced before camp, and today it seems to be the most natural way for me.") and may even be incorporated in one's Jewish practice ("The Conservative Movement was new to me, and I learned a great deal about it at camp. I was exposed to Judaism and to my Jewish roots. It influenced my Jewish identity and since then I observe some minhagim.") There are other indicators of such effects in the current data. For example, close to half of respondents have prayed in a Conservative synagogue since their sheliḥut, while only about a quarter had done so prior to camp (fig. 2). Of these, the largest number report doing so on numerous occasions. In the words of one shaliaḥ, "I was opened to the Conservative Movement and loved what I saw at camp. Ever since I returned to Israel I try to go to Conservative shuls for tefillah whenever I can."

While this response shows the shaliaḥ's enthusiasm for the Conservative Movement, it also alludes to a recurring theme in the responses of the sheliḥim, the idea that "whenever I can" may not be very often, as many respondents report that they do not have a Conservative synagogue in their area. In fact, the increase in attendance at Conservative services must be interpreted along with comments written by several respondents that such attendance took place only at structured events (e.g., staffing a Conservative-affiliated program or attending a family or friend's event).

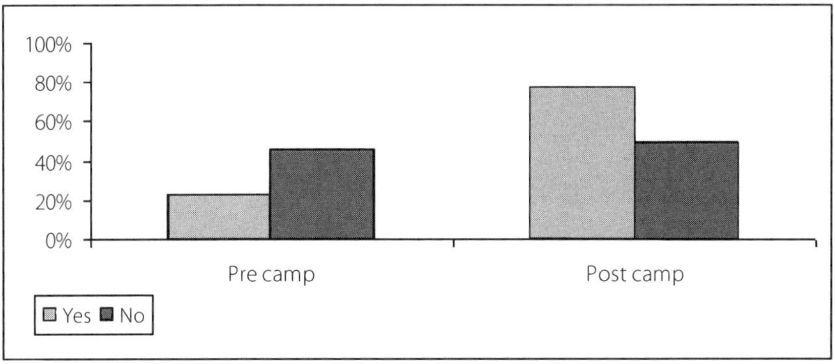

Figure 2. Attending Conservative Synagogue

Discussion and Recommendations

Every year Camp Ramah hosts a group of devoted, energetic, and charismatic young Israelis. Some of these sheliḥim encounter expressions of Judaism—egalitarian and spiritually joyous—that run counter to their preconceptions of what life could be like in an engaged Jewish community. Others encounter rituals that seem foreign and even uncomfortable at first but develop an appreciation for their value. What happens to these sheliḥim upon their return to Israel? Some of the Orthodox sheliḥim discussed not only being more accepting of Jews of differing denominations, but also that they educated others in their communities about tolerance of religious pluralism. Many sheliḥim—both secular and traditional—leave camp deeply influenced by camp religious life and motivated to implement their new religious experiences and minhagim within the Conservative Movement after returning to Israel. However, many of these same sheliḥim discuss, often with frustration, their inability to sustain this pattern of change and describe their return to their familiar frameworks of Israeli Orthodox or secular life. The pattern may be punctuated by particular events (e.g., attending a Conservative-sponsored program or the family event of a Conservative friend or even another summer at Ramah), so perhaps part of the impact of Ramah can be seen as linking the shaliaḥ with other opportunities to engage in Conservative Jewish practice.

However, it should be noted that the transition from camp is far from seamless; and for many of the participants in this study, it does not bring with it the opportunities to retain the engagement and excitement initiated at camp. These participants do not see the institutions of Conservative Judaism as available to them either because they lack information about local Conservative congregations or because no such congregation exists in their area.

Further, a shaliaḥ's decision to stay involved in the Conservative Movement in Israel might have to do with perceptions of community in addition to the existence of actual communal organizations. It was the warm, embracing, community feel that seems to have facilitated much of Ramah's impact. To sustain that, relationships must be fostered, for example, through reunions or Web-based networking.

The Conservative Movement has the opportunity not only to influence the lives of Israeli Jews, but also to use the sheliḥim to increase its own presence in Israel. Many sheliḥim are deeply moved by warm, communal, and egalitarian expressions of Judaism at Ramah that run counter to their preconceptions and their expectations regarding the Jewish communities from which they come. However, such enthusiasm cannot be sustained in an environment in which there are few opportunities to re-experience these positive moments and in which the status quo is quite different from what exists at Ramah. If the Conservative Movement wishes to build on the experience of its sheliḥim, it must become more proactive in building the scaffolding for the connections and transitions between camp and Israel in the lives of the sheliḥim.

For other first-hand accounts of the impact of Ramah on sheliḥim, see the contributions by Benny Gamlieli and Maya Aviv in the Reflections section.

Notes

[1] Translated from: http://www.jewishagency.org/JewishAgency/Hebrew/Education/Shlichim/Summer+Camps/Want_to_be_shaliach/jobs.

[2] Interestingly, a similar issue would exist if capitalization were not used in English. Would "I am C/conservative" refer to a denomination or a political leaning?

[3] In this report, percentages reported as Conservative are those indicating conservativi in Hebrew; those reporting masorati are those who indicated that term.

[4] Due to a problem with the online survey, only those completing paper surveys responded to this item.

References

Ezrachi, E. 1994. Encounters between American Jews and Israelis: Israelis in American Jewish summer camps. PhD diss., Jewish Theological Seminary.

Bram, C., and E. Neria. 2003. Veni Vedi Li: *Israeli shelichim identity encounters in U.S. Jewish summer camps.* Research presented to the Research Unit in the Department of Education in the Jewish Agency.

SETH ADELSON

The Evolution of the Ramah Nature Experience

יומא חד הוה אזל באורחא, חזייה להוא גברא דהוה נטע חרובא, אמר ליה: האי,
עד כמה שנין טעין? – אמר ליה: עד שבעין שנין. – אמר ליה: פשיטא לך דחיית
שבעין שנין? – אמר ליה: האי גברא עלמא בחרובא אשכחתיה, כי היכי דשתלי לי
אבהתי – שתלי נמי לבראי.

One day, as [Ḥoni the Circle-Maker] was walking on the road, he saw a man planting a carob tree. He asked him, "How long will it take this tree to bear fruit?" The man replied, "Seventy years." He asked, "Are you quite sure you will live another seventy years to eat its fruit?" The man replied, "I myself found fully grown carob trees in the world; as my forebears planted for me, so am I planting for my children."[1] (BT *Ta'anit* 23a)

Ramah and Nature

ONE OF THE ESSENTIAL FEATURES of summer camp is its location. Camp would simply not be camp if it took place in a suburb. For sixty years, Ramah has taken mostly suburban kids away from their homes, away from creature comforts and the car culture, depositing them in the woods for the summer. The camps are located in rural areas, some quite far from the nearest shopping mall, and closer to the natural world than most *ḥanichim* (campers) have ever lived.

In today's climate of specialization among summer camps, the Ramah camps are distinctive because they offer a full range of programming. Most camp activities take place outdoors, and although the majority of programs do not focus upon the environment as the essential feature of the activity, the surroundings are an inseparable part of the experience. Many specialty camps, and particularly those that are not outdoor-oriented, are not located in rural settings;

RABBI SETH ADELSON *serves as the associate rabbi at Temple Israel of Great Neck, New York. He received cantorial investiture in 2004 and rabbinic ordination in 2007 from The Jewish Theological Seminary and has spent many wonderful summers at Camp Ramah in New England, working as rosh maḥana'ut and the Jewish Environmental and Nature Education Fellow, among other positions.*

the camper lives in an environment similar to that of his or her suburban home. As the camping industry retreats from nature, Ramah remains steadfastly in the woods.

Given the growing prominence of environmental issues facing American society and the whole world, the influence that camp can exert in developing sensitivity to these issues is more important than ever. Many Ramahniks had their first experiences hiking, camping, gardening, and otherwise exploring nature under the auspices of camp, whether directly through nature-oriented programming or indirectly through other programs that take place outdoors. Whereas some alumni point to *ḥug teva* (an optional activity period for nature) as having had an impact, others invoke the *ḥiddush* (innovation) of holding morning *tefillot* (prayers) at a campsite on top of a mountain or taking a dip in a remote waterfall during a camping expedition. As we often hear, some Ramahniks think that you can't recite *havdalah* (the Saturday evening ceremony that separates the Sabbath from the rest of the week) without a lake.

Although there have been several studies to determine the value of camp with respect to furthering Jewish education and continuity,[2] little has been published exploring the role of camp in developing the camper's relationship to nature and the environment. How does camp put children in touch with nature? What have nature educators noticed with regard to how children respond to these experiences? What innovations has Ramah implemented to contribute to our growing sensitivity to the environment?

In the course of producing the present work, these questions were posed to a number of people who have been involved with Ramah's outdoor and nature programs, to determine what Ramahniks have taken back with them from their summers in the woods. The interviewees included nature and outdoor educators from all of the North American Ramah camps, many of whom had received special fellowships and training for their jobs. The results show that in the last decade, Ramah has demonstrated much creativity and innovation in inspiring its charges to consider their relationships with nature.

Areas of Nature Education[3]

There are two primary venues through which ḥanichim are exposed to nature: camping/outdoor adventure programs (which go by different names in different camps) that challenge the camper to take part intimately in physical outdoor activities and nature/environmental education that presents the camper with useful knowledge about the natural world and seeks to develop a heightened appreciation for it. These two are not necessarily associated with each other; in some camps they fall under the auspices of the same staff and in others, not. Regardless, they often cross paths in terms of educational objectives.

Although these areas are traditional camp fare, they both have changed markedly in recent years. Training has improved so that nature educators at camp are likely to know more about their subject; new programs were developed, especially in areas relevant to environmental concerns; today safety is a higher priority; and integration with other areas of camp is more common. These changes have developed due to the growing international consciousness regarding the environment and the greater appreciation of the opportunities presented for nature education at camp. As the suburbanization of America continues, the awareness of camp as an outpost in the woods increases; improvements in nature education are a natural outgrowth of the need to reconnect with the environment even as we move further away from it.

An additional, less formal path of exposure to the outdoors is the location of the camp itself. Virtually all campers and staff come from environments that are far removed from regular, intimate contact with nature, and camp is often the only place where they encounter flora and fauna that are not somehow contained. This type of incidental exposure to the natural world is increasingly limited to the time spent in camp, making camp a more significant venue for learning to understand the outdoors. Many a Ramahnik remembers the time that the black bear was spotted ambling across the *migrash* (open field surrounded by camper bunks) or that unfortunate incident with poison ivy. Furthermore, camp programming is often influenced by the weather, and the disappointment of a rained-out soccer game may have been alleviated by the clear night sky that permitted a view of the Perseids meteor shower that occurs faithfully every summer. For children growing up in a climate-controlled world, these experiences (less frequent outside of camp) help them to understand that although humans can manipulate their environments with ever greater skill and technology, this is still God's earth.

Modern Jewish environmental consciousness emerged within the last thirty years in conjunction with a growing universal environmental sensitivity. Pioneers in the field searched Jewish literature to find sources that pointed to such sensitivity in the Torah and later texts.[4] This effort to connect environmentalism and Jewish tradition also touched Ramah, and the result is that in recent years, Ramah nature staff has reformulated nature and outdoor education to emphasize this new, Jewish-inflected awareness. Although recycling, composting, and low-impact camping were largely unheard of thirty years ago, the Ramah camps have changed in this regard. These new initiatives often refer to the standard-bearing negative commandment of *bal tashḥit,* the injunction against wasting natural resources.[5]

Ramah has always aimed high with its multipronged educational objectives and though nature education was never front-and-center, it is a consistent offering. In recent years, nature education at Ramah has responded to the greater urgency of *tikkun olam* (repairing the world) by developing a new sophistication. The result is that more Ramahniks are learning about nature experientially than ever before.

Camping/outdoor programs

Camping and outdoor programs, known in the individual camps as *maḥana'ut, etgar, al hagovah,* or *kav reches,* long have existed at Ramah. Traditionally, the older *edot* (divisions) would take trips out of camp for a few days: campers would be transported by bus to a hiking location, hike without packs, and at the conclusion of the hike would board the bus again to ride to their camp site. Food would be prepared by the staff, usually hamburgers and hot dogs. Little or no planned, systematic attention was paid to nature education, to minimizing impact on the environment, or to motivating ḥanichim to appreciate the outdoors. One exception to these limited programs was Camp Ramah in Canada's "tripping" program. For decades, in keeping with the culture of Ontario camps, Ramah Canada offered extensive off-site canoeing trips of four to six days for its teenage campers.

Today, the outdoor programs encompass a wide range of activities, including bicycling, canoeing, and rock climbing in addition to the traditional hiking and camping. Greater attention is paid to safety, and educational nature programming is often included as part of the outdoor plan. Furthermore, many camps have on-site outdoor activities that supplement the out-of-camp programming, including ropes courses and tree houses. Some camps also have in-camp overnight programs, especially for the younger edot, which use the more secluded areas of camp to create an outdoor experience. The variety of offerings and the depth of programming have blossomed in recent years.

Nature and environmental education

The nature programs at camp of which I am aware traditionally were small and operated in the shadow of the more glamorous camp departments. Whereas high-profile operations such as sports and *ḥinnuch* (education) might have numerous personnel and generous budgets, the *teva* (nature) instructor generally was relegated to a poorly-located, run-down shack with only his or her wits and a halfway-decent knife to plan *ḥugim* (activities). Until the infusion of foundation money beginning in 2000, the *rosh teva* (nature instructor) likely had not received formal training in nature education.

For example, during my years at Camp Ramah in New England, a nature program was offered only sporadically and when it did exist, it attracted only a few ḥanichim. It was offered as a ḥug, and nature study was not part of any other sphere of camp. Prior to the arrival of a Jewish Environmental and Nature Education (JENE) fellowship (provided by the Foundation for Jewish Camping in 2004), no teva program was offered for several summers—the last ḥug teva had been led by a part-time teacher who visited camp a few days per week.

In recent years, nature education at Ramah dramatically expanded its repertoire. Gardening and recycling programs were introduced at several camps, and a whole new range of nature-based activities—including crafts, songs, and games—are offered at Ramah camps. The offerings are not only new and more exciting, but they are being taught by staff who are better prepared and have more training than in the past. Current trends in environmental consciousness have led to the recognition of a need for improved nature education, and Ramah has stepped in to fill that need.

Nature Education Fellowships

In recent years there also has been a flurry of funding activity on the part of philanthropic organizations to improve nature education in North American camps, and Ramah has benefited from these programs. Typically, these programs include external training and specify the requirements and responsibilities of the nature staff member. Two organizations in particular, the Foundation for Jewish Camping and the Nathan Cummings Foundation, have provided staff and training to Ramah camps.

The Nathan Cummings Foundation funded the Nathan Cummings Environmental Fellowship for three summers (2000–2002), providing several Ramah camps with nature education staff. Like its successor, the JENE Fellowship, Nathan Cummings provided a pre-camp, experiential training seminar for all of the fellows, including resource materials, activities, games, knowledge about flora and fauna, and so forth. The Nathan Cummings fellows were required to find and/or make their own supplies for training. At least five Nathan Cummings fellows served in Ramah camps. These participants took their knowledge and skills to Ramah camps for six summers, bringing a wealth of new programs, activities, and knowledge to an area that previously had received minimal attention.

The JENE Fellowship, provided by the Foundation for Jewish Camping, was a program that lasted only three summers (2003–2005) but appears to have had a significant impact upon nature programs at Ramah camps. The fellowship, in addition to a generous stipend, included a week of pre-season training by America's foremost Jewish nature educators with other JENE fellows at a camp in California, provision of sourcebooks and programming materials, and stipulations about ways in which the JENE fellow could be used in camp. Training took place over a week of residence in camp and covered a wide range of subjects. The fellows worked in gardens, built compost piles, made fire from scratch, camped out under the stars, hiked, swapped recipes and songs, learned exciting nature-based activities and crafts, and discussed important environmental issues and educational techniques, among other activities. The goal was to produce a cadre of trained, nature education staff for North American Jewish camps, something that was sorely lacking. JENE produced at least three fellows that served in Ramah camps.

Innovations in Nature and Outdoor Programming at Ramah

Through interviews with nature and outdoor educators from all of the Ramah camps and drawing upon my own experience in the field, I have endeavored to present a portrait of the state of nature education at Ramah. The interviews revealed that there is a wide range of new methods and activities designed to bring kids to an understanding of nature and the environment. In addition to the gardens, compost piles, and recycling plans, some have re-imagined their camping trips as educational experiences; today many of the camps have ropes courses and climbing walls, designed not only to develop physical skills but also to foster team-building and to help individuals confront their fears. But the greatest innovation is the effort to raise the consciousness of the camp community regarding nature and the environment. The following is an examination of individual programming successes at various camps.

Eliav Bock, a rabbinical student at The Jewish Theological Seminary (JTS) and a JENE fellow in 2005, implemented a number of new programs at Camp Ramah in Canada, including a camp-wide recycling program, a *yom teva* (Nature Day) for younger edot, and a garden ("a miserable failure," he reports). Since Eliav ran both the in-camp teva program, as well as maḥana'ut, he could enrich the latter with a good deal of nature/environmental educational content, and he ensured that his outdoor staff was well-equipped to teach.

The recycling program was particularly successful:

> During staff week, I made plaques . . . each one started with the Hebrew word, *hayada'ta*—"Did you know?"—and then would give some statistic about camp. For example, it might say, "Hayada'ta . . . at camp we throw away 10,000 bottles each summer?" and then below, it said "Reduce, reuse, recycle."

Bock encouraged the involvement of interested *madrichim* (counselors) in designing the program, and with their "buy-in," the program took off. By the end of the summer, ḥanichim from the oldest *edah* (division) were overseeing the program, which collected bottles, cans, and paper. Bock also managed to further improve the visibility of nature education by making tie-ins with other areas of camp, particularly in the area of *tefillah* (prayer).

JTS rabbinical student Jill Levy, a Nathan Cummings fellow in 2002, initiated the teva program at Ramah Darom. In addition to creating a garden, a recycling program, and a unique siddur specifically for what she calls, "nature *tefillot*." Although she was not responsible for maḥana'ut, Levy also spent time training the maḥana'ut staff in nature-oriented games and tree and insect identification. Having an interest in entomology, she "had that as a large focus of the program and was able to create a culture in camp of appreciating insects instead of fearing and killing them."

One accomplishment about which Levy is especially proud is a minor victory for conservation enthusiasts, but a major one for a summer camp nature educator. She was able to convince the camp director to purchase individual coffee mugs for the staff and to set up hooks in the *ḥadar ochel* (dining hall) for them so that when staff members had coffee every morning at breakfast, they would not be wasting Styrofoam cups. This small cultural change is a prime example of the ways in which nature educators have helped Ramah camps understand that the principle of bal tashḥit applies not only to fruit trees surrounding a besieged city, but also to all of the things that we use.

Rabbi Shalom Kantor, a Nathan Cummings Environmental fellow, taught the ropes course and also managed the camping program during his summers at Ramah California. His innovations in the camping program included increasing the environmental education content of outdoor trips:

> I began the process of infusing outdoor awareness education into the overnight programs, which really had not existed before, as I understood the programs. This included but was not limited to nature/surrounding awareness, biodiversity education, outdoor basic skills, [and] group and individual trust and cooperation programming.

Kantor reports that other programs introduced under his watch were a morning "hike and tefillah" program and the hiring of an additional outdoors educator to teach environmental awareness. In addition, Kantor introduced a small innovation to the camping trip of Tzofim (the rising-ninth-grade division):

> We were able to expand the overnight program so that the boys and girls were separate from each other for one night and then together for one night. This allowed each gender to have an experience that was void of the intergender pressures that are a constant part of the camp experience, especially in the outdoor setting.

Even a minor ḥiddush like this can have a great impact on the outdoor experience; in some cases, putting aside awkward social pressures allows room for ḥanichim to learn more about themselves in the context of nature.[6]

Aaron Philmus, also a JTS rabbinical student, was a JENE fellow who worked as a teva educator at the Ramah Day Camp in Nyack, New York in

2005. He points to the *ginnat besamim* (spice garden) that was built with the cooperation of ḥanichim and rosh teva, Gail Kohler, as a successful innovation during his summer there.

> We performed all parts of the planting with the kids: from clearing the grass to planting seeds and watering. We also made a big compost heap (a "soil machine") with hay and leftovers from the animal feedings and learned about decomposition and the connection between adam (person) and adamah (earth). We also learned about the *berachah* [blessing] for *besamim* [fragrant things, such as spices]. Gail raised butterflies that loved to hang out on our flowers. Overall, a big success.

Aaron's gardening experience was echoed in the garden at Camp Ramah in New England, where herbs, flowers, and vegetables were planted by ḥanichim. The produce occasionally ended up on Shabbat tables in the ḥadar ochel. The kitchen contributed back by donating vegetable peelings and the outer leaves of lettuce and cabbage to the camp's compost piles that were tended by the ḥug teva.

Hannah Steigmann, a rabbinical student at JTS, spent the summer of 2004 developing a new recycling program at Ramah in New England. She created a character known as Captain Planet and appeared in character to introduce different groups within camp to the concept of *miḥzur* (recycling). Steigmann, assisted by Adat Machon (the second-oldest division in camp) through their service project program, placed recycling boxes for mixed paper and mixed glass, plastic, and aluminum in individual *tzerifim* (bunks). These containers were emptied during *nikkayon* (clean-up time). By the end of the summer, the program was wildly successful, with collection bins filling up faster than the hauling company could empty them.

Rabbi Todd Zeff, director of Camp Ramah in the Poconos, served as *rosh maḥana'ut* (head of outdoor camping) at Camp Ramah in Wisconsin for four summers in the late 1990s and oversaw both the teva program and the outdoor trips. Zeff points to the importance of including the nature educational element in the context of camping trips and trained his own staff to teach ḥanichim about the various flora they encountered along the trail.

As part of these trips, Zeff would have ḥanichim pray individually, out of sight and hearing range from one another. He found that this enabled the children to connect prayer with the beauty of creation and gave them a particularly memorable experience that they would not otherwise encounter during regular camp tefillot.

Rabbi Harry Pell, who served as *rosh al hagovah* (director of outdoor and camping programs) at Camp Ramah in the Berkshires in 2000 and 2001, tells of the dramatic turnaround of this program that has occurred over the last fifteen years. Although al hagovah always offered trips for all of the edot, it was a small operation that Pell described as "two guys and a shack"; today it is an all-encompassing program with a staff of twelve to fourteen. In the early 1990s, Seth Adelsberg began this turnaround by expanding al hagovah to include rock climbing and small, ten-person trips for Bogrim (the third-oldest division in camp) along the celebrated Appalachian Trail, which passes close to camp. The program, known as Etgar Ramah ("Ramah challenge"), expanded to other edot, with the continued and gradual purchase of equipment, such that today the four edot comprised of older campers all have Etgar Ramah tracks within al hagovah. Ḥanichim in these edot may choose from two-, three-, or four-day hiking or biking trips, and they pack and carry all of their own gear and food. Pell also points to the Judaic content of these trips, noting that tefillot and daily *shi'urim* (lessons) are an essential part of the experience, and how the trips focus on developing individual self-confidence and trust skills within the group. "I'm very proud of al hagovah," he said. "There's nothing else that I've been involved with that has seen so much growth and development. Everybody involved has contributed to it and made it grow."

Pell also adds that out-of-camp, outdoor experiences can be far more rewarding than an in-camp ropes course, for example, which is an artificial construction. Al hagovah offers caving at caves located not far from camp, where campers are given the same team-building challenges that they face on the ropes course, but with a difference:

> You take the bunk to a cave, and it's suddenly real. They come together to help each other. . . . They also gain a sense of appreciation of the cave—you leave it as you find it. They are more cohesive as they come out, having overcome their vulnerability.

After spending one summer as rosh maḥana'ut at Camp Ramah in New England, I served as a JENE fellow for two subsequent summers and developed the teva program by bringing the wealth of programming activities from the JENE training to camp. Among the new programs that we initiated in 2004 were the A-side garden and the B-side compost pile. However, the programs with the widest reach and greatest success, in terms of both educational achievement and enjoyment by participants, were the in-camp overnights for each of the younger edot that we implemented in 2005. Rather than merely taking the kids out to *maḥaneh gimel* (an open, undeveloped field that is set apart from the rest of camp), feeding them macaroni and cheese cooked over propane stoves, and putting them to sleep under the stars, my assistant Deb Laufer and I crafted a more comprehensive program that, despite the in-camp location, took the ḥanichim out of their element and gave them multiple new perspectives.

Based around the camp's tree house that is in a remote wooded location on the opposite side of the mysterious and serene Mosquito Lake, the overnight generally included nature games, a night walk, star-gazing, ḥanichim preparing their own food over the campfire that they built, sleeping in tents that they assembled, and tefillot that highlighted nature themes that appear in the weekday liturgy.

As part of the activities, ḥanichim were given a solid dose of environmental education over the course of the overnight. In most cases, we began the program with a game supplied by the JENE resources that asked and answered questions about nature and the environment. We evaluated ways in which human activities affect the environment, including garbage production (we estimated how much garbage we made over the course of the program), light pollution that was clearly visible at night, and our own use of the camp's natural resources.

Feedback from this program was tremendously positive. Kids who were not interested in, or who were afraid of, the outdoors found something that appealed to them; veteran madrichim, who were skeptical of the whole idea of an in-camp overnight, admitted that it was much more fun and educational than any of the out-of-camp trips they had experienced. Ḥug teva received a corresponding bounce in interest.

Preliminary Indications of Success

The new approaches to nature education are exciting and fun for campers, but what have they learned? According to those interviewed, what have Ramahniks brought back with them from the woods?

Camping trips offer a more experiential classroom than in-camp teva activities, due to their highly physical investment in hiking and canoeing through picturesque places coupled with sleeping outdoors and learning to use a trowel. Among his ḥanichim, Eliav Bock has seen a greater awareness of their interaction with the environment. "Kids on my canoeing trips took away a greater sense of awe and appreciation for nature; a sense for how to live in the outdoors while leaving a smaller footprint on the resources around us."

The same sentiment was reported by virtually all of the interviewees. On the in-camp overnight program in New England, I saw a heightened interest in understanding the natural world. At the conclusion of the program, I would ask campers what they had learned, and the answers often surprised me; the overnight had sparked, in many of them, a sensitivity to the environment that had not existed the day before. The ḥanichim, in addition to having a great time cooking their dinner over an open fire, participating in a flashlight-free night walk, and visiting a "Bedouin tent," had assimilated numerous tidbits about nature, the environment, and Judaism, from the source of bal tashḥit, to the antidote for poison ivy, to the natural imagery appearing in *Pesukei Dezimrah* (the preliminary part of morning prayers).

Several of the nature educators mentioned ḥanichim who, in later years, recalled their positive nature experiences. Rabbi Zeff says that one camper told him that his program had "changed her life and helped her find direction." Some of these ḥanichim became madrichim and shared their experiences with their own ḥanichim. Bock shared this touching story:

> A first-year counselor told me that he had just returned from a camping trip with his ten-year-old campers. He told me how he had sat with them during a storm and watched the rain come down on the lake. He asked me whether I had remembered when I had sat with him some five years earlier when he was twelve and had helped him to see that being caught in a rain storm was not just a scary thing, but also an amazing act of God. I remembered clearly comforting him while he sat crying, because he had been so afraid of the rain. It made my summer to think that now he was passing this along to his own campers.

Rabbi Pell, having spent enough summers at Ramah in the Berkshires to see ḥanichim come through the al hagovah program, also mentioned the willingness of some of these ḥanichim to "give back." Those who are inspired by their outdoor experiences are often willing, as madrichim or even as al hagovah staff, to share their inspiration with others. And thus the inspiration to understand and appreciate nature is transmitted to a new generation of Ramahniks.

Long-Term Trends

As global consciousness of environmental issues grows, the need for further education is unquestionable, and what better place for it than summer camp? Certainly, the success of the programs described above speaks to their value; they are fun and educational. Because the environmental fellowships have been suspended, at least for now, the future for nature education will depend on the willingness of individual camps to hire and train committed staff.

Regarding camping and outdoor trips, Rabbi Zeff sees a greater emphasis today on safety, as well as an improved focus on helping ḥanichim develop their personal independence. Given that most kids who come to Ramah grow up in the suburbs, the encounter with nature can be an empowering one, if they are given the tools to understand and appreciate it.

Hannah Steigmann admits that the recycling program was expensive and therefore not favored by her camp's business manager, but the will of many ḥanichim and madrichim was behind it. As economic and governmental forces make recycling more financially attractive, the pilot programs of recent years will become the established practice of the future.

Perhaps one example of good things to come is the new solar generator at Camp Ramah in California. Designed to eventually produce 300 kilowatts of electricity and initially to save the camp about $30,000 per year in energy expenses, the generator also will spare the atmosphere 4.3 million pounds of carbon dioxide annually. The generator came online in May 2006 and quietly serves as a demonstration of bal tashḥit in action, an icon that will be as much a teaching tool as an economic asset to camp. According to camp director Rabbi Daniel Greyber, by both using and educating about solar energy during future encampments, he and his staff believe they will create generations of Jewish leaders who are environmentally conscious and who will seek to move more and more institutions to environmentally friendly energy options. As the project develops into its second and third phase, Rabbi Greyber expects that the camp will perform an energy audit to learn about other ways the camp can reduce its consumption. "Just as we ask our *tzevet* [staff] to be role models, we believe that our camp plant should be a model for the type of world we want to create."

Conclusion

We are in a period of dramatic change with respect to environmental awareness. Although the theory and reality of global warming have been bandied about by the scientific community for more than half a century, it is only within the last two years that the realization of the seriousness of this problem has entered the public mind on a large scale. The need for nature education and an experiential understanding of the environment is greater now than ever before, and Ramah is meeting this challenge.

The renewed emphasis upon nature education, assisted by the environmental fellowships available in recent years, has produced palpable results in Ramah camps, including a variety of new programs. The specialists who managed these innovations have sought new access points within camp, generating interest among campers who otherwise would not have been reached. They have sought integration with other areas of camp, planting gardens in cooperation with the ḥinnuch staff, composting with the members of the Tikvah program (a division for campers with special needs), and bringing new perspectives to tefillot.

Integration with tefillot as a primary tool was mentioned across the board by all of the specialists. Indeed, the environment and prayer are natural allies; they comment upon and reinforce each other. Tefillot in natural settings, as many camp alumni can tell you, can be more inspiring than in any interior space; likewise, the language of tefillah frequently draws upon images from nature: the awesome power and the subtleties of the natural world, the human connection to Creation, and the infusion of the Divine in everything.

Meanwhile, the camping experience has been heightened by the fresh infusion of nature education. With trip leaders focused upon using the outdoor experience as a path to understanding the natural world, ḥanichim are coming away from these trips with greater sensitivity than ever.

Now is the time, as Ramah turns sixty and eyes the next decade, to seek these opportunities for greater identification with our environment. The world cannot wait.

Resource List[7]

Nature education from a Jewish perspective

Challenge: Torah Views on Science and Its Problems. Edited by Aryeh Carmell and Cyril Domb. New York: Feldheim, 1976.

Conservative Judaism 44:1. Fall 1991. Special issue dedicated to Jewish environmental thought and action.

Ecology and the Jewish Spirit: Where Nature and the Sacred Meet. Edited by Ellen Bernstein. Woodstock, VT: Jewish Lights Publishing, 1998.

A Garden of Choice Fruits. Edited by David E. S. Stein. Shomrei Adamah, 1991. Out of print but available at http://davidesstein.name/A_Garden_of_Choice_Fruits--Stein.pdf.

The Green Shalom Guide: A How-To Manual for Greening Local Jewish Synagogues, Schools and Offices. Edited by Naomi Friedman and De Fischler Herman. Takoma Park, MD: Shomrei Adamah, 1995.

It's a Mitzvah! Step-by-Step to Jewish Living. Bradley Shavit Artson. New York: Rabbinical Assembly, 1995, chapter 17 on *bal tashḥit* (prohibition of waste).

The Jewish Sourcebook on the Environment and Ecology. Ronald H. Isaacs. Northvale, NJ: Jason Aronson, 1998.

Jews, Money, and Social Responsibility: Developing a "Torah of Money" for Contemporary Life. Lawrence Bush and Jeffrey Dekro. Philadelphia: Shefa Fund, 1993.

Judaism and Ecology Volume: Religions of the World and Ecology Series. Edited by Hava Tirosh-Samuelson. Center for the Study of World Religions, Harvard Divinity School, 2002.

Judaism and Ecology. Study guide. New York: Hadassah and Shomrei Adamah.

Let The Earth Teach You Torah. Ellen Bernstein and Dan Fink. Available through COEJL.

Listen to the Trees: Jews and the Earth. Molly Cone. New York: URJ Press, 1995.

The Sabbath: Its Meaning for Modern Man. Abraham Joshua Heschel. New York: Farrar, Straus, Giroux, 1951.

Seasons of Our Joy: A Handbook of Jewish Festivals. Arthur Waskow. Boston: Beacon Press, 1982.

Seek My Face, Speak My Name. Arthur Green. Northvale, NJ: Jason Aronson, 1992.

Spirit and Nature: Why the Environment is a Religious Issue. Edited by Steven C. Rockefeller and John N. Elder. Esp. "Learning to Live with Less" by Ismar Schorsch. Boston: Beacon Press, 1992.

Spirit in Nature: Teaching Judaism and Ecology on the Trail. Matt Biers-Ariel, Deborah Newbrun, and Michal Fox-Smart. New York: Behrman House, 2000.

Texts and Commentaries on Biological Diversity and Human Responsibility: A Study Guide. 1996. Available through COEJL.

This Sacred Earth: Religion, Nature, Environment. Edited by Roger Gottlieb. New York: Routledge, 1995.

To Till and To Tend: A Guide to Jewish Environmental Study and Action. COEJL, 1994.

Torah and Flora. Louis I. Rabinowitz. Sanhedrin Press, 1979.

Torah of the Earth: Exploring 4,000 Years of Ecology in Jewish Thought. Vols. 1 and 2. Edited by Arthur Waskow. Woodstock, VT: Jewish Lights, 2000.

Trees, Earth and Torah: A Tu B'Shvat Anthology. Edited by Ari Elon, Naomi Hyman, and Arthur Waskow. Philadelphia: The Jewish Publication Society, 1999.

Who Renews Creation? Earl Schwartz and Barry Cytron. New York: United Synagogue Youth, 1993.

"With all Your Possessions": Jewish Ethics and Economic Life. Meir Tamari. New York: Free Press, 1987.

General environmental education: Activities and stories

Bubbles, Rainbows, and Worms: Science Experiments for Preschool Children. Sam Ed Brown. Gryphon House, 2004.

Earth Book for Kids: Activities to Help Heal the Environment. Linda Schwartz. Santa Barbara, CA: Learning Works, 1990.

Hug a Tree and Other Things to Do Outdoors with Young Children. Robert E. Rockwell, Elizabeth A. Sherwood, and Robert A. Williams. Gryphon House, 1983.

Keepers of the Animals: Native American Stories and Wildlife Activities for Children. Michael J. Caduto and Joseph Bruchac. Fulcrum, 1997.

Keepers of the Earth: Native American Stories and Environmental Activities. Michael J. Caduto, Ka-Hon-Hes, Joseph Bruchac, and Carol Wood. Fulcrum, 1989.

Nature Specialist: A Complete Guide to Program and Activities. Lenore Hendler Miller. American Camping Association, 1998.

Nature with Children of All Ages. Edith A. Sisson. Prentice Hall, 1982.

Sharing the Joy of Nature. Joseph Cornell. Nevada City, CA: Dawn Publications, 1989.

Sharing Nature with Children. Joseph Cornell. Nevada City, CA: Dawn Publications, 1998.

Silver Bullets. Karl Rohnke. Kendall/Hunt Publishing, 1984.

Snips and Snails and Walnut Whales: Nature Crafts for Children. Phyllis Fiarotta and Noel Fiarotta. Workman Publishing, 1975.

Notes

[1] Babylonian Talmud, *Massekhet Ta'anit* 23a. English translation from Hayim Nahman Bialik and Yehoshua Hana Ravnitzky, eds., *The Book of Legends,* William G. Braude, trans. (New York: Schocken Books, 1992), 203.

[2] For example, see Ariela Keysar and Barry A. Kosmin, "Research Findings on the Impact of Camp Ramah: A Companion Study to the 2004 '*Eight Up*' Report on the Attitudes and Practices of Conservative Jewish College Students" (New York: National Ramah Commission, 2005) and its summary in this volume; and Steven M. Cohen, "Camp Ramah and Adult Jewish Identity: Long-Term Influences on Conservative Congregants in North America," in *Ramah, Reflections at 50: Visions for a New Century,* ed. Sheldon A. Dorph (New York: National Ramah Commission, 2000), 95–129.

[3] "Nature education" is a general term that may refer to a wide variety of activities and is used in this article to refer not only to familiarizing students with the features of the natural world (i.e., flora and fauna, terrain, climate, natural phenomena, etc.), but also to what may be further sub-categorized as "environmental education" (investigating how humans interact with and affect nature). "Outdoor education" is a term that refers to recreational involvement with nature, like hiking, canoeing, mountain climbing, etc.

[4] To my knowledge, although no author has attempted a history of contemporary Jewish environmental awareness, I have learned through personal communications with Dr. Gabe Goldman, Ellen Bernstein, and Barbara Lerman-Golomb that the seeds of this movement were planted in the 1970s, with the writings of Rabbi Everett Gendler and Dr. David Ehrenfeld and the development of ecologically themed Tu Bishvat seders; the founding of Shomrei Adamah in 1988 and of Coalition on the Environment and Jewish Life (COEJL) in 1993 were subsequent milestones.

[5] While *bal tashḥit,* from Deut. 20:19–20, is the prohibition of destroying fruit trees in the context of laying siege to a city, subsequent commentators extended its application to waste of any kind. It has been adopted by Jewish environmentalists as a universal prohibition against destruction of the environment and applied as support for a variety of positive and negative environmental "commandments." For example, recycling reduces waste and is therefore a manifestation of bal tashḥit.

[6] At the suggestion of the *rosh edah,* we divided the same age group by sex for the in-camp overnight at Camp Ramah in New England in 2005, and likewise the results were remarkable. It seems that this approach can be especially effective for children of this age.

[7] This list was culled from a variety of sources, including the COEJL website (www.coejl.org) and a bibliography by Terry Lieberstein. Not all of these works are in print.

HOWARD I. BLAS

Campers with Developmental Disabilities: The Tikvah Program

Disabilities: What the Ancient Rabbis Knew

AT A PRE-SEASON RETREAT, twenty senior staff members of Camp Ramah in New England spent a weekend discussing the educational theme for the upcoming summer—the biblical concept of *betzelem elohim*—the idea that everyone is created in the image of God.[1] As the participants studied a series of biblical and rabbinic texts, it became clear that the rabbis of the second through sixth centuries debated the implications of similarities and differences in people. The ancient rabbis puzzled over which blessing to say upon encountering people who were blind, were missing limbs, or had "unusual skin." It may seem strange to say a blessing in such circumstances, yet a person was expected to acknowledge the entirety of God's human creations.[2]

In the Mishneh Torah, Moses Maimonides, a respected rabbi, Bible commentator, physician, and philosopher, who lived in Egypt and Spain from 1138–1204, discusses the blessing recited upon seeing people who are different in some way. He suggests that one blessing is said upon encountering a person who is *born* a certain way, and an entirely different blessing is recited upon seeing a person who *becomes* "different" (i.e., someone who loses his or her sight or limb). In the former case, one is expected to say the blessing, "Blessed are you God, King of the world, who makes living creatures different," whereas in the latter case, one says, "Blessed are you, the True Judge."[3]

As documented by Eleanor Eells in *History of Organized Camping: The First 100 Years,* camp programs for children with various special needs began to

HOWARD I. BLAS *is a social worker and special education teacher living in New Haven, Connecticut. He worked as a counselor and rosh edah in the Tikvah Program at Camp Ramah in New England from 1984–1988 and has been the director of the Tikvah Program since 2001. In July 2009, he was named to the first cohort of Jim Joseph Foundation Fellows at the Lookstein Center at Bar Ilan University, a program that focuses on leadership, community building, Jewish literacy, and technology.*

emerge in the late nineteenth century, and there has been slow, steady growth since then.[4] Fortunately, now parents of children with all types of special needs easily can access information about camping programs through various print and online directories.[5] It is not possible to pinpoint a date when integration began in so-called regular or typical camps.[6] However, it is clear that "a number of camps operated by religious organizations were in the vanguard of running planned integration programs."[7]

One of the first Jewish summer camps to offer an overnight camping option to campers with special needs was Camp Ramah in New England.[8] The Tikvah Program, now in its fortieth year, is an eight-week overnight camping program for campers with developmental disabilities such as mental retardation, autism and autism-spectrum disorders, and neurological impairments. After four decades, Tikvah is such a natural part of the Ramah community that it is difficult to imagine the camp *without* Tikvah. Yet, when the Tikvah Program was started in 1970, the concept of a program for campers with special needs, as part of a typical camp, was not embraced universally or welcomed.

The next section provides more details of the pioneering Tikvah Program at Ramah in New England. The section after that offers an overview of special needs programs at other Ramah camps. Finally, we look at the lessons that the Ramah Camping Movement has learned from the Tikvah experience, as evidenced by the stories of Ramah and Tikvah staff members, as well as Tikvah families.

The Tikvah Program at Camp Ramah in New England

The Tikvah concept and the early years

According to Herb and Barbara Greenberg, the founders and the directors of the Tikvah Program for twenty-nine years, the concept of a camping program for Jewish adolescents with special needs first was proposed in the late 1960s. The subcommittee on Special Education of the United Synagogue of America Commission on Jewish Education requested that a Jewish summer camp incorporate a group of adolescents with developmental disabilities into its population. Various Jewish camps already had rejected this proposal. In early 1970, the proposal was presented to the National Ramah Commission. Ramah camp boards and directors expressed fears that the presence of a group of mentally and/or emotionally handicapped children in the camp community would disrupt the structure of the camp.[9] Greenberg further reports, "The leaders of Ramah felt that a program that introduced children with disabilities into the camp would create anxiety, both among the other campers and among the staff. They also worried that some parents might be afraid to send their children to camp if these children were there."[10]

Donald Adelman, *z"l,* the director of Camp Ramah in Glen Spey, New York, "was the lone dissenter, the only Ramah director who really wanted this program," according to the Greenbergs. "He took an enormous risk, and he staked his whole career on it. . . . He saw it as a moral responsibility toward those with special needs."[11] In an interview, Herb Greenberg reports, "Years later, we learned that Don had insisted that if there was no room at Ramah for Tikvah, then the whole point of the camp would be lost. 'This is what Ramah should be, and I insist on having it.'"[12]

Tikvah originally was designed to be an overnight camping program, serving a preadolescent population of mentally retarded campers. However, "[i]n the months before the opening of the Tikvah Program in 1970, it became apparent in recruiting campers that a somewhat different population was more receptive to and more in need of a special camp program."[13] Thus, the initial group of campers consisted of children classified by their respective school systems as brain injured, learning disabled, and emotionally disturbed.

The first year of the Tikvah Program took place at Camp Ramah in Glen Spey, New York and included eight campers and five staff members. When the Glen Spey site closed, the Tikvah Program moved to its current site at Camp Ramah in New England in Massachusetts and has operated there continuously since then. In the early years of the program, Tikvah included campers with a wide range of developmental problems. Greenberg notes, "At the outset of the program, we admitted very impaired teenagers including those with Down Syndrome, autism, schizophrenia, and those classified as emotionally disturbed."[14]

In the early years, the Greenbergs spent many hours helping campers and staff members become more comfortable with the idea of a program for campers with special needs as part of the larger Ramah camp. The work was not easy. Even some camp doctors felt uneasy with the Tikvah campers. They feared lawsuits and insisted that the child's primary physician be contacted before any treatment or medical intervention could be taken. Many Israeli staff members also expressed discomfort about working with Tikvah campers. Greenberg reports, "At the time, Israelis were still coming off the euphoria of the Six-Day War (1967) . . . they couldn't tolerate any overt display of weakness, and they even said so."[15]

Some members of the camp community warmly welcomed members of the new program. Bruce Lipton, head of the Ramah New England kitchen from 1968–2006, recalls, "Back then, we didn't think one way or another about special needs—they were just kids—we taught him [a Tikvah camper he employed] how to work in the kitchen—and he is now employed by a large grocery store in the Midwest." Lipton proudly reports that this man came to camp nearly every summer to help set up the kitchen.[16]

The program continued to grow each summer with as many as forty campers with very different special needs participating. The camper population also was quite diverse geographically and religiously. Campers attended Ramah New England from across the United States (as well as from Israel and Mexico) and from across the Jewish religious spectrum—from the unaffiliated and non-observant to those who identified as Reform, Reconstructionist, Conservative, Orthodox, and Hasidic. The Tikvah Program has always strived to create a positive bunk and division experience while also remaining sensitive to the individual needs of each camper. Greenberg notes how, in the early years, Tikvah campers were "desperate for their own peer group."[17] Some campers with learning disabilities who were socially adept were placed in regular bunks, while youngsters with learning disabilities but limited social capabilities remained in bunks designed specifically for Tikvah campers."[18]

The inclusion of Tikvah campers in all aspects of camp life historically has provided the parents of Tikvah campers with a model of what was possible in their home communities. And Tikvah parents historically have worked to help and support each other, through conversations during the year, and by coming together at the Tikvah Parent Conference, a two-day meeting held each summer, where Tikvah parents from across the country share experiences, resources, and advocacy skills. According to the Greenbergs, the experiences of both the campers and their parents in the camp program would impact on and empower families and lead to changes in "every institution in the larger community—schools, group homes, et cetera."[19]

It is interesting to note that while the camp was pioneering inclusion and integration for campers with special needs and offering support for parents, the same children were experiencing separation from their so-called typically developing peers in their home communities and school districts. Several years before Tikvah was founded, a series of court cases, beginning with Brown v. the Board of Education of Topeka, Kansas in 1954, challenged the notion of the segregation of students. In the Brown decision, separation of students based on race was challenged. This case ushered in a period of "intense concern and questioning among parents of children with disabilities who asked why the same principles of equal access to education did not apply to their children."[20]

In 1972, the Pennsylvania Association for Retarded Citizens brought a class action suit against the Commonwealth of Pennsylvania. The suit established the right of free public education for all children with mental retardation. In 1975, the PL-94-142 Education for All Handicapped Children Act mandated free, appropriate public education for all children with disabilities, ages six to twenty-one. It also protected the rights of children with disabilities and their parents in educational decision making, required the development of an individualized education program (IEP) for each child with a disability, and stated that students with disabilities must receive educational services in the least restrictive environment.[21] Congress reauthorized the amendment and renamed it four times, most recently in 1997, when it was restructured and renamed IDEA—Individuals with Disabilities Education Act (PL 105-17).

The range of services for campers with special needs

The Tikvah Program is part of the Camp Ramah in New England community. Currently, the program consists of four components: the Amitzim camping division for campers ages thirteen to eighteen; the Vocational Training Program known as *tochnit avodah* (and by the more informal Voc Ed) for qualified eighteen- to twenty-one-year-old graduates of the camping program; Post Voc Ed, a program that offers a select group of Voc Ed graduates an opportunity to work as salaried camp employees; and Inclusion, a program through which nine- to twelve-year-old campers with a wide range of special needs are included in the daily life of typical bunks and *edot* (divisions).

Activities for Tikvah campers. The Tikvah schedule strives to maintain predictability and routine. Amitzim participate in the entire range of camper activities. At Ramah New England, for example, campers wake up, daven (using a special Tikvah siddur), eat in the *ḥadar ochel,* and return to their bunks—specifically designated for Tikvah campers—for *nikkayon* (bunk cleanup). Three morning *perakim* (periods) typically include *ḥug* (arts and crafts, woodworking, nature, newspaper, video, drama, etc.), sports, and *shirah* and *rikkud* (singing and Israeli dancing). Bogrim Buddies (fourteen-year-old peers) and Machon Helpers (fifteen-year-old peers) participate with Tikvah campers in *ḥugim* and sports several times a week.

Following *aruḥat tzohorayim* (lunch) and *she'at menuḥah* (rest hour, which includes letter-writing time), campers participate in a rotation of four afternoon periods that always include swimming and a Jewish studies class. Although most Tikvah campers participate in these activities with other members of the Tikvah Program, some campers are mainstreamed with other edot for such activities as rikkud, *ommanut* (arts and crafts), and Jewish learning. Other activities in the rotation include *pe'ulot tzerif* (bunk activities, which might include time at the ropes course, alpine tower, and trampoline), ommanut, and a period where campers work at various job sites in camp. After dinner, campers participate in a *pe'ulat erev* (evening activity), sing *Rad hayom* in a closing circle, shower, and conclude their day with winding-down time (usually consisting of a bedtime story or a calming musical piece), and the recitation of Shema before lights out.

Tikvah camper interaction with the larger camp community. The location of Tikvah Village, which consists of two male and two female *tzerifim* (bunks) and a large *mo'adon* (multi-purpose room), fosters interaction with the camp community. Tikvah Village intentionally was constructed on what is called B-Side, the home of the thirteen- to sixteen-year-old "typically developing" campers. (A-Side, a ten minute walk from B-Side, houses the nine- to twelve-year-old "typically developing" campers). Many classes, electives, and camp-wide activities take place in the pine grove and in the buildings just behind the Tikvah bunks. Thus, socialization and interaction occur as campers walk past the Tikvah bunks, en route to division or camp-wide activities or Friday night services. Interaction also takes place on the porches of the Tikvah bunks and in the areas in front of the Tikvah bunks.

There are numerous additional formal and informal opportunities for interaction between members of the Tikvah Program and other campers. As an individual's comfort level increases, his or her level of involvement with the Tikvah Program increases.

On the most basic level, campers and staff members share the physical camp site with the Tikvah Program. Therefore, they see and interact (at first, sometimes from a distance) with Tikvah campers throughout the day—on walkways, ball fields and classrooms, in the dining room, and at all camp-wide activities. Observing Tikvah campers at camp-wide activities can be quite powerful and instructive to members of the camp community. For example, when Tikvah campers compete in the camp-wide sports day, campers in other divisions sometimes see how fast or skilled at volleyball or softball a person with disabilities can be. When a member of the Tikvah Program leads prayers or blessings for the entire camp, a younger camper, perhaps not yet possessing such skills or confidence, sees how people with disabilities possess many abilities. For the past two summers, a member of the Tikvah Program who has been taking dance lessons for many years, performed a solo tap dance for the entire camp at the *zimkudiyyah* (song and dance festival).

Beyond observing from a distance, there are numerous opportunities, both planned and spontaneous, for campers and staff to interact with Tikvah campers. The youngest campers (entering third grade), who attend camp for a two-week mini-session, traditionally visit with members of the Tikvah Program and tour the Tikvah bunks as part of their Jewish Studies curriculum on the theme of being created "in God's image." This curriculum focuses on similarities and differences between human beings. Tikvah counselors visit the bunks of the youngest campers to answer questions the evening before these campers visit Tikvah Village. When the campers experience Tikvah Village, they have an opportunity (often for the first time in their lives) to walk up the ramp, hold the grab bar in the bathroom, and sit on the shower chair. The campers compare and contrast these bunks to their own. (They are often jealous to see how spacious, well-lit, and climate-controlled the bunks are!) Later in the week, the campers join Tikvah campers for prayer services.

Campers ages nine to twelve interact with Tikvah campers through participation in counselor-planned bunk or division activities. Younger campers typically enjoy many of the same activities as the Tikvah campers. Campers in the thirteen- to sixteen-year-old divisions can study rabbinic sources dealing with disabilities in their Jewish Studies classes and participate in a dialogue with a panel of Tikvah campers and graduates. In addition, fourteen- and fifteen-year-old campers can elect to participate in a buddy program. Each camper electing to be a buddy spends forty-five minutes, twice a week, socializing and/or working one-on-one (on a skill, sport, etc.) with a Tikvah camper.

Sixteen-year-old campers have the option to work with Tikvah campers as part of their counselor-in–training (CIT) experience. These CITs learn the skills that are required to serve campers with special needs, and they work two full days per week with their Tikvah bunk (at such crucial times as wake up, rest period, and preparation for bedtime). Although CITs may exhibit typical sixteen-year-old behavior in their own divisions, they tend to display their best, most responsible behavior in their CIT role. They serve as excellent models of appropriate dress, behavior, and language for the Tikvah campers. In the summer of 2007, an unprecedented twenty campers volunteered to serve as CITs. Parents of Tikvah campers always are pleased that their children have opportunities to interact extensively with "typically developing" teenagers.

Although Tikvah campers are clearly the recipients of the assistance and coaching offered by peers from other divisions, it is important to emphasize that the relationships are beneficial to "typically developing" campers as well. Volunteering brings out the best in the teenagers, who often feel proud that they have succeeded in what may have appeared to be a difficult area. Such direct involvement with campers with special needs tends to demystify this population. These teenagers often choose to donate money to the Tikvah Program as part of a bar/bat mitzvah project, they sometimes choose to volunteer or perform additional community service with a similar population in their home communities, and many former buddies and CITs return to camp to serve as Tikvah counselors.

Vocational education and inclusion programs. Nearly twenty years ago, Tikvah started a vocational education (Voc Ed) program. Select graduates of the camping program live in a group-home–like setting where they are responsible for their own laundry, cleaning of shared rooms and the common area, light cooking, and kitchen chores. "Voc Eders" work at various jobs throughout camp. Some graduates of this program are hired as salaried workers of camp. In New England, several members of the Post Voc Ed Program are in charge of operating and maintaining the newly constructed, six-unit guest house, while others work in the art department, the mail room/information center, the *gan* (camp program for staff children), and the infirmary. Post Voc Eders live in staff housing, work with a job coach, and receive support around problem solving, socialization issues, and negotiating days off. Similarly, graduates of the other Tikvah programs are hired by the camps.

Developments in the field and in the lives of children and families with special needs encourage the program to challenge its established practices and consider additional programs and models of service delivery. When families of current and prospective campers began raising questions about Tikvah's "separateness" from same-age peers in typical divisions, the camp explored the possibility of starting an inclusion program. A small inclusion program for campers too young for Tikvah, funded by a grant, was started at Ramah New England in 2005. Such a program allows same-age campers (with and without identified disabilities) to begin camp together at a young age and "travel" through the various edot together.

Currently, the Tikvah Program is examining its age of graduation policy. Although graduation from high school (at twenty-one or twenty-two, depending on one's home school district) has historically been considered to be the end of eligibility for Tikvah; it has become increasingly apparent that some campers can continue to benefit from the program. In addition, many campers with developmental delays exhibit uncanny growth in their late teens and early twenties. On a case-by-case basis, some campers have remained in camp beyond the graduation age.

Teaching values and decision-making: Tikvah campers as givers. Campers with different areas of strength and weakness tend to help and receive help from others. They also help and receive help from members of the larger Ramah community. For example, a particularly strong female camper who was not very verbal took it upon herself to push the adult-sized stroller of a camper with cerebral palsy. Tikvah campers tend to reach out to visitors by showing them the correct page in the Tikvah siddur and by introducing themselves with words and a handshake to guests who attend Tikvah Shabbat morning services.

Although Tikvah campers are recipients of the kindness of others, they also are taught to contribute. They help clean the camp on Fridays, often set up benches and prayer books, and clean candle holders for Shabbat. One summer, Tikvah campers regularly volunteered to make a minyan for a staff member saying kaddish. Tikvah campers study the Jewish concept of *tikkun olam* (repairing the world) and participate in various charitable activities. On Fridays, Tikvah campers bake hallah to raise money for *tzedakah*. Campers who participate in the Tikvah Israel trip during the winter routinely deliver gifts to children (including Israeli Arabs) in a pediatric unit of a hospital, plant trees, and engage in other forms of *gemilut ḥasadim* (acts of kindness).

Tikvah campers also contribute by donating their talents to the camp community. One camper, a skilled tennis player, volunteered to teach tennis to nine- and ten-year-old campers several times a week; another camper, an excellent volleyball player, served as an assistant coach for the camp volleyball team. Several members of the Voc Ed program play in the weekly staff softball game and have made major contributions to their teams. A mother proudly tells the story of how her son was helped in preparing for his bar mitzvah by a Tikvah camper who possessed excellent synagogue skills. (That young bar mitzvah student returned to camp years later to serve as a Tikvah counselor!)

The Development of Other Ramah Programs for Campers with Special Needs

In 1973, a second Tikvah program was established at Camp Ramah in Wisconsin. The current Ramah Wisconsin program is primarily for adolescents with learning problems and social difficulties, specializing in the needs of campers with Asperger's Syndrome. In addition to an eight-week camping program, Wisconsin also offers a four-week "Taste of Tikvah" option for first-time campers who are in junior high school. In the early 1980s, a program was started at Camp Ramah in California; another was started at Camp Ramah in Canada in 1993. The Tikvah programs in Canada and California, like that of New England, offer overnight camping experiences for adolescents with developmental disabilities. Ramah Canada offers a six-week Tikvah program for campers ages twelve to twenty-one. Campers aged eighteen to twenty-one also participate in a vocational education program. Current Tikvah campers may remain in the program until age twenty-four, whereas new campers are accepted through age twenty-one.

Camp Ramah in California offers a four-week program for adolescents ages eleven to fifteen with learning, emotional, and developmental disabilities, as well as a similar program for fifteen- to eighteen-year-olds. "Ezra," a seven-week vocational training and independent living program, is offered to eighteen- to twenty-four-year-olds. Ezra participants live in a new dorm built in the

Rabbi Mitchell Cohen, former director of Camp Ramah in Canada, reflects on establishing Tikvah at Canada:

When I became the director of Ramah Canada in 1990 after having spent seven summers at Ramah California, I immediately felt the absence of a Tikvah program. Tikvah in California had a large impact on me as an educator, particularly in the ways in which the program impacted on the entire camp.

I began planning for a Tikvah program at Ramah Canada. I received Board approval, as long as I could find the funding to create such an expensive new program. In particular, Ab Flatt, my Board president, and Gloria Silverman, an executive committee member and senior camp educator, were strong supporters of this idea. The Federation proved to be very supportive, and I submitted a proposal for approximately $60,000 over three years, which was approved. The main obstacle was finding a director.

Dr. Mitch Parker, a teacher at camp, was a psychologist who worked in a school with a special needs population in Buffalo, and I asked him whether he knew of anyone who might be interested in directing a new Tikvah program. I'll never forget the phone call, a few days later, when he called me back and said, 'How about me?' I was thrilled, and that call was the beginning of an eight-year relationship [at Ramah Canada]. It was critical to have someone with the professionalism and specific expertise that Mitch possesses to allay the fears of many parents, board members, and staff members that perhaps we could not handle youngsters with developmental challenges at camp.

Now, after many successful summers of the Tikvah Program, an entire generation of campers and staff can't imagine Camp Ramah in Canada without Tikvah! The Tikvah Program has provided many special experiences for all members of the camp community. One highlight for me was the bar mitzvah of Brian, a Tikvah camper from Toronto, whose parents were disappointed that he could not have his bar mitzvah at a Toronto synagogue. They approached me about doing a bar mitzvah at camp, and needless to say, it was one of the most emotional events of my career. The entire camp came to tefillot to be part of this experience, and when Brian raised his hands in triumph in front of the Torah, there wasn't a dry eye in the room.

These experiences continue at Ramah Canada and at special needs programs throughout the Ramah camping system.

summer of 2008. In anticipation of the building of the new dorm, Elana Naftalin-Kelman, director of Camp Ramah in California's Tikvah/Special Needs programs, said, "To have a space of their own within camp where the Ezra participants can learn to cook their own meals, do their own laundry, and host their friends and family—all while continuing to learn how to live Jewish lives is an invaluable component of our program. This dorm will radically expand and enhance each participant's experience at camp and their impact upon camp as well."

In 2003, Camp Ramah in the Berkshires established the four-week overnight Breira program for campers with learning and/or social challenges. Each summer, Breira serves twenty campers through age fifteen. Common diagnoses of Breira campers include attention deficit disorder (ADD), pervasive developmental disorder (PDD), Asperger's Syndrome, language-based learning disabilities, and anxiety disorders. According to Dr. Beth Jaret, the director of the Breira B'Ramah program, as quoted in the program brochure, the goals of Breira are "to honor attitude over aptitude, effort over ability, and cooperation over competition; to utilize feedback from campers and staff in order to increase self-awareness regarding personal hygiene, social responsibility, and social growth; and to provide the tools that are necessary to enable Breira campers to strengthen their identity, observance, and commitment to Judaism."

Rabbi Paul Resnick, the director of Ramah Berkshires, has said, "Before this program began, parents had to make the choice between a place that would support their child's needs and a camp with a Jewish soul."[22] He writes of the early planning stages of Breira:

> What was discussed in 1999 was a program to serve mainstreamed children in a mainstream camp. It was nothing short of a radical change in camping. . . . We [met] in the offices of Camp Ramah in the Berkshires in the Union Theological Seminary dreaming about something new. . . . We were committed and we knew that this would become a groundbreaking program in the world of informal Jewish education.[23]

In the past five years, several Ramah camps have established family camp programs designed for families with children with special needs. Camp Ramah Darom in Georgia runs Camp Yofi, a family camp for children with autism, their parents, and siblings. Rabbi Loren Sykes, director of Camp Ramah in Wisconsin and former executive director of Ramah Darom, was recognized by the Covenant Foundation in 2006 for this innovative program. After the program's first year in 2005, Rabbi Sykes wrote:

> There is nothing small about each victory for a child with autism, a sibling, or a parent. Each win is major and significant. . . . As we entered Shabbat that week, it became clear that I had never been involved in anything more meaningful or moving than Camp Yofi. I met an incredible group of families parenting at a level most of us can never understand. The first gathering of Jewish families with children with autism had, in a very short time, created one of the most spiritual communities I have ever joined.[24]

Camp Ramah in California runs Camp Ohr Lanu, a week-long camp for families who have children with special needs. Camp Ramah in the Poconos announced the opening of its Tikvah Family Camp for the summer of 2009 for the families of children with developmental disorders and/or social learning disorders. Kesher, a program for campers with deafness, existed for several summers at Camp Ramah in the Poconos but is no longer in existence.

Each of the Ramah special needs programs has unique features. Ramah California, Wisconsin, and New England have offered Israel programs to a wide range of Tikvah campers and alumni. Additionally, various camps offer a vocational training program with employment *in* camp. Wisconsin has experimented with transporting program participants to jobs *outside* of camp in the Eagle River, Wisconsin community. As mentioned earlier, Ramah California has a special Café Ezra, run entirely by members of the vocational training program. At the Ramah Day Camp in Wheeling, Illinois, a program for children ages five to eleven is offered in partnership with Keshet, a Chicago-area program for Jewish children with special needs. This inclusion program is for children with a wide range of disabilities.

Each Ramah camp has stories to share about in-camp Tikvah bar and bat mitzvah celebrations. And each camp proudly offers stories of people whose lives have been changed by Tikvah—from Tikvah staff members, to Tikvah campers and families, to campers in other divisions, staff members, Israeli *sheliḥim,* and Shabbat visitors. The following section demonstrates that the impact of Tikvah is indeed extraordinary, and the Tikvah model teaches many valuable lessons.

Special Needs at Ramah: Lessons for the Field

Tikvah campers and the various Tikvah programs clearly have had a strong impact on the Ramah community. Several generations of Ramah campers and staff members have benefited from the presence of the Tikvah Program as part of the larger Ramah community. Important lessons (which may be applied to a variety of settings) can be learned from the Tikvah experience.

Lesson 1

All beginnings are hard but usually are worth it. (Or, *na'aseh venishma:* Do it now! Collaborate with other believers to work out the difficulties as they arise.)

Herb and Barbara Greenberg's description of the early years of Tikvah indicate an initial reluctance and even a resistance to establishing a program for campers with special needs as part of the larger camp community. These feelings could derive from nervousness or fear.

Rabbi Mitch Cohen, the current National Ramah Director, who was the director of Camp Ramah in Canada when that camp initiated its Tikvah Program, notes:

> To our shock and dismay, many staff members—particularly those who had been on staff for many years—thought we might be hurting camp in some way, shifting the focus of Ramah, or taking on more than we could handle. I was appalled that something as wonderful as Tikvah could be the focus of such a negative reaction. Thankfully, these fears quickly dissipated when the Tikvah participants arrived. Our Tikvah staff was fantastic with them and with integrating them into the camp community. Almost everyone in camp saw that we could handle this new population and that their presence in camp would only add value to Ramah. That has been the legacy of Tikvah . . . as now an entire generation of campers and staff couldn't imagine Camp Ramah in Canada without Tikvah!

Dr. Mitch Parker, former director of the Tikvah Program at Ramah Canada, recalls the jitters felt by the entire Ramah Canada community as they prepared for their first group of Tikvah campers. He recalls a conversation between a Tikvah counselor and a veteran Ramah counselor just before the campers arrived, "Why are you doing this? Tikvah is going to ruin the Camp Ramah experience for everyone!" Parker recounts:

> We put on a brave front, but no one was really sure what challenges day one, day two, or day three would bring. . . . Today and for the past fifteen years, the Tikvah Program is an integral part of Camp Ramah in Canada. Every summer, when the campers in Tikvah return home at the end of the sixth week of the season, there is a palpable sense of loss among the campers and staff. The rest of the summer, despite many exciting activities and events, is just a little bit less bright.

Herb Greenberg observes, "It is a testimony to the Ramah community in that it demonstrated tremendous patience, sensitivity, and resilience in learning how to deal with this population."[25]

Lesson 2

The impact on the camp community as a whole is great. Tikvah shapes attitudes and influences career choices. Tikvah offers a great deal not only to campers with special needs but also to the larger Ramah community. Campers regularly write and call to share stories of the impact of Tikvah on their growth and development and sometimes on their career choices. They recall an interaction or experience with a certain Tikvah camper—from time spent as a Bogrim Buddy, to a more informal interaction—dancing together in the hadar ochel, playing catch on the *migrash,* sitting together on the tennis court during a camp-wide barbecue, or watching a Tikvah play. Some campers and staff members return to their home communities or college campuses and volunteer in various capacities to work with people with special needs (e.g., Special Olympics or tutoring for bar and bat mitzvah). Many campers serve informally as "attitude and language monitors" in their homes and communities, "correcting" parents, neighbors, and fellow congregants when words like "disabled" are used to describe people with disabilities. Many such campers request to work as Tikvah counselors when they return to camp as staff members.

To more systematically study the attitudes of campers, Ramah New England administered the Learning and Development at Camp Ramah Inventory (a survey of social and emotional issues) to one hundred fifth-through seventh-grade campers.[26] Results were significant for a very high rate of agreement to the twelve questions that were included to better understand attitudes of typical campers toward the Tikvah Program and to assess the likely impact of the Tikvah Program on their life paths. Key findings include:

- Seventy-nine percent strongly agreed or agreed that "[t]he Ramah experience has helped me to feel more comfortable around people with special needs."
- Sixty-three percent strongly agreed or agreed that "[m]y experiences with campers from this camp's special needs program will carry over into other areas of my life."
- Fifty-eight percent strongly agreed or agreed that "[m]y experiences with campers from this camp's special needs program have made me a better person (for example, more patient, more tolerant)."

Although the study included only campers, we know anecdotally that counselors from both the Tikvah Program and other divisions and specialty staffs sometimes pursue studies and seek employment in special education and related fields. Ilana Blidner, the director of the 2008 Tikvah Program at Ramah Canada, is one of the countless people who have decided on career paths as a result of the Tikvah experience. Blidner reports, "I had no idea where four years as a counselor would lead. That first experience working as a counselor in Tikvah provided me with a completely alternate perspective to my life goals and ambitions." She went on to pursue degrees in psychology, child study, and special education and notes:

> I dream of opening my own learning center one day that caters to the social and emotional development of children with special needs. . . . I can say with complete certainty that if it wasn't for my opportunity four years ago to enter the Tikvah Program, I would not be where I am today, academically and professionally.

Blidner captures the essence of the impact of Tikvah on Ramah quite eloquently when she says:

> I think the camp benefits from having Tikvah there. I know that our campers bring a different energy to our camp. They are the most appreciative

> individuals who benefit from many aspects of Camp Ramah life. I have had countless experiences where our campers have participated in an event with another edah or had members of [the] *mishlaḥat* engage in activity with them—and everyone leaves with large smiles, laughter, and a sense of fulfillment. The campers of Tikvah have this tremendous ability to empower others in our camp. Magshimim campers, Nitzanim campers, campers of all ages have approached me in the past to relay a special experience they had with one of our campers or to ask if they can participate in our pe'ulot erev or tefillot. It always seems that other campers and staff in camp gravitate toward the Tikvah edah. It is remarkable. I believe that a significant benefit that camp receives from having Tikvah as a part of our camp is the awareness it brings to others—that is, it sheds light on the diversity that surrounds our communities and provides an opportunity for individuals, who don't usually have the opportunity at home, to spend time with our campers, to learn from them, and spend time with them. It is wonderful for such young campers (and campers and staff of all ages) to learn about various developmental disabilities and observe individuals with different strengths and needs.

Rose Sharon, Tikvah Program co-director at Camp Ramah in Wisconsin, captures how integral and involved Tikvah is in all aspects of camp life—from the integrated Machon-Tikvah play, to the fact that former Tikvah campers work on staff. This level of involvement in the community continues outside of camp, where campers are welcomed and included in United Synagogue Youth (USY) activities. A Tikvah Wisconsin camper, Mitch Paschen, was invited to deliver a speech at the USY international convention some time ago.

Ralph Schwartz, a former counselor and rosh edah in the New England Tikvah Program, the founding director of the Breira Program at Ramah Berkshires, and the current co-director of the Tikvah Program at Ramah Wisconsin observes, "In each of these Ramah camps, the rest of the campers and the staff have gained tremendous understanding, sensitivity, caring, and respect for Tikvah campers." Speaking personally, Schwartz notes, "My work in Tikvah affects my life, my relationships with others, and my understanding of our world. All of us are truly created in the image of God."

Lesson 3

Tikvah families need Tikvah. Without it, their children would not reach their Jewish potential nor feel included in the Jewish community. After families find Tikvah, they feel as if they've "won the lottery." Although historically families learned of Tikvah by word of mouth from families with children in the program, through rabbis, or through other members of the Jewish community, increasingly they are learning of Tikvah through online searches and through directories of camp and special needs programs. Some families report feeling satisfied that their rabbi or cantor knew of Tikvah through their own Ramah experiences, whereas other families report disappointment and are upset that their clergy never mentioned Tikvah *despite* their involvement with Ramah and their awareness of the congregant's child with special needs. Families typically report a shortage of Jewish camping programs (day and overnight) for children with special needs. Some families come to Tikvah after what they describe as "failed" experiences at other overnight camps.

Tikvah families, especially those who have discovered the program when their children are still young enough to benefit from many years in the program, tend to be very pleased with their child's growth and development as a result of their Tikvah experience. Parents report their children's increased socialization and independence through their camp experience. One mother reports that "sleepover camp is [my son's] opportunity to expand his social 'circle' and do so in an independent setting—away from mom and dad and school." They are pleased that he has the same opportunities as other children to attend summer camp. Parents highlight opportunities to grow and mature socially, emotionally, physically, and psychologically, and to develop self-care skills, independence, and confidence. They are pleased with their children's opportunities to be with "typical" peers and to be involved in "real interactions."

Many Tikvah families express their gratitude that Ramah provides their children with "exposure to Jewish learning, values, traditions, history, and ritual." Whereas some campers participate in Jewish rituals year-round at home, one family (though quite involved Jewishly) notes that their son attends a boarding school and does not have ongoing exposure to Jewish rituals. Several families expressed frustration at the lack of ongoing Jewish educational opportunities in their home communities. "At camp, [my daughter] has received a wonderful Jewish education. This is very important to us—because she has not been able to attend religious school and receive a Jewish education because of her disabilities."

Tikvah parents also recognize the benefit of Tikvah for the other Ramah campers. One mother observes:

> Other kids learn to be more accepting and tolerant—it opens their eyes to something they may otherwise never be exposed to. Walls of ignorance and lack of understanding are broken down when they all live and play in the same environment. I have to believe that interactions with Tikvah campers help make the other campers and counselors more sensitive to and understanding of those with special needs and appreciative of their own abilities.

Excerpts from a letter dated September 1994 to Rabbi Mitchell Cohen, then director of Camp Ramah in Canada, from Paula David, a Ramah Canada Tikvah parent:

We have always loved Brian and been proud of his accomplishments. We, as his family, never had the imagination, the skills and the courage to push him in new directions that Ramah seems to have done just by existing. He arrived home from camp and immediately set the table, wolfed down supper and followed with *birkat hamazon* (grace after meals). As he pulled his various papers and craft projects out of his duffle bags, he serenaded us with appropriate Hebrew prayers, songs and words that had been part of his camp life. In spite of his deafness and speech problems, we were all able to recognize the tunes and words he meant. . . .

This is from a child that we thought would never have the capacity to understand what goes on in shul, never mind have a sense of Jewish identity. This is now the child that inspires his four siblings to accompany him to synagogue services and learn his camp songs so that they can all sing together. This is the child who gathers *kippot* for family dinners and makes sure everyone has a siddur in front of their plate. This is the child who wraps himself up in his *tallit* and *tefillin* and quietly davens when he is sad . . . His family never really enjoyed or felt connected to a synagogue, mainly because of the reception (or lack thereof) that Brian receives. Camp Ramah has given Brian a magical belonging that we were unable to provide and are thrilled to see . . .

I know you look for special staff and you follow through with special training for the Tikvah staff. In this case, the word 'special' becomes overused, and there aren't really words to describe the bond and the unconditional acceptance that we've seen Brian enjoy with his counselors. Yaniv has become an ongoing part of Brian's circle, taking him out most week-ends and supporting him in Special Olympic bowling and swimming. Even though Brian was heartbroken when he finally accepted that Yaniv wasn't returning to camp this year, we were able to see how he was proud and excited to introduce and talk about Michael and Rafi. In many ways, our family now feels that Brian's counselors join our ranks, because they have lived with him and recognize the gifts he brings into others' lives. Brian's circle, and therefore his family's because of Camp Ramah, continues to widen and strengthen. Until the Tikvah Program, Brian, although he knew he was loved, never knew the wonder of having loving friends and peers.

Other parents note, "By having Tikvah in the larger camp community, there are great benefits—from understanding that there are differences in people, to acceptance of the differences, to working with the differences. . . . It's a win-win situation for all concerned. Welcome to the 'real world', where there are differences!" And, "Typical campers can see firsthand that people with special needs are not a monolithic entity, and each camper brings his/her uniqueness, as well as those special aspects of personality, adolescence, and social needs that all campers share."

Conclusion

When the Tikvah Program first was created, there were few overnight camping programs that offered services to campers with special needs and that also were part of a regular summer camp. Programs geared specifically to Jewish campers were even harder to find. Now, after forty years, the Tikvah programs, and other programs serving campers with special needs, are integral parts of their respective Ramah camps. These programs offer opportunities and benefits for all members of the Ramah community. Nonetheless, such programs present special issues and challenges. The Ramah Camping Movement continues to grow and evolve to meet these challenges and the changing requirements of campers with special needs. The impact of the Tikvah Program, as well as other Ramah programs for people with special needs, is tremendous and is clearly felt throughout the Ramah Camping Movement and the entire Jewish world.

Notes

1 Campers at all Ramah camps spend one period each day learning in a Jewish Studies class and a Hebrew language class. The staff retreat served to kick off the theme of the coming summer, where campers would be exploring what it means to be created "in God's image."

2 There are many categories of blessings in the Jewish tradition. Some are for expressing thanks and enjoyment; others are recited as part of the three-times-a-day, fixed-prayer service; and others were formulated by the ancient rabbis for such rituals as lighting Sabbath or Hanukkah candles, using the four biblical species on the Sukkot (Tabernacles) holiday, etc. Just as it is a commandment to show thanks to God for things we experience through our various senses, such as food and beverages, pleasant fragrances, and rainbows, so too it is expected that people say blessings when they encounter the important or famous (e.g., presidents and prime ministers), as well as those who appear "different."

3 Maimonides writes, "One who sees an Ethiopian (a person with a different color of skin from what the rabbis were accustomed to seeing) or a person with a disfigured face or limbs recites the blessing, 'Blessed are you God, King of the world, who makes living creatures different.'" One who sees a blind person or an amputee (this may refer to someone who is "crippled" or paralyzed as well) says the blessing, "Blessed are you, the True Judge."

4 Eleanor Eells, *History of Organized Camping: The First 100 Years* (Martinsville, IN: American Camping Association, 1986).

5 For example, the organization Resources for Children with Special Needs (www.resourcesnyc.org/rcsn.htm) publishes a camp guide that is updated every year. At www.mysummercamps.com, one can access a link to "special needs camps," and click one of twenty-four subcategories, such as Asperger's, autism, cerebral palsy, developmental disabilities, etc.

6 Jim Blake, "Opening Doors: Integration of Persons with a Disability in Organized Children's Camping in Canada." *Journal of Leisurability* 23 no. 2 (1996): 1–9.

7 Ibid., 3. Blake refers to a personal communication with the director of a Mennonite camp who said he became involved in integration because, "it's just who we are and what we believe in."

[8] According to Rabbi Mitch Cohen, the National Ramah Director, the Tikvah Program actually opened its doors on the campus of Camp Ramah in Glen Spey, New York. The Glen Spey site was closed in 1971, and all campers were transferred to either Camp Ramah in the Berkshires or Camp Ramah in New England. Tikvah was relocated to the New England site in Massachusetts.

[9] Herb and Barbara Greenberg, "Our Tikvah Mission: A Recipe for Leadership," in *Ramah Reflections at 50: Visions for a New Century,* ed. Sheldon A. Dorph (New York: National Ramah Commission, 2000), 140. See also "The Tikvah Program," *The Pedagogic Reporter* (American Association for Jewish Education) 30 no. 1 (Fall, 1979): 31–33. Also, Barbara Greenberg, "*Yesh Tikvah*—There is Hope," *Women's League Outlook* (Winter, 1987): 10–12.

[10] Personal communication with Herb Greenberg.

[11] *The Tikvah Program at 25 Dinner Journal,* Herb and Barbara Greenberg Talk with William Novak, 4–5.

[12] Ibid.

[13] Herb and Barbara Greenberg, *The Pedagogic Reporter,* 31.

[14] Personal communication with Herb Greenberg.

[15] Ramah camps bring a delegation of thirty to fifty Israelis to camp each summer. The comfort level of the Israelis working with the Tikvah Program has increased every year since the program was established. Some returning Israelis even request to serve as counselors or live-ins in the Tikvah bunks.

[16] Personal communication with Bruce Lipton, November, 2006. Also, in B. Greenberg, "*Yesh Tikvah*—There is Hope," 12.

[17] Personal communication with Herb Greenberg.

[18] Personal communication with Herb Greenberg. There were many variables that determined placement in bunks outside of Tikvah, and they included and were not limited to the following: (1) parental inclusion or suppression of data from schools and specialists; (2) school placement (children who were successfully mainstreamed throughout the school year were given an opportunity for regular placement); (3) medication factors (anti-depressants, Ritalin dosage, other central nervous system (CNS) stimulants, seizure disorders, etc.) were determinants in placement because of monitoring issues; (4) background in Jewish education; (5) successful integration in USY programs in the home community. Full regular cabin placement was always limited through the end of my tenure. One of the main factors was the fact that the camp had to deal with many socially and emotionally troubled kids who had never been considered for Tikvah placement.

[19] Personal communication with Herb Greenberg.

[20] William H. Howard, *Exceptional Children: An Introduction to Special Education* (Upper Saddle River, NJ: Merrill Prentice Hall, 2003), 20.

[21] Ibid., 32.

[22] Tammy Arnow, "Breira B'Ramah Adds Another Dimension to Camp," *Mifgash Ramah: The Voice of Camp Ramah in the Berkshires* (August 2005): 9.

[23] Personal communication with Rabbi Paul Resnick.

[24] Loren Sykes, "Parashat Ekev," *Derishat Shalom* [e-mail newsletter] (August 26, 2005).

[25] Personal communication with Herb Greenberg.

[26] Additional results from this survey are discussed in the chapter entitled "Social Climate at Ramah: Relationships and Motivation" by Jeffrey S. Kress and Michael Ben-Avie in this volume.

JOSHUA CAHAN

Reclaiming Piety

OVER THE LAST DECADE, Ramah Wisconsin has strengthened its tradition of excellence in Jewish study and programming significantly. An essential component of this revitalization has been the presence of the Beit Midrash Program (BMP) and the Northwoods Kollel. Over the past eight years, these programs have transformed the religious culture of the camp, inspiring a whole generation of campers through yeshiva-style Torah study and intense religious living within a context of thoughtfulness and open-mindedness.

The effect has been profound. Through these experiences, more campers have come to value the religious, as well as the social opportunities camp offers. Through Jewish study and spirituality, they have discovered exciting ways to express their Jewishness. And the impact stretches beyond the summer: more of our alumni are organizing study groups and Shabbat activities at home during the year; studying Torah in Israel after high school; and playing leadership roles in campus religious life. The following are a few examples: (a) Our Shabbat afternoon singing has become enormously popular—the slow and emotional melodies of *se'udah shelishit* (the third meal)—drawing almost 200 people, campers as well as staff every Shabbat. Numerous campers have described that hour of song as the spiritual highlight of their week. And that energy has had a ripple effect. In the last few years, many Ramah Seminar and USY Pilgrimage groups have made se'udah shelishit a regular part of their Shabbat programs, mostly at the urging of Ramah Wisconsin alumni. I also am aware of at least seven campuses and six synagogues where alumni have been involved in organizing se'udah shelishit programs. (b) An alumna of our program, a student at an Orthodox day school, found in the *beit midrash* a community with which to talk through her struggles and concerns about how to fit her desire for gender equality into her ideas of traditional Judaism. Three years of challenging study at

RABBI JOSHUA CAHAN *is the director of the Beit Midrash of The Jewish Theological Seminary, where he is a doctoral candidate in Talmud. Since 2000, Rabbi Cahan has been the director of the Northwoods Kollel, a summer yeshiva program at Camp Ramah in Wisconsin. He is also the editor of the recently published* Yedid Nefesh *bentsher.*

camp led her to study at the Conservative Yeshiva through the Nativ program and ultimately led her to a more mature and positive relationship to Torah study and observance and to a deepened commitment to egalitarian study and prayer. (c) Another alumnus recently returned from Israel and is beginning college. He reports that he had many wonderful and inspiring experiences in Israel and learned and grew a great deal. But in many ways, he still sees the openness and excitement of his religious experience at camp to be the ideal. He will head to campus (a small campus where Chabad is the best option for Shabbat) with a certainty that no matter what community he finds himself in temporarily, the values he learned at Ramah will remain central to his ultimate vision of his religious identity.

Conservative institutions and programs often exert a lot of effort in outreach, making Jewish experiences accessible to the less knowledgeable, but sometimes forgetting that the key to building a secure future is in-reach—creating frameworks that foster the continued religious growth of young people who want more of what we have given them. They are asking for the resources to continue to grow and learn within a context that reinforces the values of equality, social justice, and halachic development that are so central to our worldview. Our experience suggests that reclaiming key aspects of yeshiva culture—like Talmud study and beit midrash-oriented learning and creating shared spiritual experiences through song and ritual—is crucial to shaping religiously committed Jews who will retain these values.

The Beit Midrash Program

I founded the BMP in 2000 together with camp alumnus Aryeh Bernstein. We were invited by the camp director, Rabbi David Soloff, to structure a Talmud-study experience that would utilize both beit midrash and classroom study to engage students directly with Talmudic texts and ideas. The initiative responded to a sense that we were not meeting the educational needs of many of our campers. There was a growing subgroup of campers who were asking for opportunities to study Talmud and engage more directly with Jewish texts, many of whom saw Talmud study as part of their religious growth process. We wanted to engage and encourage their exploration while helping them to approach Talmud and notions of tradition and halachah in a thoughtful and open-minded way. Also, some of our brightest and most engaged campers were finding formal study at camp intellectually unsatisfying. We wanted to offer an intensive, self-directed study environment that would challenge them and deepen their thinking about their Jewish selves.

In our first summer, we attracted about twenty students. In recent years, approximately fifty-five campers from three *edot* (divisions), one-quarter of all those eligible, have signed up each summer for the program, committing one and a half hours daily to Talmud study. The core of the program is intensive Talmud study, offered as an alternative to standard camp classes in Judaica and Hebrew, focusing on developing the skills to understand and think critically about rabbinic texts. We use original texts without translation, providing glossaries and guiding questions to help students navigate the unfamiliar terrain. Study time is divided evenly between work in *ḥavruta* (study pairs) and class discussion, allowing participants the freedom to develop their own ideas while trying to keep the sense of challenge from turning into frustration.

At the same time, we always work to connect the texts and ideas to contemporary, real-world problems, to ask how the tradition speaks to us, and to learn how our world forces us to reexamine elements of our tradition. We encourage students to struggle with texts and ideas, which means asking serious questions that both embrace and challenge the tradition. We also developed informal groups outside the classroom where religious questions can be discussed openly. We push campers to articulate and explain their own views about Judaism and to listen to their peers. This has challenged many of their preconceptions, encouraged self-awareness, and taught them to listen seriously and respectfully to differing viewpoints. This may be the most important lesson we teach—after they learn to dialogue with reflection and respect, our more outspoken campers discover that their most rewarding relationships are with those who see religion very differently.

The beit midrash concept met with significant skepticism from several sources. Some feared that the program would lower the level of the Judaic text classes outside of the BMP because the strongest students would opt for the BMP, leaving the original program and its teachers with less motivated students. There was also a fear that having a separate Talmud track would be a cause for polarization among campers; being in Talmud track either would be seen as a social stigma to be avoided or as a badge for anyone who wanted to be seen as a "serious Jew."

We tried to be very conscious of these concerns in publicizing the program, talking about alternative learning models and avoiding language that suggested that one model was better than another. We emphasized the focus on Talmudic methodology and skills and on independent study. In practice, there was some impact on regular text classes, but this was greatly offset by a marked improvement in the organization and quality of the entire text program. In recent years, many campers have actually felt torn because of the attractiveness of both the Beit Midrash and the text programs. We sense that more campers now have a positive view of their Jewish study experience because of these choices.

We have seen no evidence that participation in the BMP creates divisions beyond the classroom. There has been a balance of male and female participants, of students from traditional or observant Jewish backgrounds and of those from alternative traditional backgrounds, and from day schools and public schools. Strong and religiously involved students also have chosen the main text program, thus avoiding any serious problems of imbalance.

Another implication of this new program is that all campers from an *edah* no longer study the same material. Some view this as a loss, as campers might miss a key component of the edah curriculum and the progression through material from summer to summer. Yet, the growth of the BMP has paralleled the recognition among the camp senior educators that it is unrealistic to expect that the camp curriculum will have significant continuity from one summer to the next, given the ten intervening months. Instead, we have begun to focus on creating powerful learning experiences that resonate positively with students, exploring a wider range of topics for younger campers, and offering a range of electives for the three oldest edot. The BMP fits much more comfortably into this mindset than into earlier educational models. It is now one of a range of different learning experiences that enable campers to find their comfort zone.

There also has been skepticism about whether Conservative kids would be interested in studying Talmud in a yeshiva-like setting and that such interest perhaps indicated a first step toward Orthodox Judaism. It is indeed a challenge to get teenagers involved in the complexities of rabbinic thought, but this is true of kids from all backgrounds. On the other hand, many of our kids are turned on by the religious energy that pervades the BMP study environment and are searching for the keys that enable them to fully share in it, while others find the intellectual challenge a good entry into appreciating Jewish tradition.

Singing and Spirituality

Spiritual expression also has become more important at camp. Our Thursday night singing and study program (an optional program open to the older age groups), called *mishmar*—after the traditional yeshiva late-night study session—draws campers from all backgrounds. It has grown in popularity to the point that this summer our library could barely hold the 150 participants. The singing is intense, the *divrei torah* are simple and provocative, the atmosphere is one of deep connectedness to God and to each other. Mishmar offers an experience that many participants didn't know they were seeking but has become the highlight of their camp week. It has fostered the kind of powerful spiritual awakening that we have long sought and is illustrated by the following phenomenon. We were worried this summer because junior counselors (JCs), who were mishmar stalwarts as campers, have their day off on Thursdays and would therefore miss it. As 10:15 p.m. rolled around, a stream of JCs filed into the beit midrash for mishmar, full of stories about how they had organized mishmar themselves on Ramah Seminar and had waited a year to return to our sacred space.

Our Shabbat afternoon singing after se'udah shelishit has expanded similarly. A program that once consisted of a small group of staff now brings together almost 200 participants each week as edah staff, responding to camper interest, have reworked their programming to enable more campers to participate. The whole camp has learned many of these beautiful songs, and campers participate by giving divrei torah and leading the singing.

Many BMP participants have come to see camp as a place of serious intellectual and religious growth and the program faculty as mentors beyond their summers at camp. During the year, faculty send out weekly divrei torah to campers, parents, and community members. These are collected on the camp website[1] and have contributed to the organization of year-long study programs in Minneapolis and Chicago. Thus, camp has become an avenue for increasing the presence and the level of Torah study not only in the Northwoods but in our feeder cities as well. And our students leave with a personal commitment to continuing their religious journey beyond camp. They carry away from Ramah a deep desire for spiritual engagement and a sense that this engagement is fully compatible with critical thought.

The Northwoods Kollel

The Northwoods Kollel began in 2001 and helps to shape the atmosphere of Torah study for the entire camp. Each year six college students come to spend the summer studying in the camp's beit midrash with a faculty of high-level scholars that has included Rabbi Jane Kanarek of Hebrew College of Boston, Dr. Rebecca Schorsch of Chicagoland Jewish High School, and Rabbi Ben Hollander, *z"l,* of the Hebrew University. They spend eight hours each day immersed in Jewish texts and also teach classes, live and eat with campers, serve as *tefillah* advisors, and participate in a range of informal programming around camp.

The Kollel students are passionate and thoughtful young people, deeply committed to being both students and role models. They set a tone of intense study and of egalitarian *frumkeit* that is felt throughout camp. They come from around North America seeking an intensive, advanced learning experience in a non-Orthodox setting. Some are graduates of Solomon Schechter or community day schools looking to develop their skills and to probe their personal beliefs. Others are Modern Orthodox students looking for a more scientific approach to study. Still others encounter Jewish text study first during college and, having taken the first steps on their own, need a framework to go further. All come in search of a community of like-minded people who share their deep commitment to integrating Torah study with the full range of human wisdom. For many, the Kollel is the first religious setting in which they feel truly at home. In the words of alumna Sigal Samuel, "Kollel for me meant not only a place where I could learn an incredible amount in a short period of time, but also a place where I could live, become, and grow into a more refined self through the company of peers and teachers alike."

The Northwoods Kollel program is modeled on a traditional yeshiva curriculum, emphasizing the study of Talmud and halachah and also exploring Midrash, Hasidic thought, and philosophy. But although the topics are traditional, the approach is decidedly modern. We look at the sources and development of each text alongside its later interpretations. We argue about halachic questions with deep respect for both the pull of tradition and the need for critique. We explore how Torah study and mitzvah observance can bring together Jews who espouse radically different theologies. These students, through their encounters with texts, teachers, and peers are preparing to be the spokespeople for a new kind of traditional Judaism. They are committed to a modern vision of religious truth and driven by a powerful spirituality that is not threatened by, but embraces, all sources of knowledge.

In the first summers of its existence, some staff resented the presence of the Kollel, feeling that it was a poor use of camp resources—students were being paid to study while others were paid to work. These attitudes have changed as it has become clear over seven years that the Kollel, while offering an important opportunity for its students, also has been a crucial element in the religious growth of campers and staff. Each summer, we have a group of enthusiastic, knowledgeable, and accessible staff members in camp who model for both campers and staff a compelling vision for religious life. During the summer, Kollel students have myriad opportunities to draw kids to religious experiences and to bring Torah to every corner of camp. The Kollel and BMP also have been part of a flowering of advanced programming throughout the camp, from more serious study in regular text classes to professional-like opportunities in the performing and visual arts.

Perhaps the most important impact of the Kollel is long term. Many Kollel participants, most of whom would not otherwise be in this or any Ramah camp, return as teachers, counselors, and even *rashei edot* (division heads). And they bring their love of Torah to everything they do. For years now, the BMP has been taught mainly by graduates of the Kollel program, including one who began his formal learning in the Kollel and is now working on his Ph.D. in Talmud, and another who began his Talmud study as an entering tenth grader in the first summer of our BMP! One former Kollel student has sworn every summer that he would not be back. Yet after three summers as a counselor, he served in 2007 as the first *rosh edah* for Garinim, a new division at Ramah Wisconsin for campers entering fifth grade.

The program also has led some alumni toward careers in Jewish education. One student, who had considered pursuing a doctorate in Classics, instead decided after college to spend a year teaching high school rabbinics and is now studying at the Pardes Institute in Jerusalem. Another wrote that "[The kollel] led me down the Jewish education path by giving me the opportunity to improve my text skills that summer but [even] more by giving me the connection to camp that allowed me to work on my teaching skills in subsequent summers."

Reclaiming Piety: A Challenge to the Conservative Movement

Some aspects of our work evoked discomfort among some members of the camp community, which gets to the heart of both the great opportunity and the looming questions in this project. Although singing, dancing, and divrei torah certainly have been standard parts of the camp program since its inception, we introduced programs that were intentionally modeled on the religious environment of Orthodox *yeshivot.* It was feared by some that by embracing this culture, we would encourage more campers to join Orthodox communities in college and beyond.

Those of us involved in the BMP believe that the opposite is true. For decades, some of Ramah's most committed kids were drawn to join Orthodox communities after high school precisely because egalitarian settings did not offer the same compelling and inspiring models of religious expression. They discovered an intensity of devotion and of study in such communities that was new to them and powerfully attractive. They may have concluded that liberal methodologies and gender equality are less important than, or not compatible with, spiritual engagement. The response must be to demonstrate that such religious expression and Torah study are equally at home in communities that embrace the fullness of their values. We have tried to do just that—our campers arrive on college campuses already comfortable with these experiences and feeling ownership over them, and they are not alienated by them. Most leave feeling confident that devotion to Torah does not require abandoning critical thought. And with stronger religious role models, many are leaving high school on a path to look for or create strong Conservative communities.

There is indeed a major challenge here. As has been the case throughout the history of Ramah, our teens leave Ramah looking for and demanding a kind of religious culture that most of our synagogues do not provide. Kids who are exposed to these experiences at camp often find the return home to be a letdown and a disappointment. Part of this is natural—there is no way that any community can replicate the intensity and excitement of the camp setting. But part of this disappointment should serve as a kind of warning. We must find ways of encouraging kids who want to take on more mitzvot, of engaging them in conversation about Torah, and of making it a priority to create opportunities for any camper looking for more Torah study.

The response to the BMP and Kollel programs of Ramah Wisconsin has revealed a hunger for a new kind of intensity and spirituality that demands a response in our camps and across the institutions of our movement. It demonstrates the power of what I would call "shared expressions of piety," a kind of religious expression not always embraced by the Conservative Movement, which excites our teenagers about Jewish study and observance and sparks a desire for spiritual engagement. This active and outward religious expressiveness is manifested in specific behaviors, such as energetic and impassioned singing and prayer, a deepening engagement with Torah study, talking openly about belief and spirituality, and taking on new ritual observances. Together, they build a deep engagement with Judaism—in study, observance, and faith—that has the potential to powerfully energize our communities.

Specifically, I want to emphasize three crucial messages:

First, when Ramah campers get excited about religious life and are interested in study and mitzvot, when Jewish texts and ideas help them to feel the beauty in the world, when rituals and songs awaken a sense of passion and excitement that is asleep within their own souls, we must create more opportunities for them within the Conservative Movement. Today, with more and more people moving freely between spiritual communities, Conservative Jews should be much more comfortable with *niggunim*, *tzitzit*, yeshiva study, and other expressive forms of piety without fearing that these forms will "make us Orthodox." And so we need to embrace these signs of piety as natural and essential elements of the religious experience that we want to offer to campers. And we must find ways to make them more a part of our synagogue culture as well.

Second, we have found that our students are not looking for answers but for a language in which to engage with the real challenges of life in authentic and sophisticated ways. They respond to the challenge and intensity of engaging with Talmud and other rabbinic texts but also expect their own views of the world to be taken seriously. Many are just beginning to ask serious questions about Judaism, about identity, and about self; they need opportunities to incorporate Jewish concepts as they explore their own self-understanding. It is not true that progressive theology can speak only to theologians, whereas only fundamentalist theology can inspire the masses. We encourage each of our campers to articulate his or her own ideas, confident that the appealing religious environment in which we guide that process ensures that the spiritual community remains at its core.

Finally, the experience of the power of religious involvement is solidified by being part of a religious community. Shared rituals—the intense joy of singing, of praying, and of creating Shabbat together, of a communal holy space—help each of its members to experience life's beauty more deeply. If religion is about the awareness of a meaning that transcends the self, these shared settings are the spaces where we can tangibly feel transcendence. This is true beyond camp: I would suggest that many or most people from a secular background, who choose observance, do so because they experience the power of shared ritual in observant communities and are elated by it. Those seeking spiritual engagement are drawn to communities that step beyond Shabbat services to eat together, sing together, and study together. By creating opportunities for shared *deveikut* (intense connection to God), we draw more and more campers to the power of that experience. We instill in more campers the desire to look for those communities outside of camp as well. And we create the potential for these teenagers to be the foundation of engaged, spiritually connected, and thoughtful communities in college and beyond.

Note

[1] http://www.ramahwisconsin.com/divreitorah.htm.

HERB GREENBERG AND **BARBARA GREENBERG**

Our Tikvah Mission: A Recipe for Leadership

WE BASK IN MUCH PRIDE and satisfaction as we reflect upon our efforts that spurred an entirely new direction in Jewish education. The era following the Six-Day War created an enormous surge of Zionist pride that led to an interest in innovation in Jewish educational and communal growth. As a result, our generation experienced a heightened degree of idealism and commitment to strengthening Jewish identity on both the personal and the collective level. In particular, informal education, as witnessed, for example, by the growth of the חבורה movement, created new opportunities for the greater Jewish community. Because of this trend, new leadership was needed to support a growing list of priorities in Jewish life. And so we began to link our professional experiences as special educators to the new agendas in the Jewish world.

In the late 1960s, a new voice emerged in the secular Jewish as well as non-Jewish communities. The de-institutionalization process had begun, and for the first time, most children and adults with special needs were being returned to their respective communities. Modest private efforts were implemented to deal with this novel situation. Jewish families were faced with enormous challenges that included the reintegration of many children with serious disabilities — and in some cases "unwanted" children — into their homes. Jewish communal and religious institutions did not have the resources to deal with these revolutionary changes in the mental health arena.

Forty-plus years ago Jewish youngsters who were developmentally challenged had no identity in their Jewish communities. The Jewish world did not acknowledge the birthright of this population. By and large, families of these children remained invisible to the Jewish community. They suffered in silence, though they craved a Jewish education and identity for their children.

HERB GREENBERG AND **BARBARA GREENBERG** *are the founding directors of the Tikvah Program at Camp Ramah in New England, where they worked for twenty-nine summers. Now living in Raanana, Israel, near their children and eleven grandchildren, they made aliyah after retiring from the Long Island public school system, where they served for more than thirty-six and twenty-eight years, respectively, as educators for adolescents with special needs.*

Until 1969, homogeneity of population had been the watchword at the Ramah camps, reflecting the reality in educational thinking of the time. The Jewish world, however, is indebted to the Ramah network for the contributions to Jewish educational innovation and leadership throughout North America, Europe, and Israel that Ramah initiated during this period. In late March of 1970, the United Synagogue Commission on Jewish Education for the Special Child found a home for the first Tikvah Program. Much credit is due to the members of this committee including, among others, Rabbi Joseph Kelman, *z"l,* Dr. Morton Siegel, Dr. Pesach Schindler, and Edya Arzt, *z"l,* who lobbied with great dedication for the creation of a new model to be known as Jewish special education.

The United Synagogue Commission on Jewish Education worked closely with the National Ramah Commission to create a novel paradigm, one that was unprecedented at the time in the secular world. The opportunity to right a wrong, to perform תיקון עולם or repair of the world, created its own momentum. From its inception, the Tikvah Program endeavored to achieve תיקון עולם on two levels simultaneously. In the broader population, the Tikvah Program sought to dispel the myths and stereotypes regarding children who have special needs. The Tikvah Program embraced those developmentally challenged youngsters who had been disenfranchised for so long from Jewish education and social interaction with their "normal" peers.

Though Jewish special education in the late 1960s was an abstract concept without any concrete foundation, under the direction of Don Adelman, *z"l,* Camp Ramah in Glen Spey, New York, agreed to host this new venture. Three months before the opening of the 1970 summer camp season, there were no Tikvah campers and no Tikvah staff. During this period we personally made many hurried phone calls to rabbis of all denominations, Jewish educators, and Jewish community leaders in an effort to identify a suitable camper population for the inaugural season of the program. But to no avail! Adolescent Jewish children with developmental disabilities, along with their families, could not be found in Jewish educational and communal settings. We then turned to the world of secular special education, our professional milieu, realizing that Jewish parents were frequently very active in the various special education organizations of the time, often seemingly out of proportion to the number of Jewish special education students represented. When we turned to this world of secular special education, we began to identify our target population, though it was by no means a homogeneous group. The eight campers whom we then found exhibited a wide range of learning and behavioral disorders, ranging from moderate to severe. Aside from the fact that these eight youngsters possessed no Jewish background, none of them had ever experienced social interactions with non-disabled peers. In addition to the differences between the intellectual and behavioral profiles of the first Tikvah campers and those of their non-Tikvah peers, the Tikvah campers also differed greatly from one another and from the rest of the camp in their educational, social, and religious experiential backgrounds. It became apparent to us that one of the first challenges we would face would be that of reconciling the varied expectations of our staff, the general Ramah community, and the parents of the non-Tikvah campers.

Next, we briefly outline our efforts to meet the new challenge of creating a model of integrated Jewish summer camping that would sustain itself for future generations. First of all, we must state that it was, and remains, our belief that an innovative educational or communal paradigm would benefit one subgroup, in this case youngsters with special educational needs, if and only if, there was a commitment among all the parties involved to share a common vision, to encourage and accept constructive criticism, to support consistent leadership, to provide the necessary financial and staff resources, to adjust goals to meet new challenges as they arose, and to inculcate the tenets of the program into the consciousness of the community at large.

The concretization of a vision is a milestone of leadership. During staff week in June of 1970, we told our staff of four counselors, "You are writing, figuratively speaking, a 'Torah' for developmentally challenged Jewish children." In general terms, we further informed our staff that the goals, achieved through specific processes and activities of the Tikvah Program, would enable this new camper population to internalize many of the skills and values that we have always treasured as a Jewish people. We also hoped that, in the process of implementing this formidable goal, we would educate the entire Ramah community, enlisting everyone as a partner in our enterprise. Ultimately, we wished everyone who constituted the community of Camp Ramah to meet the challenge we presented, that of accepting the reality that members of the Tikvah Program must be guaranteed equal opportunity throughout the camp. As a starting point, we expected our staff to serve as role models for the entire camp, by demonstrating through their own efforts in daily interactions with Tikvah youngsters, that anyone who worked in Camp Ramah could draw upon his or her unique strengths to support this population. In so doing, every staff member would, by example, encourage the non-Tikvah campers to dispel any fears they harbored toward peers with significant deficits.

We must conclude after having founded and then having directed the Tikvah Program at Camp Ramah in New England for twenty-nine summers (1970–98) that the Ramah Camping Movement has proven itself to be an incubator for the creation and nurturing of leaders in all walks of Jewish life. For us and for many others, our years at Ramah coalesced into a transformative experience. Despite certain bureaucratic restrictions inherent in any organization, Camp Ramah was open to institutional change and afforded us opportunities for experimentation and innovation, while at the same time, it provided the chance for almost any staff member to participate, either individually or as part of a group, in activities with the Tikvah campers. Camp Ramah encouraged our personal growth. In a very practical sense, our entire family—including our children Seth Greenberg and Gabie Greenberg Sykora—was changed by our Ramah experience. We all became fluent in Hebrew and internalized an ardent dedication to Israel, culminating in our עליה or settling in Israel (1992, 1993, and 1999, respectively). One of the missions of Ramah during our early tenure there was to encourage עליה, and the institution can share in our נחת or joy, as we now number nineteen family members, including eleven grandchildren, nine of whom are sabras, all living in Ra'anana, Israel.

During the first few years of the Tikvah Program, a leadership model evolved. This model enabled the project to resonate as a mission, a vision, and as a new reality for the Ramah community. To realize our vision, we had to consider many professional, as well as personal factors. We had to keep our goals clearly in mind while exhibiting some degree of flexibility in the means we employed to achieve them. We had to consider, for example, competing interests. In addition, on at least some level, there is always initial resistance to innovation, often accompanied by some degree of skepticism regarding the validity of the aims of any new program. It was, nevertheless, vital to maintain our consistency of purpose. In addition to these professional considerations, we had to sort out family issues because the implementation of this effort required an extraordinary investment of time, effort, and patience.

During the first years of the Tikvah Program, we waged a difficult struggle on many fronts. On the one hand, following the existing educational model, understandably the camp administration instinctively viewed the program as a self-contained entity within the total structure. Contrary to this attitude, however, the leadership of the Tikvah Program advocated on several fronts for inclusion of the Tikvah campers in all camp-wide activities and their acceptance as a legitimate division within the camp. We also campaigned for professional partnership in all administrative decisions and insisted on the right of the Tikvah Program to share the specialty resources of the camp. Though all of these expectations were enthusiastically supported by Don Adelman, *z"l*, the director of Camp Ramah in Glen Spey and later in New England, consensus among the rest of the senior leadership of the camp was lacking. It was not uncommon, for example, for camp-wide decisions to be implemented without regard for the unique requirements of the Tikvah Program. Such oversight undoubtedly was due to adherence to the decision-making model that had existed prior to the advent of the Tikvah Program.

During the initial stages of our efforts, most non-Tikvah staff felt ill-equipped both emotionally and intellectually to offer their services to the Tikvah population. Don Adelman, *z"l,* as the camp director, set the tone the very first week. He told everyone on staff at the camp that the incorporation of the Tikvah Program provided a structure whereby the entire community could concretize many of the Jewish values inherent in the Jewish educational curriculum of the camp. Our vision was validated from the top, and our faith was confirmed that Camp Ramah truly demonstrated a resiliency imbued with both a desire for, and an ability to, withstand change.

In our leadership model, we demonstrated trust in our staff by delegating to them many roles and responsibilities. First, we trained staff to work with the entire camp community. Although camp counselors, specialists, and educators expressed discomfort and insecurity at the prospect of working with youngsters with special needs, the Tikvah leadership addressed all the well-known stereotypes of that era regarding people who were developmentally challenged. To this end, we refused to use—and would not countenance the use by others—the medical labels universally accepted in the field of special education at that time, such as mental retardation, emotional disturbance, brain damage, and so forth. We insisted that everyone refer to the campers in our program in a generic manner and that they address the learning and social challenges displayed by the members of our group in an individualized, descriptive fashion.

Through role playing, we established the basic principles of communication between our staff and each member of the Tikvah Program, such as, "You must establish eye contact with Moshe before you give him a set of directions." Because Tikvah campers frequently communicated through touch, a means of approach often not accepted comfortably by relative strangers, we encouraged staff throughout the camp to respond in a calm voice, "I don't like to be touched. Do not do that again. If you touch me, I will not talk to you, and I will go away." We developed such strategies in partnership with the entire camp to ensure some level of consistency and to facilitate a shared community responsibility to this group. Our Tikvah staff attended all camp-wide orientation sessions, and we modeled for the general staff techniques of communication, as well as advocacy, to enable them to support our roles during the summer. As our staff became more comfortable in their roles as crisis managers, we encouraged selected staff and campers in the Camp Ramah community at large to work with our population as volunteers. Voluntarism always has been an important value at the Ramah camps, and we provided many opportunities for volunteers to become sensitized to differences and to appreciate, in a practical sense, both the endless variation of God's creation and the fact that we are all responsible for one another.

We owe a special debt of gratitude to Rabbi Burton Visotzky, who served as a counselor during the first summer of Tikvah, went on to become a division head, and also assumed major fund-raising responsibilities. But perhaps his greatest contribution to the first Tikvah Program was the impetus he provided to advance the nascent field of Jewish education for youngsters with special needs. His wise counsel accelerated our efforts to provide training for the Tikvah campers in such areas as תפילות (prayers), the use of Hebrew as a spoken language, and Shabbat observance; as well as to promote their participation in informal activities that focused on the development of their emerging Jewish identity.

During the first weeks, Burt unwittingly found himself drawn into a thought-provoking and heart-wrenching discussion with the Tikvah campers that was to lead the Tikvah Program to a new height of honesty and integrity that remains its hallmark to this day. One of the campers asked Burt, "Why did God make me retarded?" This question opened the door to many Tikvah staff-camper discussions revolving around self-image, one's rightful place in the community, the challenges of independent living, and of course, a deeper interest in religious issues. How could we ever have anticipated engaging this group in a discussion about צלם אלוקים (the image of God) and the fact that we, regardless of our individual strengths or deficits, are partners with God in enriching our lives?

Rabbi David Halivni, who was the professor-in-residence during the early years of the Tikvah Program, gave us much support and insight in helping us understand how we could overcome the halachic restrictions placed upon the חרש and the שוטה (the hearing impaired and the person who does not speak). He offered us the concept of a "religious IQ," and he believed that modern psychology and educational methodology opened up new frontiers for this population. It was therefore reasonable, he proposed, to create higher religious expectations for our target population, the campers of the Tikvah Program, than had previously been thought possible, through the integration of special and Jewish education.

We first applied this principle during the early years of the Tikvah Program. Rabbi Steven Shulman, then a Tikvah counselor, designed the prototype of the first Tikvah סידור (siddur) and prepared one of his campers to become the first Tikvah bar mitzvah during a ceremony that took place at camp. Another staff member, in this case a member of the משלחת (staff sent from Israel), who had a profound influence on the direction of the Tikvah Program was Yankele Berlowitz, *z"l*. Yankele, an Israeli ראש עדה (division head), resolutely promoted Zionism and עליה. He expressed an unwavering dedication to ארץ ישראל, and he took upon himself the mission of imparting this zeal to as many members of the Ramah community as possible.

During that first summer in 1970, Yankele resisted the integration of the Tikvah Program into the camp. We engaged in many heated discussions; however at the time, he could not understand the potential of our group. Most Israelis, like many Americans, during the early years of Tikvah reflected the thinking of the time that youngsters with special needs should be separated from the community. Yankele forced us to analyze the Tikvah Program from his Israeli perspective, with its emphasis on fierce independence and mental and physical capabilities, a perspective that had never crossed our minds. The courage of our convictions prevailed. In subsequent years, Yankele directed day camp programs in Israel in which he included youngsters with special educational needs. Throughout the years, the remarkable and varied talents of the משלחת provided much enrichment and emotional support to Tikvah staff and campers alike.

At Camp Ramah in New England, two of the most influential members of the משלחת, in addition to Yankele, were Yehuda Gubani and Yedida Tzivoni. For more than twenty years, Yehuda has inspired a love of the Hebrew language in Tikvah and non-Tikvah campers alike. Yedida has enthusiastically welcomed Tikvah campers into the arts program and has encouraged some of the older ones to serve as assistants. Over and above their responsibilities in Hebrew and the arts, respectively, both Yehuda and Yedida consistently have served as two of the most vocal advocates for the Tikvah Program within Camp Ramah in New England. Howard Blas, the present director of the Tikvah Program, has done a superb job of extending the scope of the program. In our estimation, he represents the epitome of Ramah leadership. The Ramah community and the Jewish community of New England will continue to be the beneficiaries in the years to come.

Unfortunately, some educators view parents as adversaries rather than as partners in the educational process. We have always rejected this notion. We have always been faithful to the dictum that we have much to learn from parents, for they usually offer the most insight into, and direction for, their children. Many of the families with whom we worked over the course of twenty-nine summers at Camp Ramah in New England have become role models for us. Many of the early Tikvah parents were Holocaust survivors who were intent on building new families. These families inspired us to embed the concept of תיקון עולם into the program. Their devotion to their children's progress provided us with incentives to chart many unexplored directions for Tikvah campers.

In addition, at the outset we committed ourselves to provide professional services for these families. Beginning with the first year of the Tikvah Program, the summer culminated in a three-day parent conference, in which together we addressed behavioral, social, educational, Judaic, and other issues that arose during the summer. We also offered the parents strategies for reinforcing at home, during the school year, strengths that their children had developed during the eight-week summer session. We provided all parents with a detailed printed narrative of the summer, together with goals to be implemented during the year both at home and in school. This parent conference took place outside the camp, and we invited professionals from a wide variety of mental health and related fields. In some cases, the Tikvah director became the child's advocate during the school year when intervention was required. On one occasion, for example, the Tikvah director testified in federal court on behalf of a Tikvah family who wanted their child educated in the least restrictive environment.

There is no question that our tenure as administrators of the Tikvah Program sharpened our professional skills in many ways. First and foremost, we realized our goal of integrating Jewish education and special education. We were able to create new training models in the camp for staff, parents, and professionals. This process created a momentum in the greater Jewish community through the efforts of Ramah and Tikvah staff who sought opportunities for further growth beyond the summer. We were invited to speak at many conferences throughout the United States to encourage the launching of new ventures on behalf of Jewish children who are developmentally challenged. Over the years, our staff members pioneered Jewish special education classes in synagogues, social activity programs in recreation centers, group homes run under Jewish auspices, day school programs for Jewish children with special needs, Tikvah Programs in most of the Ramah camps, programs in Israel, integrated Jewish youth programs in all the denominations, as well as trips to Israel. We collaborated and consulted with Tikvah staff members and local Jewish leaders in support of these efforts.

The success of the Tikvah Program encouraged us to expand our vision and to imagine and develop new horizons for the Tikvah population, always in response to the needs of these campers as we perceived them. At each stage, we had to overcome initial opposition and skepticism. The "aging out" of the camper population presented a particular challenge to us. Families of older Tikvah campers were troubled by the prospect of their children's tenure in the program coming to an end. These new directions included vocational educational training, referred to as the Voc Ed Program, for the eighteen- to twenty-one-year-old population, and the building of a training residence to prepare many graduates of the camper program for semi–independent or independent living. Beginning in 1984, some older campers and graduates of the Tikvah Program were invited to participate in organized Tikvah trips to Israel. During this past decade, selected Tikvah graduates of the Voc Ed Program were invited to become members of the Camp Ramah staff. In 2006, eight years after our retirement from Tikvah, our final vision was realized. The completion of the new guesthouse at Camp Ramah in New England, a project intended to provide training for employment opportunities in the hotel service industry for qualified Tikvah graduates, as well as much-needed guest facilities for the camp, clearly demonstrates "If you will it, it is no dream," which became the slogan of the Zionist movement—the striving for a Jewish national home in Israel. The quote comes from Theodor Herzl's book *The Old New Land* (*Altneuland*), published in 1902.

The partnership that we nurtured between the Camps Ramah and the Tikvah Program has provided us with much spiritual gratification, which has proved to be our ultimate reward. Each morning we begin our תפילות by reciting מה טובו אוהליך יעקב, משכנותיך ישראל "How goodly are your tents, O Jacob, your dwelling places, O Israel." Malbim suggests that the "tents of Jacob" refer to the Israelites' temporary dwellings in the desert, whereas the "sanctuaries of Israel" refer to our permanent homes in Israel. We see a parallel here with the role of the Tikvah Program as a training ground in which campers with special needs can hone their social, vocational, and other skills and thereby facilitate their eventual integration into the adult Jewish community.

We never anticipated how the inclusion of the Tikvah Program in all its various aspects would stir the spiritual senses of the Ramah community and encourage so many of its members to discover enriched value and significance in the מצוות. We derived much satisfaction and נחת as numerous traditional Jewish values came to life in the Ramah community. They include גמילות חסדים (acts of lovingkindness), כבוד הבריות (respect for one's fellow man), and ערבות (the sense of mutual responsibility among members of a community). In diverse ways these values permeate the life of each Ramah camp that hosts a Tikvah Program. The Tikvah campers absorb these values through a combination of formal and informal education, including drama; and the rest of the camp does so, in part, by observing the Tikvah campers. This learning by observation and example is mutual, and each population within the camp has much to learn from the other. Rabbi Abraham Chill, *z"l,* grandfather of a former Tikvah camper, wrote *The Mitzvot* in 1974, in which he cited ויקרא

(Leviticus 19:18), ואהבת לרעך כמוך "You shall love your neighbor as yourself." Rabbi Chill comments, "Our sages are almost unanimous in their agreement that [this] biblical commandment . . . is the basic pillar upon which the entire Torah is built." Similarly, we recognize that it was our Torah tradition that provided the moral imperative for our efforts to confer dignity and self-esteem to a neglected population of children.

In our leadership model, we always emphasized to campers and staff that all of us have an obligation to give something back to the community that has nurtured us and helped us achieve our potential. In our remarks at the dedication of the guesthouse at Camp Ramah in New England, we observed that we had gained at least as much from our Ramah-Tikvah experience as we had imparted. On that occasion we concluded, "It has been a privilege for us to have shared our ideals and visions with this community. It is our hope that this building will enable Camp Ramah in New England to extend its reach as a leader in Jewish educational innovation for all its constituents."

DANIEL GREYBER

Reflections on Eight Summers of Lishma, 1999–2007

Background

THE SUMMER OF 2007 marked the ninth summer of the Lishma program—a joint program of Camp Ramah in California and the Ziegler School of Rabbinic Studies (ZSRS). Lishma is another in a long list of educationally innovative programs fostered by the creative spirit of Ramah camping, and the sixtieth anniversary of Ramah presents an appropriate time to reflect on Lishma's successes and challenges nine years later. What is Lishma? Lishma is an egalitarian, yeshiva-study, summer program where young adult Jews explore their Jewish identities through the lens of traditional Jewish text study, prayer, and practice. To date, more than 110 young adults have participated in the Lishma program, many of whom then continued to study for rabbinical ordination at The Jewish Theological Seminary (JTS), ZSRS, Boston Hebrew College, Reconstructionist Rabbinical College (RRC), and Hebrew Union College (HUC), or master's degrees in Jewish education at JTS and American Jewish University (AJU) and Jewish communal service at AJU and HUC. Just as important (if not more), most alumni are young, highly involved lay leaders in organized Jewish life, and some have made aliyah. This essay reviews the story of how and why Lishma first began, provides an assessment of its successes and challenges, including the place for Lishma and programs like it within the Ramah camping system, and presents suggestions for the future.

The Conservative Yeshiva: Seeds of an idea

In the spring of 1995, I was twenty-three years old and had completed a program of study at the World Union for Jewish Students (WUJS) Institute in Arad, Israel, with a thirst to study in a yeshiva to gain a deeper understanding

RABBI DANIEL GREYBER *is the executive director of Camp Ramah in California and of the Max & Pauline Zimmer Conference Center of American Jewish University. He is the founder and creator of Lishma, a joint venture of the Ziegler School of Rabbinic Studies and Camp Ramah in California.*

of traditional Jewish texts and a grounding that would enable lifetime learning. No options existed within the Conservative Movement at the time. With the spiritual and financial support (and to the credit) of my childhood rabbi, Leonard Cahan of Congregation Har Shalom in Potomac, Maryland, I attended Yeshivat Hamivtar in Efrat, known to many as Brovender's Yeshiva for one of its *rashei yeshivah,* Rabbi Chaim Brovender. Studying at Brovender's was an enriching experience and although I joined late in the year and struggled in many classes, I gained a sense of the richness and complexity of Jewish thought and a love for being part of a passionate learning community. But I did not feel at home. Although as a male, I did not feel a sense of exclusion from public prayer in an Orthodox environment, my becoming more religious was a change from my family's practice, and I felt the Orthodox yeshiva to be too severe a break from the way in which I was raised. For these reasons, when I heard rumors in the summer of 1995 that a Conservative yeshiva would be founded in Jerusalem that fall, I stopped by the Fuchsberg Center on Agron Street and asked Dr. Pesach Schindler if I could enroll. I was thrilled to be accepted starting in early September.

At the Conservative Yeshiva in 1995, fifteen young adults gathered around a few tables in a humble building that bears little resemblance to the beautifully remodeled Fuchsberg Center that stands proudly in the center of Jerusalem today. We studied liturgy with Dr. Ze'ev Falk, *z"l,* a teacher of remarkable humility, wisdom, and gentleness, who instilled in me a lifelong love of *tefillah.* Dr. Shai Wald taught a stimulating introductory class in Mishnah, as well as a second, more advanced section in Talmud. Dr. Pesach Schindler taught *ḥumash* and was a wise rebbe who expressed a genuine interest in, and acceptance of, each of the varied personalities around the table and our stories of who we were and where we were going. Beyond the teachers and our sparse environs, what I remember most is the excitement of being part of something that was truly unique: men and women praying together and studying Torah—not for an academic degree, but for its own sake—together around a table where each person's voice was equally valued and had equal access to the texts of our tradition. Though I departed mid-year for the United States for a job in the advertising world, my experience at the Conservative Yeshiva left me with a lasting vision of what the Conservative Movement could create—places where interested, non-professional Jews could seriously engage with and deepen their relationship with Jewish texts from a distinctly religious point of view.

A few years later, I would begin study at the newly formed ZSRS at the University of Judaism (now AJU). Rabbi Daniel Gordis, then dean of the school, had written an article in which he presented the case of the emerging need for yeshiva-style study in non-Orthodox settings.[1] Rabbi Gordis witnessed the need for yeshiva-style learning in non-Orthodox settings first hand as a member of the senior staff of Camp Ramah in California and as the dean of the Brandeis Collegiate Institute from 1990 to 1994. After reading Rabbi Gordis's article, I raised with him the idea of founding a Conservative yeshiva-study program in the United States. His immediate, enthusiastic response was to approach Brian Greene, the director of Camp Ramah in California. During his tenure, Brian Greene had started the innovative Meytiv social action program for campers entering the eleventh and twelfth grades and had expressed interest to Rabbi Gordis in developing a program for eighteen- to twenty-five-year olds. Under the leadership of Brian Greene and Rabbi Gordis, along with significant grant-writing support from AJU, seed funding for the Lishma program was sought in the spring of 1998 from the Covenant Foundation. The proposal included an assessment of the need for opportunities for serious Jewish learning, particularly among the young adult population within non-Orthodox communities, and an outline of essential components of the core program.

The need for Lishma

In our proposal we argued first and foremost for the need for a program like Lishma in the American Jewish community. Our argument was based upon the reality that the college years are a time when young adults first begin to form their own identities, develop their personal beliefs, and establish their own homes. Unfortunately, it is during this period and the years immediately following college that non-Orthodox Jews demonstrate the greatest decline in Jewish involvement. We argued:

> In contrast to the liberal Jewish world, the vitality of the Modern Orthodox movement is largely due to young adults in their 20s and 30s. Many of these young adults are products of the *yeshivah*—a place where participants worship together, live together, form a dynamic religious community, and most importantly, study together. The Orthodox community recognizes that ongoing commitment to Jewish life is powerfully fueled by a *spiritual* engagement with Jewish texts—rather than by the almost exclusively intellectual engagement the liberal community currently offers in academic settings.
>
> Young people beginning their religious quest are not searching for academic rigor. They thirst for *meaning*. They want to encounter the Jewish tradition not exclusively as an historical or intellectual venture, but as a religious one—an all-encompassing experience that can help them formulate preliminary answers to the questions of meaning all of us address throughout our lives. In America—the largest Jewish population in the entire world—there is not a single institution for the 94% of Jews who are

> not Orthodox to study Torah in a non-academic setting, as a religious enterprise. This is not for lack of desire on the part of young Jews. Every year, groups of newly energized young Jews emerge from programs such as Camp Ramah, the Brandeis Collegiate Institute, Jewish high schools and college programs, and ask, "What do I do next? How do I continue?"[2]

It was to fill this need that the Lishma program was created. We believed Lishma would make a powerful impact upon the culture of Camp Ramah in California, and we also believed it was a program that could easily be replicated in other Ramah camps and in many other Jewish summer camps around the country. In subsequent summers, two other Ramah camps, Ramah Wisconsin and Ramah Nyack, started other models of yeshiva-study programs as part of their camp communities, and the one at Wisconsin continues as of this writing.

The vision

Because Lishma could be replicated, we envisioned a transformation of the future leadership of the liberal American Jewish community and, through its work, a transformation of non-Orthodox communities for the twenty-first century. In initial discussions with the Covenant Foundation and subsequent discussions with Lishma funders, such as the Righteous Persons Foundation, the Jewish Community Foundation of Los Angeles, and Joshua Venture, we argued that Lishma—and programs like it—could create a cadre of young adults who would live within the Jewish community and establish a hospitable environment for other young people who are seeking a way to become involved—for instance, those who have come back from inspirational experiences such as a trip to Israel or a summer at Ramah. This cadre would be the next generation of leadership for the liberal Jewish community, individuals who can provide religious vision as lay people, not necessarily as rabbis or academics. They would be able to articulate the role and significance Judaism plays in the choices, large and small, that comprise daily life.

Finally, Lishma offered exciting opportunities on an organizational level. First, as a collaboration between a summer camp and a rabbinical seminary, the program offered new opportunities for synergy and understanding between institutions with similar goals but dissimilar constituencies. Summer camp is an intense setting that catalyzes personal growth in a way that a graduate school cannot hope to match. Rabbinical education offers the bridge to Jewish text and tradition on which commitment to Jewish life is founded. Together, they can make a deep impact. Second, the curriculum of Lishma seeks to bridge two fissures that run through the liberal Jewish community. One is the fissure between non-Orthodox Jews and the tradition of learning that, as noted above, so powerfully fuels the young adults of the Orthodox Movement. The other is the fissure between radically different conceptions of what Jewish investment is all about: the focus of the religious community on study and learning and the focus of the liberal community on the Jewish social action model, which has little ongoing engagement with the religious tradition. Each conception is anemic without the enrichment that the other provides, and a model is required that shows the two are complementary. Reproduced nation-wide, we hoped Lishma might begin to merge these critical rifts in the liberal Jewish community.

The first summer: Preparation

In the summer of 1998, Lishma received its first grant—$72,000—from the Covenant Foundation to fund the program for the summers of 1999 and 2000. Funding was not to be used for operating expenses but rather to provide full scholarships for every participant and to fund $500-stipends for each participant. In hindsight, the Covenant Foundation understood the immediate needs and eventual challenges of starting and running a program for Jews ages eighteen to twenty-five. Young adults not only lack funds to pay for supplemental programs; they feel pressure to find jobs and begin providing their own financial resources.[3] The ability to offer prospective participants a $500-stipend to help underwrite their studies provided a powerful tool for recruiting young adults to a brand new program.

Recruitment took place through a variety of means including campus recruitment. Out of geographic necessity, recruitment focused on campuses in the Southwest, as well as meeting people at college leadership conferences such as Koach Kallah, phone calls and e-mail messages to solicit potential candidates from Hillel directors and Jewish Campus Service Corps (JCSC) fellows, and limited print advertising. A formal interview—either face-to-face or more often by telephone—was a crucial part of the application process, both to allow the participant to ask questions she or he had about Lishma and also to ensure the applicant understood what the program was about and to assess his or her suitability for living in a close-knit, intense, communal setting for six weeks.

Lishma participants were not required to have an extensive background in text learning or Jewish practice but also were not to be totally unfamiliar with traditional Jewish study and practice; minimally, they were required to be able to read Hebrew phonetically. During the application process (often during the formal interview), participants were told that although there was no expectation that participants regularly prayed, kept Shabbat or kashrut, or practiced the traditional observance that would be part of the six-week program, nonetheless, regular participation in these activities was an expected part of the program. Those who were unwilling to experiment with these practices during the program were dissuaded from attending. On the other end of the spectrum, a few applicants (and eventual participants) were Orthodox in their orientation to Jewish life. In interviews, these participants were told clearly that the community would be egalitarian in philosophy and practice. Whereas these individuals were not expected to violate their own religious principles (e.g., women were not obligated to accept an aliyah), they also could not opt out of participation in the community.

Similar to the experience of many Ramah campers and staff members, the aim of Lishma was to create a community in which members benefited from the isolation and the artificial nature of camp. Cut off from the social pressures of the outside world, Lishma participants could "re-invent" themselves; they could experiment with their identity and discover how regular prayer, study, and practice would affect their souls. Cut off from the time pressures of school and jobs that demand productivity and results, Lishma participants were given a summer-long Shabbat—"an island in time" at a pivotal moment in their identity formation—in which to evaluate who they were and where they wanted to go in their relationship with the Jewish tradition and the Jewish people. They agreed to become for their six weeks at camp someone they were not; we asked them to let go—to some extent—of who they were before the program and to be open to becoming someone different. We also told them that we had little expectation that after they left the program, they would remain exactly who they had been during the summer. What was expected was that during the summer they would demonstrate courage, openness, honesty, and authenticity in relation to each other and to the Judaism they encountered.

Programmatic Elements

The lead scholar and the beit midrash

After the participants were recruited, the next step was creating a program. We envisioned a program built around the core experience of yeshiva study. In addition to the living, praying, and recreating together, a yeshiva is distinguished by its active, participatory method of learning. Hebrew text is deciphered in *ḥavruta* study, in which students form pairs and help each other translate and make sense of short passages through (often excited) discussion and the use of reference guides. When many pairs of students are learning together in a study hall, there is a buzz in the air from the spirited debate. Then, when the whole group is gathered later, all students take turns reading aloud and discussing the text with a scholar.

The program would be staffed by a rotation of lead scholars who would guide and teach morning and afternoon text sessions that would form the core of the program. Three lead scholars were found for Lishma's first summer: Reb Mimi Feigelson, Dr. Joel Gereboff, and Rabbi Joel Rembaum. In our grant application, and in initial discussions with the scholars, we suggested a traditional yeshiva curriculum structured around different texts with morning sessions focused on either Mishnah or Talmud and afternoon sessions focused on either ḥumash with Rashi or Jewish philosophers such as Maimonides. Reb Mimi, an Orthodox scholar and a student of Rabbi Shlomo Carlebach, expressed interest in teaching at Lishma but insisted that the teaching be structured by theme, rather than by text.

Reb Mimi, who taught the first two weeks of the 1999 and 2000 summers, focused her *shi'urim* on the subjects of forgiveness and compassion, and she taught texts that ranged from stories from the Tanach, passages from the Talmud, chapters from the Mishneh Torah of Maimonides, to passages from Hasidic literature. These sessions were immensely successful for a number of reasons. First, in terms of building participants' overall understanding of the Jewish textual tradition, students were exposed to a much broader range of Jewish texts than a more rigid curriculum would have allowed. Second, teaching thematically prevented sessions from getting bogged down in "academic" debates; in seeking to understand the meaning of the day's text, students also struggled with their own understandings of the limits of forgiveness in their own friendships and families. Finally, Reb Mimi brought unanticipated, and clearly vital, elements to Lishma: music and storytelling. I will never forget the first day of the first *shi'ur* as the group finally sat around the table after weeks and months of effort, and Reb Mimi took out her guitar and started to play and sing. Because there were no words to learn and because the *niggunim* repeated themselves, it was easy for everyone to join in, and so we did. Singing became the way that each day's session would begin and end, often interspersed with Hasidic stories appropriate to the day's discussion. The addition of music and stories to the learning, something that one would rarely, if ever, find in a Jewish studies course in a university setting, communicated a powerful message that our learning was not only an intellectual exercise. It was meant to open our hearts and to engage our total selves.

Starting with Reb Mimi was a tremendous beginning, but it also created problems for those teachers who had different styles. Transitions from one type of teacher to another were difficult and in future summers were minimized. In future summers, the number of scholars was reduced to one or two, which led to more continuity and the possibility to go into greater depth with one scholar. During the first summer, Dr. Joel Gereboff, the second Lishma scholar and a regular teacher in the Mador program at Ramah California for many summers, focused on a traditional introductory chapter of Talmud—*Ellu metzi'ot*—from tractate *Bava Metzi'a* and engaged students in discussions about fairness and conflict resolution. Rabbi Joel Rembaum introduced students to the documentary hypothesis and forced students to struggle, many for the first time, with different theories of revelation and how a scientific approach to texts could be integrated into a life committed to Torah and traditional observance.

In subsequent summers, scholars focused on themes such as *deveikut* (clinging to God), *tzedakah,* the student-teacher relationship, honoring parents, leadership, and other topics, each of which exposed Lishma participants to a range of Jewish texts and engaged them intellectually, emotionally, and religiously. One potential weakness of the thematic model for text study is that in not moving through texts more "organically," (i.e., studying a chapter of Talmud or Mishnah from beginning to end rather than choosing a particularly interesting *sugya*), some students experienced disappointment when, either during the program or after the program, they were confronted with texts that did not focus so directly upon existential issues. Although the other two scholars in Lishma's first summer also chose to teach thematically, the fact that students were forced to confront texts that focused on more technical aspects of Jewish law challenged the students' ability to see the relevance of Jewish text study as a whole. Overall, the teaching of the first summer achieved its goals—students walked away having been engaged as people and Jews and having been touched by the texts they had learned. A charismatic and engaging lead scholar was a key part of that success.

Ziegler rabbinical students and mentoring meetings

In addition to a lead scholar, the program was staffed by two—typically one male and one female—rabbinical students at ZSRS. These students were meant to be role models and mentors to Lishma participants. We felt it was essential to the sense of community that Lishma staff members live at camp and be accessible to students at all times. Since instruction at the Ziegler School is also based on a yeshiva model, Ziegler rabbinical students were familiar with the openness and supportive demeanor necessary to make intensive study a positive experience for newcomers. Having the rabbinical students live in close proximity to Lishma participants meant that the whole community ate together, learned together, prayed together, and "hung out" together—much like counselors and campers at camp. These close relationships communicated a message that the learning was meant to engage the whole self, not only the mind.

Mentor meetings served to further the relationships between ZSRS rabbinical students and Lishma participants. Each Lishma participant would meet with one of the two ZSRS rabbinical students three times over the course of the six weeks to connect personally about their experience. Meetings were structured—they were not an optional element of the program and certain, consistent, questions were explored with each participant. However, questions and the content of the meetings were open-ended and non-judgmental. The first meeting allowed the student to tell his or her "story" more thoroughly and invited the participant to share his or her goals for the program. Sample questions included:

- Tell me how you decided to participate in the Lishma program.
- What is your "Jewish story"?
- How is the program going so far?
- What did you really enjoy the first few days? What has been a challenge? What is different than you expected, and what is similar to what you expected?
- What are your goals for the summer? What hopes do you have?
- Are there concrete skills that you want to learn that we can help you with?

The second meeting served as a check-in meeting and helped Lishma staff to make mid-course corrections to the program. During the course of the first summer, one issue that surfaced in mid-summer meetings was that many participants were overwhelmed by the amount of prayer required. In response to hearing similar sentiments from many participants, a meeting was convened to hear concerns and figure out a solution. Each participant acknowledged that he or she was aware, intellectually, that regular prayer was an expectation of the program, but many felt emotionally overwhelmed by the intensity of the program and expressed a need for flexibility. Other participants were worried that if the prayer requirements were loosened, their own experience would be compromised. They expressed that they came to the program to have a strong "minyan experience" and did not want any of the prayer services cancelled. The group decided that regular *shaḥarit, minḥah,* and *arvit* services would be maintained but that the whole group would only be required to come for shaḥarit. For the afternoon and evening services, the group would work together to maintain a minyan, and if some needed to take a break and either not pray or pray individually, they would do so only if there was a minyan. In addition to hearing about participants' individual experiences, the middle check-in mentoring meeting also enabled us to received important feedback from the group as a whole.

The last mentoring meeting was an opportunity for Lishma staff and students to reflect on and synthesize their Lishma experience. Participants were asked about their future, post-Lishma, plans. They had a chance to discuss the challenges of returning to regular life and integrating lessons learned from the summer into daily life. In post-summer evaluations, participants expressed how creating a structured space in which they were invited to articulate their fears, expectations, successes, and challenges made them feel heard and understood, not just as program participants, but as Jews and as people. Rachel Bat-Or, Lishma coordinator from 2002 to 2005, wrote, "So often a Lishmanik came to talk to me about what they had learned during that day that excited or upset them. We would talk about how it affected them, how they could understand it, and how to integrate it into the rest of their ideas." An important element of many Christian seminary curricula and spiritual mentoring meetings are worthy of further exploration for inclusion in rabbinic training and even in synagogue settings to give individual Jews a structured opportunity to discuss issues of faith and practice.

A camp program: Building community

Notwithstanding the central focus on text study, Lishma still distinguishes itself as a camp program, with its participants sharing many of the goals and challenges that campers have during the course of a summer. Just as campers in a bunk often struggle to live together in a shared space and cohesive community, Lishma also struggled to build community within itself and within the larger camp community. We worked to ensure that the program was not a suffocating experience for those unaccustomed to the rigors of traditional communal Jewish life, but also to ensure that Lishma provided a strong communal experience for those who came seeking it. The Lishma coordinator, Rachel Bat Or wrote:

> One of the changes that I made that I feel particularly proud of was adding a question onto the application about community building. I noticed that during my first summer, people did not have an easy time creating community. There seemed to be a split between those who wanted to reach consensus about a decision and those who wanted to do things their own way without group agreement. . . . The biggest problem was not the differences themselves but that those who wanted to bypass group discussion did not respect or want to hear from those who wanted to talk things through. There was no framework, no preexisting agreements to help us discuss the differences. Having a question on the application and a discussion during the interview about how each person helped to create community set up the context for conscious conversations about community building, and the tension of my first summer did not emerge again.

Beyond the beit midrash

To further address the critical issue of young adults' involvement in Jewish life after the program, Lishma must be more than just an enjoyable summer experience built around Jewish study. The following components were included that aim to expand the relevance and importance of Jewish study outside of the Lishma program:

Social Action. Participants devoted every Tuesday entirely to a community service project. Monday's evening program was often dedicated to the study of classic texts that speak to the importance and religious significance of social action as a way of introducing the activity for the following day. Texts illustrated social action as a religious expression that is as vital to Judaism as are study and prayer. Projects included activities such as picking oranges at a farm that dedicated a portion of its produce to a local homeless shelter, learning Torah with residents at Beit Teshuva—the only Jewish halfway-house in the country dedicated to helping Jews struggling with addiction, and visiting residents at a Jewish home for the aged.

Evening Programs. Often a highlight of the summer, evening programs were informal and exposed Lishma participants to guest speakers and to a wide variety of topics addressing the reality of bringing Judaism into everyday life. An additional aspect of evening programs featured in the first few summers was a book-author series in which Lishma participants studied with a series of local authors such as Rabbis David Wolpe, Brad Artson, Elliot Dorff, and Stewart Vogel. Each participant was given a copy of one of the author's books after the session with the author. This program gave participants a tangible beginning to building a Jewish library and beginning a lifetime journey of Jewish reading. Other evening programs (from the first and subsequent summers) included thought-provoking activities such as viewing *Trembling before God,* a film about homosexuality in Orthodox communities, and a subsequent discussion about Judaism and homosexuality. Other programs were less intense such as baking hallah for Shabbat, Israeli folk dancing, painting, making ceramics, and enjoying a camp-wide concert with Rick Recht.

Practical Halachah. Sometimes the challenge to Jewish observance is not motivation or means but knowing how. Several times over the course of the summer, time was set aside for participants to hear a halachic overview of Shabbat, tzedakah, kashrut and other aspects of Jewish life and to have an open discussion about the barriers to observance, its deep communal and spiritual meaning, and how it can be accomplished amid the pressures of daily life.

Channel Islands camping trip

One of the most memorable parts of the program for participants and staff alike is a Shabbat camping trip at the nearby Channel Islands National Park. The trip took place the first summer of Lishma and was repeated every summer thereafter. It includes a one-hour journey by boat from the Ventura harbor to Santa Cruz Island, the largest of the Channel Islands, often with the boat surrounded by hundreds of channel dolphins. Spending Shabbat on an island is easier because according to some halachic authorities, an island serves as a natural *eruv,* and carrying is permitted. Nonetheless, seeing the moment as an educational opportunity, Lishma scholar Dr. Aaron Amit (2005–7) constructed an eruv and taught participants the principles of how an eruv works. Highlights of a Shabbat of the camping trip includes a spirited Carlebach-style *kabbalat shabbat* as the sun sets over the Pacific Ocean, stunning hikes to remote ocean beaches, and on Sunday morning, helping the National Park service perform trail maintenance and rid the island of damaging, non-native plants. The Shabbat serves as a mid-summer break from the study routine and an opportunity for participants to bond with each other and return to camp renewed for the second half of the program.

Integration with camp

When we started Lishma, we anticipated that Lishma students would serve as important role models to the hundreds of campers and staff in residence at Camp Ramah in California. We hoped that campers and staff would be curious about these college kids who were spending their summer in intensive Jewish study, would engage them in discussion, and over the course of time, might begin to consider a similar experience for themselves. Lishma evening programs were made available to the general Ramah staff, and Ramah staff members could receive staff education credit for participation in Lishma classes. Lishma participants were invited to the Friday night *oneg* and Saturday night activities for Ramah's general staff. To facilitate interaction with Ramah campers, Lishma participants either taught or participated in *limmud* on Shabbat afternoons when the entire camp studies Pirkei Avot or some other Jewish text while sitting in circles on "The Hill"—a central, grassy area at camp.

These efforts at integration were only marginally effective. First of all, many Ramah campers were not aware of the existence of Lishma or if they were, they were not fully aware of what the program was and who the participants were. Either by choice or by necessity, Lishma participated in few of the core camp-wide activities. The allocation of space required that Lishma sit in the small dining room and that the group eat lunch and dinner one-half hour prior to the rest of camp instead of joining campers and staff in the main dining room. Because we hoped that meals would bc a setting for continuing discussions from the beit midrash and for getting to know one another, the noisy and fun but chaotic atmosphere of the main dining room was not necessarily the preferred place for Lishma to eat. When the rest of camp gathered on Friday nights to daven together in Kikkar Tziyyon, Lishma gathered in the small observatory at the top of camp for a spirited, intimate prayer service. These decisions served the Lishma program well internally but served to separate Lishma from the rest of the camp. When Lishma participants studied with campers as part of limmud on Saturday afternoon, campers often did not understand why Lishma participants were there, a curiosity that sometimes invited important conversations but at other times created distance. Furthermore, Ramah staff members often socialize by talking about their common challenges and successes in caring for and working with campers, providing little common ground with Lishma participants. What Lishma gained in creating a stronger program for itself, the overall Ramah camp lost as an opportunity for having Lishma participants become role models.

Students and teachers

The difference between academic learning and Lishma learning was felt not only by students but also by its teachers. Lishma scholar Dr. Aaron Amit is a professor of Talmud at Bar Ilan University and formerly a faculty member of Machon Schechter in Israel. After the 2007 summer, he wrote about the impact that teaching at Lishma had on him.

> Teaching on this program . . . has affected me deeply and given me a perspective on teaching that I had never experienced before. In the course of a month we went through many situations together and in the process of learning, davening, eating and traveling together we fulfilled *lilmod, lelammed vela'asot* [to study, to teach and to do] in their full sense! And not just any students—the students who came to study at Lishma gave up summer jobs and mindless relaxation, committing themselves to four weeks of intense learning and spiritual growth. I have been so moved by the summers of Lishma that I find myself spending much of the time between summers thinking how I am going to teach it "this time" and what material I will add and change. I have been given a gift and I want to use it in the best way possible.
>
> *Lishma* means learning Torah with no ulterior motives—learning Torah not in order to get a reward but for the love of the learning itself. The participants in Lishma learn over the summer the pleasures of learning for

its own sake. And yet, as the days pass and the participants speak—each letting their own unique view of Torah be heard, I find that the definition of *lishma* changes. If I had to try for a succinct definition, I would say that in this context *torah lishma* means—giving the Torah its own name. Torah lishma is the process by which each individual who learns Torah gives themselves the freedom to give Torah a new and unique name. If we allow ourselves to give Torah a new name, we have fulfilled the command to study because we have learned to integrate Torah into our own life.

But doing this is no easy task—it means being an active participant in the dialogue about life—about meaning—about God—it means coming to terms with difficult and obscure texts, it means addressing the deepest side of our existence and trying to understand our inner voice. It means allowing each person to understand that they matter and they have great untapped potential to teach the world a unique message. Many people go through the motions of daily routines without thinking about what they are doing. Torah lishma is about changing that and thinking about each one of our acts. Over the summers I have let myself express my deepest feelings and thoughts in a serious way in front of an amazing group of students. People share and grow together both individually and as a group. In the end there is no one who remains the same person who began the program and I am convinced that every participant will make Judaism a part of their life afterwards. I have stayed in contact with many of the participants and I see that the love of learning planted by the first experience of Lishma leads to a thirst for more.

Beyond North America

In the summer of 2004, three women from the former Soviet Union came to study at Lishma after reading about it on the Internet. In the summer of 2005, as part of a larger partnership between the Los Angeles Jewish Federation and the Baltic communities of Lithuania, Latvia, and Estonia, three more participants came to Lishma from overseas. These participants brought an important dimension of diversity to Lishma. The Eastern Europeans had the opportunity to view an egalitarian Judaism that does not exist in the former Soviet Union. They also learned to deal with the culture shock of a different language, weather, culture, type of food, and way of observance. They sometimes struggled with all of that but at the end of the program, they brought a deep commitment to Jewish practice back to their communities. As for the Americans—they welcomed the newcomers and helped them to acclimate to American ways of doing things. They learned some Russian and taught the visitors what to expect when we went to Los Angeles for our social action days. The cultural exchange became an important part of the Lishma experience for both the Americans and those from the former Soviet Union.

Lishma through the Years

The Early Years—1999 to 2001

As one might expect, during the summers of 1999 and 2000 when participants were offered $500-stipends to participate in Lishma, enrollment was high.

Lishma Enrollment by Year

1999	18
2000	16
2001	9
2002	9
2003	16
2004	15
2005	16
2006	11
2007	7
Total Alumni	**117**

During those years, the program also required participants to commit for six weeks instead of the current four-week model. In 2000, an additional New and Innovative Program grant of $25,000 was secured from the Jewish Community Foundation. These funds were used for funding year-round-staff costs and to create a scholarship fund for future summers. Although financial aid was made available to needy students, enrollment declined in 2001 as the program shifted from paying stipends to participants to charging tuition of $2,000. In 2001, as the founding Lishma coordinator, I was named a Joshua Venture Fellow. Funding from this fellowship sustained my continued involvement with the program until I became the executive director of Camp Ramah in California in the spring of 2002.

From 2002 to 2007

From 2002 to 2007, Lishma enrollment fluctuated depending on the fee structure, the year-round Lishma coordinator, and the existence of competing programs. Between summers, Lishma was directed by ZSRS students including Rachel Bat Or (2002–5), Scott Perlo (fall 2005), and Lizzie Heydemann and Jordan Gerson (spring 2006 to fall 2007). Funding for year-round coordinators was limited as Lishma transitioned from a "new and innovative" program, which gained substantial support from major foundations, to one of many yeshiva-study programs available around the country (see below). Lishma alumni made small donations but because they were young adults, they lacked the resources to form a core of regular donors to support the program.

In addition, having a ZSRS student as the year-round coordinator presented significant challenges. First, ZSRS students graduate after five years and also are unable to work on Lishma during their third year of the program while they study in Israel. Second, a Lishma coordinator is charged, most importantly, with recruiting, interviewing, and registering participants for the following summer and as the summer grows closer, preparing for the summer program. These tasks represent significant time commitments, take time to learn, and leave little time for additional tasks such as coordinating alumni reunions, publishing alumni newsletters, updating alumni databases, and sending letters to alumni and other Lishma supporters to help generate financial support. Valuable data about Lishma's alumni from 1999 to 2007 is not up to date because a viable staffing structure to accomplish these tasks did not exist and would be difficult to maintain, considering the small size and budget of the program. A committee of staff and lay leaders from Camp Ramah in California and ZSRS is currently meeting as of this writing to examine these challenges and chart a better way forward.

Challenges for the future: At camp and beyond

Lishma has extended a key element of the Ramah mission: cultivating the future professional and lay leadership of the Conservative Movement. Lishma graduates have gone on to become rabbis, educators, Jewish communal professionals, and perhaps most significantly, young lay leaders. Beth Allen, a 2006 Lishma participant wrote,

> After a month, we're returning to our own communities strengthened. We know more deeply the practical halachic issues such as kashrut, davening (prayer) and Shabbat. We are also grounded in rabbinic logic, and more open to interpretation. We are educated enough to know that there's something that we bring to the Jewish table, and that Conservative Judaism wants to be a home for us. We will lead the future because Conservative Judaism embraced us—not as potential rabbis, but as lay people who are seeking and growing.

It is clear that the Lishma experience has strengthened an intense commitment to Jewish life amid many of its 100+ alumni. Yet despite its successes, Lishma's enrollment has suffered from a lack of funding, especially since 2002, and faces other significant challenges for its continued viability, including:

Staffing/recruitment. Lishma is run during the year on a part-time basis by rabbinical students with an extremely limited schedule. Because of limited funding and because of an already full academic schedule with limited time for travel, staff struggles to meet and recruit students "face-to-face" on campus and at conferences.

Integration into camp. Lishma struggles to find its place within the summer camp community and perhaps most importantly, within Ramah California's board of directors. Within camp, Lishma participants are recognized by Ramah staff, but except for their weekly participation in Shabbat limmud, the Lishma program is largely unrecognized by Ramah campers. Ramah staff members are accepting of Lishma participants but have little in common with them because they lack a common, shared experience upon which to form bonds. Within the board of directors, the Lishma program enjoys some support, including some members who have funded individual Lishma participants each year since the inception of the program. Perhaps because of the lack of integration with the core summer program, most board members, although not hostile to Lishma, remain cautious of diverting resources—for example, financial and summer adult housing—away from the core summer camp program.

In addition, realities outside of camp pose challenges to Lishma as well:

A changed landscape. The landscape in 2007 looks very different than it did nine years ago. When Lishma began, we could write, "In America—the largest Jewish population in the entire world—there is not a single institution for the 94% of Jews who are not Orthodox to study Torah in a non-academic setting, as a religious enterprise." Now that is no longer the case. In North America, the Northwoods Kollel continues to attract six to eight staff members to Ramah Wisconsin each summer to engage in serious text study for part of the day and to work as teachers for the remainder of the day. Machon Hadar, an independent yeshiva-study program for young adult Jews on the upper West Side of Manhattan, opened for the first time in the summer of 2007 and was filled to capacity. Participants received substantial living stipends due to significant support from the New York Federation. The Conservative Yeshiva in Jerusalem is running a summer program and although not in the United States, it is reaching a similar constituency and is also experiencing high enrollment.

Returning to the Movement. Like graduates of many Ramah camps, upon completing the program, Lishma participants struggle to find communities within the Conservative Movement to which they can return. Services in the main sanctuary lack opportunities for participation and leadership by interested lay people, and many adult education courses lack a track for engagement with traditional Jewish texts. Having taken on a commitment to traditional Shabbat observance, many Lishma graduates—and many Ramah graduates—feel lonely in Conservative synagogues and too often, our most committed young people, committed both to observance and the Conservative Movement, gravitate to Modern Orthodox communities, not for theological reasons but rather, because they are seeking community.

Finally, the Conservative Movement is, frankly, unorganized in its approach to the population of committed young adults it produces. The current Lishma coordinator, Elizabeth Heydemann, writes,

> A deeper issue lies with the relationship of Lishma to the Conservative Movement. . . . We invest so much in the foundations of our kids' Jewish lives by sending them to Ramah and to Israel, only to let Jewish learning and living fall by the wayside in college and beyond. Lishma is a life-changing, knowledge-building, identity-strengthening program, whose ripples extend far beyond the bounds of our movement. Lishma should be on every rabbi's list of programs to recommend to their young congregants and their middle-aged congregants' kids and grandkids.

Greater coordination is required if we are to succeed on the level of a movement in reaching this crucial age group as they consider whom to marry and what their religious commitment will be as they grow into adulthood.

Concluding Comments

Nine years ago, we wrote:

> The broad, overarching goal of Lishma is to create a cadre of young adults who will live within the Jewish community and establish a hospitable environment for other young people who are seeking a way to become involved—for instance, those who have come back from inspirational experiences such as a trip to Israel or a summer at Ramah. This cadre will be the next generation of leadership for the liberal Jewish community, individuals who can provide religious vision as lay people, not necessarily as rabbis or academics.

To a great extent, Lishma has succeeded. Young adults at a critical stage in life have been inspired and educated. In transition between their parents' homes and establishing their own, they often lack financial resources and seek meaning and direction. Investing in their growth and development is a crucial element for gaining the long-term commitment of a population vital to the creativity and vibrancy of our community. It is our hope that Lishma and similar programs will become more and more important to our movement's agenda—*ken yirbu* (so should they multiply)!

Notes

[1] Daniel Gordis, "Honey from the Word: Yeshiva Learning from Liberal Judaism?" *Jewish Spectator* (Spring 1994): 6–11.

[2] Grant application to the Covenant Foundation, submitted spring 1998.

[3] Ramah camps and USY summer programs continue to be powerful environments for reaching young adult Jews by giving them an opportunity to earn money as staff members while living and teaching in educational Jewish communities. Although salary levels are relatively low, the opportunity to earn money, rather than be a drain on family or personal resources should not be underestimated as a factor in why young adults choose to come to Ramah and USY summer programs.

CHERYL MAGEN

Bridging Academia and the Field: The Davidson School and Camp Ramah

SINCE THE INCEPTION of Ramah as a system of camps in the 1950s, The Jewish Theological Seminary (JTS) has been a supporter, partner, and provider of oversight for each of the camps. The relationship over the years has taken different forms, but the connection always has been a driving presence. The partnership was renewed and strengthened in 2003 with the appointment of Dr. Steve Brown as the dean of the William Davidson Graduate School of Jewish Education and of Rabbi Mitch Cohen as the director of the National Ramah Commission (NRC). Both are products of the Ramah Camping Movement, and this partnership was a natural outgrowth of their dedication to the educational mission of Ramah. The same year that Steve Brown and Mitch Cohen began serving in their positions, I came to the Davidson School after serving for nineteen summers as the director of Ramah Poconos. Both Steve and Mitch decided that I would serve as the Davidson educational consultant to Ramah. And so, a new element in the Ramah–JTS/Davidson partnership was formed.

Mitch, Steve, and I began to meet on a regular basis to outline projects that would be useful to the Ramah camps and that when possible, would involve the collaboration of some of the Davidson students. There was also an understanding that the Ramah camps would serve as fertile ground for possible recruitment of new students to Davidson to pursue either a master's degree or a doctorate in Jewish education. Working closely with the admissions professional from the Davidson School, as well as the admissions directors of the other JTS schools, each summer we forged connections with Ramah camp

CHERYL MAGEN *serves on the education staff of the William Davidson Graduate School of Jewish Education of The Jewish Theological Seminary as the educational consultant to the National Ramah Commission. In addition, she is the director of the master's degree program in Camp Administration and Leadership at Touro University–Nevada. She served as the director of Camp Ramah in the Poconos for nineteen years.*

directors and *rashei ḥinnuch* (heads of education) to identify potential candidates for pursuing graduate degrees in Jewish education. Beyond assisting with recruitment, my position includes three main portfolios, *ḥinnuch* (education), *hadrachah* (leadership training), and *tefillah* (prayer). Each of these portfolios has yielded significant opportunities for year-round collaboration. I describe each of these portfolios in turn.

Ḥinnuch: Creating Contexts for Collaboration

The rashei ḥinnuch, like many other staff members, are not year-round, full-time Ramah employees. Although there is much to be gained by bringing educators together to enhance their work, geography and the schedule between summers make it difficult to create meaningful connections among these rashei ḥinnuch.

In the spring of 2004, through the generosity of the Davidson School, the rashei ḥinnuch from all seven of the Ramah overnight camps and the Nyack day camp were invited to a two-day conference at JTS. This was a new opportunity to share the goals of the educational missions of the different camps, compare curricula, work together to solve challenges, and plan strategically for the future. Since then, the rashei ḥinnuch meet regularly each fall and spring for two days of sharing, collaboration, and professional development. Meetings in the fall afford an opportunity to "unpack" and process the summer experience and plan for the next summer, set goals for the shared work of the group, and share materials developed over the summer. Each rosh ḥinnuch is given a flash drive so that he or she can share curriculum easily with other educators and contribute material to a centralized resource bank. The spring meetings are devoted to discussions about faculty training, including the integration of staff and curriculum into all arenas of the camp, as well as about team-building ideas and staff week schedules.

There is professional development for the rashei ḥinnuch at both the fall and spring gatherings. Faculty and staff from the Davidson School and JTS spend time teaching and leading sessions to enrich the educators' knowledge and to support their summer efforts. For example, after attending a poignant experiential learning session with Dr. Neil Gillman, former chair of the Department of Philosophy at JTS, the rosh ḥinnuch at each camp emphasized the importance of including God in formal and informal discussions with campers and staff. In a session with Dr. Carol Ingall, a professor of Jewish Education at JTS, the group learned the "8 E's" (guidelines for moral education) from her book, *Transmission and Transformation*. This information became the basis for the creation of a *berit* (covenant) for each *yahadut* (Judaica) class at Camp Ramah in New England.

Curriculum development

The sessions with the rashei ḥinnuch also led to curriculum development. A unit for each of the *edot* on *shemirat halashon* (avoiding offensive language) was developed collaboratively by all the rashei ḥinnuch after a learning session with Dr. Steve Brown. As stated in the introduction to the materials, the shemirat halashon curriculum addresses the following concern:

> Being away from parents and the rigors of school limits, the camp atmosphere often feels permissive when it comes to trying on behaviors and testing new limits. After all, in a peer community such as Ramah, it seems natural to try language and behaviors that are closely watched at home under parental supervision. Specifically, campers tend to use more foul language than is acceptable at home and tend to be intensely motivated to share details about others—whether true or false—more readily than at home as well.

The shemirat halashon curriculum has four units. Each unit is intended for short-term use by the educators in *shi'urim* and by the *madrichim* in the *tzerifim*. The units can be used in *tefillot* and other *pe'ulot* as well. One of the hallmarks of a Ramah experience is learning to look at one's choices in life through a Jewish lens. These units present one window into the issues that surround the use of foul language and the existence of gossip and rumors, and the units include actions to make camp a "cleaner" environment when people speak.

Another example of curriculum developed by this group is "Jews and Social Justice," which is designed for rising tenth-graders so as to enable all camps to implement the study before the campers go to Israel on Ramah Seminar. The curriculum analyzes the issues of poverty, hunger, homelessness, and the impact of terrorism in the United States, Canada, and Israel. An important goal of the "Jews and Social Justice" curriculum is the integration of ḥinnuch into the everyday life of a camper. Therefore, it includes not only the study of formal texts but also pe'ulot for the bunk and the edah using different perspectives and modalities. In this way, campers with various learning styles and abilities can connect to the material. One pe'ulat erev focuses on terrorism in Israel and examines four different aspects—social, economic, political, and cultural—of what happens to the victims and the differences before and after a terrorist attack. The materials also include readings from investigative reporter Barbara Ehrenreich's best-seller *Nickel and Dimed,*[1] the use of the Disney movie *Beauty and the Beast,* and the lyrics of "Don't Laugh at Me," a song by Peter, Paul, and Mary. All the materials are provided so that this educational kit is extremely easy to use at camp. As an outgrowth of this educational initiative, the Israel Seminar program added more opportunities for volunteer work in Israel.

The other major outcome of bringing the rashei ḥinnuch together was a clear mission statement of the educational goals for Ramah. Even though the camps are different in many ways and serve different regional populations, we came to a shared vision of education in the Ramah camps. The following statement emerged from these deliberations:

The educational "viSSion" of Camp Ramah

The "viSSion"[2] of education at Camp Ramah is to create an observant, Conservative, Jewish, learning community with an overarching purpose to convey appreciation for the joy and richness of Jewish life.

When immersed in a positive, informal, and fun Jewish learning environment, campers and staff can successfully make connections between tefillah, song, *mitzvot,* and *middot,* incorporating them into their daily lives, which we hope will carry over into a lifelong pursuit of Jewish learning.

The viSSion of informal education at Camp Ramah is also to foster a love for and an appreciation of the Hebrew language, and to recognize and appreciate one's place in Jewish history in order to create the future leaders of the Jewish community.

Through integrated educational experiences, Ramah hopes to instill enthusiasm for and a desire to spend time in Israel in any of many capacities (e.g., touring, studying, aliyah), as well as to develop a sense of pride in one's Jewish identity and a passion to advocate for it.

All of these learning experiences are carefully designed to contribute to the social and emotional character development and positive self-esteem of the campers and staff who spend time in Ramah programs.

The master binder: A collaborative resource bank

The eight educational directors have collaborated on the creation of a master binder for use by ḥinnuch faculty at the Ramah camps. This compilation consists of two parts: (1) Ramah-specific pieces, such as the viSSion statement, a list of educational websites, and a rubric for planning electives; and (2) pieces specific to the individual camp that every educator needs, such as the logistics for duplicating materials and how to arrange for snacks for a *siyyum.* In developing this master binder, faculty members at each camp gained a better understanding of the Ramah Camping Movement and the knowledge that they were contributing to a movement-wide effort.

Developments in Staff Training

Staff training is a second key component of the Ramah–Davidson/JTS partnership. The Bert B. Weinstein Counselor Training Institute and the Louis and Shoshana Winer Training Institute for Rashei Edah serve as important vehicles for the training of staff for the Ramah Camping Movement. As the representative of the Davidson School, I helped National Ramah with various staff training programs—developing training materials and leading sessions. In particular, I worked closely with Mitch Cohen and Amy Skopp Cooper, National Ramah Assistant Director, to create a set curriculum for the Winer Institute, which is held annually prior to the start of the summer season. The Winer curriculum is intended to supplement the staff development programs that camp directors lead for their own rashei edah. At the end of each summer, rashei edah who have attended Winer have reported that the training was invaluable, enabling them to understand the complex nature of this senior staff position. For staff members who feel overwhelmed and unprepared before stepping into the role of rosh edah, the Winer Institute not only provides specific direction for working with staff and the directors for the good of a particular age group, but also gives participants a sense of being part of the larger Ramah Camping Movement.

In 2006, the new director of Ramah New England, Rabbi Ed Gelb, implemented regularly scheduled formal training for counselors and junior counselors. This change was facilitated by the reintroduction of educator-led shi'urim into the daytime program. Previously, shi'urim were led by the madrichim themselves, who now were available for intensive, ongoing hadrachah. To support this effort, Mitch Cohen asked me to create a set of formal sessions to be used in hadrachah at the New England camp. With the guidance and input of Meryl Sussman, the Poconos staff training coordinator, I adapted material that had been developed over time at Ramah Poconos to design twenty-one sessions for junior counselors and sixteen sessions for senior counselors on topics ranging from "Disciplining with Dignity" and "Seizing the Teachable Moment" to "The Emotional Bank Account" and "Your Future with Ramah." This new curriculum also is used at Ramah Darom and Ramah Poconos to augment their existing training programs.

B'racha B'Ramah: An Important Resource for Tefillah Education

The third portfolio, tefillah, yielded a fruitful three-year collaboration among students from all five schools at JTS and professionals from the William Davidson Graduate School. JTS graduate students who spent their summers at Ramah as participants in the Alexander M. Shapiro Fellowship Program gathered together in the fall of 2004 under the leadership of Rabbi Mitch Cohen to talk about the importance of establishing National Ramah guidelines for tefillah education in the camps. The tefillah initiative that became known as B'racha B'Ramah developed as a result of these conversations. B'racha B'Ramah, a compilation of gradated tefillah resource materials, is intended to guide, empower, and provide support to camp staff to enhance the quality and quantity of tefillah education.

The initial discussions about the nature of the curriculum to be developed and the focus for each edah were a particularly interesting part of the process. For guidance, we turned to Dr. Steve Brown, an expert in tefillah education. Steve suggested that we "just start at the beginning" by teaching the opening of the *shaḥarit* service to the youngest edah and proceeding from there, rather than targeting specific prayers for specific age groups based on the content or meaning of the prayer (as other tefillah educators might suggest). Steve reasoned that if campers spend the typical five to eight years at a camp, then they would know virtually the entire service by the time they "graduated." In addition, it became important to advocate that any prayer could be taught in any summer to any age group. The edah guidelines were suggestions for organizing the materials, but they were not intended to be limiting. The goal was to empower the edah staff to teach tefillah and to avoid repeating the same material summer after summer.

In April 2005, Rabbi Dahlia Kronish submitted her Davidson School master's thesis entitled "How to Teach Birkhot Hashachar to Rising 4th and 5th Graders," which became the very first component of the B'racha B'Ramah curriculum. B'racha B'Ramah was produced through monthly meetings with students from List College, the Graduate School, the Davidson School, the Rabbinical School, and the H. L. Miller Cantorial School. Some of the students were former Ramah campers or staff, and some had never been to Ramah but were committed to the idea of tefillah education. Each student worked on one aspect of the materials. As developed by Rabbi Kronish in her thesis, text pages are designed like a page of Talmud with the commentary around the center box including key words, central themes, sources, choreography, and fun facts about the tefillah. A sample page from the fourth- to fifth-grade unit appears on the following page.

B'racha B'Ramah consists of 300 pages of resource materials and two music CDs. The curriculum for each edah focuses on a particular section of the weekday shaḥarit service. Each unit includes several selections of prayers from that part of the service, ideas for *divrei tefillah,* stories for use in tefillot or before bedtime, and program ideas for pe'ulot tzerif, pe'ulot edah, and pe'ulot erev. These materials follow the model of integrating ḥinnuch in all program areas throughout the day. The areas of focus for each age group are summarized in the following table:

THE NATIONAL RAMAH COMMISSION

In partnership with the William Davidson Graduate School of Jewish Education

רעיונות מרכזיים

מה טבו is a prayer that helps us take a look at our surroundings and turn an ordinary place into a מקום תפילה.

Reflects the beauty of communal worship and communal institutions.

Written in the first person – highlights personal connection. (ואני...ואני...ואני).

The collection of verses in this prayer expresses love and reverence for the synagogue that in the absence of the Temple is the place where God's Glory resides among Israel (Scherman, 1998, p. 12).

Our מקום תפילה as a place of God's presence, God's dwelling, God's compassion and Grace.

The power of turning a curse into a blessing as provided by the allusion to Balaam.

The power of words.

מה טבו functions as a way of preparing us for entering into a prayer space – physically and spiritually. In this *tefillah* we begin to articulate our relationship with God (we kneel, bow before, bless the Creator).

God is a God of Kindness חסד and Salvation ישועה.

הידעת?

The tradition of saying מה טבו upon entering the synagogue is derived from the Talmudic interpretation of "your tents" as houses of study and "your dwelling places" as synagogues. (Brown, 1996, p. 140).

בימוי

This prayer was appended to the fixed liturgy when the preliminary preparation to *Shacharit* (otherwise known as *birkot hashachar*) was moved to the synagogue.

Depending on custom of the place, מה טבו can be recited individually prior to putting on *tallit* and *tefillin*, or communally after the two have been donned.

מַה טֹּבוּ אֹהָלֶיךָ יַעֲקֹב, מִשְׁכְּנֹתֶיךָ יִשְׂרָאֵל. וַאֲנִי בְּרֹב חַסְדְּךָ אָבוֹא בֵיתֶךָ, אֶשְׁתַּחֲוֶה אֶל הֵיכַל קָדְשְׁךָ בְּיִרְאָתֶךָ. ה׳ אָהַבְתִּי מְעוֹן בֵּיתֶךָ, וּמְקוֹם מִשְׁכַּן כְּבוֹדֶךָ. וַאֲנִי אֶשְׁתַּחֲוֶה וְאֶכְרָעָה, אֶבְרְכָה לִפְנֵי ה׳ עֹשִׂי. וַאֲנִי, תְפִלָּתִי לְךָ ה׳, עֵת רָצוֹן, אֱלֹהִים בְּרָב חַסְדֶּךָ, עֲנֵנִי בֶּאֱמֶת יִשְׁעֶךָ.

How wonderful are your tents, Jacob, your abodes, Israel! I, by Your great love, enter Your house, and bow down reverently before Your holy shrine. Adonai, I love Your house of dwelling, the abode of Your glory. I will humbly bow down low before Adonai, my Maker (L. Hoffman, 2002, p. 50).

מילות מפתח

מַה טֹּבוּ -- טוב
How wonderful!

אֹהָלֶיךָ – אוהל, אוהל מועד
Tents; Tent of Meeting (*Mishkan*).

יִרְאָתֶךָ – י.ר.א
To revere.

חַסְדֶּךָ – ח.ס.ד (חסיד, גמילות חסדים)
Kindness.

יִשְׁעֶךָ – י.ש.ע. (ישועה, מושיע)
To redeem.

מקורות

במדבר כ״ד פסוק ה׳: מַה־טבו אֹהָלֶיךָ יַעֲקֹב מִשְׁכְּנֹתֶיךָ יִשְׂרָאֵל:
See Numbers chapters 22-24 for the full Balaam story.

תהילים ה׳ פסוק ח: וַאֲנִי בְּרֹב חַסְדְּךָ אָבוֹא בֵיתֶךָ אֶשְׁתַּחֲוֶה אֶל־הֵיכַל קָדְשְׁךָ בְּיִרְאָתֶךָ:
Psalms 5:8 -- Here the verse appears as part of a lament asking God to let the worshipper pray at the Temple (L. Hoffman, 2002, p. 52).

תהילים כ״ו פסוק ח: ה׳ אָהַבְתִּי מְעוֹן בֵּיתֶךָ וּמְקוֹם מִשְׁכַּן כְּבוֹדֶךָ:
Psalms 26:8 – Here the verse appears as part of a lament requesting God's help based on the worshiper's past piety, namely how much he loved going to God's Temple (L. Hoffman, 2002, p. 52).

תהילים צ״ה פסוק ו: בֹּאוּ נִשְׁתַּחֲוֶה וְנִכְרָעָה נִבְרְכָה לִפְנֵי ה׳ עֹשֵׂנוּ:
Psalms 95:6 – Notice how the Biblical verse is written in the plural voice, whereas in the *tefillah*, it is changed to the singular.

תהילים ס״ט פסוק י״ד: וַאֲנִי תְפִלָּתִי־לְךָ ה׳ עֵת רָצוֹן אֱלֹהִים בְּרָב־חַסְדֶּךָ עֲנֵנִי בֶּאֱמֶת יִשְׁעֶךָ:

Sample page from B'racha B'Ramah (fourth- to fifth-grade unit)

Areas of Focus of B'racha B'Ramah By Age Group

AGE GROUP	AREA OF FOCUS
Rising 4th and 5th graders	Birchot Hashaḥar
Rising 6th graders	Pesukei Dezimra
Rising 7th graders	Shema Uvirchoteha
Rising 8th graders	Amidah
Rising 9th graders	Torah Service
Rising 10th graders	Minḥah and Ma'ariv
Rising 11th graders	Concepts of Israel in Tefillah

The first of the two CDs accompanying the curriculum, "The Nusaḥ of the Weekday Shaḥarit Service" was produced at JTS by recently graduated cantors studying in the Davidson School for their master's degrees, along with several students in the Miller Cantorial School. It contains the nusaḥ used at the various Ramah camps. This CD can be used to teach those who want to hone their davening skills or their ability to lead tefillot. The second CD is "The Music of the Weekday Shaḥarit Service" and contains original music for tefillot found in shaḥarit by noted musicians Debbie Friedman, Rick Recht, and Craig Taubman.

The materials were piloted in the camps in 2005 and were fully in place by the summer of 2007. The ongoing challenge will be for each rosh edah, and ultimately for each director, to make sure that the resources are being utilized on a consistent basis. After that happens, we can plan assessments and updates and then, perhaps, move toward similar materials for Shabbat. Currently, the materials are utilized as intended—by the staff as resources to help in the educational venture of tefillah at camp. Each Ramah camp is at a different place in terms of how its staff teaches tefillah and who delivers the educational messages and resources regarding prayer. Hopefully, the B'racha B'Ramah resources will become the standard for this instruction.

Conclusion

The partnership between the Davidson School and the Ramah camps and programs is a strong example of true collaboration with committed professionals working together toward the goal of developing inspired campers and staff, the future leaders of the Conservative Movement—rabbis, cantors, educators, and educated lay people, who then will help raise a new generation of leaders. Institutional collaboration can be an example of how the whole is greater than the sum of its parts. Each group brings their unique perspective to the table that can serve as a check and balance system. In this case, you have the rich academic resources of the Davidson School working alongside the creative practitioners of the Ramah camps.

Overall, the collaboration enriched both of the partners and hopefully, will lead to the development of more educational materials in the future. The Davidson School is committed to supporting the work of Ramah by dedicating personnel, research time, and student-faculty collaboration. In return, the school will continue to benefit from Ramah's best and brightest who choose careers in Jewish education.

Notes

[1] B. Ehrenreich, *Nickel and Dimed: On (Not) Getting by in America* (New York: Henry Holt & Company, 2001).

[2] ViSSion = a combination of "mission" (a focused and specific set of outcomes) and "vision" (global, all-encompassing goals). This term was coined by Dr. Jeff Kress and Cheryl Magen in their work with the Informal and Communal Education program at the William Davidson Graduate School of Jewish Education.

ALBERT THALER AND **AMY SKOPP COOPER**

Ramah Day Camp in Nyack: Creating a Unique Community of Staff

1. RABBI ALBERT THALER

In the winter of 1970, I was invited by Rabbi David Mogilner, *z"l,* to assume responsibility for Ramah Day Camp in Nyack. At the time, I was completely unaware that there was a Ramah day camp program in existence. I did know that Nyack had been the site of the American Seminar, which was a program for youngsters who, for various reasons, were either unable or chose not to participate in Ramah's Israel Seminar.

After the Six-Day War in 1967, the number of participants in Ramah's Israel Seminar increased dramatically. During the post-war period of euphoria, student travel to Israel became more popular, while a summer at Nyack became less and less attractive. The American Seminar, a small program, became progressively smaller. Opening a day camp was proposed to take advantage of both the Seminar staff of young educators and the underused camp site. Members of the education staff were recruited to help with the fledgling day camp, which at the time drew children from the local community.

When I began to serve as the director in 1971, a small day camp program had already been in operation for a few years. However, by this time, the American Seminar no longer existed, and the facility had become available for an expanded day camp program. Although the camp was in poor physical condition, it was conceivable that we could house a staff large enough to support an increased camper population. Ramah in the Berkshires had its beginnings as a Ramah overnight camp in Nyack. If the Nyack site could house an overnight Ramah camp for several summers, as in fact it had, the facility could certainly house the required number of counselors, specialists, and educators

RABBI ALBERT THALER *served as the director of Ramah Day Camp in Nyack for twenty-seven years. He has been the spiritual leader of Temple Gates of Prayer in Flushing, New York since 1980, after having served for twenty-six years at the Queensboro Jewish Center. Upon his retirement from Ramah Nyack in 1997, he received the Max Arzt Distinguished Rabbinic Service Award from The Jewish Theological Seminary.*

to serve a large number of day campers. Along with Rabbi Stanley Bramnick, whom I had asked to serve as camp administrator, I set into motion a slow, but ongoing, series of renovations using funds that the camp itself generated. We received no funds from any source other than camper tuition fees. During my years as director, we put approximately one and a half million dollars into the facility. This program of renovating, building, and adding activity areas began in the early seventies and continues to this day under the leadership of Amy Skopp Cooper as director and Mark Friedman as business manager.

I invited a few of the American Seminar teachers to continue to work at the day camp. There were approximately eighty children registered for the day camp program in the summer prior to my arrival. The model of a small staff in residence had already been established because holdovers from the American Seminar were spending summers at camp. We decided to seize the opportunity. Our plan was to grow the day camp program and recruit staff by offering them the best of both worlds. They could live at camp, working with children during the day, and then participate in a program of education and recreation after camp hours, creating and becoming part of a vibrant community. It was abundantly clear that to create an exciting summer day camp program for children, we had to cast a net wide enough to attract quality staff people with the knowledge, talent, and skills necessary to implement a Ramah program. We could not rely solely on the local community to provide that staff. Further, we wanted to include a *mishlaḥat* (staff from Israel) to bring the reality of Israel and its message into our camp community. All of this, of course, meant providing decent housing with a functioning kitchen and dining room staff.

The opportunity for young adults that we offered was unique, and though difficult, our search for staff was successful. Simultaneously with this search, we began to recruit campers in geographic areas beyond Rockland County. We reached out to communities in New Jersey, Queens, Westchester, and Manhattan. Within a few years the number of children grew to well over 600 campers with a staff of more than 200. Essentially we were running two camps—one for children and one for the staff members. We were on to a most exciting idea. Every summer we were creating an active Jewish community whose participants worked, played, studied, taught, inspired, and in turn were themselves inspired. I looked upon the effort as a project of *livnot ulhibbanot* (to build [others] and to be built [ourselves]). During my twenty-seven years as director I felt that our work with the staff was as important, if not more important than our work with the children, for they too were "our children." A significant byproduct is the approximately forty marriages that resulted from people meeting during summers at Nyack. Many children of those marriages are today's Ramah campers.

There were other factors at work. The attraction of Shabbat at camp with only staff members present was an enormous plus. Shabbat could be enjoyed in its essence and in its fullness. There were beautiful Ramah *tefillot*; spirited *zemirot* (Sabbath songs) at meals; softball and volleyball games in the afternoon; the availability of a swimming pool; and time for reading, personal study, formal classes, and informal discussions. Shabbat would draw to a close with *se'udah shelishit* (the third Sabbath meal) and a *havdalah* service with its special mystique. In the eyes of many outside of our camp community, the Ramah overnight camps were "the real thing." For us, Nyack was just as real and every bit a Ramah experience. It was exciting, rewarding, fun, and for many of us, it was home. We developed a loyal, creative, caring, and giving staff.

While all this was happening, the day camp program was greatly enhanced by having the staff available to meet, plan, and work after camp hours so as to prepare for upcoming events. *Yom yisra'el,* Maccabiah, *zimriyyah, rikkudiyyah,* Senior Citizen's Day, *ongei shabbat,* the Tish'ah Be'av service, and other special programs required much planning and work. The staff was invested, and their enthusiasm was infectious. Their zeal contributed to the anticipation and excitement with which our children arrived each morning.

Although there are now two other Ramah day camps, the Nyack program with its resident staff remains unique. Where possible, Nyack's model is eminently worthy of replication. Its continuing success speaks for itself.

2. AMY SKOPP COOPER

RABBI THALER RETIRED AS DIRECTOR in 1997. His visionary leadership, charismatic personality, and creative brilliance have left an enduring mark on Ramah Nyack. Admittedly, transitioning into the role of the director who followed him was challenging. Rabbi Thaler served as my teacher and behind-the-scenes mentor during my first years as director. Many talented and loyal senior staff members remained in their positions and offered me invaluable guidance and support.

During the past twelve years, we have invested considerable time, energy, and resources into the physical plant and camp program. We built the Ramot Ramah third tier of camp, which now includes multiple sport fields, tennis courts, a high ropes course, gymnastics wing, and by the 2010 season, a brand new staff facility that will sleep seventy staff members and house fall and

AMY SKOPP COOPER *is the national assistant director of the National Ramah Commission and the director of Ramah Day Camp in Nyack. She has also served as the education director of Congregation Bnai Israel in Millburn, New Jersey, and as the assistant director of the high school Prozdor program at the Hebrew College in Boston.*

spring family retreats. The camp continues to attract a talented and committed pool of young adults to serve on staff. Over the past few years, our camper population has grown, and as a result, we now hire close to 350 staff members annually; approximately 200 reside in camp.

Creating a vibrant, dynamic, egalitarian, and serious Jewish community for our residential staff remains a top priority for Ramah Nyack. We hire young adults who understand that their day does not end at 4 p.m. Instead, the expectation is that staff will study, participate in numerous after-camp programs, plan activities for campers and peers, participate in *hadrachah* (leadership development) sessions, and become active partners in planning their summer experience. On any evening of the week, from 4 p.m. until 1 a.m., staff members are engaged in a plethora of programs. These include weekly guest lectures by educators from The Jewish Theological Seminary (JTS), an ulpan, on-going dialogue with *shelihim* (Israeli staff members), social action, guided *havruta* (study-with-a-partner) learning, a staff choir, an Israeli dance troupe, a staff band, and *tzedakah* events. As I walk through camp late each evening, I note with great satisfaction that virtually every porch and indoor space is being used for programs, that the walkway is a hub of activity, and that young adults are sitting on steps playing guitars and singing Israeli songs.

Nyack also has positioned itself as a resource and learning center for the greater Jewish community. A variety of Jewish professional education conferences are hosted at camp each summer, affording educators the opportunity to observe camper and staff programs and meet with our senior staff. The community is invited to weekly staff lectures and evening programs, to daven with staff on weekday mornings, and to join us on Tish'ah Be'av. In turn, Nyack staff members volunteer within the greater Rockland community. Staff members visit the local Jewish senior home every Friday afternoon to lead pre–*kabbalat shabbat* services and train as mitzvah clowns in connection with *bikkur holim* (visiting the sick) at local hospitals.

Staff members are also encouraged to spend time during the summer preparing for religious school teaching positions and youth work. Knowing that many of our staff members will be offered teaching and youth-group advisor positions, we offer an ongoing group training program to our university-age staff members, through which staff are introduced to theories of education, lesson-plan development, and effective teaching strategies. They meet with mentors on a regular basis. Each summer we identify staff members whom we encourage to consider professional careers in the rabbinate, Jewish education, and Jewish communal service. During the summer, professors and deans from JTS come to camp to teach and meet individually with these prospective students.

In particular, I want to mention the evolving role of the mishlaḥat at Nyack. Our priority has become to hire young sheliḥim who are committed to fully integrating into the staff community. Consequently, in recent years, we have moved away from hiring Israeli families and now select singles, newly out of the army. The members of the mishlaḥat no longer live together and eat together as a distinct group. They are expected to become full participants in the staff community, working closely with their North American peers, socializing with them, studying and developing programs together. We have noted that our North American staff has become increasingly connected with our sheliḥim and as a result, with Eretz Yisra'el. In turn, we have observed that our sheliḥim have connected much more with the egalitarian religious life at camp, which has had a significant impact on them.

Shabbat continues to be a hallmark of the Nyack staff experience. Over 200 young adults daven together, eat together in a leisurely manner, study with a Shabbat guest lecturer, sing and dance, participate in a late Friday evening *tish* and enjoy one another's company. Shabbat programs are planned by staff members; young adults are encouraged to offer *divrei torah,* lead *shirah,* learn how to read Torah, and become *sheliḥei tzibbur* (prayer leaders). Over the years, we have celebrated incredible Shabbat moments, including celebrations of bar and bat mitzvah and engagement announcements! The Shabbat guest community continues to swell with Ramah *vatikim* (camp "veterans") and prospective staff members.

Approximately 70 percent of staff members return to camp for three consecutive summers. Unfortunately, this limits the number of new staff we can hire each summer. However, for the young adults who spend most of their college summers with us, we know that Nyack is a formative experience in their Jewish lives. They have participated in a unique, peer-run, engaging, and serious Jewish community. They are empowered and seek Nyack-like communities year round.

As we face the future, we are proud to look back on four decades of extraordinary success at Ramah Nyack, educating and inspiring children and their families. The most outstanding success is Nyack's model of staff education, which continues to be unique in the world of Jewish informal education. Ramah Nyack provides nurturing Jewish experiences for hundreds of staff members ages sixteen and up who themselves provide excellence in day camp programming. On a personal level, maintaining and building upon the wonderful model developed during Rabbi Thaler's tenure has provided great satisfaction. We look forward to the next decade of success.

RAMAH 60 רמה

In Memoriam

JEROME ABRAMS

Professor Seymour Fox, z"l (1929–2006)

At the age of twenty, Seymour Fox, *z"l,* already was the educational director/cantor of a synagogue in Chicago. In the fall of 1952, Fox entered the Rabbinical School of The Jewish Theological Seminary (JTS). The following summer he was the adviser for the junior counselors at Camp Ramah in Wisconsin. This was the beginning of Seymour Fox's career as a major force in the growth and development of the Ramah Camping Movement. In 1954, Fox became the director of Ramah Wisconsin. In 1956, upon completion of rabbinical school, Fox assumed the position of assistant to the JTS Chancellor. His major responsibility was supervising the Ramah camps. Fox made it his top priority. That year, Dr. M. Bernard Resnikoff, *z"l,* was appointed as the first full-time National Ramah director reporting to Seymour Fox.

Fox was appointed the associate dean of the Teachers Institute of JTS in 1960. Under the guidance of the renowned Bruno Bettelheim, he received his doctorate from the University of Chicago in 1965. In 1966, he was appointed dean of the Teachers Institute. In 1967, Fox accepted the position of director of the School of Education at the Hebrew University and made aliyah. When the philanthropist Morton L. Mandel was the chair of the Jewish Agency's Committee on Education, he brought in Seymour Fox as a senior adviser. In 1990, Fox became the president of the Mandel Foundation in Israel and in 2002, the director for programming of the Mandel Foundation worldwide.

Seymour Fox's boundless energy, his powerful personality, and his innovative and creative mind are legendary. These personal qualities, along with his passionate commitment to Jewish education and to creating a new vision for this field, made him a major figure in the Ramah Camping Movement and the educational system of the State of Israel. At Ramah, he initiated and developed such programs as the American Seminar, the Israel Seminar, the Mador, and seminars during which directors studied regularly with the distinguished philosopher of education, Joseph Schwab. Fox developed retreats and seminars with the Teachers Institute faculty, the Melton Research Center staff, and the Ramah directors participating together. He elevated the Ramah directorship into a profession. In 1958, when I became the director of Camp Ramah in Connecticut (now Camp Ramah in New England), and David Mogilner, *z"l,* succeeded me as the director of Camp Ramah in Wisconsin, Fox convinced the leaders at JTS that the job of being a Ramah director is a full-time position.

In 1963, Fox founded the Melton Research Center at JTS. He developed an unusual, integrated organizational structure of the educational facilities at the Seminary. Under one umbrella, he combined the resources of the Teachers Institute faculty as the academic base, the Melton Research Center as the educational research base, and Ramah as the "theory in practice" base. Under this educational umbrella, he also assembled an outstanding array of scholars, thinkers, and practitioners from both the secular and Jewish worlds who were active participants in these programs. Seymour Fox, without a doubt, was one of the major figures in making Ramah the "crown jewel" of the Conservative Movement.

At Hebrew University, Fox established the Melton Research Center for Jewish Education in the Diaspora. He started the Jerusalem Fellows program, funded mainly by the Jewish Agency in Israel. In addition, he founded the Mandel Foundation, and under its auspices, the Mandel School for Educational Leadership. Fox served as an adviser to ministers of education in Israel. In all of Fox's educational enterprises, two of his philosophical and methodological hallmarks were always evident. One was his commitment to inquiry, to questioning accepted theories and practices, and a passion for creating new visions of education. Second, he would manage to gather the best minds and practitioners from a variety of disciplines and have them interact directly with the participants, very often on a one-to-one basis. The trainees would experience firsthand, with these great minds, what it means to inquire, to question, to explore, and to probe for new ways and ideas—in other words, to be an out-of-the-box, creative professional, in addition to being proficient in the content, skills, and methods of the field. Fox was especially successful in developing this innovative educational process.

I conclude with the following personal musing: There is an old Yiddish expression, *"Mentsh tracht und Gott lacht."* In 2006, approaching the age of 76, Seymour Fox finally decided to enjoy a little rest and recreation and announced his retirement. Suddenly, just two weeks later, he passed away. *Ḥaval.*

RABBI JEROME ABRAMS *opened Camp Ramah in the Berkshires in 1964 and retired as director emeritus in 1994. He spent his entire career of over thirty-five years as a Ramah director and senior leader. He started his career as the director of Camp Ramah in Wisconsin from 1956 to 1957 and subsequently directed Camp Ramah in Connecticut (now New England) from 1958 to 1960 and Camp Ramah in Nyack from 1961 to 1963.*

TODD ZEFF

Michael Levin, z"l (1984–2006)

Michael Levin spent many years as a Ramah Poconos camper and staff member before making aliyah and joining the Israel Defense Forces. He lost his life in combat in Lebanon on August 1, 2006. On August 2, 2006, Rabbi Todd Zeff, the director of Camp Ramah in the Poconos, sent the following letter to the Ramah Poconos community.

With great sadness we write to tell you that Michael Levin, a long-time member of the Ramah Poconos community, who made aliyah and was serving in the army, was killed on Tuesday, August 1, in Lebanon. Michael had joined an elite combat unit of paratroopers who fought a fierce battle with Hezbollah terrorists in the southern Lebanese village of Ayta-al-Shaab. Michael was killed in battle, together with two other Israeli soldiers.

Michael was deeply connected to Camp Ramah, having attended as a camper for many years and having worked here until his aliyah after camp, in 2002. Mike also worked at the Ramah Day Camp in Philadelphia. Ramah and Conservative Judaism were central aspects of his life and the basis of so many of his friendships.

Michael came to visit Ramah Poconos on Visiting Day two weeks ago. His friends took such pride in his decision to live in Israel and fight to defend Israel from its enemies. He was a driven, wonderful young man who pursued his Zionist dreams. He had a wonderful, warm heart and an infectious smile. The impact of his life, and death, is reverberating throughout our camp and the wider Ramah community. He will be greatly missed.

Michael is survived by his parents, Mark and Harriet Levin, and by his two sisters, Dara and Elisa. Dara, his twin sister, has been working this summer at the Ramah Day Camp. Michael's family and some close friends are traveling to Israel to attend his military funeral, which will take place at Mount Herzl in Jerusalem. They will return home to continue shivah in the community.

Many staff members at both Ramah Poconos and Ramah Day Camp were shocked and saddened by the news of the death of their friend. Camp administrators, social workers, and rabbis came together to discuss the best ways of discussing Michael's death with the camp population. Close friends have been given enough breathing space to mourn their loss, while many others who knew Michael have been discussing his bravery, his heroism, and his commitment to Israel. As the camp enters the saddest day of the Jewish calendar, Tish'ah Be'av, many will be contemplating Michael's role as a link in a long chain of those who have given their lives to defend the Jewish people and the Jewish state.

According to Michael's long-time close friend from Ramah, Lital Rashi,

> Mike was such a good friend. His community was made up of friends from Ramah and USY, as well as the new friends he made in Israel. Mike believed in the Jewish community and our need to dedicate ourselves to our future. I can't believe that he's gone.

Kevin Waloff, another close friend, said, "Mike did what he believed in. We should all be so fortunate to follow our dreams and pursue our Judaism passionately."

In Michael's Nativ yearbook, he is pictured with an Israeli flag, with the quote, "You can't fulfill your dream unless you dare to risk it all."

As the campers at the Ramah Day Camp and Camp Ramah in the Poconos continue to laugh and sing and enjoy everything about Camp Ramah as Michael once did, many in these communities will recall, with great sadness, the ultimate sacrifice made by a close friend.

To read more about Michael, see Yossi Katz's contribution in the Reflections section of this volume.

BURTON COHEN

Louis Newman, z"l (1918–2007)

Histories of the Ramah Camping Movement show that Louis Newman served the Ramah camps formally in three capacities: director of Camp Ramah in Wisconsin (1951–53), director of Camp Ramah in Connecticut (1955), and director of the Mador (National Ramah Counselor Training Program, located at Camp Ramah in the Poconos, 1963–64). His achievements in these important positions within the movement would certainly suffice to establish his role as an important figure in the development of Ramah camping. However, his influence extended far beyond the acts of administrative and educational leadership that he performed at these three locations.

Newman's influence upon the development of Ramah camping is best grasped when perceived in the framework of his total career. Ramah was only one of the areas in which Newman made a significant contribution to American Jewish education. His tenure at Ramah Wisconsin was preceded by and paralleled his work as founding director of the Akiba Hebrew Academy in Philadelphia. It was Newman's design for Akiba that provided the model for the new Jewish community day high schools that have proliferated from coast to coast in the last decade. From directing Akiba, Newman went on to become the first director of the Melton Center for Research in Jewish Education at The Jewish Theological Seminary (JTS), which led to his long tenure as head of the Boston Bureau of Jewish Education. So, whereas the Ramah community can take pride in Newman's work in Wisconsin, Connecticut, and Mador, we ought not forget that it was only one aspect of a long, multifaceted, and distinguished career in Jewish education.

One other aspect of Newman's work at Ramah should be recalled: he was a part-time director. When he undertook to lead Camp Ramah in Wisconsin, his "day" job was serving as principal of the Akiba Hebrew Academy High School. Ramah was what he did in the winter months on Sundays and in the months of July and August, which should have been his vacation period. (There was nothing unusual about this arrangement; until recently, most camp directors were part-time workers. One of my own goals during the early years that I served as National Ramah Director was to convert all of the Ramah directorships to full-time positions.)

When Lou Newman came to Wisconsin, Camp Ramah had already functioned for four successful seasons under directors Henry Goldberg and Hillel Silverman. JTS administrators, Sylvia Ettenberg and Moshe Davis, had done a yeoman's job of creating a Conservative camping movement. They had established that there was a place in the Conservative Movement for an eight-week summer camp for Hebrew school students, which along with all of the other regular camp activities, was conducted in Hebrew and included morning services and Hebrew and Judaica classes in its daily schedule, as well as halachic observance of Shabbat, kashrut, and the other *mitzvot.*

What did Lou Newman bring to Ramah? Lou Newman was an experienced Jewish educator who also was well experienced in Jewish educational camping. He had no reluctance to offer activities of Jewish content in the camp setting. (He had already served on the staffs of similar camps in the East and was a great Hasid for teaching modern Hebrew.) Newman's chief contribution was that he saw the Jewish educational camp setting as providing the opportunity for offering a much richer educational program than usually envisioned for such camps. He was an intrepid student of modern educational philosophy and educational psychology. His studies convinced him that camp must offer more than a veneer of Jewish study and practice, layered over the normal camp program. He aimed to create a curriculum in which the campers would be challenged to assume a large degree of responsibility for the creation of their own activities. He aimed to create an atmosphere in which cooperation, not competition, was the keynote of the program. He aimed to create an environment in which staff was sensitive and responsive to the needs and problems of every individual camper. (It was Newman who hired the first psychologist to work at Ramah.) At Ramah Wisconsin, he introduced challenging and stimulating recreational equipment for the camp, such as aluminum canoes and woodworking machines. He made these innovations and many others, always with the greatest integrity, sensitivity, and determination.

The late Rabbi Alexander Shapiro, then a JTS rabbinical student who served as a counselor during Newman's first summers in Wisconsin, wrote a memoir in which he looked back on Newman's approach and impact in those early summers.

> Lou's admonition to be receptive to the life of the child and his needs was remote from a call for permissiveness. Quite to the contrary, I am hard put to remember another educational endeavor that had as much preoccupation with moral issues and with moral responsibility of children. It extended into every single area of the camp community, from the cleanup of the grounds to the impassioned debate on the morality of color wars. We were then but dimly conscious of the fact we were engaged in the kind of serious educational experiment that was ultimately to have a serious impact upon others. We seriously debated whether it was a moral act for us to take a day off once a week. . . . Lou's approach was entirely that of stimulating within the individual group worker [i.e., counselor] his own overwhelming sense of responsibility for what transpired in camp, one that tended to be much more far-reaching than any set of demands put forward by any [previous Ramah] camp administrator. (Shapiro and Cohen 1984, ix)*

Lou Newman had great skill in selecting staff and in inspiring those whom he chose to be successful implementers of the ideas that he so fervently espoused. Before his first summer as director of Ramah Wisconsin, Newman wrote about the kind of staff members that he hoped to hire for his staff:

> A person may challenge me and say, "You supply me with the goals which concern you and I will achieve them." If a person said this to me before the camp season opened, I would immediately answer, "You are honest, diligent and have many fine qualities. Find yourself a job elsewhere." I would then put a few dollars in the JNF [Jewish National Fund] box in gratitude for having discovered early this value-less person. It is impossible for one person to successfully educate another to be a particular kind of human being,

> without a consciously and personally formulated philosophy. (Shapiro and Cohen 1984, 195)*

The four directors who followed Newman in Wisconsin (Seymour Fox, Jerry Abrams, David Mogilner, and I) all served *with* him in Wisconsin in various capacities during his three summers there. Two of them, Abrams and Mogilner, went forth from Wisconsin to direct east coast Ramah camps, spreading Lou's educational approach throughout the Ramah Camping Movement. They taught Lou's broad approach to Jewish educational camping to their staff members, some of whom went on to be Ramah directors themselves. The centralized character of the Ramah Camping Movement, with its hub at JTS, facilitated the spread of Newman's ideas among the camps and their staffs.

In a true sense it could be said, *ki miviskonsin tetzei torat Lou Newman.*

*Quotations that appear in this tribute are taken from Alexander M. Shapiro and Burton I. Cohen, *Studies in Jewish Education and Judaica in Honor of Louis Newman* (New York: Ktav Publishing, 1984). That book contains a number of important studies describing Newman's work in Jewish education at Ramah and in other settings, as well as some short extracts from his writings.

RABBI BURTON COHEN, *Ph.D., is an associate professor emeritus of Jewish education and the former chair of the Department of Jewish Education at The Jewish Theological Seminary. He served on the staffs of Ramah Wisconsin (1951–53) and Ramah Connecticut (1954) when Lou Newman was director of those camps. Dr. Cohen was the director of Camp Ramah in Wisconsin from 1959 to 1974. From 1974 to 1989, he served as the director of the National Ramah Commission.*

Excerpts from condolences sent to the Newman family

[F]or those of us who attended Akiba Hebrew Academy in Philadelphia between 1951 and 1963 when Lou Newman was the principal, or Ramah in Wisconsin in the years when he was the director, Lou was the institution. . . . [H]is influence on us was powerful and lasting. He taught us to think, to analyze, and to be critical. . . . I am eternally thankful to Lou, and immensely proud of my friendship with him.

Rabbi Marim Charry
Great Neck, New York

[I]t was Lou, of course, [who helped me] determine that my professional career would be with Ramah, for which I am eternally grateful. . . . We all also recalled what an exemplary human being he was: ethical, a man of integrity, caring. I always considered Lou the best listener I ever related to.

Rabbi Jerome Abrams
Director Emeritus, Camp Ramah in the Berkshires

I was fortunate to sit in on some of [Lou's] training sessions for educators at Ramah in the Berkshires when my dad attended as an educator and I schlepped along as a sidekick. Finally, it was a privilege to have been Lou's student at the Seminary College. I may not have always agreed with how Lou read the texts that we studied in class, but I came away with a profound appreciation for how he applied the inquiry method even if our conclusions differed. The world of Jewish education has grown tremendously because of Lou's contributions.

Edwin R. Frankel
Ritual Director, Congregation Agudas Achim, Bexley, Ohio

60

MORTON M. STEINBERG

Irving Robbin, z"l (1922–1990)

Irving Robbin served as president of Camp Ramah in Wisconsin for eighteen years, longer than any other president of any Ramah camp. He then served as president of the National Ramah Commission from 1987 to 1989. He died suddenly of a heart attack in 1990 while on a vacation in Hawaii.

As a camp president, Irv Robbin was a visionary who dreamed dreams, shared them with his board, and challenged his fellow board members to turn those dreams into reality. He oversaw a great expansion of Ramah Wisconsin, both in facilities and in enrollment. He served as a guide to Rabbi Burton Cohen during his final summers as camp director at Wisconsin, as well as to Rabbi David Soloff, during his first years as camp director.

"He was a decisive leader and extremely ethical," recalls Rabbi Soloff. "He was deeply committed to planning. He would say, 'You have to have a plan. *Ḥevreh,* how are we going to get this done?' Once the vision was clear, his comments were directed to accomplishing the task. And he was always the first person to step forward with resources to implement the plan."

Irv's leadership garnered him the respect, admiration, and loyalty of his board; the professional leaders of the camp; and an entire generation of campers' parents.

Irv grew up in an Orthodox family on the "old west side" of Chicago. He became a very successful businessman. Beginning in the 1950s, he built his business into one of the foremost independent jewelers in the Chicago area. But his passion was Jewish education. He was a founder and the first president of the Northwest Suburban Jewish Congregation in Morton Grove, Illinois. He later moved to Highland Park and became active at North Suburban Synagogue Beth El, eventually becoming the chairman of its board of education. He also served as president of the Chicagoland Solomon Schechter Day Schools and was a founder of the first Schechter high school in the Midwest. He first became involved in Camp Ramah in the early 1960s when seeking a summer camp for his daughters to attend. He was a pillar of the Chicago Jewish community. But he was more than that.

Irv Robbin impressed people as being mild mannered yet self-assured, a caring person, meticulous in habit and dress. He possessed a reassuring quality and always displayed casual confidence about himself and his views. He spoke calmly, but with an intensity that at times he could barely contain, especially when he spoke about Camp Ramah or Jewish education or Rabbi Phillip L. Lipis, *z"l,* or General George S. Patton.

Irv's appearance, lifestyle, interests, and pursuits did not reveal his experiences in World War II, and he seldom spoke publicly about that aspect of his life. He no doubt felt he had done just what every other American in their twenties or thirties did from 1942 to 1945: they accepted their duty to serve their country, and they performed it modestly, without flourish or fanfare. But it was his experiences in that war that impacted the direction of his life and that eventually would affect the development of Camp Ramah.

Irv was only nineteen years old when the United States entered World War II. He soon enlisted in the Army. He became a member of F Company, 110th Regiment, 28th Infantry Division—part of the famous Third Army under the command of General Patton.

The 28th Infantry Division landed at Omaha Beach in Normandy, France, just a few weeks after D-Day. It entered combat against the German army on July 22, 1944. Private Irving Robbin fought the Nazis in Normandy and across northern France. He helped liberate Paris in August 1944, fought on into Belgium, and fought in the devastating Battle of the Hurtgen Forest, where one soldier recalled: "The days were so terrible that I would pray for darkness, and the nights were so bad I would pray for daylight."

In December 1944, when victory seemed assured and the fighting was at a lull, the 28th Infantry Division was stationed in and around the small town of Wiltz, Luxembourg. But on December 16, Hitler launched the largest and most brutal counteroffensive of World War II. It became known as the Battle of the Bulge. Over 200,000 heavily armed German combat troops, supported by thousands of tanks, attacked directly into the American lines. The very center of that powerful onslaught was at Wiltz. This is how the U.S. Army's official historian described the resistance put up by Irv's regiment: "The 110th Infantry . . . held off four German regiments. . . . That was around two thousand [American] men versus at least ten thousand [Germans]. . . . Considering the odds, nowhere on the first day of the German offensive was there a more remarkable achievement by the American soldier." But despite their determination, Irv's platoon of perhaps forty men was surrounded by German soldiers outside of the small town of Clervaux. On December 22, they were forced to surrender.

The first thing the Germans demanded of their new prisoners was to identify the Jewish soldiers, but the captured Americans, bonded by combat into an unshakable brotherhood, refused to do so. They all threw their identification tags into the deep snow. Irv's life was spared by his comrades' loyalty.

For the next three weeks, in the bitter cold of winter, the American captives were marched over frozen roads toward the German city of Koblenz. The Germans did not provide adequate rations to the prisoners, who were forced to scrounge what they could on their own to survive. Irv had studied German in high school and spoke Yiddish. He was able to obtain food for his unit by writing out notes for German civilians addressed to "General Patton" informing the general that the holders of the notes should not be treated harshly because they had assisted American soldiers. At Koblenz, the prisoners were packed into unheated railroad box cars and transported to Stalag 2A, a prisoner of war camp in Neubrandenburg, about fifty miles north of Berlin. Irv wrote that in the box cars "one body was pressed against the other — our rations were tea, two slices of bread and three pieces of cheese. One can easily imagine the stench. . . . When [Allied] air planes flew overhead . . . we were like dead ducks waiting to be strafed by our own planes. . . . [W]ith God's help we finally arrived at Neubrandenburg." And there they remained, under extraordinarily harsh conditions, for the next four months.

At Stalag 2A, Irv cared for the sick POWs. He was respected by the men, not only for his performance as a soldier, but also because of his principles. (After liberation, and while still in the prison camp, he was appointed Regimental Sergeant Major, the highest enlisted rank in that unit.) Throughout his tour of duty, Irv carried a miniature pair of tefillin. Even after he was captured, he was able to keep his tefillin with him by hiding them under his armpit.

On April 28, 1945, with the Russian Army approaching from the east, the German guards abandoned Stalag 2A. On that day, Irv began writing a diary with the following words: "The hour of our liberation is rapidly approaching." Irv's diary is a beautifully written story of courage, compassion, dignity, and love. It relates his day-by-day, at times hour-by-hour, experiences in leaving Stalag 2A and returning to the United States. It is a remarkable and fascinating story of the return of a combat soldier, an American hero, from World War II. A copy of that diary is in the permanent collection of the library at Camp Ramah in Wisconsin. It was following his release from Stalag 2A that Irv visited sites revealing the horrors of the Holocaust, and it was there, on the ashes of our people, that twenty-two-year-old Irving Robbin vowed to make Jewish education a priority in his life.

Following the war, Irv married his childhood sweetheart, Janet Schwartzberg, and together they raised their daughters, Karen and Sheryl. Both of their children attended Ramah Wisconsin and met their future husbands there. Karen married Dr. David Benson, and today they reside in Highland Park, Illinois. Sheryl married Rabbi Daniel Landes, who serves as director of the Pardes Institute for Jewish Learning in Jerusalem, where they make their home. In the early 1970s, Janet was instrumental in establishing the Tikvah program at Ramah Wisconsin.

It was with Ramah that Irv's passion for Jewish education, kindled many years earlier, found its greatest reward and where he so delighted in his achievements. He devoted his time and energies and resources to Ramah. He enlisted others to join him in his mission, others who became leaders of Ramah in their own right to carry on the vision of a great leader. Irv Robbin was a hero of his country, a hero to his people, and a hero of Camp Ramah. *Zecher tzaddik livrachah.*

MORTON M. STEINBERG *is a senior partner at the law firm DLA Piper LLP (US). He served as president of Camp Ramah in Wisconsin for nine years and then as president of the National Ramah Commission (NRC) from 2003 to 2007. He is currently chairman of the board of trustees of the NRC. While president of the NRC, he also served on the Leadership Council for Conservative Judaism and was an elected delegate of MERCAZ USA to the 35th Zionist Congress in Jerusalem. A product of the Conservative Movement, Mr. Steinberg was a camper, counselor, and waterfront director at Camp Ramah in Wisconsin.*

REUVEN ROHN AND **RUTH ROHN**

Aryeh Rohn, z"l (1919–2003)

A bald, stocky, yet diminutive middle-aged man grasps the pulley and zooms down the cable suspended among the trees. There goes Aryeh Rohn checking out the safety of the main attraction of *yom yarid* (Carnival Day) at Camp Ramah in the Poconos. The line supports his weight, and the ride is smooth and exhilarating. Smiling, he jumps down and calls back up the line, *"Hakol beseder!"* Part of his job description? Not exactly. But any job that has to do with ensuring the safety of the campers and staff is too important for Aryeh to delegate to others. Besides, this particular task involves the physical exertion and fun that he loves. But how did this Viennese-accented, Hebrew-speaking, *yeke khevreman* come to be in this setting?

Aryeh grew up in Vienna in the 1920s and 1930s, in a home imbued with Zionist ideals. Active in the Zionist youth movement and scouts, he displayed maturity and talent for leadership and became a *madrich* while still a young teen. This experience would serve to prepare him well for his life's work in Jewish education, especially at Camp Ramah.

In 1938, he made aliyah and joined a *kevutzah* of other Austrian and German *olim,* intending to become a vintner. In the evenings, after a long day's work, Aryeh and a few others entertained their *ḥevreh* with songs, jokes, and stories well into the night. Some nights, the strong swimmers, Aryeh among them, would help illegal Jewish immigrants (*ma'pilim*) swim to shore under the cover of darkness, eluding the British. Could he have possibly imagined at those moments that these skills would eventually earn him his first job at Camp Ramah?

Rahel, a *kevutzah* member also from Vienna, was charmed by Aryeh's sense of humor and fun. They fell in love, they married, and after a few years, moved to Pardes Hanna where their son Reuven was born, and where work in education beckoned. Aryeh started teaching in the local elementary school. He loved guiding and educating his students and enjoyed using his creativity and musical abilities to create plays and holiday ceremonies for the school. Here, Aryeh made two enduring resolutions: to Hebraicize the family name to Rohn and to devote his life to education.

Aryeh's family in Austria had survived the Shoah by fleeing to the United States. When Aryeh received word that his father was ailing, he and Rachel faced a difficult choice. Leaving Israel was wrenching, but they agreed that obligations to immediate family came first. Yet the love affair with Israel that began in their youth continued throughout their lives. They would return frequently under the auspices of the Ramah Communities Program, often leading groups of American youth.

In the United States, Aryeh taught at both day and afternoon schools while studying and earning a doctorate in education. He threw himself into his work and brought his vitality, knowledge, and love of Judaism, Israel, and the Hebrew language to all the students he taught. He eventually became Educational Director at East Midwood Jewish Center in Brooklyn. One of his teaching colleagues told him about Camp Ramah. This was to be a life-changing piece of information!

In 1954, with his skill and strength as a swimmer, Aryeh easily earned Red Cross certification as a lifeguard and swimming instructor, qualifying him to be *rosh agam* at Ramah Connecticut. Peter Geffen still remembers Aryeh teaching him how to swim during that summer. Aryeh, Rachel, nine-year-old Reuven, and three-year-old Ruthie experienced their first taste of Ramah and were hooked. This would mark the beginning of a long association with Ramah, one that continues to this day, for the family of Aryeh and Rachel Rohn.

In 1955, Aryeh became *rosh madrichim* in Ramah Poconos. There he began to work hand-in-hand with *rosh maḥaneh* Levi Soshuk. Aryeh found in Levi a kindred spirit, and the two men became close friends. They shared a love of Hebrew and the same passion for Jewish education. Their personalities and styles complemented one another and their work together, first in the Poconos and then in Ramah Canada, became legendary.

Aryeh firmly believed in the motto, "*Maḥaneh Ramah: maḥaneh dati, ivri, ḥinnuchi.*" He believed in Ramah's mission as a religious, Hebrew, and educational milieu. As a full-time Jewish educator in formal school settings, he believed in what Ramah uniquely could provide: an all-encompassing Jewish and Hebrew-speaking environment in which Jewish youth could live, learn, and have fun together. He resonated so strongly with the goals of Ramah that he brought hundreds of his own students from East Midwood Jewish Center to the Poconos, to Canada, and to the Berkshires to benefit from all that Ramah could offer.

In the context of his work at Ramah, Aryeh was able to draw upon his youth movement and scout experiences—teaching informally and using outdoor activities and games—to create meaningful learning that was always punctuated by fun. Ramahniks, both *ḥanichim* and madrichim, clamored to be in his classes.

Aryeh's fun-loving inventiveness is mythic. As but one example of many, one summer he created the *va'ad hageshem,* (the Rain Committee) whose function was to oversee the weather whenever an important outdoor activity was scheduled. On a particular yom yarid, which happened to coincide with Visitors Day, the forecast was for rain. However, Aryeh announced over the *ramkol* (public address system) that the *va'ad hageshem* had met and declared that it would not rain until the carnival was over. A camp full of witnesses will vouch for the fact that the day was gorgeous until just after the carnival ended; then it proceeded to pour for half an hour. From then on, whenever Aryeh announced a *va'ad hageshem* prediction, everyone believed him. The ability to cultivate an image of omniscience was yet another of Aryeh's legendary skills.

A beloved feature of camp life in those years was the *kuntz*. One of the first and biggest *kuntzim* that Aryeh helped organize took place in 1955. One morning, a large bulletin board in the *ḥadar ochel* announced *be'od 15 yom mikreh gadol*. Each and every day thereafter a countdown took place in Hebrew. Everyone was trying to guess what this event could possibly be. Early on the morning of the appointed day, a flying saucer suddenly appeared floating in the agam. Now, everyone was even more curious as to what was going on. After *tefillot*, at breakfast in the ḥadar ochel, the room fell quiet as part of the ceiling opened up and three men in their space suits descended, claiming to come from Mars. They brought a singularly important message for the whole camp: "*Ivri, dabber ivrit!*" It was a great kuntz that helped solidify the central place of ivrit at camp and fostered a *ruaḥ ivrit* for everyone all summer.

As a Jewish educator, Aryeh's actions reflected his commitment to serving as a *dugmah*, a role model. Jimmy Stark (*ḥanich* Poconos) and Elliot Judd (ḥanich Poconos and Canada, *tzevet* Berkshires), *z"l*, each recall an example of this. On two separate *shabbatot*, each suffered a freak accident with severe injuries. In each case, the camp doctor determined that a visit to the hospital was necessary. Driving each of them the twenty miles to the nearest hospital was another responsibility Aryeh insisted upon performing himself, acting as a concerned parent would, while teaching by example the important Jewish principle: *pikkuaḥ nefesh doḥeh shabbat*. The obligation to save a human life in jeopardy overrides other mitzvot, even Shabbat observance.

Aryeh strongly believed in the concept of *in loco parentis*. He took very seriously the responsibility to provide a safe and orderly environment for the ḥanichim as well as the tzevet, and he ran a tight ship. As a good father would, he also believed that camp should be fun. Somehow he managed to balance these goals. The stories told about him by former campers and colleagues at camp reflect this delicate balance.

Aryeh had unique skills in handling people, whether in groups or as individuals. When controlling the crowd in the ḥadar ochel or anywhere there was a large gathering, he almost never raised his voice. Sometimes, he would quietly begin to make up a story: *pa'am aḥat bemaḥaneh aḥer*, once upon a time in another camp. . . . Within thirty seconds the room would fall silent as everyone tried to hear the story. At other times an *edah* or *tzerif* might inappropriately start a cheer while Aryeh's arm was raised to signal silence. He would chime in and sing-song along with their cheer and within seconds, they would fall silent, realizing their rudeness. On rare occasions he would call, "Mordechai Kestenbaum, *nah lehafsik!*" Ḥanichim got the message even as they wondered who this Mordechai was, and why he was being singled out. In fact, Mordechai was Aryeh's fictitious foil. Without subjecting anyone to public embarrassment, Aryeh would scold Mordechai Kestenbaum, and order was restored.

Bill Davidovitz, a former Ramah Canada ḥanich and member of the tzevet recounts:

> One *erev shabbat* I came to *mifkad,* to our flag-raising ceremony, wearing a colored shirt, rather than the required white shirt. Aryeh approached me and asked, *"Lamah attah lo lavush kullecha belavan?"* He wanted to know why I wasn't dressed in white. Trying to defend myself, I pointed out that he himself was wearing khaki pants. 'Ah yes,' he replied, 'but I don't have a figure like yours.' His little self-deprecating remark left me open to receiving his message and made this incident so memorable. Aryeh would make his point without hitting you over the head. He took the edge off, by calling you on your mistake while preserving your dignity.

Aryeh's sensitivity also contributed to his admirable skill as a mentor. One summer, Aryeh served as supervising director at Ramah Berkshires when Rabbi Shelly Dorph became camp director. Shelly described feeling frustrated and overwhelmed at times. He was thankful that Aryeh made himself available for advice at all times, yet kept a low profile in the camp at large. Aryeh's staying well in the background allowed Shelly to learn from his own mistakes, as well as take credit for all the successes. Shelly credits his success as a new director and the mastery he achieved in this role to the sensitive and skillful mentoring he received from Aryeh.

Aryeh Rohn was proud to be involved with Camp Ramah. His greatest pleasure was watching ḥanichim grow to become knowledgeable, committed Jewish adults who in turn would contribute to the enrichment of Jewish life in North America. Many of the students he brought to Ramah, first from Newark and later from East Midwood, have become leaders in the Ramah world (e.g., Roger Fine, Hugh Pollack, and others) or leading Jewish scholars and educators (e.g., Rabbi Art Green, Lawrence Fine, Robert Goldenberg, Daniel Grossberg, Vicky Kelman, and others).

Peter Geffen remembers Aryeh as the moral conscience of Ramah. "He had a wonderful spirit and brought maturity and dignity to camp life." Jane Paznik-Bondarin (*ḥanichat* Poconos and Canada, and *tzevet* Canada) recalls:

> Aryeh was so omnipresent and coincident with my whole Ramah experience, and it felt to me as if he were part of the very fabric of Ramah, certainly my Ramah. He embodied everything I thought of as Ramah, as authentic Jewish life. In my mind he was always striding, even when he was standing still. He was leading . . . leading us all in activity, in thought. He

> was the moral conscience of the camp. I am fairly certain more people than just I, figured he knew what we were thinking, whenever we were thinking about shirking an obligation or doing something for which we did not have permission. The standards he taught us by example, the way we learned to be with one another under his watch, these have all stayed with me and guided my professional and personal life.

Aryeh, with a touch of pride and a twinkle in his eye might quip in response, in Hebrew, of course: "I see that Mordechai Kestenbaum finally shaped up. Hakol beseder!"

REUVEN ROHN, *M.D., son of Aryeh Rohn, z"l, is a pediatric endocrinologist and a professor of pediatrics in Norfolk, Virginia, and has spent thirty-seven years in various capacities at Ramah. His children have all attended Ramah camps.*

RUTH ROHN, *daughter of Aryeh Rohn, z"l, is a Jewish educator and consultant in Toronto, Ontario, Canada, and has spent seventeen years in various capacities at Ramah. Her children have all attended Ramah camps as well.*

60

DAVID ACKERMAN

Rabbi Alexander Shapiro, z"l (1929–1992)

My first encounter with Rabbi Alexander Shapiro took place at Camp Ramah in the Berkshires. I was a second-year rabbinical student and a first-time *rosh edah;* he was the president of the Rabbinical Assembly. Alex had come to camp along with a distinguished group of Conservative rabbis to work on what would become *Emet Ve-Emunah,* the movement's ideological statement of the mid-1980s. I vividly remember his comfort and ease in the camp setting, a quality that to my eye set him apart from many of the other rabbis in attendance at that gathering. Little did I know then that Alex had spent his entire adult life engaged with Ramah, an engagement that went back to his early years as a rabbinical student.

For a young man who rarely and barely left Brooklyn until well past his bar mitzvah, the trip to Conover, Wisconsin in the summer of 1950 must have been momentous. Alex Shapiro's experience at Ramah in Wisconsin over the next four summers changed his life in deep and fundamental ways. Along with other Jewish Theological Seminary (JTS) students, among them his future wife Ruth Goldenberg, Shapiro joined the 1950 Wisconsin staff as a counselor.

He and Ruth returned each summer until 1953, working closely with Louis Newman who became Ramah Wisconsin's director in 1951. By the late 1950s, Ruth and Alex Shapiro, now settled in Philadelphia, became senior staff mainstays at Camp Ramah in the Poconos, where Rabbi Shapiro ultimately served as Director in the late 1960s.

Shapiro held many specific jobs during those years in Wisconsin and the Poconos—counselor, teacher, camp rabbi, advisor—but his one true ongoing role was to live out and model for others the enduring ideal of Torah as a way of life that has stood at Ramah's center from the beginning. Louis Newman himself expressed Rabbi Shapiro's intuitive grasp of Ramah's vision and approach with a wonderfully evocative anecdote:

> Some would say that Rabbi Shapiro went out of his way to find the difficult tasks to undertake. He did, and they were a special kind, and they made him dear to me. . . . The first [personal experience] took place over forty [now fifty] years ago when we worked together in Camp Ramah. I was director. He was a counselor: a lapsed engineer become a rabbinical student, very much interested in character formation. Campers and counselors were invited to offer fresh ideas to achieve the camp's educational goals, and Rabbi Shapiro's initiative was among those I valued most. He requested time and funds with which to buy cement and lumber to construct a stairway. It was a bothersome and sometimes dangerous slope from the dining room to the shower building, down which the kids would slide, run, fall, and tumble. Convinced of the worth of [A. D.] Gordon's Zionist philosophy of labor, with no one around who had any experience in such an undertaking, he directed the enterprise. He did it sensibly, energetically, with campers who volunteered: children twelve, thirteen, fourteen years old. Why did he do this? He did it for *ivrit.* He was teaching Hebrew on the job, educating for values (Zionism and solidarity with the workers in Israel) and demonstrating, which he always did, that "one shouldn't delay carrying out actions that are important." From then until this day I never knew my friend Eli to recoil from a worthy initiative, no matter how novel and how difficult it seemed.

Decades later, Rabbi Shapiro put pen to paper and formulated, as part of a volume of essays in Newman's honor, his own recollection of those early summers at Ramah Wisconsin:

> We were all terribly young and untried; yet we had the feeling that we were at the cutting edge of a whole new point of view, a whole new way of seeing the educational process. . . . Notions of a child's involvement in his own educational destiny came as something revolutionary. . . . We believed deeply that we were changing the lives of human beings, and through them, that we were literally changing the world. Strangely enough . . . our own belief in ourselves struck a responsive chord in the children entrusted to

> our care. They, too, came to believe in themselves and in the community of which they were a part.

That sense of Ramah's revolutionary character was a theme that Rabbi Shapiro returned to frequently over the years, speaking of those summers in Wisconsin with a detectable gleam in his eye. The cohesiveness of the Ramah community, coupled with its intensity, was another point of emphasis for Shapiro.

> Over the course of a very short period of time, everyone in the community, from the youngest child to the oldest member of the professional staff, considered himself to be part of the community. I remember well the meetings of the entire camp community that were called each week to talk of the problems that we shared. How well I remember the intensity of those meetings! How well I recollect the marvel of one of the youngest children in camp . . . having his questions answered seriously and patiently by the director while the exchange was heard without condescension by the child's older campmates, as well as by his counselors.

Ramah's earnest concern with the ethical responsibilities of counselors, along with the abiding sense of significance that the work of camp held for young staff members, prompted this commentary from Rabbi Shapiro:

> I am hard put to remember another educational endeavor that had quite as much preoccupation with moral issues and with the moral responsibility of children. It extended into every single area of the camp community, from the cleanup of the grounds to the impassioned debates on the morality of color wars. We were then but dimly conscious of the fact that we were engaged in the kind of serious educational experiment that was ultimately to have significant impact on others. How far-reaching that influence was to be we could not possibly imagine. What we all knew was that it was far more than a summer job that drew us together. We seriously debated whether it was a moral act for us to take a day off once a week. After all, the children were put in our charge for twenty-four hours a day. Is it not irresponsible, we seriously asked, to leave even for a while? Those of us who had the temerity to take the day off came rushing back at the end of the day to discover what new development we had missed.

Not everything about Ramah Wisconsin in those years was sweetness and light. In Rabbi Shapiro's memory, the external conditions of the camp were every bit as dismal as the educational components were glorious.

> What made the entire experience unique from the perspective of later educational endeavors was that the conditions under which all of us worked were totally primitive. The camp grounds were indifferently maintained, sports equipment minimal, food indifferent at best, and housing conditions terrible! Moreover, every single one of us could have earned significantly more than the pitiful salaries we were paid in any one of a number of other

institutions. Yet, all of that faded into insignificance in comparison to the enterprise of which we were a part.

Indeed, Rabbi Shapiro's brief memoir concludes by returning to the theme of Ramah's religious and educational goals:

> In fact, Ramah represented the first serious attempt I had ever encountered to apply religion to life, not in the abstract but in the very concrete. . . . The possibility that its insights could be applied to the world of children and, in fact, to the world of adults, too, in the context of the daily life of a society came as a revolutionary idea in those days. The intensity of religious concern was overwhelming, particularly since it did not stimulate simply the fulfillment of mitzvah but rather the deepest possible understanding of what was behind the ethical command.

For Rabbi Alex Shapiro, the lessons learned from his summers at Ramah Wisconsin and Ramah Poconos shaped his rabbinate and his life. His commitment to and focus on the needs and concerns of each individual he encountered in his work were a direct extension of Ramah's emphasis on each unique camper. His desire to build and nurture synagogue communities that included each and every one and excluded no one was a direct extension of Ramah's success at establishing cohesive and inclusive communities. His abiding, even overwhelming sense of responsibility for the members of his congregations was a direct extension of the debates about days off that he recalled from those early summers in Wisconsin. And finally, and perhaps most importantly, his religious attitude marked by a passionate commitment both to ritual observance and ethical imperative was a direct extension of the revolution that he helped to shape nearly sixty years ago at Camp Ramah.

Alex and Ruth Shapiro bequeathed their love of Ramah and their lifelong commitment to its ideals to their children and grandchildren all of whom have collectively spent dozens of summers at Camp Ramah in the Poconos. Often living in the same five-star staff bunks that Rabbi Shapiro so lovingly described, and often playing some of the same camp roles as Ruth and Alex, members of the Shapiro-Saks-Ackerman clan continue the rich tradition begun in the summer of 1950 at Camp Ramah in Wisconsin. Here's hoping that a fourth generation will experience the same joys.

RABBI DAVID ACKERMAN, *son-in-law of Rabbi Alexander Shapiro, z"l, is the spiritual leader of Beth Am Israel in Penn Valley, Pennsylvania. He previously served as rabbi for national outreach at The Jewish Theological Seminary, as the long-time spiritual leader of Tiferet Bet Israel in Blue Bell, Pennsylvania, and as a staff member at Camp Ramah in the Poconos.*

SAUL SHAPIRO

Dr. Miriam Klein Shapiro, z"l (1938–2005)

Miriam Klein Shapiro was a true pioneer at Camp Ramah; she began attending camp in 1947. By the time she retired in 1988, she had missed only one summer. She served in five different camps—as a camper, waiter, counselor, teacher, and for her last twelve years of service, she was the director of education at Camp Ramah in the Berkshires. By her count, she and her immediate family had accumulated over 250 summers at Ramah camps. Miriam influenced thousands of lives through her teaching, but many more by the way she lived her life.

Miriam was born in Springfield, Massachusetts, the daughter of Henriette and Rabbi Isaac Klein. She moved to Buffalo, New York, while in high school. Rabbi Klein was an expert in Jewish law, and his wife was an educational leader in the Conservative Movement. Miriam was born just before the start of the World War II. This was a time when American Jews worried about the fate of Jews throughout the world. So Miriam was given the middle name Hope in English and *Neḥamah* (comfort) in Hebrew.

She received undergraduate degrees from Barnard College and The Jewish Theological Seminary (JTS). She received a master of social work from Columbia University and earned master's and doctoral degrees in Bible from JTS.

Miriam was a master educator, a scholar, and a woman of many accomplishments. She viewed Ramah as the ultimate example of putting educational theory into practice, in and out of the classroom. She worked hard to ensure that education had its proper place of importance in camp life and spent countless hours throughout the year recruiting an excellent staff and developing curriculum and educational programs. Her dedication and skill as an educator—professionally, as well as in every other aspect of her life—made her a person from whom everyone could learn. As Edward Edelstein, the director of the Jewish Educators Assembly, said in his *hesped* (eulogy), "[A] whole generation of educators have turned to Miriam for guidance, looked up to her educational expertise, admired her convictions, and respected her scholarship. Many in Jewish education strive to acquire just one or two of those traits. Miriam attained them all." Miriam not only taught her students, but she also touched their lives and influenced their lifestyles and life choices. Her students respected and loved her. Former students still come up to members of her family and tell them how much of an influence she was on them. Just a couple of weeks before she died, Miriam went to Camp Ramah in the Berkshires for visiting day; many former colleagues and students stopped by to see her while she sat on the porch of the bunk she occupied for so many years and where her daughter now spends her summers.

Miriam loved studying and teaching Bible. She taught at the State University of New York at Purchase, The Jewish Theological Seminary, the Academy for Jewish Religion, and Manhattanville College, lecturing on biblical and Judaic issues.

In her professional life outside of Camp Ramah, she served in many key roles in the world of Jewish education, including Hebrew school teacher, day school principal, and board of Jewish education curriculum specialist. She worked as a teacher and an educational consultant for the Board of Jewish Education of Greater New York for more than twenty years, creating and serving as director of the Board's Jewish Family Education program and its Teacher Center in Westchester, New York.

Although she lived in the United States for her entire life, Miriam's deep love of Israel was expressed in her frequent trips there, where she and her family enjoyed living in their second home in Jerusalem, and she often incorporated Israel-related themes into her work at Ramah.

Throughout her lifetime, Miriam was actively involved in Jewish communal life. She served as the first female chairperson of the Education Commission of the United Synagogue of Conservative Judaism, the second president of the Union for Traditional Judaism, the first female president of the Conservative Movement's Jewish Educators Assembly, and the president of the United States National Board of License for teachers and principals of Jewish schools. She also served on numerous boards, including those of the Westchester Hebrew High School and the United Synagogue Standards Committee. In addition, throughout her lifetime, she received numerous honors and awards.

Although each of her accomplishments is impressive, perhaps the most important of Miriam's accomplishments was her devotion to her family. This was the role that brought her the greatest satisfaction in her life. Her five children, her three children by marriage, her nine grandchildren, and our marriage of forty-seven years (a relationship of fifty years, if one counts from when we first met at Ramah) were her greatest pride and joy.

Together, we built a Jewish home, gave our children a day-school education, and took enormous pride in the fact that we transferred to the next generation the lessons that she had learned from her parents.

Rachel Shapiro Kirzner provided the following additional reflections on her mother's relationship with Camp Ramah:

My first and last memories of my mother are intertwined with Camp Ramah. I'd like to say that I remember my first days at camp with my family, but I can't because I was only two weeks old when we arrived at the newly opened Camp Ramah in the Berkshires in the summer of 1964. I do know that my mother promptly caught a severe case of poison ivy, and our sixteen-year-old babysitter, Paula Scharf Kohn, was unexpectedly the primary caregiver of my newborn self, Sara (two), and Ephraim (four). Apparently I cried so much in those early days that my parents joked, *"Kol beramah nishma . . . Rachel mevakkah,"* (a voice in Ramah is heard . . . Rachel is crying). Not exactly what was meant in Jeremiah 31, but my mother and father always loved a good biblical pun, especially one involving things that were important to them.

I always viewed Ramah as my summer home, not surprisingly because we were never anywhere else once June arrived. We couldn't be there enough, and always stayed through the Camp USY session each summer. I remember the back room at Lake Side C with five young children crammed into it after Sim and RD arrived, and also later with no children, transformed into a teachers' resource room. Both of those uses encompass what was most dear in the heart of my mother—family, education, and in particular education at Ramah. I remember accompanying my mother as she taught her classes in the early days of Ramah. One memorable but typical lesson in the old Beit Gesher consisted of "Simon Says" in Hebrew, to teach campers the parts of the body in a fun way, one where they barely felt they were learning. As the years went on, and she became *rosh ḥinnuch* (head of education) rather than a line teacher, she never lost her fondness for teaching the campers, but translated that dedication into training a new generation of educators. Long after her on-site tenure at Camp Ramah ended, her methods and influence still permeate the education in the camp.

My father, may he live and be well for many more years, also made his stamp on Camp Ramah. Although I later learned that he was Chair of Ramah Berkshires, and then of the National Ramah Commission, as a child I thought he had the most important job at camp: fixing the camp plumbing and washing machines. That he later added directing traffic at the golf-course parking lot each visiting day only enhanced his stature in my eyes. His modesty and enthusiasm for all facets of running a camp like Ramah were such that he never corrected my childhood misconceptions, and it was only much later that I understood his key role in the development and continuing strength of the

Ramah system. Every Shabbat afternoon when I was a camper, I would visit my parents at Lake Side C. I would walk over from A or B side, depending on the year, and my mother would be sitting on the porch waiting for me. We would sit and talk on the porch, but were often interrupted by her many fans among the campers and staff as they walked by the bunk. Her dual role as a camp parent and staffer was a balancing act but one that was cherished by her, and it was with bittersweet feelings that she finally ended her summers at Ramah. Among the many professionally engraved plaques and inscribed awards we found recently when going through my mother's belongings, one that stood out in a place of pride was a handmade wall hanging, clearly a product of the *ommanut* (arts and crafts) studio at camp, that marked her twenty-five-year anniversary in the Ramah system.

My mother treasured her involvement in Ramah, perhaps above all of her other professional commitments. I will never forget that in the last month of her life, when her strength was waning, she made sure to visit camp for one last visiting day, both to visit her children and grandchildren there, and to see her beloved camp one more time. In my mind's eye I can still see her on that day, and many others like it, surrounded by family and friends, once again holding court on the front porch of Lake Side C.

DR. SAUL SHAPIRO, *husband of Dr. Miriam Klein Shapiro, z"l, is a former National Ramah Commission president and a past president of the board of Camp Ramah in the Berkshires. Members of the families of Saul and Miriam's children, Ephraim Shapiro, Sara Shapiro Shuter, Rachel Shapiro Kirzner, Sim Shapiro, and Rivka Shapiro, also contributed to this article. Shapiro family members have attended the following Ramah camps and programs: Berkshires, Canada, Connecticut, Israel Seminar, Maine, Nyack (both overnight and day camp), and Poconos.*

60

SILVERMAN FAMILY

Gloria (Sussman) Silverman, z"l (1936–2008)

Gloria (Sussman) Silverman, *z"l,* beloved wife of Rabbi Israel Silverman, *z"l* (whom she met at Camp Ramah), mother of five (raised at Camp Ramah), and *savta* of thirteen alumni of Camp Ramah (with three more to go), spent over fifty years of her life at Camp Ramah.

Gloria began her affiliation at Ramah in Connecticut and also worked at Ramah camps in the Berkshires, the Poconos, and in Canada, where she spent over thirty summers. Her roles at camp included *yo'etzet, morah,* and developer/coordinator of programming for visitors and for fine arts. During the rest of the year, she served as a winter director, recruiter, and board member for Camp Ramah in Canada.

Following her death in December 2008, we (her children and grandchildren), as well as Camp Ramah, received hundreds of tributes to her, some of which are quoted here. These reflections capture her dedication to the ideals and vision of Camp Ramah and to their practical application.

Gloria's career at Ramah began in the late 1950s in Connecticut. One of her former campers, Gail Josephson Lipsitz, recalls:

> It would be impossible to capture in words the positive influence Gloria had on me. I met her when she was Gloria Sussman, my counselor at Camp Ramah in Connecticut during my very first summer there, in 1958. . . . It was my joy and privilege to have this most amazing young woman as my guide on [my Ramah] journey. Gloria was warm, wise, spiritual, and earthy at the same time. She became a friend, mentor, and mother all in one. She conveyed to me and my bunkmates a deep love of Judaism and modeled how to live a Jewish life 24/7. I vividly remember her hugs, her beautiful voice when she played her guitar and taught us Hebrew songs, her staying in with us at night to read us *The Diary of Anne Frank,* her helping us understand one bunkmate's social difficulties and how to deal with her compassionately, her sense of fun, her creativity. All the other bunks envied us and we became a little community, so bonded.
>
> I kept in touch with Gloria, and I still have the book she sent me for my bat mitzvah. She had such an impact on me that I wrote my college application essay about her.

She went on to become *rosh edah bet.* Her dear friend and colleague, Rabbi Mayer Rabinowitz, remembers her as

> a most warm and loving individual who always had a smile on her face and was beloved by campers and staff. She could diffuse a situation with her sense of humor and her smile. She also had a mischievous streak that played itself out at camp. She and the junior counselors decided to put a canoe in the swimming pool and remove all silverware from the dining room except for knives. They placed alarm clocks all over the director's house set to go off at different times and removed the hinges from some of the doors in the house so they would fall when opened.

It was during the summer of 1962 that Gloria met her future husband, Rabbi Israel Silverman, *z"l.* They married the following summer and returned to Ramah camps together each summer until his death in 2003.

During the early 1970s, Gloria was a yo'etzet at Camp Ramah in the Poconos. Michael Miller remembers his early years with Ramah when, after his job application was initially rejected, he was invited to be the staff activities coordinator and part-time driver.

> Danny Margolis [the director] suggested various options for me at Ramah, and he sent me to a woman I had not yet met—Gloria. Little did I know that I was being interviewed and needed her approval if I was to have a future in Ramah. We sat and spoke about my background, skills, interests, and educational philosophy. I was so impressed by her insights and knowledge of the educational process. I left that meeting convinced that this was the most insightful, thoughtful, sensitive, and maybe above all, honest Jewish educator I had ever met. No nonsense, no platitudes, no glib answers but an honest assessment as to what Ramah could and could not do, and how to best use the eight weeks we had.
>
> Soon after, I became a rosh edah, and Gloria was my yo'etzet. She was the most wonderful sounding board you could imagine. She told me straight out what was good about my running the edah and what was not. She had no problem telling me, "Michael, that is a dumb idea" or "what you are doing is not going to work." She taught me how to work and train staff, how to run a successful edah meeting (an incredible life skill), . . . how to delegate tasks and what to do myself, [and] above all she taught me how to evaluate, be critical and honest about my work, and yet at the same time always to be supportive of my staff. She taught me that my most important job was to be the *madrich* for my *madrichim.* She taught me what it meant to be a leader, to take responsibility, to admit when I did something wrong, and to always give the credit to my staff for our successes. Gloria kept me going after my failures, helped me save overworked counselors when they fell apart, and was ever present as our guide, mentor, mother, teacher, and friend.
>
> Gloria has a very special place in my heart and my Ramah memories, and I consider her to be one of the two or three most extraordinary educators with whom I have ever worked. She truly has a place in the Ramah Hall of Fame.

Between 1975 and 2005, Gloria was a fixture at Camp Ramah in Canada, as much a part of the landscape in Utterson, Ontario as the *ḥadar ochel* or Skeleton Lake. She continued to work as a yo'etzet for *rashei edah* and for directors. Shelly Dorph, the former director of the National Ramah Commission, recalls:

> I have such fond memories of Gloria and Israel sitting on the porch of their "condo" at Ramah—reading, playing with the grandkids, or meeting with counselors and staff who needed consultation, support, good advice, or whatever. For me as National Director, having Gloria at camp was like

> having the best part of Ramah's total wisdom and experience in support of the director and staff. Gloria was such a powerful, wise educator and *neshamah.* Her memory is surely a blessing to the thousands who knew and learned from her, myself included.

Rabbi Neil Cooper, the director of Camp Ramah in Canada from 1981 to 1982, notes:

> During my first years on staff, Gloria was a constant source of encouragement and advice. As I studied Talmud with Israel and learned Torah from him, I gained invaluable lessons regarding camping and Jewish education from the wealth of insights and expertise which she carried and shared. I remember that after directing a *pe'ulat erev,* after addressing the staff, or following a *hanhalah* meeting, I would shoot a glance at Gloria hoping for her sought-after approval and her loving smile. Indispensable to my personal and professional growth during those formative years was the impact of Gloria and Israel.

In the words of Judy Markose, the director of Camp Ramah in Canada from 1985 to 1989:

> Gloria was a one-of-a-kind leader and role model, a mentor and advisor to me in ways that I will never forget. Even at my young age, she saw potential in me. Gloria challenged me to be strong and decisive, sensitive, and insightful. She taught me about the politics of working with lay people, about how to interact with the parents of our campers, and so many other basics of running camp. She was always honest and straightforward and also supportive and encouraging. Somehow I wasn't intimidated, but it did mean a lot to me to gain Gloria's approval. For me as a woman trying to juggle career and family, Gloria represented the all-important value of balancing both spheres. It was clear to me that her husband and children came before anything else—though she could have gone down any career path she chose, as a creative, innovative, and fearless educator. It was a privilege to be taken under the protective wing of Gloria (and Israel) Silverman.

Rabbi Mitch Cohen, the director of Camp Ramah in Canada from 1990 to 2000, adds:

> Gloria's warmth and wisdom was a gift to me as director and to the camp community in numerous ways. Mostly, she was always there for me to advise me, to brainstorm with me, and to help me negotiate difficult situations. She was truly a remarkable woman who made Ramah, and so many educators including myself, better.

In addition to the work she did with the lay and professional leaders of Camp Ramah, Gloria actively recruited the youth of her home community, Hamilton, Ontario, where she was the principal of Beth Jacob Congregation's

Hebrew School during the 1970s and 1980s. She targeted the usual suspects, to be sure, but perhaps more importantly, she drew others to Ramah.

Rabbi Arye Berk recalls:

> I would not have ever worked at Camp Ramah in Canada except for "divine intervention" caused by a suggestion of Gloria Silverman. I never attended the camp as a camper, but I spent part of three wonderful summers at Camp Ramah in Canada in the mid 1980s as a driver. This was my first experience seeing the joy of Shabbat, and I know Ramah was one of the first stepping stones on my path to becoming a rabbi.
>
> As the driver of the camp, I picked up the campers after their trips in Algonquin and Killarney Provincial Parks. One summer Gloria decided to join the campers on their hardest trip in Killarney Park, and I did not think Gloria would be able to handle this canoe trip. But, when I arrived at Killarney to pick up the campers, there was Gloria, a little tired but smiling at her accomplishment. I should not have been surprised—she had a very strong will! I will always be grateful to Mrs. Silverman for making it possible for me to enter the world of Camp Ramah in Canada.

Gloria was also responsible for bringing a group of celebrated artists to Camp Ramah in Canada to advance existing efforts for programs and activities. David Moss observes:

> Gloria intuitively recognized the value of the arts, and especially the visual arts, for educating and inspiring Jewishly. She enthusiastically embraced not only my art, but warmly welcomed me and my family into the Ramah community and into her life. From the very moment we met, Gloria did whatever she thought necessary to make sure that my skills could be shared at camp—not only with campers and staff, but with other Judaic artists as well. Her warm, wise, and efficient structuring of the programs we created together truly brought about a flowering of the creative visual arts at Ramah. I cherish our years of working together and will always remember the excitement of the challenges, the pride of accomplishment, and the deep friendship and love that grew between us.

Karen Trager, Gloria's camper in 1962, sums up what countless others have said:

> I am indebted to her, and I will continue to miss her for as long as I'm alive. I credit her for so much of my own Jewish journey, and like so many of her former students, I know I am a Jewish educator today because of her example, her oh-so-subtle influence, her caring. She reached out to me and opened up a whole new world.

Gloria's life was blessed by Camp Ramah, and she brought blessings to the Ramah Camping Movement as well. Gloria was afforded myriad opportunities to learn and to grow, and in return, Ramah was a vehicle for her to teach and to influence.

Yehi zichrah baruch—may her memory continue to serve as a blessing for all who knew her.

SILVERMAN FAMILY *members attend or are alumni of the following Ramah camps and programs: Berkshires, Canada, Connecticut, Israel, New England, Nyack, Poconos, and Wisconsin:*

Judah and Margo Silverman, Daniel and Rachel, Tova, Leah
Lanie and Joel Goldberg, Rina, David and Rebecca, Joshua, Sarah
Aviva Silverman and Mark Smiley, Yael, Dov, Benjamin
Riva Silverman and Abram Heisler, Naomi, Jacob, Adina
Devorah Silverman and Reuben Rotman, Zachary, Dalia, Maya

60

ELIOT MALOMET

Rabbi Israel Silverman, z"l (1928–2003)

Rabbi Israel Silverman was chairman of the Rabbinical Assembly Committee on Law and Standards, a member of the Rabbinical Assembly's Va'ad Hakavod, one of the deans of the Canadian rabbinate, and one of the most respected, revered, and admired rabbis of his generation. But for almost a biblical generation—forty years—we at Camp Ramah in Canada had the privilege of calling him our *rav.* Rabbi Israel Silverman, of blessed memory, had a lifelong association with the Ramah Camping Movement and from the mid-1960s to before his death in 2003, he was the *rav hamaḥaneh* at Camp Ramah in Canada.

Naturally, Rabbi Silverman oversaw the kashrut of the camp and functioned as our decision maker in matters of halachah. But as rav hamaḥaneh he understood that his role was much more than a *mashgiaḥ* and a *posek.* He saw himself first and foremost as a teacher, and for many of us, he would be the single most important *dugmah,* religious-ethical-Torah exemplar, that we would ever have. He taught everyone, from those on the *hanhalah* to the lay leadership, from teachers to specialists, and from counselors to campers. He mentored and guided us and modeled for us the life of Torah and the path of *mitzvot.*

Rabbi Silverman was a brilliant and masterful teacher. Whether it was Tanach, Mishnah, Talmud, or Maimonides's Mishneh Torah, he had the extraordinary ability to take the most arcane, pedantic, or seemingly distant text and make it come alive before our very eyes. Long before it became fashionable to adorn texts with attractive graphic layouts and visual stimuli, Rabbi Silverman relied on the power of oral transmission; rigorous explication and logic; the drama of question and answer, anecdote, and illustration; and the power of personal example to elucidate a text. He believed that a classic text had an inherent power to communicate itself; he saw himself simply as an agent to let that take place. Although he set high standards for us, Rabbi Silverman had exceptional patience and was willing to go over and over a text until, in his words, it was absolutely "crystal clear." One could read a text a hundred times and still learn something new on the one hundred and first time, he would say. To study Torah with Rav Silverman was to experience the excitement and pleasure of Torah. Teaching Torah was his greatest joy and the greatest satisfaction of his soul. His greatest legacy is that he taught us how to love Torah.

Rabbi Silverman was our link to The Jewish Theological Seminary (JTS) and beyond. Rarely did a class transpire without a quote from one of his many revered teachers: Saul Lieberman, Louis Finkelstein, Abraham Joshua Heschel, Mordecai Kaplan, Alexander Marx, and H. L. Ginsberg, all of blessed memory, among others. He was a reservoir of JTS lore and rabbinic stories and when he augmented his teaching with colorful vignettes, he conveyed to us his deep spiritual authenticity. We, his students, became recipients of this tradition, and through him we became linked to these great scholars, their teachers, and to those before them as well, all the way back to Sinai.

Rabbi Silverman embodied the values of Conservative Judaism. The creative tension between halachah and aggadah resided in his soul; both Hillel and Shammai dwelled in his personality. He thought through the issues of the day with deep, pensive, and disciplined halachic logic, yet he tempered his positions with wise, gentle, and joyful aggadic compassion. During the rest of the year, he was a congregational rabbi in the "real world," who taught Torah from Shabbat to Shabbat, presided over the life-cycle events of his congregants, and applied halachah to the everyday lives of individual Jews in the reality of their settings. But during the summer, he lived in the "ideal world," a self-contained environment in which Judaism could thrive unencumbered by the daily demands of life. He thought of Camp Ramah as the greatest attempt undertaken by North American Jewry to create an ideal Jewish educational community, with the Hebrew language at its core. And how he was committed to Hebrew! He loved the opportunity to live in an environment where Hebrew was taught and learned and spoken, and where Hebrew was the vehicle of the camp culture and sport, especially baseball! How he loved to umpire the games in Hebrew!

It was our feeling—notwithstanding all of the important positions Rabbi Silverman held in the Conservative Movement and all the roles he played outside of camp—that the most important place in the world for him was Camp Ramah in Canada. He loved everything about our camp: its natural Canadian beauty, its serenity, and most of all, its potential for cultivating generations of Jews and imprinting upon them the joy of Torah and the love of Jewish life. His influence on a biblical generation of campers and staff was profound, but in his characteristic humility, he would be the last to take credit for it. Like Rabbi Akiva said of Rachel, he owed it all, he would say, to his beloved wife, Gloria, *z"l*. He would boast proudly that the most important reason why he loved Ramah was because of Gloria, the most important and influential *yo'etzet* (advisor) that Camp Ramah has ever known.

To remember Rabbi Silverman at Camp Ramah in Canada is to remember his profound influence on our lives, the extraordinary power of his intellect and erudition, and the way he would light up with passion and excitement and vigor and strength when he studied a classic text of the Talmud or the Rambam. To remember him is to see him seated on the *mirpeset* of the *sifriyyah* with a tractate before him or at a small table in his own *tzerif* presiding at a wonderful Shabbat *kiddush*. To remember Rabbi Israel Silverman is to lovingly recall how he and Gloria would walk hand in hand from their little tzerif toward the *bamah* on the eve of Shabbat, facing Skeleton Bay, a corner of God's own creation, as if the wings of the Divine Presence herself hovered over them both.

May the memory of Rabbi Israel Silverman be a blessing.

RABBI ELIOT MALOMET *is the spiritual leader of the Highland Park Conservative Temple–Congregation Anshe Emeth, Highland Park, New Jersey, and an alumnus of Camp Ramah in Canada.*

BARBRA WALTERS

Sidney Zweig, z"l (1921–1992)

You are not required to complete the work, but you are not free to abandon it.
Pirkei Avot 2:16

This quotation from *Pirkei Avot* is helpful in understanding how Sidney Zweig, *z"l,* lived his life. Even though Sid's profession was accountancy, Camp Ramah was his "job," and Sidney Zweig was determined to do the best job he could. Sid served as chairman of Camp Ramah in Canada from 1968 to 1989. During his tenure as chairman, he worked with seven directors: M. Donald Adelman, *z"l;* Lenny Berkowitz; Walter Ackerman, *z"l;* David Zisenwine; Seymour Epstein; Neil Cooper; and Judy Markose.

I became a member of the Ramah Canada board in 1978. I served on many board committees for Ramah and stayed on the personnel committee for the last few years of Sid's chairmanship. During this time, I was always impressed with Sid's ability to focus on the ideals of Camp Ramah. He never became overwhelmed by the problems that running a camp presented. He knew we had to find the "right" camp director, or make repairs to the physical plant, or eventually solve our ongoing sewage problems—huge obstacles! But Sid never lost sight of the hundreds of Jewish children who would come to Ramah to celebrate eight *Shabbatot*, eat kosher food, sing and learn Hebrew, and enjoy the total experience provided by a Ramah summer. Mostly, he wanted our Jewish young people to be influenced by Ramah.

When he invited the *hanhalah* to his home for his annual pre-camp barbecue, he was always thrilled at the quality of these remarkable young people who would be making the Ramah experience come alive. His eyes would sparkle as he would tell me of their many talents, and how proud he was of each one who would give their time and energy to make our camp program as excellent as it could be.

Sid was a smart man. He was a logical thinker, a good listener, and he was not afraid to make decisions—Jewish decisions! He was a man of strong convictions. He was a man who said what he meant in a few words—a man who kept his word.

Sid always did his research. He consulted with people whom he respected and who respected him, particularly Gloria Silverman, *z"l.* Over the years of her dedicated service to Camp Ramah in Canada and throughout Sid's chairmanship, among all her other roles, she acted as his mentor and confidant. It was Gloria who first encouraged, and then convinced, Sid to interview and then to employ our first female camp director, Judy Markose.

Sid and his wife Lorna became loyal friends of mine and of my husband Manley. We laughed and cried together. Sid would be very happy and joyful to see not only my own grandchildren soaking up Ramah, but also the grandchildren of many others of our generation. Given his infectious youthful spirit, he would be delighted to see a board with many young and "not so young" parents of Ramahniks. To quote the philosopher William James, "The greatest use of life is to spend it for something that will outlast it." Sidney Zweig used his life well, and I believe his legacy continues to inspire future generations.

There were, of course, others who worked closely with Sid and were touched by this great man. Sid Zweig's Ramah story would not be complete without some reminiscences from a few of these people. I chose to include the following five, in alphabetical order:

> In thirty-three summers at Camp Ramah in Canada, I have been truly blessed to have studied with great rabbis and to have learned from generations of inspiring campers. I have been fortunate to have my life influenced by many impressive individuals. One such individual was Sidney Zweig. There is no one who surpasses the commitment and dedication of Sid Zweig to his beloved camp. Sid was a friend and a mentor who encouraged me to pursue a career in the rabbinate and always supported me in my long Ramah career. Sid was a straight-shooter, had a dry sense of humor, and a true love for Ramah in Canada. I was lucky to know him as well as I did, and his memory still serves me as a blessing!
> *Rabbi Chuck Diamond*
> *Pittsburgh, Pennsylvania*

> Sid Zweig loved Camp Ramah in Canada and worked tirelessly to promote and protect it. I had known Sid for many years as the father of one of my classmates, Netta, and then in his role as the "man in charge" at camp. When I was *rosh agam* in the late 1970s, we needed a new ski boat. Sid told me to do my research and present him with my findings. We researched the least expensive option (assuming that was the way we would have to go), but also wanted to move our program to the next level—a step that would involve a more expensive specialized ski boat and a more powerful engine. I expected Sid to insist on the cheaper option, but he accepted our recommendation and permitted us to make the more expensive purchase—and more importantly, encouraged us to move our program forward. In this decision, not only did Sid encourage and support us as senior staff, but he showed vision and understanding of the camp program. I'm sure that this is just one small example of how Sid helped to build Camp Ramah in Canada.
>
> My career as a member of the lay leadership of Camp Ramah began with the encouragement and support of Sid Zweig. A number of years after

my time as a staff member at camp, Sid encouraged me to become involved with the lay leadership of Camp Ramah in Canada. I was made a member of various committees of the board, a board member, and eventually the president of the camp. Camp Ramah in Canada has been the focus of my community involvement for many years, and today I sit as the senior vice president of the National Ramah Commission—the first Canadian to serve in this position. I owe Sid a huge debt of gratitude for mentoring me and believing in a strong Canadian Camp Ramah.
Sheldon L. Disenhouse
Senior Vice President, National Ramah Commission

When I was the director of Camp Ramah in Canada from 1978 to 1980, Sid Zweig was chairman. He had already been connected to the lay governance of the camp for many years. While we had our differences from time to time, the most impressive thing about Sid was his complete devotion to Ramah, the campers, and the staff. Always foremost in his mind was the fact that Ramah was a great source of fun and sound Jewish education for the kids. His volunteer time and energy was totally given to the camp. Even when his views differed from those of the camp board, the staff, or JTS, it was his deep concern for the camp and its viability that motivated him. His was a special kind of leadership that brought his attention to every micro detail of the camp administration, always challenging us to find the most efficient and effective ways to run the camp. Because Sid was an accountant, I learned a great deal about pre-computer accounting techniques—skills that I value to this day. Sid Zweig cared deeply for Ramah and gave the camp a big part of his life.
Seymour "Epi" Epstein, Ed.D.
Former Director, Camp Ramah in Canada

I first met Sid Zweig when he was an accountant for our group of drug stores over fifty years ago. He later took over as chairman for Camp Ramah in Canada from Barney Goldhar, the camp's founding chairman and benefactor. Sid was a brilliant professional who convinced me of the virtues of Camp Ramah for my young family. This began a great love affair with Ramah that has lasted for close to forty years, for our children, and then our grandchildren.

Sid was very passionate about Ramah and remained [as the] chairman for approximately two decades. He kept the camp cohesive throughout its formative years. He surrounded himself with a young group of committee members who are still very active with the Ramah Camping Movement, both locally and at the national level. I was fortunate to be the beneficiary of Sid's wisdom when I assumed the chairmanship of the camp shortly before Sid passed away. He was a "great guy," my mentor and friend.
Ab Flatt
Past Chairman, Camp Ramah in Canada

My father passed on to me his love and dedication for Camp Ramah in Canada, where he had a long tenure as Chairman of the Board. I still return to camp on staff each summer! In addition, my father was my role model when I became the Chair of the Board of my daughter's school. On many occasions, I found myself thinking about what my father would have done. Until I became the Chair, I was not even aware of how much I had absorbed, as if by osmosis, of my father's leadership style. The legacy he left for the present Camp Ramah in Canada Board has been mentioned to me as recently as in the last few years, when a current Board member said that someone had stood up at a meeting, saying "Sid Zweig would never have let this happen!" Every summer, when I come up to camp, I always go to the staff lounge, to check on the sign that notes that the building is dedicated to his memory.

Netta Zweig
Administrative Director, Camp Ramah in Canada

BARBRA WALTERS *of Toronto, Canada, served as a member of the Board of Directors of Camp Ramah in Canada for more than twenty years.*

RAMAH60רמה
Reflections

MORTON M. STEINBERG

Introduction

The full story of Camp Ramah is composed of the personal stories of the tens of thousands of individuals who attended Ramah as campers or staff members over the past sixty years. Of course, not all of these stories can be told, but a number of Ramahniks have graciously submitted essays that reveal at least part of that story. The National Ramah Commission is proud to present these essays as an important historical record in connection with Ramah's sixtieth-anniversary celebration.

In reading these essays, several common themes quickly become apparent: the lasting friendships formed at camp, the important influence of staff members on campers and of senior staff members on their younger colleagues, and the profound impact on Jewish self-identity and practice resulting from the passion and appreciation felt for one's individual Ramah experience. Although virtually every essay reflects at least one of these themes, and most incorporate more than one, each story is still unique.

My own Ramah story had its improbable start on a Tuesday morning in June 1955 at the old Chicago and Northwestern Railway station in Chicago. My parents were going to make their first trip to Israel so at the urging of our rabbi, Phillip L. Lipis, *z"l,* they decided to send me and my older brother to Camp Ramah in Wisconsin. I was crying when I boarded the train that morning. I was ten years of age and had never been "sent away" before. Except for my brother, who was assigned to a different train car, I did not know anyone else on the train.[1]

MORTON M. STEINBERG *is a senior partner at the law firm DLA Piper LLP (US). He served as president of Camp Ramah in Wisconsin for nine years and then as president of the National Ramah Commission (NRC) from 2003 to 2007. He is currently chairman of the board of trustees of the NRC. While president of the NRC, he also served on the Leadership Council for Conservative Judaism and was an elected delegate of MERCAZ USA to the 35th Zionist Congress in Jerusalem. A product of the Conservative Movement, Mr. Steinberg was a camper, counselor, and waterfront director at Camp Ramah in Wisconsin.*

Night was falling when the train finally arrived in Conover. We gathered our belongings, got off the train, and squeezed onto school buses for the ride to camp. When we reached camp, we were directed through the darkness to a place called the *ḥadar ochel.* Not knowing we were walking across a tennis court, I tripped over the net, smashing my small carrying case and the new tennis racket my mother had bought for me. (I didn't play tennis, but it was on the list of things to bring to camp!)

After a noisy dinner of cold hamburgers, my bunkmates and I followed our counselor to our cabin. In those days, our clothes and bedding were shipped to camp a week or so before the campers arrived so that the counselors could make the kids' beds in advance. I was tired as I entered the cabin but relieved to see the row of bunk beds neatly made up, with pajamas lying on each camper's pillow—except for one: on my bunk was just a plain mattress. Although my parents had shipped my trunk to camp, they didn't trust the U.S. mail with the keys. Instead, they entrusted them to my older brother. So while the other kids quickly got into their warm beds and fell asleep, I went back out into the night looking for Joseph in *tzerif gimel* to get the keys to my trunk.

The next morning, I asked my counselor Danny Merritt if we were going to breakfast. He said yes, but first we were going to morning services. I said, "You must be mistaken—today is Wednesday, not Saturday." And he said, "At Ramah we have services *every* morning!" and with that, he led us up to the *beit am* where I saw the older boys mysteriously wrapping leather straps around their arms. I was totally bewildered. What was I doing at this place?

After those first twenty-four hours, things rapidly improved for me. I returned to camp for the next six summers and participated in the first Ramah Israel Seminar in 1962. I was a bunk counselor for three summers and eventually served as waterfront director and as a member of the *hanhalah* under Rabbi Burton Cohen, the camp director. I was invited to join the Ramah Wisconsin Committee in 1974 and served as its president from 1994 to 2003.

I had fabulous times at camp. My Ramah friends and I lived for the summer: for baseball, swimming, canoe trips, singing, hikes, and, eventually, even classes, discussion groups, and davening. To this day my closest friends are from Ramah. I met my wife Miriam at camp and both of our children were campers and staff members at Ramah Wisconsin.

My story varies little from the theme of the essays that follow. Although anecdotal, these personal remembrances supplement and give substance and personality to the scholarly studies that describe the impact Ramah has had on its campers and staff, some of which appear in this volume. The essays also validate what the lay and professional leadership of Ramah has known for the past six decades: Ramah works!

Ramah was and is summer camping at its best. Like many other camps, it builds camaraderie, develops athletic and artistic skills, teaches fair play and ethical conduct, and promotes responsibility and independence of action and thought in a safe environment. It exposes kids to the beauty of nature and the thrill of the outdoors. But what makes Ramah unique is that it also presents a pathway to Jewish living—a *derech ḥayyim* to all who attend. Ramah opens doors to ideas and concepts not otherwise available to the majority of its campers. Hebrew language and Jewish ritual become a natural part of each day. Some campers find the exposure to Jewish life and thought so attractive that they devote their professional lives to it, attending rabbinical school or pursuing a career in Jewish education. Many find a calling to fill positions of lay leadership in the synagogue or other Jewish community organizations. Many are inspired to make aliyah to Israel. Some migrate to the Orthodox community. Others lose interest and find their own way in life; Ramah is not for everyone. But the opportunity for a Jewish lifestyle is there. Ramah can be transformative, and regardless of the path subsequently taken in life, the Ramah experience gives meaning and richness to the lives of its alumni and staff. Ramah, the great success of the Conservative Movement, benefits all streams of Judaism in North America and in Israel.

And how is this done? It is done by the people one encounters and lives with at Ramah and by the educational and religious principles that are refined and implemented at camp. Some of the most influential people in my life were the counselors and teachers I met at Ramah—not just because of what they said, but because of the examples they provided: in formal classes, on the ball field, in the dining hall, and in the cabin. Many of these counselors and teachers are now some of the most outstanding leaders in academia, as well as in local and national Jewish communal organizations.

Several years ago, the Jewish newspaper *Forward* reported on the controversial debate in the Conservative Movement over homosexuality and Jewish law. Three top Jewish thinkers were quoted extensively because of their divergent views: Rabbi David Novak, a leader of the Union for Traditional Judaism; Rabbi Elliot Dorff, rector of the University of Judaism (now renamed the American Jewish University); and Dr. Joel Roth, "perhaps the [Conservative] movement's most respected arbiter of *Halacha*." Unmentioned in the article was the fact that all three of these individuals attended Camp Ramah in Wisconsin and all, to some degree, had the doorway to their Jewish life opened to them at camp.

The purpose of presenting the essays published in this volume goes beyond entertainment. In his recent volume *The Landscape of History*,[2] the respected historian John Lewis Gaddis wrote:

> [I]f we can widen the range of experience beyond what we as individuals have encountered, if we can draw upon the experiences of others who've had to confront comparable situations in the past, then — although there are no guarantees — our chances of acting wisely is increased proportionately.

Ramah helped shape the lives of tens of thousands of young Americans, Canadians, and Israelis, many of whom became leaders in their own communities, and most of whom live a Jewish life at least to some extent based on their camp experience. These stories are an important part of the history of the Ramah Camping Movement, and hopefully, not only give testimony to the effectiveness and impact of Ramah but also provide guidance, perhaps inspiration, to future generations in acting wisely with respect to Ramah. The challenge of the National Ramah Commission and of each individual Ramah oversight committee is to promote, improve, and expand the overall Ramah program. By reading these essays, we can dwell not only for a moment on the nostalgia of our youth, but we can also gain insights into meeting that challenge.

Ramah has been a part of my life since the day I boarded that train to Conover fifty-five years ago. It is a legacy that I share proudly with the authors whose articles follow, as well as with thousands of others throughout the Jewish world. All of us at the National Ramah Commission hope you enjoy reading these articles and hope that perhaps they will be instructive to future Ramah leaders as the story of Ramah continues to unfold for many generations to come.

Notes

[1] Alan Birndorf, who was my junior counselor that summer, was the only person who befriended me on that train ride. Alan remained very active in Ramah alumni activities and attended Ramah's sixtieth-anniversary celebration in New York in October 2007; he passed away suddenly three weeks later.

[2] John Lewis Gaddis, *The Landscape of History: How Historians Map the Past* (New York: Oxford University Press, 2002), 9.

POCONOS

RABBI MAYER ABRAMOWITZ
Rabbi Emeritus, Temple Menorah, Miami Beach, Florida

In April of 1951, I returned to the United States after a six-year stint in Europe. I had served as a U.S. Army chaplain in Germany and Austria and then as the chief emigration officer for the Joint Distribution Committee in Italy. During those six years, I had lost contact with the American Jewish community, including The Jewish Theological Seminary (JTS).

I returned to the States and needed a job to provide for my wife and four-month-old daughter. Saul Teplitz told me about Camp Ramah. I approached Rabbi Bernard Siegel, then the executive director of United Synagogue, requesting a job at Ramah as a camp rabbi. "Mike," he replied, "Rabbis we have enough. Lifeguards we need."

I took out my Red Cross Life Savers card. Rabbi Siegel grasped the card, and noticing the expiration date of 1942, he said: "Get it renewed and you have a job as waterfront man at Ramah in the Poconos." So at the ripe old age of thirty-one, I passed the test and immediately took off for Ramah.

It was a never-to-be-forgotten summer.

David Fish, the camp manager, and his family were our table partners and that relationship became a lifelong friendship. We made friends with staff members, and these relationships also lasted long after the summer program.

In addition to being the guest waterfront man, I also doubled as song leader in the dining room—introduced with the chant *anu rotzim me'ir.* As a confirmed egoist, I reveled (and still do) recalling that chant.

Also, as an added bit of excitement, I studied Gemara with some staff members who were preparing to take their tests for entry into JTS. In later years, meeting them as rabbis was a true delight. Ramah remained with me and my wife as a great highlight of our life.

60

CALIFORNIA

RABBI BRADLEY SHAVIT ARTSON

Abner and Roslyn Goldstine Dean's Chair, Ziegler School of Rabbinic Studies; Vice President, American Jewish University

[Adapted with the permission of the author from "Special Torah Column: High Holy Day Season, 2007/5768," in Today's Torah weekly e-mail from the Ziegler School of Rabbinic Studies, Los Angeles, CA, September 17, 2007.]

I have fifteen-year-old twins—Jacob and Shira—in my opinion, both of them wonderful, extraordinary children and both of them in their own way, very devoted to Jewish life—in very distinct ways—but devoted nonetheless. Jacob wrestles with having autism, and as a result of his autism, he has had to give up certain dreams. How ironic that the child who most loves Torah study and who most loves daily *tefillot,* has not been able to participate in formal Jewish education or Jewish camping because nobody offers a program that he is able to be part of. Because he misses her, summer after summer, Jacob watched his sister go off to Camp Ramah with sorrow—but also with envy. Other kids go to Camp Ramah despite the tefillot and despite the *limmud.* The first time Jacob was told that there are non-Jewish camps, he asked:

"Do they have Torah studies?"
"No."
"Do they do *shaḥarit?*"
"No."
"Then why bother going to camp?"

And I, of course, as the *abba,* eventually made my peace with the particular strengths and challenges of each of my children, and one of those challenges meant that at Camp Ramah, the summer camp that I most love, there was no place for my son who loves Torah—until this summer. This summer, for the first time, the Amitzim Program (for children with special needs) allowed a child to attend with an aide, thus making the inclusion inclusive and enabling Jacob to participate. Jacob says that this summer was the greatest summer of his life and that the greatest week of the greatest summer of his life was his time at Camp Ramah because he could spend a week with his sister at Camp Ramah, which was, he said, "The dream of a lifetime!"

It was indeed the dream of a lifetime, not only his, but mine as well. So I want to share with you the exact moment that was for me, *dayyenu.*

After serving as camp rabbi for one week each summer for as long as my kids have been alive, my daughter, Shira, last year, banished me from camp. I was not allowed to be camp rabbi because for God's sake, she is a fourteen-year-old girl, and who wants her dad hanging around at camp? But this summer she is a mature fifteen-year-old girl, which makes all the difference, and she decided that since this was her last summer as a camper that I would be allowed to come back as camp rabbi for the final week of the session (in part because she did not want to take the bus home). Those of you who are parents know that tainted love is good enough!

So, I was there as camp rabbi for a week, and Jacob and Elana were invited to join me for Shabbat. Jacob had already enjoyed his week at camp with Amitzim, but he came back with Elana, his mom, my wife. An extremely raucous *minḥah* (afternoon service) is part of the last transitional celebration that takes place during one's final summer as a camper (in the Machon *edah*). Those of you who have never seen a Far West USY (or a Camp Ramah in California) minḥah service are missing extraordinary worship. Teens jump over tables, literally. Their singing is non-stop, their creativity and humor is amazing, and the energy level is astonishing. Camp Ramah in Ojai has a *beit keneset* (house of prayer) in the round. When you shut all the doors and windows, the noise level reverberates in your sternum. You don't have to rely on your outer ears; your inner ear can hear each and every shout and stomp, and your inner ears want to be covered just as much as your outer ones.

As the minḥah service is about to start, Shira is sitting in the middle of the beit keneset with her friends on one of the iron-hard benches. She stands and emerges from the beit keneset and says to me, "Where's Jacob?" I point out where he is on a nearby path, and she walks over to him and takes him by the hand, saying, "Come with me." Then she leads her brother into the beit keneset, which is a noisy *balagan*.

For those of you who do not know, autistic kids have trouble with loud noise.

So, Jacob walks in, Shira holding his hand—he doesn't really have a choice in this—and she continues to pull him through the crowd. Shira uses her other hand to move the dancing, singing, shouting teens out of the way. Jacob uses his spare hand to try to cover both ears, but he makes himself walk with his sister through the room. When Shira reaches her bench in the middle of the noise and the chaos and the jumping and the shouting, she asks one of her friends to move over, and they make room for her and her brother. Shira sits Jacob down, and she sits next to him with her arms around him, causing Jacob to get so excited that he leaps up and tries to bolt.

I am standing next to the bench beside the twins, and Elana is on the far side of the room, against a wall. Every time Jacob leaps up, Shira helps calm him down and bring him back. Occasionally, I have to go and smile at him and help him come back. The entire time that Jacob is there, he has a smile on his face so big, you could see it from the *ḥadar ochel* (dining hall), which is a long way away.

And at that moment, if I had dropped dead—dayyenu, it would have been sufficient.

To see my twins at the minḥah service at Camp Ramah, in the Machon year, sitting together; to watch the other "Machonies" smiling at Jacob, encouraging him with their warmth, telling him sometimes, "It's good that you're here," and even when they were not telling him verbally, smiling to let him know how welcome he was, to see Jacob mustering superhuman strength to stay in that noise—despite his intense feelings—because his sister had given him the greatest *kavod* in the world; to see my girl so loving and sweet that she was able to transcend the self-absorption of most teenagers; to know that she could contribute something that no other person on the planet could do at that moment; and then to look across the room to see Elana with a smile as big as Jacob's, and to know that our family was complete, that we were all there together, and that our complete family included Camp Ramah, included all of the Jewish people—that was dayyenu!

In an instant, a dream that I had abandoned and a prayer that I had stopped saying was granted me. Dayyenu. It's enough. If I never have another dayyenu moment, I will look back on that one and say, whatever else life brings, it was worth it—for that shimmering pure moment of bliss.

60

DAROM

MAYA AVIV

Former *mishlaḥat* member

[Translated from the Hebrew by Rabbi Mitchell Cohen, National Ramah Director.]

Before I arrived at Ramah Darom, I was very disconnected from the world of religion. Although my mother grew up in a religious home, I never personally related to the religious aspects of Judaism. Kashrut, Friday-night kiddush, and fasting on Yom Kippur were not part of my life. During our training for Camp Ramah, we learned about Conservative Judaism. This created a great conflict for me as I struggled with the notion of attending *tefillot* and observing Shabbat during the two months of camp. After observing a Shabbat during the training seminar, I called my father, crying hysterically, and asked "How am I going to do this?"

Amazingly, during the two months of camp, my perspective changed radically. I quickly adjusted to the routine of attending morning services, reciting *birkat hamazon* after each meal, observing Shabbat, saying the *Shema,* and so on. I recall waiting with great anticipation for the beginning of Shabbat and for the beautiful *havdalah* service. These activities that were so foreign to me at first became an integral part of who I am and ever since, have added beauty and meaning to my life. Camp Ramah awakened within me my Jewish soul.

When I returned to Israel after camp, I reentered the world of "Maya the secular Israeli." Slowly, over time, I found myself being drawn closer and closer to Shabbat observance, daily prayer, and other Jewish rituals. . . .

I owe a great debt of gratitude to Camp Ramah for the religious inspiration that has changed my life so powerfully.

60

DAROM

RABBI DAVID BAUM

Congregation Shaarei Kodesh, Boca Raton, Florida

[Interview conducted by Rabbi Mitchell Cohen, National Ramah Director, June 2007.]

At the time of this interview, David Baum was a fourth-year rabbinical student at The Jewish Theological Seminary (JTS) and was spending his ninth summer at Camp Ramah Darom. As a freshman at the University of Florida in the late 1990s, never in his wildest dreams did he think that he would pursue a career as a Jewish professional, much less as a rabbi! Yet that is exactly his current career path and way of life, inspired mostly by his years of experiential learning and leadership at Camp Ramah and by the impact of his mentor and friend, Rabbi Loren Sykes.

During the summer of 2007, Dave served as the *rosh tefillah,* helping with *tefillah* education for all the campers and staff as part of Ramah's overall efforts to teach prayer skills and to instill a deepened sense of spirituality. Over the years, Dave has also served as a counselor, a *rosh edah,* director of staff learning, a *yo'etz* (parent liaison and staff trainer), and a Judaica teacher.

During the inaugural summer of Ramah Darom, Dave's childhood friend, Karen Eliav from his home town of Plantation, Florida, attended camp as a counselor. She said that it was an "amazing experience," and she convinced a number of her friends, including Dave, to come and work at camp the following summer. Dave recalled:

> The summer of 1998 was incredible. I loved being at Camp Ramah as a counselor. Then I really got hooked on Ramah when I was chosen to

> represent Ramah Darom at the Weinstein Institute for Counselor Training when we got together in the winter with counselors from all the other Ramah camps. This really made me realize that being at Ramah was helping me to become part of something much bigger, affecting young people all over North America.

After that experience, Dave considered going to Ramah Canada because he had met some wonderful people who attended that camp in Utterson, Ontario. "But Rabbi Sykes asked me to come back as a counselor for Gesher, the oldest edah, and I couldn't turn him down. Eventually, he asked me to be a rosh edah, an experience that completely solidified my desire to pursue a career in Jewish leadership."

Motivated to become a Jewish educator, Dave, who had been planning a career in the business world, knew he would be disappointing his father by coming back to camp year after year. In 2002, after a "difficult" telephone conversation with his dad, he wrote his dad a passionate letter explaining his reasons for returning to camp and taking on a leadership role:

> Dear Dad:
>
> You didn't seem too happy with the conversation we just had. I gave more thought to why I want to return to camp and therefore postpone my college graduation. In essence, becoming a rosh edah at camp is about making a difference in children's lives. I'm going to help give many children a sense of Judaism that some have never gotten, and I'm going to help my staff develop leadership skills, and hopefully instill inspiration. I want to bring happiness and Yiddishkeit to these kids because that is what you and mom have taught me throughout my life. Although this is going to be hard work and long hours, and although I'm going to be one of the youngest division heads ever, I am doing this gladly. Some of my friends have parent role models who have instilled in them greed and selfishness, and they don't treat others with respect. Yet you have taught me better values, and that is why I want to share these values with others. So I guess you can look at this as a blessing or a curse. If delaying my graduation makes school a little bit harder for me, but in the process I get to bring happiness and values to children at camp, then I will gladly take on that responsibility. So thank you for instilling within me true Yiddishkeit and wonderful values. I hope that in the future, I can give this gift to my own children, just the same way you have instilled it within Sandy, Richie and me.
>
> Your son,
> David

Dave reflected back on this letter as a key moment in his life, when he was willing to take what he thought was the right path, and try to convince his parents to support this decision. Five years later, Dave is one of the most senior leaders and educators at Ramah Darom and soon will be ordained by JTS as a rabbi.

The other key Ramah moment in Dave's life occurred when his grandfather, Frank Baum, came to visit him at Ramah. Dave became quite emotional as he recalled the time:

> My grandfather was a survivor of the Holocaust, but he never ever, in all my life, spoke about his experiences during the war. After spending Shabbat at camp with me and my younger sister, Sandy, who was a camper, my grandfather stunned us by saying that he wanted to talk about his experiences in the Holocaust to the children at camp. The word "camp" had deep associations for him, and the stark contrast between the "death camp" he had experienced and "this camp of unbelievably vibrant Jewish life" moved him to speak for the first time about his experiences during the war.

The Ramah experience worked its magic on Dave Baum. The tension between choosing a career with the greatest possible financial rewards and a career in a helping profession works itself out differently for every young person. Simply being aware of this tension and making young people aware of their potential for spiritual, educational, or other types of leadership is one of the true signs of success for any Ramah educator. Thanks to the nurturing mentorship of Rabbi Loren Sykes and the powerful experiences at Ramah Darom, Dave Baum will be helping and educating others for many years.

60

BERKSHIRES

CAROL FANGER BELL
Jewish day school educator, Norwood, Massachusetts

I am sure that your essays about Ramah experiences usually come from those who came to Ramah as children. I found Camp Ramah as an adult, yet it has influenced my life significantly. I have taught at Jewish day schools for many years. In recent years, I have been on a personal Jewish journey, which has led me to realize that I love being Jewish, a concept that I always hope to instill in my students.

In May 2002, my school was invited to send our fourth-graders to Ramah Berkshires for a Shabbaton. My principal sent me as a chaperone, saying that she knew I'd love camp as much, if not more, than the children. She was right. Davening outdoors and watching the female counselors with their *tallitot* made a tremendous impression on me. I contacted Ramah Berkshires during the year to see if they had a place for me for the summer. About two weeks before the camp season started, I got a call offering me a position with the Gan program, assisting the *gannenet.*

So I quickly shifted into gear, packed up my classroom, and went to camp, leaving my husband, twenty-five-year old son, and twenty-one-year old daughter. Before the first week was over, the gannenet left unexpectedly, and I inherited the job!

That summer was the best gift that I have ever given myself. It gave me another place where I can enjoy being Jewish. I am only sorry that it took me so long to discover the specialness of the Ramah camps; it seemed like all the other adults there had been coming for years.

60

GLEN SPEY

BEN S. BERNANKE, PH.D.
Chairman, Board of Governors, U.S. Federal Reserve System

I did attend Camp Ramah one summer. It was a good experience for me, as there were relatively few Jewish young people in the town (Dillon, South Carolina) where I grew up, and the summer gave me a chance to be immersed in a Jewish, Hebrew-speaking environment (although my modern Hebrew wasn't that good—I had learned biblical Hebrew from my grandfather). I enjoyed the sports, social events, and participating in a theater production.

60

CALIFORNIA · CONNECTICUT POCONOS · WISCONSIN

ANNE SCHIFFMAN BONOWITZ
Jewish educator, Columbus, Ohio

Camp Ramah in the Poconos, 1950: I was twelve and had received a scholarship from my synagogue so I could attend camp that summer. I think I was the only girl in my bunk who was not the daughter of a rabbi, a cantor, or some other Jewish professional. I certainly was sure that I knew less Hebrew than anyone else. It wasn't until sometime in the fifth week that I even understood the most basic announcements in the dining room. At a time when each camper received an *ayin* if she spoke enough *ivrit* for one day, I received three for the entire summer.

Camp Ramah in the Poconos, 1954: I was a camper-waiter in Machon, thanks to a scholarship arranged by my teacher, Levi Soshuk, *z"l.* We were having an *edah* meeting. I stood before the entire Machon and chastised them for not setting a good example for the younger campers because we were not speaking enough Hebrew.

Autumn, 1954: I entered the Seminary College of The Jewish Theological Seminary (JTS) in the Aleph class while completing my senior year in high school. I was active in Leaders Training Fellowship (LTF) and tutored Hebrew school students to earn some money. I did all this because of the wonderful experiences I had at Ramah.

During my college years, I worked at the Ramah camps in Connecticut, Wisconsin, and California. After my last summer at camp in 1960, having graduated from Brooklyn College and JTS, I moved to Columbus, Ohio, to be one of the first teachers in the Melton pilot school where I met my husband.

When our oldest son, Alan, went to Ramah Wisconsin in 1974, we went to visit him. For me, it was like coming home. The best part was when Burt Cohen, the camp director, asked if we would be on staff the following year. That began my second career at Ramah. I served as teacher and head teacher from 1975 to 1982. My husband Marv served as camp nurse and also as the musical accompanist for all the musical shows. (I really think Burt needed Marv more than he needed me on staff.)

Ramah has played a part in every phase of my life from childhood to middle-age, and even now, as I approach seventy, I often find myself thinking back to those wonderful experiences and friendships.

60

CANADA

SHARON CHAI

Assistant Professor, Tel Hai Academic College, Upper Galilee

I have no doubt that Judaism is the basis for both my personal and professional life and the motivating force of my soul. As a child brought up in the Diaspora, I am indebted to my parents for choosing to educate me at Jewish schools and to send me to Camp Ramah in Canada, where the history of the Jewish people and more importantly, Jewish values, were inculcated into my consciousness and became an integral part of my being. My belief in humanity, in pluralism, and in education emanate from the experiences I accrued during those crucial years. I was profoundly influenced by Ramah staff members who, motivated by their Judaism, chose to go to the South to convince black Americans of the importance of voting, thus empowering them to evoke change. It was these same staff members who escorted Martin Luther King's cortege upon his death.

At Camp Ramah on Tish'ah Be'av, after the reading of *Eichah* on the floor of the *beit am,* the staff chose to show pictures and to read poems from the renowned book *I Never Saw Another Butterfly,* a collection of children's poetry and drawings from Terezinstadt, the German concentration camp in Czechoslovakia. This was an emotional experience that was to have an ever-lasting impact on my life. As a nine-year-old, I could not conceptualize the difference between myself, an affluent child in the serene and beautiful surroundings of Camp Ramah and those nine-year-old children who were tortured and brutally murdered, only because they were Jewish. From the depths of my soul, and from the innocence and naivete possible only in one's early years, I vowed to avenge their deaths and to give meaning and pay homage to their lives and deaths.

I never lost sight of my vow, and it is from that promise that I chose to make Israel my home and to bring up my children there. It is the values of Judaism and my identification with basic tenets of our humanity that effected ever-lasting change in me. It is the tradition of prayer, the connection to my God, and Judaism, which I love and cherish, that form the perspective of my essence. It is also the spirit of my own personal interpretation of Judaism that is the driving force of my professional life.

NYACK

STACEY COHEN
Graphic designer, New York, New York

When I think of camp, my mind instantly races to any given Friday. It is a hectic work day for everyone. For swim staff, the day begins early; classes are jumbled with free swims, and you only get five minutes to eat lunch, which you must eat in the pool house instead of in the *ḥadar ochel.* While the rest of camp is at the Friday afternoon *oneg,* swim staff is in a meeting, assessing the past week, making preparations for the one to come, and admittedly goofing off in the water before the pool reopens for after-camp swimming. As the end of the camp day approaches, the lifeguards collectively cross the *gesher* to join the rest of the *ḥanichim* and *tzevet* to dance our hearts out.

In accordance with tradition, Friday afternoon dancing ends with Michael Edelstein lowering the flag, everyone singing "Hatikvah," and of course, dancing to "Amen" and welcoming Shabbat.

The hours between the ḥanichim leaving the campgrounds and lighting candles are always filled with delightful high-paced activity: visiting the local old age home, decorating the ḥadar ochel, handing out Shabbat-o-grams, racing to shower while there is still hot water. I personally fill time by waiting on the *migrash* with a friend for the hustle and bustle to clear as we lie on our backs in the shade and enjoy each other's company.

At 6:15 p.m. every Friday during the eight weeks Camp Ramah in Nyack is in session, a miracle happens. Everyone in camp is in the same place, at the same time. No one is carrying a cell phone or car keys. We are all dressed in our finest summer threads; and with that well-known approving smile of our director, Amy Skopp Cooper, the community opens their *siddurim* and begins to chant "Yedid Nefesh."

This may sound like an exaggeration, but this is very possibly the moment I live for. It's not just a moment I look forward to at the end of each summer week, it is an experience I cling to during the year as well, when the reality of life separates our Ramah community, and we spend our Friday nights singing "Yedid Nefesh" in different communities. No matter where I might physically be on any given Shabbat, my heart is in the *beit keneset* of Camp Ramah in Nyack.

Camp is my home. I have spent some of the most influential years of my life there and made the longest lasting friendships I probably will ever have. Ramah has given me love and nourishment for five years, and it will continue to be a part of me for the rest of my life.

60

CANADA

JESSICA M. COOPERMAN, M.D.
Child & Adolescent Family Services, Markham Stouffville Hospital, Markham, Ontario

I want to share this story because Ramah Canada is one of my most favorite places in the world, and my experience there was life changing and one of the highlights of growing up.

My first year at camp was 1983. I was twelve years old. My dad described Ramah to me and my sister Liza as a place where we would pray, study Hebrew, and hopefully, find husbands. Needless to say with that introduction, I wasn't completely enthusiastic. Within a few hours of being at camp, I realized that he was right. We would pray and study Hebrew, but his description didn't do justice to the wonderful environment that made *tefillah* and learning so much fun. I also had no idea that at Ramah I would meet some of my best friends, including my very best friend Judi Price (Rosen).

From our first summer together in Arazim, Judi and I were inseparable. Our friendship has mainly been long-distance. When we met, she lived in Burlington, and I lived in Ottawa. We always counted the days until we could be together again at camp. During our university years, we were lucky enough to live together in the same city for a couple of years, but schooling and fate again forced us to resort to our old ways of communicating, mainly by mail and by phone. Just when we thought we would finally be in the same place at the same time again, Judi married a wonderful man and moved to Winnipeg. I was so pleased to be the maid of honor at her wedding—seventeen years after we had met. Three years later, she returned the favor and entertained my wedding guests with tales of my idiosyncrasies dating back to camp. So here we are, twenty-four years later: in two different provinces, two husbands (one each!) and now, two babies! My friendship with Judi is the best thing I took from my years at *maḥaneh Ramah. Tov li!*

60

WISCONSIN

BENJAMIN DERMAN

Medical student, Northwestern University, Feinberg School of Medicine

I was a camper at Camp Ramah in Wisconsin from 1999–2004, a participant on Ramah Seminar in 2005, and a counselor in 2006.

It was a rather cool Saturday evening, and only a few minutes were left before Shabbat would come to a close. My friend and I were sitting on slightly wobbly benches as we discussed our favorite contemporary musicians. Suddenly, we heard a symphonic crash, and our eyes darted toward the usually calm Lake Buckatabon to find a powerful storm brewing. We were not frightened but rather curious at how nature's display could be so completely out of sync: the dazzling lightning bolts seemed to be completely independent from the booming thunder as the two of them advanced toward camp.

And then I heard a faint note—it was my friend who began to softly hum the tune to one of our favorite *se'udah shelishit* songs. I couldn't help but join in. I no longer felt the wobbly bench, nor did I notice the fact that I had not dressed properly to face the storm that was rapidly approaching. For those last few minutes of Shabbat, I felt an experience more powerful than ever before; a moment when I felt as though there were an everlasting bond between man and the Almighty, but even more so, a perfect harmony between man and his fellow man.

60

CALIFORNIA • POCONOS • WISCONSIN

RABBI ELLIOT DORFF, PH.D.

Rector and Distinguished Professor of Philosophy, American Jewish University

[Adapted with the permission of the author and the publisher from Elliot N. Dorff, *Knowing God: Jewish Journeys to the Unknowable* (Lanham, MD: Rowman and Littlefield, 1992), 10–11.]

I grew up in a typical "second-generation" Jewish home in Milwaukee. The vast majority of my contemporaries dropped out of Jewish education after their bar or bat mitzvah, and they generally remember the experience of religious school as meaningless and boring.

My own case was very different because my parents sent me to Camp Ramah in Wisconsin. I was twelve years old during my first summer at Camp Ramah, and I am convinced that had I not been there then, I would have dropped out of Jewish religious life after my bar mitzvah ceremony the following June, following the example of virtually all of my friends. It was not that I had some kind of religious revelation at Ramah; at the beginning it was simply a nice camping experience. Even at age twelve, however, I was impressed by the fact that Judaism was truly a way of life for the people at camp. It was not restricted to prayer and study, although we did more of those than I had ever done before; Judaism affected every aspect of life at camp, from discussions with friends to the evening activities to the sports field. I loved the singing and the dancing; the Hebrew that I was learning to speak in classes, at the waterfront, and on the baseball diamond; and the beauty of the traditional Sabbath observances. It was all so natural and unselfconscious. For the first time in my life, Judaism was a source of guidance and joy and not simply a burden that I carried as a member of a minority in a Christian culture.

Through my summers at Ramah as a camper and counselor, and through my Jewish studies during the academic years that intervened, I came to recognize the factors that were involving me more and more in religious life. I liked the depth of the relationships the Jewish environment created. We were certainly not saints in any sense of the term, but at Ramah we had a heightened awareness of moral norms and of the need to be sensitive to other people's needs. We were not embarrassed by talking about behavior and helping people with their problems; it was simply part of what was expected of every one of us.

The intellectual stimulation grew by leaps and bounds as I became older. Indeed, the most exciting and mind-stretching conversations I had took place at camp. Ironically, in this religious environment, rather than anywhere else, I felt more able to raise any questions that occurred to me. The leaders of the camp, in fact, prodded us to confront our problems with religious commitment. We were encouraged to ask questions we had never dared to discuss publicly, and the leaders themselves raised issues none of us had ever thought of. This exciting intellectual ferment was coupled with a sense of structure, of rootedness, and of purpose to life that was missing in the lives of all of my non-religious friends. Consequently, when I decided to become a rabbi, my chief aim was to reproduce the experiences Ramah had given me — to share the spoils, as it were.

60

WISCONSIN

SIDRA DEKOVEN EZRAHI, PH.D.
Professor, The Hebrew University of Jerusalem

I definitely would not have moved to Israel if it were not for Camp Ramah. Looking back on all these years, I think that camp, like Israel, was a kind of utopia. It was a perfect world; it was a perfectly artificial world that was created for use by people who had great intuitions and a great vision.

60

EDWIN R. FRANKEL
Ritual Director, Congregation Agudas Achim, Bexley, Ohio

I was sixteen when I first attended a Ramah camp. It was an eye-opening experience for me. It was the beginning of more than twenty summers in which I thrived at four Ramah camps, not to mention an occasional Shabbat at Nyack as a Jewish Theological Seminary (JTS) student.

It was amazing. I was living among Jews who were serious about their Judaism, Jews who had not grown up as *shomerei mitzvot* or breaking their teeth on Hebrew or leading *tefillot.*

I grew up with *shul* as home away from home. I spoke Hebrew from the time I started school. To me, Hebrew was not a foreign language but a second language. To me, participating in shul life is like breathing; I could not go on without it. Still, Ramah was wild. Printing and reading daily *hoda'ot* in Hebrew, hearing Hebrew announcements in the *ḥadar ochel,* or just chatting in Hebrew with fellow staff, particularly *mishlaḥat* members, were all experiences I could not have expected. Nowhere except in Israel had I lived in an atmosphere that was so fully dedicated to using Hebrew as a natural part of life.

I believed then, as I do still today, in the Ramah of my earliest youth. I was a devotee of Ramah long before I first got there. Campers who came to United Synagogue Youth (USY) *kinnusim* with songs and ideas they learned at Ramah motivated me. I was amazed by the Ramahniks' devotion to Hebrew. I was captivated by the high standards required to be invited to attend Ramah. Heck, back then, I even remember synagogue members who were turned down by Ramah for insufficient Hebrew skills. Ramah valued Hebrew, and that impressed me no end.

Ramah's devotion to Hebrew diminished a bit over the years. I never heard English spoken publicly during my first years at Ramah, but by my last summer at camp there were camp leaders who struggled to express themselves in Hebrew. Yet, even their struggle to use Hebrew was motivating. I hope I did my part to encourage Hebrew usage. I know it was a major aspect of my work in radio where I forbade broadcasters to use English on the air. (Remember the big Beatles hit *"Hi ohevet otecha"*?)

My experience at Ramah helped shape my professional career. I still consider myself a Jewish educator. At Ramah I recognized the impact that Jewish education can have on students and their families, particularly when conducted outside the classroom. At Ramah, I was able to live a dream where the process of learning was more important than the content. At Ramah, I could create programs in which there was room for *tanach* and *torah shebe'al peh,* but also for *rikkud* and *serigah.*

What is the biggest impact? I am several years past fifty, and if I had the means and opportunity, I would bring my bride of three years to camp and do it all again. Perhaps with the right push, I could even get my own kids (now grown) to join us on staff.

60

BERKSHIRES · CANADA

RABBI MATTHEW FUTTERMAN
Anshe Emet Synagogue, Chicago, Illinois

My friends' stories about life at summer camps with Indian-sounding names hardly prepared me for my first summer at Ramah in the Berkshires. I had expected that like my friends from home, I, too, would learn survival skills and improve my performance on the ball field. Although Ramah offered sports and swimming, camping and hiking, and we put on lots of Broadway musicals, that was not what Ramah was all about.

Ramah was about building and shaping community—the ideal Jewish community. That is what was at the heart of my Ramah experiences between 1966 (my first summer as a Ramah camper) and 2004 (my most recent summer as a staff member).

I originally went to camp to make my parents proud—especially my father. My father spent many summers at Camp Kindervelt, a Yiddish-speaking camp with a labor Zionist orientation that had a profound impact on his Jewish outlook. Perhaps because we did not speak Yiddish at home, my parents did not send me to Kindervelt.

I grew up in a very different Jewish world than my father. To my grandfather's great dismay, my parents chose to send me to Hebrew school instead of *folk schule.* I attended junior congregation weekly and learned to read Torah at the same age that my father learned to read Sholem Aleichem. According to family legend, after my grandfather heard that I had been registered to begin Hebrew school at the synagogue, he called from Florida to berate my parents and angrily shouted at them, "You want he should become a rabbi!?"

No thought was further from their minds at the time when they proudly informed me that Rabbi Sam Schafler, *z"l,* our rabbi at Temple Gates of Prayer in Flushing, had called and wanted me to go to Ramah. My parents understood that this was a very prestigious honor. And, in my father's mind, Ramah would be my Kindervelt.

Ramah became the laboratory in which I prepared for my "real life." The stories which my counselors told about their experiences in Israel on Ramah Seminar gave birth to my Zionist yearnings. The *sheliḥim* who arrived in camp following the Six-Day War further stoked those flames. My dreams of actually living in Israel were given shape by talks delivered by both our head sports counselor, Rabbi Alex Kaplan, and my swimming teachers, Rabbi Phil and Barbara Spectre, who spoke about Israel and their aliyah with great passion.

I had my first inkling that Ramah was different and special during my first Shabbat baseball game at Ramah. When we arrived at the field, we were informed by our counselors that we would not be keeping score. Being eleven years old, that did not make sense to me. But sports on Shabbat was not about competition—it was about playing ball just for the fun of playing ball.

That lesson was driven home later that day at the weekly Shabbat staff game. The counselors, who also did not keep score, made sure that every (male) staff member who wanted to play was given a chance no matter how skilled or unskilled he was at baseball. Until that day, baseball had always been about athletic prowess. That was the day that I learned that doing the right thing was more important than doing things right.

This was a new world for me. The staff played ball for fun. And these were the same staff members who read Torah, taught Hebrew, and delivered *divrei tefillah* at our morning services. This was the Ramah philosophy at its best—well-rounded, multi-talented individuals, who were skilled athletes and expert daveners, were walking the talk.

During my first summer as a staff member, I took part in the Mador counselor training program run by Rabbi David Mogilner, *z"l.* I learned that what made Ramah special was that it was about making a difference. Mogilner defined education as the process of effecting behavioral changes meaningfully and purposefully. He taught us to think like educators by identifying our goals. At our first group meeting he asked, "What should be my first question?" We were stymied until he taught us the obvious and said, "It depends on my purpose."

More than anyone else that summer, my advisor Rabbi Steven Brown, now head of school at the Jack M. Barrack Hebrew Academy in Philadelphia, facilitated my growth and shaped the way I approached every aspect of camp routine. Nothing prepared me more for my years as a teacher and even more so as a parent than spending that summer with Steve Brown. Perhaps the most important publication issued by Ramah was the counselor's manual edited by Steve in which he incorporated many of the lessons used to turn *madornikim* into *madrichim.*

I had the great fortune that summer to be assigned to work with an experienced senior counselor, Paul Kurland, now the rabbi of the Nanuet Hebrew Center. Paul was the role model who showed me up close how to rise to each challenge posed by camp life during the many summers we worked together. And for the last thirty-five years, he has been my dearest friend and sounding board for the subsequent challenges we have tackled together and separately as rabbis and educators.

Whether establishing *bikkur ḥolim* groups or forming *niḥum avelim* committees in my community, I always think back to the visions of two other mentors and friends, Rabbi David Zisenwine, director of several Ramah camps in the 1970s and 1980s, and David August, *z"l,* Berkshires director from 1972 to 1976. Both were visionaries who believed that the essence of Ramah was the focus on "community." Zisenwine had dreamt of giving campers in the oldest *edah* (division) a summer of autonomous living, with all the responsibilities inherent in such an arrangement on the shoulders of the campers. It was a bold idea. August treated us all like family. We were not just campers or staff members—we were his children. He would take long walks with us and listen as we pondered our futures. Having made the transition from head schoolmaster in Montreal to family therapist, August taught me the importance of always looking for new challenges. I have missed his warm and knowing smile for far too many years.

Throughout my years in the rabbinate I have forced myself to identify my goals and make sure that my methods were in alignment with those goals. I continually return to the tools gifted to me by my teachers, mentors, and dear friends from Ramah. And I have endeavored to find ways to replicate Ramah's approach to life and learning in my congregations, schools, and communities.

My Ramah mentors had one thing in common: They were shaping the future of Conservative Judaism by teaching us how to live as committed Conservative Jews. They were contributing to the spiritual life of the State of Israel by shaping the values of so many educated Jews who chose to make aliyah or who came from Israel to work in Ramah camps. They helped to give direction to American Jewry by designing the laboratories in which future lay leaders and professional rabbis experimented while still novices in their fields of dreams.

Rabbi Nahman of Bratslav is famous for saying, *lechol makom she'elav ani holech, ani holech le'eretz yisra'el.* ("Everywhere I go, I go to the Land of Israel.") In my case, I say, "Everywhere I go, I call upon my Ramah training."

CANADA

BENNY GAMLIELI

Former *mishlaḥat* member

[Translated from the Hebrew by Rabbi Mitchell Cohen, National Ramah Director.]

Camp Ramah has had a major impact on my family. From a social perspective, my two sons Omer and Itai developed many close friendships at camp and have kept many of those friendships well beyond their camper years. When their North American friends from camp came to Israel, they always called and often visited, which was great for my sons and also helped to connect their American and Canadian friends to real life in Israel.

But the biggest influence that Ramah had upon my sons was in the area of religious development, particularly prayer. Omer and Itai had one set of grandparents from Yemen and one set from Romania. Each summer when we traveled to Camp Ramah, my boys would get excited about the Conservative prayers, which were more understandable to them than the liturgy they were used to. They enjoyed praying with boys and girls together, and they particularly loved all of the camp melodies. When we'd return to Eilat after the summer, we would return home from our Yemenite synagogue, and they would sing with all their hearts—*birkat hamazon, havdalah,* and other prayers that they had learned at camp—using the tunes that reminded them of the summer.

To this day my sons, who are now grown up and living in New York, make me extraordinarily happy and proud because they put on tefillin each morning, even though I do not. And every Friday and Saturday, they go to *beit keneset.* This is all because of the influence of Camp Ramah in Canada. I have no doubt that the "window" that was opened for them on their souls at Camp Ramah in Canada helps them to this day and maintains within them a strong sense of their religious roots, even though they are living far from home. And I have no doubt that Ramah continues to have a very strong impact on Israelis of all ages who come to camp.

WISCONSIN

MINDA WOLFF GARR
Instructor, The Paul Baerwald School of Social Work and Social Welfare,
The Hebrew University of Jerusalem

Looking back to my Ramah experiences, I can trace a clear connection to my years in Ramah and my eventual aliyah. I began a long (and still ongoing) career with Ramah in 1957 at the age of ten at Camp Ramah in Wisconsin. In my seven years as a camper, I had the benefit of being exposed to a variety of Hebrew enthusiasts and Israelis who insisted that I talk to them in Hebrew. Although I went to Hebrew school, in those days we didn't learn conversational Hebrew. Yet I had counselors and *rashei edah,* as well as teachers, who insisted that I make the effort. Among those that I remember were Ruti, *z"l,* and Benni Mushkin. I also grew to love Israeli songs and dances.

When the opportunity arose to go to Israel with the Ramah Seminar, I did not hesitate. From the moment I arrived in Israel I felt I had come home. I was able to carry on conversations (on a basic level) in Hebrew with relatives, and I was familiar with the culture of song and dance. Later, during my years as a counselor at Ramah Wisconsin, some of us would talk about starting a kibbutz together in Israel so we could carry on the atmosphere of camp "forever." We weren't the ones who did that, but during my sophomore year of college, one of my camp friends, Avi Davis, called and asked if "we" were going to Israel for our junior year. Then the calls went back and forth, and eventually, several of us came as a group for our junior year to Hebrew University. Again, I felt that I had come home. Hebrew came to me easily, and I felt at home in the culture. Many a Friday night I would sit with relatives who had fought in the War of Independence and sing song after song together with them. They were always astounded at the broad repertoire of songs that we could sing together.

Through my Ramah experiences, I always felt a very deep connection to Israel and to its language and culture. When I came to Israel in my junior year, it became clear to me within the first month of *ulpan* that this is where I belong. That feeling has never changed. I stayed until I married my husband Ronnie four years later (we had met at Ramah), and we came back to Israel thirty years ago. We have been privileged to spend the last twenty-eight summers at Ramah Wisconsin and to give our children the benefit of integrating the best of the American Jewish experience into their lives.

CONNECTICUT
NEW ENGLAND · POCONOS

RELA MINTZ GEFFEN, PH.D.
Former President, Baltimore Hebrew University

Says she will go anywhere for the sake of the movement." I read this statement during staff week at Ramah Poconos in the summer of 1976. As a member of the *hanhalah,* I had access to the camp personnel files, and I was reading the notes that Rabbi David Mogilner, *z"l,* had placed in my file after an exit interview with me in 1960, when I was seventeen. I had spent that summer as a counselor-in-training (CIT) for a bunk of ten-year-olds in the Connecticut camp. Suffice it to say that it had not been a great summer for me. I was about to leave for Israel for a year as a representative of United Synagogue Youth (USY) to the *machon lemadrichei ḥutz la'aretz.* I told David that I wanted to return as a counselor after the year in Israel but not to Connecticut and definitely not to work with ten-year-olds. He said, "Okay, you'll come to my camp." I did, and he made me a counselor in the Machon at Ramah in the Poconos. That is how I, a New Yorker, came to be at the Poconos camp during the summers of 1962 and 1963.

I must confess that as a child I refused to go to Ramah, having heard that they had classes every day. I ended up in Massad from the ages of ten to fourteen because nobody told me that *siḥot* were actually classes.

During the summers of 1962 and 1963, Mogilner taught a counselor education class several times a week. None of us would ever be the same. To this day I can hear him exhorting us to be "honorable and accessible role models." I can close my eyes and see him in his red jacket in the *ḥadar ochel* reminding all of us to dress warmly because *"im kar li, kar lachem"* or moving us along to the next activity by saying *"hasha'ah achshav, lefi she'oni, shehu be'etzem she'on hamaḥaneh. . . ."*

During those idyllic summers, there were two full counselors and two Madorniks in every bunk! Counselor musicals were directed by the multi-talented Rabbi Efry Spectre, *z"l.* Professor Gershon Cohen taught one of the counselor classes, and Dr. Israel Francus taught another. It was during the summer of 1963 that I became seriously involved with another Machon counselor—Michael Monson. One day we came late to Mogilner's class. This was a serious infraction. We explained by saying we had been up late studying gemara for Rav Francus. From then on "studying gemara" became a euphemism for behavior that usually took place in the bushes!

Michael and I were married in June of 1964. In June of 1967, we went to Camp Ramah in Palmer, he as the administrator of the lower camp and

I as a teacher. What a summer! We had a super group of teachers working with Rabbi Neal Kaunfer as *rosh ḥinuch.* We taught the Joseph stories to the upper camp and ate, slept, and drank Joseph for nine weeks. All of us read the Thomas Mann version in *Joseph and His Brothers* and had the great good fortune to study the text with Professor José Faur.

Following camp we left for Israel for Michael's fourth year of rabbinical school. It was just after the Six-Day War and an amazing time to be living in Jerusalem. We stayed the next summer to be counselors on Ramah Seminar. I became pregnant with our older son Uri that summer. I went to the group leader and asked if I could be excused from climbing Masada as I thought I was pregnant. "That's too serious a decision for me to make," said the *rosh kevutzah.* "You'd better ask David." Yup, David Mogilner was directing the Israel Seminar program. Our lives were still running in tandem!

Several years later, in 1976, Michael and I were living in Philadelphia. I got a call from David. He was coming to America to direct Ramah in the Poconos for one summer. He wanted me to be *rosh ḥinuch* and Michael to be an advisor in the Mador. "But I don't know how to be a *rosh ḥinuch,*" I replied. "Don't worry," he said. "I'll help you." And so he did until that terrible day at the end of the sixth week of camp when he collapsed, and we, the *hanhalah,* had to absorb the shock, break the news to the campers and staff, and manage the camp for the remainder of the summer. I remember walking around the campus with Michael Brown, who was directing the Mador. We were all in shock. Every place we looked we saw David's shadow. And I still do. Quite regularly, a word, phrase, or action by an educator or other leader triggers an automatic response in me, which I know was instilled by David Mogilner. And I am not the only one. A whole generation of Jewish educators, rabbis, and lay leaders were shaped by his dynamic personality and charismatic teaching. His memory is more than a blessing, it is an on-going inspiration.

60

CALIFORNIA · NEW ENGLAND · NYACK

SUSAN NORTH GILBOA
Jewish educator, special needs program director, and dance instructor
Encino, California

My life's journey took me down a path of no return when I spent my first summer as a camper at Ramah in Palmer, Massachusetts, in 1968. From that point on, I felt the only time I matured each year and learned about life and friendships was during the eight weeks I was at Camp Ramah. At age twelve, I was buddies with a camper in the Tikvah program. Although I thought that I needed to help her do or learn things, it was she who taught me to look at what someone with special needs can do. I was blessed with the opportunity to dance with Tirza Hodes, who was among the pioneers of Israeli dance and was a member of the Palmer *mishlaḥat.* She shared her love of dance, of Israel, of children, and of life. She had a strong personality coupled with a smile that could make anyone dance. Tirza became my first Israeli dance mentor, teaching me Israeli dances while teaching me about our culture and our people.

I had another life-changing experience when I went to Israel for the first time with Ramah Seminar in 1973. Seeing Israel with close friends with whom I had already shared such intense experiences at camp, meeting relatives for the first time and being proud to tell them I was traveling for six weeks with other American teenagers, and meeting Israelis who shared their passion for the land and its people—all contributed to creating my strong connection with Israel.

I can honestly say that the choices I made as a teenager and later in my adult life have largely been the result of my experiences with Ramah. I have dedicated my life to giving back to Ramah, the Jewish community, and to Israel. I became a counselor at Ramah Nyack in the summer of 1974 and went on to be a *seganit rosh edah* for one year. Shulamit Kivel (also my Israeli dance mentor) supported and encouraged me to be *rosh rikkud,* a position I held for six years.

After living in Israel, where I taught pre-school children with special needs and received an Israeli Dance Instructor's Certification from the Ministry of Education, I returned to the United States to earn my Master's degree in Special Education and Creative Movement. Then I accepted a teaching job in California, where I met and married Rami Gilboa. Early in our relationship, it was clear to Rami that Ramah was going to be a part of our lives. In 1990 I became rosh rikkud at Ramah in Ojai, California for the summer camp program, as well as the yearly Family Camp. Our children's early years were spent in the loving arms of campers and staff at Ramah. After seven years of being a camper, Talia went on Ramah Seminar 2005 and Aviv went on Seminar 2007. (I must say that receiving daily e-mails is quite different than the communication system we had when I was on Seminar in 1973.) Following their summers on Seminar, without hesitation, both Talia and Aviv applied to be counselors. They would say that it was not only important to their parents but that it was also important to them to give back to Ramah, and that the best way to give back was to give other kids the kinds of experiences that they had when they were campers.

I'm proud to be a Jewish educator who has had the opportunity for the past thirty-five years to teach and share the love of Israeli dance with hundreds and hundreds of Jewish children and adults.

The influence of my family, the synagogue where I grew up, and my rabbi, Albert Thaler, who first suggested that I go to Ramah and later was director of Ramah Nyack, cannot be understated in my choice of career. As a Jewish educator, the passion and love I have when teaching Israeli dance, along with my desire to create and direct programs for children with special needs, comes directly from my earliest experiences at Camp Ramah.

60

WISCONSIN

RABBI NEIL GILLMAN, PH.D.
Professor of Jewish Thought, The Jewish Theological Seminary

I first came to Camp Ramah in the summer of 1956 after having spent eleven summers in a conventional summer camp in Canada. By conventional, I mean a camp that featured a robust sports program, a color war, dances every Saturday night, and a culture that encouraged competition, hazing, and socializing with the girls at a camp located across the lake. As I grew older, I discovered that the lake was eminently bridgeable. I have very few fond memories of those eleven summers.

I entered the Rabbinical School at The Jewish Theological Seminary (JTS) in the fall of 1954 with almost no prior knowledge of the institutions of the Conservative Movement. During my second year there, my classmates urged me to accompany them to Ramah, and there seemed to be no question that by Ramah, they meant Wisconsin.

After overcoming my memories of my earlier camp experiences, I applied to join the Wisconsin staff. I discovered that I had to undergo an interview with the camp *hanhalah*. Seated around the table was an imposing group of Ramah veterans—Jerry Abrams (then the director of Ramah Wisconsin), Burt Cohen and the late David Mogilner (the *rashei edah*), Jack Bloom, Bezalel "Buzzy" Porten, and others. I knew nothing about how to be a counselor, and nothing about education. The interview was grueling, as grueling as my admissions interview to the Rabbinical School, and I'm sure I made a fool of myself. But I was accepted and assigned a Machon bunk.

To my amazement, the camp staff began to meet in mid-winter for two hours on Sunday nights in a JTS classroom. Every piece of counseling—not only the Jewish education issues—was discussed, including how to wake up the kids, how to put them to sleep (we called it *hashkavah* in those days), how to handle the first night, the first meal, the table experience (*hashulḥan beramah*) in camp, how to deal with scapegoats, and the rest. What I learned then, and what has remained with me to this day, was that every single encounter with every camper is potentially an educational opportunity; and there is a Jewish way of structuring each of these moments. Jewish education took place every moment of every day, not only in the classroom—not even mainly in the classroom.

The first clash between my old camp culture and the Ramah experience occurred in the first few days of camp when my bunk played basketball against a neighboring bunk. Using my color war experience, I urged my campers to be more physical and to use their elbows under the baskets. David Mogilner took me aside and murmured, "That's not the way we play basketball in Ramah." "No?" I responded, "In other words, in Ramah, the point of the game is to lose!" "Right on," he smiled. So there was a Jewish way of playing basketball, of eating, of speaking to your campers, and so forth.

I spent the summers of 1956, 1957, and 1958 in camp. We were bunk counselors, we taught classes, and we planned our campers' evening and Shabbat programs. I was naive, but we were made to feel that the overall goal of the camp experience was to change the world. Transform enough Ramah campers, and we will transform the American Jewish community; transform the American Jewish community, and we will transform America; transform America, and we will transform the world. It was as simple as that. It was this impulse that made it possible to endure the cold and the exhaustion; that, and the sense of collegiality that united an extraordinarily talented staff. I particularly remember Morty and Margie Tutnauer's wedding, which was held by the lake on the last night of camp in 1957, and was preceded by a week of classes on weddings, marriage, love, and sex in Judaism. The wedding was held under a *ḥuppah* created by their campers, followed by a wedding *se'udah* with *sheva berachot* and the whole shebang.

The campers and the staff members from those summers included other men and women who became prominent Jewish educators, rabbis, academicians, and community leaders: Lee Shulman, the late Dan Elazar, Jack Bloom, Jeff Tigay, Leon (Label) Waldman, Joe Young (later to join the staff of the National Institutes of Health [NIH]), and many others.

In my second summer in Wisconsin, I met the woman who was to become my wife. We were married in late 1958, and our Ramah career was interrupted for a number of years until we had young children. My wife then returned to Ramah Berkshires for a number of years as a *yo'etzet* in the Mador.

Our children later attended Ramah Berkshires, and I subsequently lectured in all of the Ramah camps. So the chain continues.

CALIFORNIA
NEW ENGLAND · WISCONSIN

GIL GRAFF, PH.D.
Executive Director, Bureau of Jewish Education, Los Angeles, California

In the course of my junior year at Hebrew University, I met dozens of Ramahniks from across the United States and Canada and was impressed with their common commitment to Jewish life, as well as by their unbridled enthusiasm about Ramah. While completing a degree in Jewish studies and earning a teaching credential in Chicago, I decided to apply to the local Ramah camp—Wisconsin—for a summer position. I was heading to law school at the University of Southern California in the fall, and I saw this as an interesting, one time experience. Little did I know. . . .

I was interviewed for a position as a counselor by the camp director, Rabbi Burton Cohen, in the spring of 1973. The interview, conducted in Hebrew, probed my understanding of the meaning and implications of a camp that defined itself as "*dati, ḥinnuchi, ivri.*" The depth of the interview was an apt prelude to the experience of being part of a community that thought about the Jewish educational significance of every activity, 24/7. From waking up campers, to seating in the dining hall, to relationships on the sports fields, to *tefillah,* Shabbat, and more—every aspect of life was the subject of deliberate action and reflection. Among the many exceptional educators whom I met that summer was Yosi Gordon, then the associate principal of Los Angeles Hebrew High School. Rabbi Gordon suggested that I join the faculty of L.A. Hebrew High, if only on a part-time basis while attending law school—an offer that I readily accepted.

Over the ensuing three years, while studying and teaching, I spent summers as a *rosh edah* at Camp Ramah, Ojai. The principal of L.A. Hebrew High, Rabbi Sheldon Dorph, was (and remains) a remarkable, educational personality. It was through contact with Rabbi Dorph, and the educational vision that animated him, that I began to think of Jewish education as a full-time calling. It was at L.A. Hebrew High and Ramah that I met Robin and, as Ramah celebrates its sixtieth anniversary, we will be marking our thirtieth.

By the early 1980s, Ramah was, for both of us, a year-round second home. One day, a call came from New York, inquiring about my possible interest in being considered for the position of director of Camp Ramah in New England. Neither Robin nor I had ever visited the area, let alone seen the Palmer camp. However, we did know from experiences at Wisconsin and Ojai, the power of the Ramah experience.

Our years at Camp Ramah in New England were extraordinary. In Palmer, as in Ramah Wisconsin and California, we interacted with outstanding, highly dedicated men and women. Some were accomplished senior educators; others were in the early stages of preparing for leadership roles in Jewish life as active *ba'alei battim,* clergy, and educators.

For the past twenty-plus years, I have served as an executive at the Los Angeles Bureau of Jewish Education. I have no doubt that my choice to engage in such work is due to the ten summers that I spent at Ramah camps. Thank you to all who have created and who help sustain the experience called Ramah.

60

BERKSHIRES · POCONOS

JULES GUTIN
Director of Youth Activities, United Synagogue of Conservative Judaism

I was a latecomer to Ramah. I didn't begin my Ramah experience until the summer of 1964 at the age of fourteen. I spent only two summers as a camper—during the first two years of Ramah in the Berkshires. For me, those two summers were critical to my growth as a Jew. As a day school graduate who went on to public high school, the unique experience at camp left a lasting impression. It was exciting to see many of my new Ramah friends throughout the year at United Synagogue Youth (USY) events and at Prozdor at The Jewish Theological Seminary (JTS). Some of those friendships endure to this day, over forty years later.

When the time came to travel to Israel in the summer of 1966, I chose Ramah Seminar. It might sound surprising that the person who currently serves as the director of USY (and was a regional USY officer at the time) chose Ramah instead of USY Pilgrimage. The truth is that it was not an unusual decision. Our Seminar group of eighty-two participants included many active USYers. We saw no conflict. Memories of that summer are still fresh in my mind. We were the last Seminar group to spend the summer in a divided

Jerusalem. Whenever I visit Israel, I still recall the barricades and walls at various intersections in Jerusalem dividing Israel from Jordan.

The summer of 1967 was spent at Ramah in the Poconos in the Mador program. That may have been the most pivotal summer of my life. The intensive staff-training program, which included regular classes dealing with educational concepts, probably convinced me to become a Jewish educator. I still remember and use many of the concepts I learned that summer.

After having been on staff for two summers at Ramah in the Berkshires, many years later (in 1990), my family began to enjoy the benefits of Ramah in the Poconos. My wife Yehudit, who never had the opportunity to attend a Ramah camp, became the *gannenet,* and our four children became campers. Yehudit eventually became a teacher and spent fourteen wonderful summers at camp. Our children all went on to serve as staff members, and I became a staff spouse, often teaching during my visits.

For all of us, our Ramah experiences were an important part of our Jewish growth. Even though we each came to camp with strong Jewish backgrounds, the overall experience added a missing dimension.

NEW ENGLAND

ISAAC "BUJI" HERZOG

Israeli Minister of Welfare and Social Services

I was a waiter at Camp Ramah in New England in the 1970s. That summer I was privileged to tutor a girl in the Tikvah special needs program. That experience taught me so much and contributed a great deal to my leadership skills and my desire to help disadvantaged populations, which plays a large role in my work as a member of Israel's current administration.

BERKSHIRES • NYACK • WISCONSIN

RABBI JEFFREY HOFFMAN, D.H.L.
Rabbi in Residence, The Academy for Jewish Religion;
Adjunct Assistant Professor of Liturgy, The Jewish Theological Seminary

I was always interested in Jewish tradition from the time I was very young although I didn't grow up in a halachically observant home. I was thrilled to go to Israel on the Ramah Community Program (part of Ramah Seminar) in 1970. There I met Rabbi Al Thaler and soon-to-be-Rabbi Herb Kavon, who later co-officiated at my wedding. But I still hadn't imbibed the kind of Ramah experience that made such an impression on me later.

During my senior year in high school, my teacher in Hebrew high school at Marathon Jewish Community Center in Little Neck, Queens, was Sandy Goldstein. She told me I *must* go to Ramah. She said the Mador program was for me. And so I applied, was accepted, and went that summer to Ramah in the Berkshires. I owe a lot to Sandy!

That first summer I was on staff in the youngest *edah,* Nitzanim. I didn't know much about daily prayer, Shabbat, and so forth. I remember that Phil Warmflash, one of the counselors in my edah, gave many of the *divrei torah* during *shaḥarit.* I probably learned more about daily prayer that summer than at any other time in my life. The same is true regarding Shabbat and *zemirot.* Later on, I made those elements mine by intense study and teaching about them. But in the summer of 1973, my soul was almost a clean slate at the perfect time to have deep Jewish experiences etched upon it.

I studied Talmud for the first time that summer. I remember sitting in the *sifriyyah* with our teacher, Ranon Katzoff. We studied part of *massechet Berachot* in the Hebrew Steinsaltz edition. I didn't follow most of it, but I fell in love with it. There was a serious-looking fellow who used to walk around with no kids to look after, and I wondered who he was. I found out he was Rabbi Neil Gillman, the professor-in-residence. Later Rabbi Gillman became a teacher of mine, then a colleague, mentor, and friend.

Among the friends I met that summer were Paul Saposh, *z"l,* Bill David, and Laurie Mark. Paul and Bill became lifelong friends. Laurie became my wife. We're proud to have a plaque up on the couples' wall at Ramah in the Berkshires.

I later served on staff at Ramah Nyack for two years. (Little did I know then that I would be the rabbi at the Conservative synagogue in Nyack from 1984 to 2004!) I transferred to Wisconsin Ramah because my girlfriend Laurie was from Minnesota, and Wisconsin was her home camp. I spent several summers on staff at Wisconsin. My love for *kabbalat shabbat* services deepened as the entire camp community gathered on Friday nights in front of Lake Buckatabon in Wisconsin.

It was at Ramah Wisconsin that Rabbi Bezalel "Buzzy" Porten provided me with a background in literary analysis of prayer and Bible that is still the basis for what I teach. Buzzy shared the beginnings of a translation and commentary on the siddur that he had written. He also exposed me to Cassuto's commentary on the Torah.

I want to say "Thank you!" to Camp Ramah. I owe a great deal of my love for Torah to you!

60

DAROM

LEONARD KAPLAN AND MAYER "BUBBA" MITCHELL, *z"l*

Founders and benefactors, Camp Ramah Darom

[Interview conducted by Rabbi Mitchell Cohen, National Ramah Director, April 2007.]

On a beautiful spring afternoon at Ramah Darom in Georgia in April 2007, I attended the camp's tenth anniversary celebration and Shabbaton for founders, funders, and key camp leaders. While sitting in the dining room with Mayer "Bubba" Mitchell, *z"l*, and Leonard Kaplan, the two key founders and financial supporters of this newest Ramah camp, and their wives, Arlene Mitchell and Tobee Kaplan, I was treated to a delightful hour of warm reminiscences and inspiration. They spoke to me about the reasons they became involved with Ramah and about their efforts to convince others of what Chancellor Ismar Schorsch of The Jewish Theological Seminary had convinced them of: that building a Ramah camp for the South "was just about the most important thing they could possibly do for their children and grandchildren and for the Jewish people."

A Deep and Enduring Friendship. Over and over, the conversation returned to a common theme: the deep and enduring friendship that developed between Bubba and Leonard because of their efforts to build Ramah Darom. "I had known Leonard as an acquaintance through our work with the American Israel Public Affairs Committee (AIPAC)," Bubba commented, "but we really became brothers through our work to create this camp." According to Leonard, "By far the most satisfying part of my work for Darom was the friendship I developed with Bubba Mitchell. He got me involved and kept me involved, and I owe him a great deal for all that I have gotten out of this incredible venture." As Tobee Kaplan phrased it, "A love affair was created between these two men which made anything possible."

As I continued to talk with the Kaplans and the Mitchells, we were joined by Bubba's brother and business partner, Abe Mitchell, who also became a major contributor to Ramah Darom and serves the camp in various leadership capacities. Abe made it clear that he wanted the camp to act responsibly, from construction decisions to business practices, as "we must make every dollar count and count efficiently." Abe, too, spoke about the great satisfaction of seeing Ramah Darom continuing to thrive ten years after its first summer in 1997. "We still have work to do," he commented, "but it sure helps to see all the smiling faces of the kids and staff as they enjoy their time at Ramah."

Why Ramah? I asked them all to reflect on their commitment to Ramah, with so many Jewish causes competing for their contributions.

Bubba explained:

> I raised four children in Mobile, a small southern town, and luckily they all married Jews. But with the intermarriage rate at over 50%, I was concerned for my eight grandchildren and Jewish children all over America. Chancellor Schorsch taught me that camping is the most important building block, more important than anything else, because kids have fun being Jewish at Ramah.

Leonard added:

> I had been giving to a wide array of Jewish causes, and I really wanted to make a difference for the Jewish future. It became clear to me that Ramah would have the biggest impact of all for two reasons: first, because of its positive influence on youngsters, and second, because of the impact on future leadership. Ramah is clearly a breeding ground for future rabbis and educators. My own rabbi, Rabbi Eli Havivi (of Greensboro, North Carolina, who grew up at Camp Ramah in the Berkshires and later served as the director of Ramah in the Poconos) helped convince me of these truths, and I have absolutely no regrets.

As our conversation continued, I asked the Mitchells and Kaplans for their advice as we begin to seek support for the building of yet another new Ramah camp, Ramah in the Rockies. "You need to find your Moshe Rabbeinu," as Leonard jokingly calls Bubba. As Leonard expressed it:

> Our relationship created all the momentum and satisfaction, and you need others in Texas, Colorado, and other places to start working together like we did. We'll tell them our story and tell them why we gave and still give. But you have to find your leaders and not be shy about asking.

As we came to the end of our discussion, Bubba summed up things this way:

> Jewish children need Camp Ramah — they need to be in a Jewish majority, and they need to have fun with each other being Jewish. That's the key to our future, and I'm indebted to Rabbi Schorsch for getting me involved and for Leonard's friendship over all these years.

When we got up from our table and left the room, hundreds of celebrants greeted Bubba and Leonard, Ramah Darom "heroes" and best friends.

[Sadly, Bubba Mitchell passed away after a long illness less than six months after Ramah Darom's tenth anniversary celebration, on September 26, 2007. — RABBI MITCHELL COHEN]

60

WISCONSIN

BETSY DOLGIN KATZ, ED.D.
Former North American Director, Florence Melton Adult Mini-School

Beginnings. The role of Camp Ramah in Wisconsin in my career began with a Hebrew test and an interview with Rabbi Burton Cohen at Ner Tamid Congregation in Chicago. I was seventeen and one of three sisters from Fairbury, Illinois: population 2,500. Ours was the only Jewish family in a 100-mile radius. I passed the test that qualified me to be a junior counselor. My knowledge was a result of tutoring during the first thirteen years of my life by my father, Seymour F. Dolgin, *z"l*, who taught me Hebrew, holidays, and history in the playroom of our house. At camp that summer, I worked hard, played hard, and did all I could to fit in with the campers and my colleagues on the staff. I discovered a wholeness, a completeness that came from being part of a community that shared Jewish activities, ideas, and values. I treasured the feeling of belonging and living a life in which Judaism was a part of everything I did. And I learned that I could even contribute to the community that came to mean so much to me.

Teachers. The greatest influences on me during my camp years were the teachers with whom I was privileged to study: Louis Newman, *z"l*, Dr. Yochanan Muffs, *z"l*, Rabbi Nathan Gordon, and others. The formal classes and informal exchanges with these great teachers shaped my career. I cannot underestimate the significance of a few moments on the porch of the newly constructed *sifriyyah* talking with Seymour Fox, *z"l*, about the meaning of *veshinantam levanecha*.

Role models. As a counselor, I was influenced by individuals with whom I worked, people who continued their Jewish education away from camp and became rabbis and teachers: Jerry Zelizer, Leon Waldman, Jeff Tigay, Joel

Roth, Phil and Barbara Spectre, Helen and Moshe Davidson, Sidra DeKoven Ezrahi, Barry Chazan, and Michael Gratz. They not only attempted to live the texts we learned but made it possible for others to do so. They taught me to see Jewish learning and teaching as a part of life—not apart from it.

Hebrew. At Camp Ramah, Hebrew also came alive. Hebrew was the language of sports, bunk activities, drama, and the arts—not isolated drills in a classroom. Yet, it was also the holy language of the prayer book and Jewish texts. I still find myself singing songs from *South Pacific, Showboat,* and *Oklahoma* and longing for *kabbalat shabbat* on the lake.

Israel. After three years together as counselors, Michael (Rabbi Michael Katz) and I had the privilege of being on the staff of the Ramah Israel Seminar just two weeks after our wedding. It was a memorable experience, considering that it was our honeymoon and our first trip to Israel. I will always carry with me first impressions of our land. Some of my deep-felt connection to Israel and my political inclinations come from standing on Mount Zion in 1964 and trying to follow the guide's instructions so we could locate the *kotel* somewhere below us.

Preparation for a career in Jewish education. As a junior counselor I went to The Jewish Theological Seminary prior to camp to learn from Dr. Joseph Schwab how to run a bunk like a home. At the University of Michigan, I taught Sunday school and studied with other Ramahniks. Because of a Ramah connection, specifically Seymour Fox, *z"l,* Michael and I went to Ohio State University for graduate work where I met another Camp Ramah leader, Dr. Saul Wachs, education director at Congregation Tifereth Israel. Returning to Chicago after graduate school, I had to choose between becoming an English teacher and becoming a Jewish educator. The Ramah factor—and my father who said "there are a lot of English teachers in the world but not so many Jewish educators"—influenced my decision.

Lifelong learning. Camp Ramah was not just for the campers. It was also a center of learning for all the adults who were there, and learning became an integral part of my life. I continue to study today. As the director of the Florence Melton Mini-School, I shared my love of learning with Jewish adults across North America. What started at Camp Ramah in Wisconsin became my lifelong pursuit, my passion, my career, and, as I hoped when I was a junior counselor, a way to contribute to a community that means so much to me.

60

POCONOS

YOSSI KATZ
Instructor, Alexander Muss High School in Israel, Hod HaSharon

The day after I graduated from Temple University in May 1978, I got on an El Al airplane and made aliyah to Israel. There were four major influences on my decision to move "home" to Israel. The first was the Jewish-Zionist education I received at home from my wonderful parents, Irv and Miriam Katz, of blessed memory. The second influence was my Hebrew school teacher, Rebbetzin Ruth Chinitz, of blessed memory, in class *heh* at Temple Beth Ami in northeast Philadelphia. The third major influence on me was my Jewish youth group, United Synagogue Youth (USY), which inculcated in me so many important Jewish values such as Zionism, Shabbat, and *tikkun olam.*

Last, but certainly not least, among the Jewish-Zionist influences on my life was Camp Ramah in the Poconos, where I spent more than fifteen years as a camper, waiter, Madornik, *madrich,* and *rosh edah.* Camp Ramah taught me that Judaism was not just a religion that I needed to celebrate on Friday nights and Saturdays but was an all-encompassing identity. Ramah showed me that I belonged to a people that had a religion and a language and a culture and a history and a land. At Ramah I spoke Hebrew not only during *tefillah* but also during sports and meals and while socializing with friends. I already knew how to be a Jew on Shabbat; Ramah taught me how to be a Jew all week long, twenty-four hours a day! As I grew older, I wanted to live in a Jewish world just like Camp Ramah, and I came to understand that I could do that only in a Jewish country—in Israel.

I attended Camp Ramah in the Poconos for the first time in 1968. It was just after the 1967 Six-Day War, and I will never forget the first time I met the Israelis on the *mishlaḥat.* I was in Tze'irim and went to *shaḥarit* in the *mercaz* on the first morning. Sitting next to me was Yitzhak Hochman, a tall, handsome, muscular mishlaḥat member. Everyone called him "Hochla." Hochla, the first religious Israeli to make the Israeli National Basketball Team, was in camp as a sports instructor. Before services I was mesmerized as he spun a basketball on his finger like a Harlem Globetrotter. But what really amazed me was when he sat down next to me and helped me put on my tefillin. He wore his tefillin on his muscular arm and davened with *kavanah* and passion. For the first time in my life I saw a person who was both an accomplished athlete and a proud and strong Jew. Later, Hochla and his fellow mishlaḥat members came to my bunk for *hashkavah* (bedtime stories) and told us about fighting in the Six-Day War. I was so excited to learn about and meet real Jewish heroes.

Camp Ramah taught me that a Jew could play sports and have muscles and also put on tefillin every morning and daven. I have not missed a day of putting on tefillin or davening shaḥarit in the past forty years and much of that, like my decision to eventually make aliyah, is due to Hochla and Camp Ramah. In the 1973 Yom Kippur War, Hochla served in an elite commando unit of *Tzahal* and fell heroically in battle in the Sinai Desert. I will never forget his heroism and sacrifice, but most of all I will always remember how he lived his life Jewishly with commitment and devotion.

After making aliyah to Israel, I won the Israeli National Boxing Championship, served in an elite reconnaissance unit of Tzahal, and for the past twenty-seven years have worked as a Jewish educator at the Alexander Muss High School in Israel (AMHSI) in Hod Hasharon. In 2001 I had a student named Michael Levin from Philadelphia in my class at AMHSI.

On his first day, Michael noticed that I was wearing a hat from Camp Ramah in the Poconos and asked me if I had been a camper there. When I replied in the affirmative, Michael told me that he, too, had grown up at Camp Ramah in the Poconos. Quickly, I learned that Michael and I shared many bonds. We both came from Philadelphia and had been active in Hagesher Region USY. Michael and I immediately became great friends and spent long nights talking about Ramah, USY, Tastykakes, Breyers ice cream, soft pretzels, mustard . . . and most of all about Israel! Michael was an A+ student, an amazing human being, and a committed Jew. Camp Ramah was a great influence on him as well, and in 2003 Michael made aliyah to Israel and joined the Israeli paratroops.

In the summer of 2006, Michael received a month leave to visit his family in Philadelphia. While in the United States, he drove up to Camp Ramah in the Poconos to see his many camp friends. On July 12, 2006, he learned that the Hizbullah had attacked Israel and kidnapped two Israeli soldiers. Michael rushed back to Israel to join his comrades in arms. On August 1, 2006, Michael Levin fell heroically in battle in Aita el Shaab in Lebanon. He was buried on Tish'ah Be'av in the national military cemetery on Mount Herzl in Jerusalem.

Two of the greatest heroes I have known in my life, Yitzhak "Hochla" Hochman and Michael Levin, both attended Camp Ramah in the Poconos. They both personified the type of Jew that we need to build our people's future. They were living examples of Ramah values—loving Torah, the Jewish people, and the State of Israel. Michael and Hochla, like Camp Ramah, will forever serve as a light and an inspiration. Ramah means "heights," and the Jewish-Zionist education I received at Camp Ramah in the Poconos helped lead me to the heights of a fulfilling Jewish life in Israel.

CALIFORNIA · CONNECTICUT NEW ENGLAND · POCONOS

RABBI STUART KELMAN
Founding Rabbi, Congregation Netivot Shalom, Berkeley, California

Robert Alter, Robert Chazan, Ray Arzt, David Mogilner, *z"l,* Walter Ackerman, *z"l,* Gloria (Sussman) Silverman, *z"l,* Zalman Schachter Shalomi, Zvi Dershowitz, Saul Wachs, Shmuel Leiter, *z"l,* Gladys Gewirtz, Shalom Schwartz, David Lieber, *z"l,* Lee Levine, Nat Entin, *z"l,* Uri Simon—these are some of the people who were my counselors, teachers, camp directors, and mentors at Camp Ramah. Barry Chazan, Jeff Tigay, Ed Bruckner, Dan Ziff, *z"l,* Gail Zaiman, Shelly Dorph, Elliot Dorff, Joel Rembaum, Robert Goldenberg, Vicky Koltun, Liz Koltun, Judy Narrowe, Alan Mintz (both of them)—memories of those whom I counted as friends, co-workers, and campers all flood back as I sit down to write this refection.

The above are only a few of the names that now float up to my consciousness. There were others—many, many others who had a profound influence on my thoughts, my actions, and my life. To those who taught me Jewish texts, to those who influenced my passion for music, to those who were able to help me synthesize that love for music with the love of liturgy and probe the deeper meaning to which liturgy was a response, to those who showed me that Judaism's message was truly revolutionary and not simply evolutionary, to those who by example were constantly striving to improve and change the world we live in, to those who gave me the tools to relate to others, and to those who gave me the hope and courage to choose a career and a life devoted to passing on these teachings and experiences—I owe a debt far greater than words can express. The words from *kaddish derabbanan* echo in my mind: *talmidei talmideihem*—the students of their students. The teachings I garnered from my teachers at Ramah live on in me, in my students, and in the students of my students.

From Ramah in Connecticut to Massachusetts, to the Poconos, and to California—memories of a river and canoe trips, of Warren Edwards the caretaker of Connecticut, the haunted house, the Sukkah, to side Aleph and side Bet, to LTF and Super-LTF, to the *beit am,* the waterfront, *etz hatefillah,* the "new" *sifriyyah,* the *matzevah,* to the "old camp," the "new camp," the long road between, Orchidtown, the "townies"—the journey of just one person going from east to west and from external to internal.

Eight messages and meanings that I've learned:

1. Judaism is all embracing in terms of how one lives and how one relates to others.

2. Hebrew is a linking mechanism, and one can't really appreciate the depths of Jewish culture without learning *leshon hakodesh.*

3. The self-contained community that Ramah offers can be construed as an ideal, which living in real life can only come close to replicating.

4. The power of the peer group (community) cannot be underestimated.

5. Experimentation is a core fact in education. Ramah encouraged us to create something fresh, not merely repeat.

6. Individuals can change the world—sure, it sounds like a 1960s bumper-sticker—but sometimes those pieces of paper hint at a deep truth.

7. People influence people to change. Modeling works. My list of names above could have started with the phrase: "I want to be like. . . ."

8. Not everything is black or white, or we would not be living in the twenty-first century. Colors and gray and variation is what makes life so interesting—and choices so hard.

I can identify the person (colleague, friend, teacher, student, camper) who passed each of the above teachings on to me. Everyone came from Ramah.

Most important: help those you love to have a comparable Camp Ramah experience but don't expect that they will take away the same things from it that you did. We all found our individual paths to Judaism. Help your community maintain strong Ramah camps for all its children.

May Ramah grow and evolve and flourish while still remaining faithful to its founding vision.

60

CALIFORNIA
NEW ENGLAND • POCONOS

VICKY KELMAN
Director, Jewish Family Education Project, Bureau of Jewish Education, San Francisco, California

What flashes in my mind when considering the impact of Camp Ramah on my life is that I became a Jewish educator because a significant teacher told me (and persuaded me): "You have the power to change the world."

The teacher was Rabbi David Mogilner, *z"l.* The setting was Camp Ramah in the Poconos, my first summer as a counselor. A gift of having come of age in the 1960s was the optimism that one individual can make a difference and that a group of individuals with shared goals can change the world.

This "can-do" attitude with which I became imbued that summer was entwined with the deep meaning that living a Jewish life came to hold for me. We were encouraged to think about Jewish life in camp as a counterculture to the Judaism of the synagogues and homes that our campers (and we ourselves) came from. We were sent home to be revolutionaries within the Jewish communities in which we lived.

I can honestly say that since that summer, in my life as wife, parent, educator, community member, communal professional, colleague, and friend, I have very rarely accepted "no" for an answer or "we don't do it that way," or "that will never work." In fact, I have always considered those kinds of statements more as a challenge to action than as a roadblock.

When I worked with teens at Camp Ramah in New England in later years, I pushed the limits of the conventional wisdom regarding what young teenagers would willingly engage in during the summer. I remember having a regular poetry discussion circle with the campers in my bunk, listening to Handel's *Messiah* when preparing for Shabbat Naḥamu (when we read those same selections from Isaiah), and organizing evening programs devoted to discussions of civil rights and the Vietnam War, issues roiling our country at the time.

In my summers at Ramah in California, we demolished the idea that counselors wouldn't come to class. We demanded it, provided good teaching, and they came. We recreated the Mador (counselor training program for twelfth graders) so that it wasn't just "the next *edah*" but was a serious professional training program. When we decided that summer camp wasn't only for kids, I dreamed about and fashioned a Ramah Family Camp that didn't just bring families to camp but filled the experience with substantial Jewish content and quality time for the families.

Ramah also made an indelible mark on my personal life. I met my husband and many of our lifelong friends at Ramah. We raised our children at Ramah and saw all four become counselors and "roshes." When we were a family with four young children and two careers and people asked me, "How do you manage it all?" I would say, "I can administrate anything, I was a *rosh edah* at Camp Ramah." We modeled our home observance on the Jewish lives we imbibed at Ramah.

When I see my two-year-old grandson Yair, running free at camp, enjoying the action and excitement, and singing "hawuyaya," his version of "Halleluyah," learned from attending *tefillot* with Amitzim (the Tikvah Program), I know that camp is embedded in the DNA of my family, and I know the torch has been passed. My three-year-old granddaughter Eliana knows the whole Machon song (and the California Ramah Machon song is very, very long)—she's ready for camp!

My husband likes to say that our family has spent a collective total of fifty-plus summers at one Ramah camp or another. WOW! Here's to the next 120!

WISCONSIN

RABBI DANIEL LANDES
Director and Rosh Hayeshiva, Pardes Institute of Jewish Studies, Jerusalem

Camp Ramah made me the Orthodox rabbi I am today. I was a weak student at my local Orthodox day school in Chicago in the early 1960s and an even worse athlete. My parents, who wanted to inject some joy in my life—I didn't laugh a lot—made the financial sacrifice to pay for eight weeks at Ramah Wisconsin in addition to day school tuition. For me, it was worth it.

They were looking for a kosher sports camp for me, and it worked. I didn't become a star, but I learned to swim (from Mort Steinberg), to make a set shot (from [Rabbi] Mel Sirner), and even made the one star catch of my life playing (what else?) right field that won the game. My brothers Steve and David had their own great experiences.

But surprise—in many ways, camp did a lot for my Yiddishkeit. For the first time I had to define (and often defend) myself for my Orthodox practice. I came from a Jewishly and generally culturally sophisticated home, but at camp I confronted *Judaism as a Civilization* by Mordecai Kaplan and Professor Heschel's critique of "pan-halakhism." I took it all seriously and came out differently, but it all made a great impression. How could it not, when it involved debating counselors who later became rabbis, such as Zicky (Isaac) Bonder, *z"l,* and Elliot Dorff?

And I had the opportunity to study with some of the great professors who visited camp or served as professors-in-residence. I learned in *ḥavruta* with Professor Avraham Goldberg, studying Mishnah and Tosefta Shabbat using a combination of classical and scientific methods that turned my head around! In those days, the camp professor would chant the last chapter of *Eichah* on Tish'ah Be'av, and I felt that camp showed real *kevod hatorah.*

But in the end, the biggest deal wasn't the learning or even *kabbalat shabbat* by the lake (where as a good Orthodox boy I stood on the side), as impressive as they were. It was the *tzerif.* I was fortunate to be in a few really good ones and one great one. The great one was my tzerif during my last year as a camper when I was in the oldest bunk—then *yud-gimel.* It was a diverse group of kids who really learned to work and play well together and to love one another. We were under the tutelage of co-counselors Rickie Aron and [Rabbi] Miles Cohen. On the first night, they welcomed us to camp and to our lone cabin on the hill with a dark picture of bats and skeletons surrounding the bunk—to the horror of someone on the educational staff who thought this was a violation of the "home haven" that the bunk represented in Ramah educational theory. We, the campers, started laughing and didn't stop for eight weeks. That was joy.

So I was rewarded. I later pursued and married the girl I met and had such serious discussions with at camp—Sheryl Robbin. And little did I know at the time that I married into a camp family—Sheryl's parents Irv, *z"l,* and Janet Robbin ran the lay side of Ramah Wisconsin for years and built the Tikvah program. And later on, our son Isaac (now in the IDF) insisted on going to Wisconsin Ramah and even returned on staff.

At Pardes I'm surrounded by Ramah. From Wisconsin, a former *madrich,* Zvi (Denny) Wolff, and our Pardes lawyer, Rickie Aron, and from another camp, Rabbi Baruch (Bruce) Feldstern, Susan Wall, and Judy Markose. We have a steady stream of former campers as students and an even greater stream going to camp as counselors, Kollel members, and so on. They all have a healthy sense of *yir'at shamayim* and *kevod haberiyyot,* and they like to laugh.

60

WISCONSIN

RABBI WILLIAM LEBEAU
Program Director, Legacy Heritage Rabbinic Fellows Program, and
Immediate Past Vice-Chancellor and Dean of the Rabbinical School,
The Jewish Theological Seminary

My fifty-year association with Ramah began in the months preceding the summer of 1957. I was nineteen years of age and in my second year as a predental student at Akron University when my philosophy professor in my only non-science class asked me to write a paper describing my understanding of God. My relationship with God during the first nineteen years of my life was remote at best. I was shaken by this assignment. A search of the philosophy section of the library led me to a chance encounter with Abraham Joshua Heschel's *God in*

Search of Man: A Philosophy of Judaism. Surprised that God was in search of me, I knew that to complete my assignment I needed to discover God.

I received an "A" on the paper, and the exercise of writing it became the impetus for my search for faith and the clarification of my Jewish identity. When I told some of my observant friends about my growing interests, they encouraged me to join them that summer at Camp Ramah in Wisconsin.

The camp needed waiters and did not require applicants to be Hebrew speakers. I agreed to abide by camp policy that I keep kosher while on staff and signed on for the summer. On the night before I left for camp, I decided to have one last supper of non-kosher food. I took a date to a favorite restaurant and ordered two dinners, one from the surf and the other from the turf menu. As I enjoyed every bite, I was certain that my kosher commitment would end with the final day of camp.

The next morning, I began my journey, not anticipating the transformative influence Ramah would have on my entire life. While waiting to transfer trains in Chicago, I ate my first "kosher" meal. Tuna fish was never my favorite, but as I ate the sandwich, I questioned the purpose of what I had just done and suddenly found myself energized by my inner encounter with God. Choosing to eat according to God's direction seemed to affirm God's existence.

After dark that evening, I finally arrived at the Conover railroad station and boarded the camp bus with other staff members. Every visitor to Ramah Wisconsin knows that Buckatabon Road, the narrow, winding, tree-lined passage that travels the circumference of the lake by the same name, is the final piece of the journey to camp. The only source of light at night is the flickering lamps in scattered homes along the way. I was nearly asleep when a spectacular array of light beams that stretched from the dark skies above directly down to the ground startled me into a state of alertness. I briefly imagined that moment as a revelatory experience in which I was the only one aware of those lights. I sensed God's immediate accessibility. It was shattering to overhear others on the bus explain that we were witnessing the wonders of the Northern Lights.

I hesitated before going to sleep that night, afraid that I could never recapture the inspiration of that day. At *shaḥarit* the next morning, a friend helped me put on tefillin. As I found myself joining with others in the davening, I made perhaps the most important discovery of that first Ramah morning. It became clear to me that religious searching happens most effectively in *ḥavruta* and community.

At the end of the first month of camp, Burt Cohen, then a *rosh edah,* asked me to become a junior counselor. Moshe Tutnauer, my senior counselor, proved to be a wonderful mentor. He has remained a lifelong friend and rabbinic role model.

I began my new assignment in time to experience the power of Tish'ah Be'av at Ramah. I learned of the significance of the day at the same time I challenged my teenagers to ask their own questions of God and Jewish observance. In the evening, we gathered at the lake to listen to the chanting of *Eichah,* the Book of Lamentations. Out on the water, Hebrew letters spelling *eichah* had been affixed to a floating platform. Late in the reading of the *Eichah* text, the visual message of our people's vulnerability transfixed us as fire engulfed the Hebrew letters. By the end of that evening, I realized that religious faith must include doubt, which challenges us to question God's role in history, as well as the excitement of inspirational moments.

Before that summer, I had already made the decision to broaden my college experience by transferring to New York University. By the end of camp, my real enthusiasm for my move to New York was the thought of studying Jewish texts at The Jewish Theological Seminary. My Ramah experience propelled me on a trajectory so strong that it would lead to a lifetime of traditional Jewish observance and Jewish service through the rabbinate.

I returned to Conover in the summer of 1959 as head waiter. By that summer, I had decided to become a rabbi. I was also very much in love with Beverly Aronson, the daughter of an Orthodox rabbi. I encouraged her to come to camp as a counselor. Ramah was an indispensable part of our decision to marry. It has continued to influence the Jewish life of the family we have created. Nothing captures my gratitude for my Ramah connection more than the joy Bev and I have known watching our five children in their own Ramah experiences.

Together with all of those associated with Ramah, I celebrate the courage and determination of those who first dreamed of Ramah as a way of helping to assure our Jewish future. I thank all who provided the resources for expanding the original vision to include many new camps and innovative programs that have increased commitment to Jewish life. Best of all, Ramah at sixty is a dynamic work still in progress.

60

POCONOS

RABBI YAIER LEHRER
Adat Shalom, Pittsburgh, Pennsylvania

My initial contact with Camp Ramah in 1963 was by virtue of the fact that both of my parents, my father Menachem Lehrer, *z"l,* and my mother Rachel, were members of the teaching staff. Their love of Judaism and Israel brought them to Ramah. I am constantly reminded of the stories my father used to tell at Ramah of his days in the underground in pre-1948 Israel. These accounts fascinated those who had never learned this part of our history. Sitting around a campfire on the far side of the lake and listening to stories of modern Jewish warriors was a dramatic moment for all who were there and a precious moment for me as well, even though I had heard the same stories countless times at home.

From the time I was eight years old, Ramah was an integral part of my life. Many of the friendships and relationships that I forged in my years as a camper, on Ramah Seminar, and as a staff member are still part of my life. As a Jewish educator, I am often in contact with colleagues throughout the world, and I remember many of them as campers and staffers. Now, of course, they are rabbis, educators, and leaders within the Conservative Movement. I venture to say that many of the most influential people in the Conservative Movement would not have reached their current positions without the immersion in Judaism and Hebrew that they received in those great summers at Camp Ramah in the Poconos.

The next time you visit any of the Ramah camps, take a good look at the campers, especially at some of the most ill-behaved ones. They are our future leaders.

60

CALIFORNIA · NYACK
POCONOS · WISCONSIN

RABBI RONALD LEVINE, PH.D.
Clinical psychologist, Van Nuys, California

It was Friday night, June 29, 1956—the first Shabbat of the first full summer of Camp Ramah in California. One hundred and fifty of us, probably dressed in white, sat nervously on benches in Kikkar Tziyyon, as that area of camp had been named, waiting for the *kabbalat shabbat* service to begin. The candles were lit. As we held orange-colored Shiloh siddurim in our hands, the service began. At some point during the service, a regal man strode to the small wooden lectern. I can see his face as if it were yesterday. He was Simon Greenberg, *zecher tzaddik livrachah,* then the vice chancellor of The Jewish Theological Seminary (JTS). Pointing to the Ojai Valley to his left, he intoned, "This is the first time these hills and valleys have ever heard the sound of Jewish prayer." At that moment

I didn't have a clue as to the significance of his statement. I do now. That was the first of the sixteen consecutive summers I spent in Ramah camps, including California, Poconos, Wisconsin, Nyack, and Ramah Israel Seminar.

I was a camper in the Machon that first summer in 1956. It was the people that I remember the best. The impressions they made on me, even at the young age of fourteen, remain with me until this day. My *rosh maḥaneh* was David Lieber, *z"l,* president emeritus of the University of Judaism. The assistant director was Rabbi Yosef Miller. In our eyes, the staff that first summer was awesome. Indeed, many of them became legends in the Conservative Movement. The head counselor was Tzvili Yardeni, *z"l.* He instilled a spirit of Eretz Yisra'el that nurtures me to this day. It was not only the Hebrew that he spoke 24/7, forcing us to learn to understand; it was his presence. My counselor was Ethan Signer, who went on to become a distinguished professor at M.I.T. My *rosh machon* was Danny Greenberg, the younger son of Simon Greenberg, *z"l.* His wife, Hannah, was a teacher. The music counselor was Efry Spectre, *z"l.* The drama counselor was a Hebraist named Avrum Doryon.

Can you imagine the intensity of the Jewish experience we had? By the end of the summer, we had all but memorized the songs in the *shiron* with the green cover. I have 8 mm film, transferred first to VHS and now on DVD, of the dances we danced on the *mirpeset* in front of the *ulam* and the plays we put on in Hebrew. Many of my fellow campers that summer went on to become pioneering leaders in the Los Angeles Jewish community: Drs. David and Daniel Farkas; Dr. Steven Spiegel; Mark, Nachum, and Luis Lainer; Rabbi Joel Rembaum; Rabbi Moshe Rothblum; Milt Hyman; Marion Shapiro Schwartz; Benita Dubinsky Getzkin; Phyllis Brunner Baim; and Rena Rosenman Snyder.

I grew up in your standard "three-day–a-year" Jewish home, which was common in that generation. We belonged to Temple Beth Am, Los Angeles, California. We weren't observant. I came home from that first summer and requested that we keep a kosher home. Fortunately, my parents agreed. All of this was because that first summer at Camp Ramah in California transformed my life.

The next summer (1957), if anything, was more invigorating than the first. We were housed in a ramshackle, wooden structure nicknamed the "Beehive" because of the bees that had taken up residence prior to us. They declined to be evicted. That summer brought other luminaries to our staff. The assistant director was Chaim Potok, *z"l.* The rosh machon was Rabbi Alex Shapiro, *z"l.* Can you imagine the intensity of the Jewish experience we had?

In the summer of 1958, Chaim created the *ḥug limmud,* a six-hour-a-day study program. I was a member of that program. That summer, our instructors were Israel Francus and Shalom Paul. I was sixteen years old and was being taught biblical and rabbinic texts by Shalom Paul and Israel Francus. Words are inadequate to describe the depth of that experience.

Summer 1959 brought yet another pioneering experience. Rabbi David Lieber, *z"l,* became the founding director of the national Mador program at Ramah in the Poconos. Eleven campers from California attended. Fellow Madorniks from other camps included Stu Kelman, Vicki Koltun Kelman, and Gail Zaiman Dorph. Shelly Dorph, a future director of National Ramah, was a junior counselor. Our teachers included Uriel Simon, *z"l,* Shmuel Leiter, *z"l,* and Deborah, *z"l,* and Bezalel "Buzzy" Porten. The level of scholarship was unparalleled. And, of course, Rabbi David Mogilner, *z"l,* was rosh maḥaneh. These are the men and women who created and nurtured my Jewish soul.

In 1960 a new director and his wife were brought to California. They would transform both my fellow campers and me and Ramah California. For the next ten years, Walter "Ackie" Ackerman and Frannie, *zichronam livrachah,* created the programs and institutions that would become unique to Camp Ramah in California. Dr. Emile Jacoby was the educational director. He installed the formal educational structure and curriculum that would last for the next thirty years. Local congregational rabbis with their wives, including Rabbi Moshe Tutnauer and Margie, Rabbi Ben Zion Bergman and Bella, Rabbi Paul Dubin and Esther, Rabbi Marvin Bornstein and Dina, were brought in to teach the staff. Scholars from the University of Judaism became frequent presenters. In the summer of 1961, the first special needs camper came to our camp, a blind camper that we all knew by his nickname, "Sparky." A special Shabbat welcoming ceremony in which the Machon lined up and sang Shabbat *zemirot* as the younger *edot* filed into Kikkar Tziyyon for kabbalat shabbat was instituted. By the time Ackie and Frannie left at the end of summer 1969, all of the programs and institutions that characterized Camp Ramah in California were in place. And, of course, the plans for the "new camp" were just on the horizon.

During my years at JTS, Seymour Fox, *z"l,* brought together a group of young men who would become the Ramah directors of the next generation, including Daniel Margolis, Shelly Dorph, Robert Abramson, and myself. This was a remarkable period in which we studied with the Ramah directors of that era: Ray Artz, David Mogilner, *z"l,* Jerry Abrams, Donny Adelman, *z"l,* and, of course, Walter Ackerman, *z"l.* Those meetings produced the educational philosophy that would guide all the Ramah camps for a generation to come. I spent my junior year in college studying in Israel. All of my courses, including a masters class in Talmud with Rabbi Abraham Goldberg, *z"l,* were in Hebrew. I learned that Hebrew at Camp Ramah in California. I am indebted to my counselors and teachers during that era for this invaluable gift that they gave me.

In 1970 I became the director of Ramah California. I left that position after one summer as I discovered that the higher up you go in Jewish education, the less you educate. Fundraising, a major focus and responsibility for most Ramah directors, was not what I had bargained for. I became a teacher at Los Angeles Hebrew High School under Shelly Dorph.

In 1971, I spent one more summer at Ramah, at the camp in Wisconsin, as assistant educational director to Moshe Davidson, *z"l.* That turned out to be the best decision I ever made in my life. I met Joyce Feinberg, from Opelika, Alabama. By the end of the summer we were engaged, and the following year we were married. It's good to go to Camp Ramah. Both of our children, Aviva and Natania, spent their childhood summers at camp and are currently on staff.

As we celebrate the sixtieth anniversary of the founding of Camp Ramah in Wisconsin, I express my heartfelt gratitude to the vision and purpose of the men and women who made Camps Ramah possible. I believe that their efforts literally saved a generation of Conservative Jews. I honor their presence and their memories.

60

CANADA

CAISSIE LEVY

Actor, New York, New York

[Imagine how delighted I was to attend the Broadway production of *Hair* starring former camper Caissie Levy from Ramah Canada. As she told me and my wife, Cari, backstage after the performance, "I first played this exact role at camp, where the show was entirely in Hebrew and look at the stage I'm on now!" Caissie grew up at Ramah Canada playing the lead in many *edah* productions. In the spring of 2009, I asked her to reflect on the impact of the Ramah experience on her life and career. — RABBI MITCHELL COHEN]

Ramah strongly influenced my career choice and career growth. The musicals we did every summer at Ramah were huge building blocks for my career onstage. I started in Arazim when I began attending Ramah at the age of eleven. Subsequently, I looked forward to performing in our all-Hebrew musicals each summer. They were the highlight of my time at camp.

Ramah, in general, was a musical place and that really influenced me. Whether we were singing *birkat hamazon,* davening Shabbat *minḥah,* or having an *oneg* in the *ḥadar ochel,* there was always song. That had a big impact on me.

In addition, Ramah made Judaism fun. I grew up in Hamilton, Ontario, in a Conservative synagogue, with traditional parents. I attended the Hamilton Hebrew Academy with my two brothers, and Judaism was a huge part of my life. But going to Ramah each summer and connecting with other Jewish kids from all over Canada and the United States made Judaism less about religious rules and more about community. Ramah brings kids together from all levels of observance and encourages them to ask questions and examine their feelings about being Jewish. Of course, it was also refreshing and freeing—especially in my high school years when I was attending public school—to have a place where I didn't feel like I was in the minority.

To this day, my Ramah friends are still my closest friends in the world. We grew up together. We're practically family. Many of them now live in New York, and they're always the first friends who come to see me in my shows. Even Ramah people I rarely keep in touch with are always popping up in the audience, and it's wonderful to see them. My friend Jon Ross, who is head of drama at Ramah Wisconsin, is still a dear friend, and we have supported each other in our theater careers in New York. We first met when I was in Magshimim when Ramah Wisconsin campers came to Ramah Canada for their annual visit. We've kept in touch ever since, and just recently he and a bunch of my other Wisconsin friends (from my bus on Israel Seminar) came to see *Hair.*

I feel as though I did most of my growing up at camp, and it shaped who I am today. Nearly all of my childhood memories revolve around Ramah. It was an amazing, magical place where kids could just be kids, explore their Judaism, make lifelong friends, and be free.

60

CALIFORNIA

GADY LEVY, ED.D.

Dean, Whizin Center for Continuing Education and
Vice President, American Jewish University

In the movies, when the hero or heroine has the defining, life-changing moment, the camera dramatically swoops in, the music swells to a crescendo, and the rain suddenly stops as birds begin to sing.

When I had my epiphany, there was no music, no singing birds, and no rain. In fact, there was a bus ride from the Los Angeles airport, a bunch of strangers, and an army tent with fifteen beds.

My family moved from Israel to Southern California when I was fifteen. Southern California is a sprawling suburbia rather than cohesive cities. The physical disconnect of the area is mirrored in its social structure. Sealed-off groups and cliques float in a sea of anomie. As a result, I felt alone.

When it came time to go to Camp Ramah in California, I expected more of the same. I could not have been more wrong. In the time it took to drive to Ojai, I met people who would become lifelong friends. Though at the time I could not articulate it, I found something that so far had eluded me in Southern California: I found people with whom I connected.

What others called arguing, we called talking. What they called pushy, we called opinion. What they called interruption, we called jazz. Conversations at Camp Ramah would often go all night, the words and ideas and possibilities so exciting that we didn't bother with something as trivial as sleep.

What I discovered at Camp Ramah was the feeling of Connection: connection to people, to ideas, to text, to culture, to activities, to history. I made it my mission to imbue the campers of Tent-10 with this power of connection. I attended Camp Ramah for ten years.

Jews are a passionate people. We may be passionate about different things, ideas, and activities, but we are passionate. Our culture gives us a shared-values base that lays a groundwork for us to connect with each other in exciting, diverse, and amazing ways.

This discovery of the power of connection and of bringing people to Judaism through their passions and interests shaped my career: from my first job as USY advisor, to Hebrew school teacher, to Director of Formal and Informal Education at Adat Ari El in Valley Village, to my current position at the American Jewish University (formerly University of Judaism and Brandeis Bardin Institute).

Based on my experience at Camp Ramah, I knew that once people experienced connection to Jewish culture through an interest or a passion, they would continue to explore and connect to other aspects of Jewish culture and community. It is my goal to help others to connect to Jewish culture and community, much as I did at Camp Ramah.

POCONOS

BRUCE LIPTON
Director of Finance and Operations, Camp Ramah in the Poconos

As Ramah celebrates sixty years, I am celebrating my twentieth working summer at Camp Ramah in the Poconos. I feel a debt of gratitude to Ramah because my association with Ramah led me from a negative past to a positive present, living a committed Conservative Jewish lifestyle. My association with Ramah led me to Israel where I lived for ten years and created a never-ending connection to the land and the people. My association with Ramah led me to my wife, and our appreciation of this fact is marked by a plaque hanging in the *gazebo zugot* (couples gazebo). We now have two children as campers.

I am currently serving as the director of finance and operations at Camp Ramah in the Poconos. My wife, Meryl Sussman, coordinates the *hadrachah* program and provides ongoing training to the staff. I am fortunate to be able to apply my professional skills, as well as my life experiences, toward the betterment of a place I love and a place that has had an important influence on my life. Ramah definitely had a positive impact on me and on my family, and this impact keeps us coming back.

60

BERKSHIRES
CONNECTICUT - NEW ENGLAND

CHARLES T. MANN, M.D.
President, National Ramah Commission

I grew up on Long Island in a relatively assimilated home. My parents went to the local Conservative synagogue three days a year. Our home was not kosher, yet my mother lit Shabbat candles each Friday night, often after getting home late from the family paint store. The Passover seder was an occasion to use the "good dishes," not to change the dishes. My father had grown up in an Orthodox home in Brooklyn, and my mother came from a totally nonobservant home. Together they were content with a typical second-generation lifestyle that was proudly Jewish and purposely minimally observant.

For a reason that still remains a mystery to me, my parents decided to send me to a new Jewish camp. It was the summer of 1955, and at the age of seven, I began my Ramah life at Ramah Connecticut. When Connecticut closed, I went on to be a bunk counselor in Palmer. It was this experience that would change my life, and then by extension, the life of my family. There were a handful of individuals who influenced me to follow my career choice of medicine. It was Ramah, however, that influenced how I would ultimately elect to live my life as a Jew and create a Jewish home. It was at Ramah that I developed a love of the Hebrew language, a commitment to Jewish observance and traditions, and a real attachment to the State of Israel.

I was introduced to my future wife by our Hillel rabbi. Barbara had never gone to Ramah; however, she had attended a Federation camp. When Barbara and I talked about getting married, I insisted that we visit Ramah together. So one Sunday in the summer of 1968, we drove up to Ramah in New England. On the way home, I informed her rather matter-of-factly that someday our children would go to Ramah. For me this was a given, not even open for discussion. Barbara developed her love for Ramah as she watched our four children go through Ramah Berkshires from Kochavim to staff. I, of course, relived my Ramah experience vicariously through my children, summer by summer.

It has been more than fifty years since I first walked into a Ramah camp. Ramah has grown, and its programming has changed with the times, but its educational mission is unchanged. Ramah continues to offer those magical summers that change the lives of both campers and staff. I hope that fifty years from now my grandchildren will still be as enchanted by Ramah as I continue to be.

CALIFORNIA

LAURA MILLER
Former Mayor, Dallas, Texas

Years ago we decided that it would be very nice to have all eleven kids on my husband's side of the family attend the same camp. Because my sister-in-law in Beverly Hills was on the board of Camp Ramah in California, we chose that camp in Ojai. Today, our kids' best friends in life are the friends they met at Camp Ramah. I don't expect them to make college friends as close as the friends they have made at Ramah.

Because of the influence of Ramah, our kids want us to invite more people to Shabbat dinner, to engage in intellectual discussions on Jewish topics, and to sing songs and do the bentshing. They now feel a duty to the community as Jews.

They now also have a very special relationship with Israel because of the Ramah Israel Seminar experience. Ramah has created for our kids a wonderful worldwide network of friends. Camp Ramah was the best thing that we have ever done for our kids. Ever!

60

BERKSHIRES
NEW ENGLAND · POCONOS

RABBI MICHAEL PANITZ, PH.D.
Temple Israel, Norfolk, Virginia

A camper at Ramah Berkshires (1966–1971), a counselor at Berkshires and Poconos (1973–1976), and then a *yo'etz* and educator at New England (1993–2000), my memories of Ramah span three phases of my life: childhood, young adulthood, and fatherhood. Ramah enhanced each of those three distinctive times.

As a camper at Ramah, I was happily surprised to find an observant Conservative Jewish community. I had been familiar with two different kinds of marginalization: a Conservative kid in an Orthodox *yeshivah ketannah* in Paterson, New Jersey, where the principal made it a point to tell the children not to attend worship services in my father's synagogue, and the rabbi's son in that congregation, where the other children and their parents expected my family to be vicariously observant for the entire membership. Ramah was a delightful glimpse of what an elite, yet real and functioning, Jewish community could be like. Kashruth, Shabbat, *tefillah,* and *talmud torah* were norms of life, along with swimming, baseball, drama, nature, and hospital corners. No wonder that I made the most intense friendships of my young life in those summers. Forty years later, I still keep up with some of my peers from camp.

As a counselor, I learned critical lessons about responsibility, about education, and about functioning in loco parentis, at just the period in my life when I was committing to a career as a Jewish educator. To this day, I consider the education class I took with Rabbi David Mogilner, *z"l,* as the most effective, single course that shaped my subsequent professional work.

As a yo'etz, and one of the "old men on campus" in a community staffed predominantly by eighteen- to twenty-three-year-olds, I gained a unique appreciation of the chain of generations upon which Jewish continuity depends. Acutely aware of both the limitations and the immense promise of the apprentice adults to whom we entrust the summertime education and care of our children,

I found it powerfully satisfying to guide them, from behind the scenes whenever possible, to grow into their own careers as shapers of the next generation.

60

BERKSHIRES • CANADA • POCONOS

BARBARA PARIS, M.D.
Director, Division of Geriatric Services, Maimonides Medical Center, Brooklyn, New York

What impact has Ramah had on my life?

When I was twelve years old, my parents sent me to Ramah Berkshires—that was 1964. I returned every summer, went on Israel Seminar in 1968, and later was a staff member for around ten summers: junior counselor and Hebrew teacher at Ramah Canada, doctor at Ramah Poconos, and then at Berkshires. My son attended Ramah Day Camp in Nyack and Ramah Berkshires, and then he was on the swim staff. My daughter attended Ramah Berkshires and then was on swim staff. Needless to say, Ramah has always played a very central role in our family life. I recently returned from a week's vacation in Israel with my husband and daughter. Shabbat in Jerusalem is always spiritually uplifting and full of joy. We enjoyed it with many friends, including Ramah friends who have made aliyah. The love of Shabbat and all of the positive energy I experienced in Israel last Shabbat began with my Ramah summers, and Shabbat in Ramah is on par with Shabbat in Jerusalem!

60

BERKSHIRES • GLEN SPEY

ELLEN SMITH RATNER
Past President, Temple Beth El, Springfield, Massachusetts

This is a story I have wanted to share for a long time, but I knew that it would be understood only by those who have been touched by the magic of a Camp Ramah experience. After all, when you try to explain how beautiful the sounds of an entire camp coming together to celebrate in the joy of Shabbat can be, or talk of the thrill of many voices singing together during *zimriyyah,* you are most certainly looked upon as slightly odd. These are not your typical stories of summer camp. Yet this is some of what has remained with me all these years after my wonderful time spent at *maḥaneh* Ramah.

Mine is a story of a wandering Jew. My family moved around quite a lot during my childhood. My parents were committed to Eretz Yisra'el and took us to live in Israel for four years when I was very young. We moved back to the United States and what remained with me were memories of a very happy time. I spoke Hebrew, went to *gan,* had friends, and fell in love with Israel. Our connection and ties remained strong. But my experience was unique and not shared by many I met. It was rare that I found others with similar feelings and knowledge about Israel. And then, the summer immediately following my bat mitzvah, I went to Camp Ramah. I attended Camp Ramah in Glen Spey for two years and then Ramah Berkshires for two more years. And it was then that I found that I had finally come to a place where it felt like home, where I belonged. I wasn't the only thirteen-year-old who spoke Hebrew, who had been to Israel, and who was proud to be Jewish. I no longer felt like a stranger in a strange land. I made a deep connection that has since guided me on my Jewish journey.

60

BERKSHIRES · NYACK · POCONOS

JOHN S. RUSKAY, PH.D.
Executive Vice President and Chief Executive Officer,
UJA–Federation of New York

[Adapted with the permission of the author and the publisher from John S. Ruskay, "From Challenge to Opportunity: To Build Inspired Communities," *Journal of Jewish Communal Service* 72, nos. 1–2 (Fall–Winter 1995–96): 22–33 (31).]

Camp Ramah, the summer camp of the Conservative Movement, had such profound significance for me. Raised in a marginal Jewish family, indifferent to the content of my Hebrew school experience, it was at Ramah that I was introduced to the rhythm of the Jewish week and the beauty and glory of Shabbat, participatory prayer, and serious Jewish study. For the first time, I participated in a vibrant Jewish community. An initial list of the qualities of Ramah in the mid-1960s that were decisive include:

• A clear vision informed by ideology, that is, a commitment to a halachic lifestyle, the Hebrew language, and Jewish study made accessible and joyful in the camp environment

• A strong educational philosophy that energized staff; staff believed that they were on the cutting edge of informal Jewish and religious education, which communicated a sense of a "greater mission" to campers

• Standards adhered to by all; everyone studied—campers, counselors, administration, and kitchen staff

• An articulated expectation of modeling interpersonal relations by fully respecting the uniqueness of "the other" (we read a great deal of Buber in those days), which raised consciousness and sensitivity to an art form

• Judaism lived fully, naturally, and authentically, without pretense.

60

BERKSHIRES · NEW ENGLAND

JONATHAN D. SARNA, PH.D.
Joseph H. & Belle R. Braun Professor of American Jewish History and Director, Hornstein Jewish Professional Leadership Program, Brandeis University

Unless you teach him how to swim, I won't take him back home again!" This was the warning supposedly issued by my late father, Professor Nahum M. Sarna, *z"l,* to his good friend the camp director, Rabbi Raphael Arzt, when he brought me to Camp Ramah in New England in 1968.

I had already been a camper at Palmer for two previous years. I had also been a camper for a year at Ramah in the Berkshires in 1964. Yet, through one ruse or another, I had always managed to evade swimming. The lake at Palmer was cold and forbidding. I preferred the library.

My father, who took seriously the rabbinic requirement that he teach his son to swim, and who lamented that he himself could not even float, was determined that I would learn to swim one way or another. Ray Arzt proved equal to the challenge.

The head of swimming was given strict instructions, and a special class was set up consisting of exactly two non-swimmers: myself and the late George Orentlicher (later the Latin valedictorian of Harvard). Swimming, at least for the two of us, became mandatory.

We tried our best to stay on the dock. George and I (who were good friends) mustered any number of persuasive arguments why we should learn other things, be in other places, not endanger our health or risk our lives, and so forth—but all to no avail. The instructor had her orders, and Ray did not want to have to take care of me all winter.

So, after our ritualistic pleas were turned down, the class got down to business. Each of us had to jump into the water ("I know it's cold, jump in anyway"), practice our strokes, and swim laps. By visiting day, we both had made substantial progress. Ray made certain that my parents took notice.

As the camp season wound down, the instructor decreed that George and I would swim across the lake. I prayed daily for rain, but the morning set for the ordeal dawned cloudless. I said *tefillot* with special fervor that day—who knew if I would ever get to say them again? Bunkmates wished us well, and we jumped in.

As it turned out, the instructor was not nearly so reckless as I had feared; she followed us in a boat. But the boat was off limits to us, and there being no other option, we had to swim. Crawl, sidestroke, backstroke—somehow, we managed to show off all of them and to propel ourselves to the inevitable destination. Huffing and puffing, we climbed out. The longest swim of my entire life was over.

"Congratulations," the instructor exclaimed, "you have now passed two levels of swimming: advanced beginners and low intermediate. You can swim!" Our campmates applauded, the instructor beamed, and Ray himself later commended our achievement. On the closing day of camp, my father inspected the two Red Cross swimming cards and happily took me home.

And then, thirteen years later, came the sequel. I was a young assistant professor by then, living in Cincinnati, Ohio. My townhouse abutted a pond. On Ḥol Hamo'ed Sukkot of that year, I invited some friends to my sukkah, one of whom came with a young child. The child broke away from her mother, raced to the side of the pond, and fell in. She struggled in the water.

Without pausing to think, I kicked off my shoes, jumped into the pond, and rescued the child; she was under water for only a few seconds. To this day, she credits me with saving her life.

"Whoever saves one life, it is as though he saved an entire universe," the Talmud teaches.

Thanks to my father, Ray Arzt, and the wonderful Camp Ramah swimming instructor, a universe was saved.

60

CALIFORNIA • WISCONSIN

PAUL SCHULTZ, M.D.
Past President, Camp Ramah in California, and
Past Vice President, National Ramah Commission

My first contact with Camp Ramah was in a January 1954 phone call from Rabbi Herman Kieval, *z"l,* to my mother indicating that he had some scholarship money ($50) in our Pittsburgh synagogue to help send me to Camp Ramah, a relatively new summer camp in northern Wisconsin, where I could keep *kashrut,* daven every day, and speak Hebrew all day. Since I did none of those things as a one-year, post-bar mitzvah, I was less enthused than my mother. Serendipitously, I had learned trope and could easily chant anything well but understood little of what I was chanting—a "splinter skill." My delivery was smooth and confident, causing most of my teachers to believe that I was fluent in Hebrew. With three other Pittsburgh youngsters, I took a train to Chicago and was met by a horde of American kids who were fluent in Hebrew and incessantly singing songs that I didn't know. We ended up at the Morrison Hotel where we davened (at last a chance to chant). We were taken to still another train headed north to Conover, Wisconsin where the eight-year-old camp was directed by Seymour (Shlomo) Fox, *z"l,* a bright young educator who had just received his rabbinic ordination. The summer was dreadful because the other campers in my cabin were fluent in Hebrew. My counselors, Paul Ritterband and Paul Herman, tried to help me. Chanting was my only chance to be heard.

Through peer influence, I returned to camp in 1955. Joel Kramer was my counselor. By then I could speak a few short sentences in Hebrew and even developed a crush on a girl from Detroit. She went on to make aliyah and eventually win recognition from the president of Israel as the country's leading educator.

I eagerly looked forward to my third year at camp, 1956, the greatest summer of my life. In Jack Bloom's cabin were an impressive group of campers that included a husky catcher from Von Steuben High School in Chicago, who went on to become a renowned litigator (Alan Silberman), and a studious though outspoken kid from Detroit who went on to become an international authority on Talmud (Joel Roth). Our single greatest achievement, however, was to translate the doo-wop song "Blue Moon" into Hebrew. I played the "bridge" on a muted trumpet. At the evening activities, the assembled group would chant, "*Anu rotzim* 'Blue Moon,'" which roughly translates to "We want to stay up another five minutes."

The next year, 1957, I became a junior counselor for a group that included a twelve-year-old boy from Chicago (Mort Steinberg), who went on to a distinguished legal career and who is a past president of the National Ramah Commission (NRC). By this time, I'd met Muffs and Mogilner (on staff) and Kripke, Dorff, Goldsmith, Zell, and many others (campers). My skills in chanting enabled me to become a *melammed* (bar mitzvah tutor) throughout college and medical school. I would also become a part-time *shammash,* learning how shuls run.

In the summer of 1960, I had a totally free month between college and medical school. I called the young new director in Wisconsin, Rabbi Burton Cohen, and asked for any job at all. When I got to camp, I found myself toiling in the kitchen under the direction of now retired Rabbi Art Olesky, a friend to this day. When Burt gave me my $25 pay check for the four weeks of work, I sincerely expressed my profound gratitude. He responded fatefully, "Don't worry, Schultzie, you'll pay us back some day."

In 1962, my counselor from six years before, Jack Bloom, officiated at our wedding when I married Joan. In 1972, we moved to California. One summer day in 1973, while cruising with family on Route 101 near Ventura, I noticed a sign that read "Ojai—13½ miles." I abruptly turned to ascend the hill, telling my wife that there might be a Camp Ramah in Ojai. As I entered the camp, I was greeted by the new director, who invited me to be a camp doctor the following summer. When I returned to camp for my first week of work in June 1974, I learned that the medical director had just quit and that I was the new medical director. I held that position from 1974 to 1986. I worked four weeks each summer and met numerous young influential Jewish professionals, including Alvin Mars, Shelly Dorph, Joel Rembaum, Stuart Kelman, Elliot Dorff (the same guy I knew from Wisconsin), and a young adult still in training, Mitch Cohen.

In 1986, I was chosen to be president of Camp Ramah in California, the first (and the last) non-Angelino to hold that office. I worked closely with, and learned a great deal from, our director, Glen Karonsky. My presidency gave me a seat on the NRC, where I found the dynamic attorney from Chicago and the studious, outspoken fellow from Detroit. So three of us from Jack Bloom's cabin were reunited on the NRC.

In 1989, when my term in California concluded, Dr. Shelly Dorph gave me the position of vice president for Ramah Programs in Israel, a position I held for sixteen years. I spent most of those years working with Dr. David Breakstone, a brilliant Jewish educator. He really taught me about Zionism when I visited Israel two to three times a year.

In summary, Camp Ramah taught me about Judaism, Israel, Zionism, and shul activity in a way that no other institution could. I made enduring friendships with numerous luminaries within the Conservative Movement. A few thousand San Diego kids have gone to Camp Ramah in Ojai, and many hundreds have gone to Israel with Ramah, perhaps some of them through my influence.

I myself am retiring from thirty-four years of neurology practice here in San Diego. There are six of us in my neurology group. Three of us were campers at Camp Ramah (two from Wisconsin, one from Poconos). What are the odds?

60

WISCONSIN

RUTH SHAPIRO
Jewish educator and clinical social worker, South Orange, New Jersey

Ramah has had an important place in my life and the life of my family for fifty-seven years; almost as long as it has existed. My first summer at Ramah was as a co-counselor of the oldest girls cabin at Ramah Wisconsin in 1950. I had completed my first year of college at Hunter College in New York City and at the Teachers' Institute at The Jewish Theological Seminary (JTS). I had met a wonderful fellow student (Rabbi Alex M. Shapiro, *z"l*) whom I would later marry. It was his idea that we both work at Ramah that summer as counselors; I knew of Ramah's reputation as a leading Hebrew-speaking camp with high educational standards and was eager to work there. Naomi Cohen, Evelyn Greenberg, Moshe Greenberg, and other JTS students and faculty were also on staff. Rabbi Hillel Silverman was camp director. It was an extraordinary summer of intellectual and social stimulation for us all, and we made lifelong friendships. The *ḥanichim* were a special group who signed on willingly and enthusiastically to the ideas of study, *ivrit,* and *tefillah.* Ramah Wisconsin was a beautiful camp located on a large, beautiful lake in a very rural area. The setting added to the specialness of that summer. We returned for three more summers, each similarly enjoyable and special in many ways.

In 1951, Louis Newman, *z"l,* became *rosh maḥaneh* and embarked on what was later termed the "Newman Revolution" at Ramah Wisconsin, which eventually sparked significant changes and creative ideas in all the Ramah camps. Many of his students went on to have a significant impact on the educational philosophy and practices of Conservative Judaism, not only at Ramah but also throughout all the educational institutions of the movement. Among the many we worked with and learned from in those summers at Ramah were Seymour (Shlomo) Fox, Sara Fox, Shalom Segal, Shalom Spiegel, and Dani Elazar.

The beloved camp song ends with *mi yittenech lemofet le'alfei revavah* (at least, it used to). Ramah has been for me, my family, and thousands of others an example of all that is good, valuable, pleasurable, and inspiring in our tradition, as lived in the macrocosm of a complete Jewish life. All that can be said looking ahead is *kol hakavod; meḥayil el ḥayil.*

MAINE · POCONOS

CHANA SIMCKES (HANNAH FIEBERMAN)

Jewish educator, Long Island, New York; Past President, Queens/Nassau Principals Council; Past Vice President, Jewish Educators Assembly

[At the fiftieth anniversary celebration of the Jewish Educators Assembly in November 2001, Chana Simckes was awarded the degree of Doctor of Pedagogy, honoris causa, by The Jewish Theological Seminary.]

In the spring of 1949, our religious school principal, Harry Malin, *z"l,* announced that two scholarships to Camp Ramah would be awarded to the two students who received the highest grades in a test to be given. I was one of the winners! Alan Lovins was the other.

And so, early one morning in July, Alan and I boarded a train in New Haven (we were both from Bridgeport). We had difficulty finding the Ramah car but eventually found the other campers on their way to Mt. Vernon, Maine.

It was quite a long trip by train, followed by a bus trip. Upon arrival at the camp, the girls were assigned to a bunk (there were only three), and the boys went to their tents.

The camp experience was difficult, but nonetheless incredible. The responsibility for creating a ball field was that of the campers. We would throw stones from the field each day! The lake was pristine, clean, and beautiful. Hiking was invigorating. Speaking Hebrew was mandatory.

By far the most wonderful experience I had was spending that summer with incredible people: Dr. Solomon Feffer, *z"l,* our director; the Katzoffs, our head counselors; Yochanan Muffs, *z"l;* and on and on.

Ramah became my lifeline to my tradition, for I came from an observant home and found the Ramah environment very supportive. When the Maine camp closed that year, the Poconos camp was opened. I remained a camper, counselor, and teacher for years to come.

In 1953 while in New York City to interview for college, I stopped at The Jewish Theological Seminary (JTS) to visit my Ramah friends. It was on that day that Dr. Judah Goldin put his arm around me, led me to his office, and revealed the signing that week of the contract with Columbia University, which led to the formation of the Joint Program. And the rest is history. I attended JTS and Columbia, married a rabbi, taught in religious schools for many years, and finally served as an educational director on Long Island for nineteen years.

For all of the above, I thank Ramah and the wonderful staff and teachers who had such a profound influence on my life so many years ago.

POCONOS

SARA RUBINOW SIMON, D.H.L.
Former Director, Special Needs Department,
Board of Jewish Education of Greater Washington, D.C.

[Miriam Kraemer Gray, Aviva Israelitan Shigon, Ellen Weinstein Pazornik, Helen Bartfeld Wolkow, and Sara Rubinow Simon, who were in Machon bunks 18 and 20 together at Camp Ramah in the Poconos in the early 1950s, got together on August 5–8, 2007, in Rehoboth, Delaware.]

The years melted away as we reconnected.

Two of us were widowed and remarried. Two of us are rabbinic spouses. We had fifteen children, and we have nineteen grandchildren thus far. Most of our grandchildren attend Jewish camps, and one of our grandchildren is a fourth-generation Ramah camper.

We agreed that the Ramah experience was a significant influence on our lives. We are all comfortable with Hebrew and actively involved in Jewish life through Jewish education, cultural arts, and synagogue and community organizational life. We have all made multiple visits to, or have lived in, Israel.

There was lots of laughing and playing of Jewish geography as we tried to identify people from the piles of old photographs we had brought with us.

We especially remembered Tish'ah Be'av and the flaming *eichah* on the lake, the somber mood, the reading of *Eichah* by flashlight, and the meaningful discussions during the day.

Shabbat was always a highlight, and we still wish we could recreate in our own lives the haunting beauty of services under the tree with everyone wearing white clothing, the Torah and ark in the tree, the delicious dinner, the lusty singing of *zemirot, havdalah* around the baseball diamond—the special feeling of *kedushah.*

We recalled *nikkayon* and the *tafkid* wheel with *ya'eh, metatei, kiyyor,* and so on—all words that don't generally appear in everyday conversation but that we still remember.

We lived in the era of polio epidemics, and we remembered Sara's father's heroic efforts to quickly locate enough gamma globulin to inoculate the whole camp. We are grateful that polio is not a worry now.

We talked about the Ramah directors, Levi Soshuk, *z"l,* and Aryeh Rohn, *z"l,* and about sitting outside for *kittot,* the sports, *ommanut,* music, the Maccabiah, our plays like *The Wizard of Oz,* the *rikkudiyyah* and, of course, the banquet and our tears when we left camp.

During our days together at the beach, we sang *birkat hamazon* and lots of Israeli and old camp songs—and even tried to do a few of the Israeli dances we had loved.

The days together passed too quickly and we felt that we had just begun to reminisce.

We are already planning our next get-together and hope that additional bunkmates from those years will join us.

[Sara Rubinow Simon is married to Rabbi Matthew Simon. It was Rabbi Simon's father, Rabbi Ralph Simon, *z"l*, of Congregation Rodfei Zedek in Chicago, Illinois, who in 1947 convinced the Chicago Council of United Synagogue to purchase a former fishing lodge in Conover, Wisconsin for use as a summer camp. According to the family, he was motivated to create a Jewish camp in the Midwest so his young son Matthew would not have to travel to the East Coast for a Jewish camping experience. Thus began Camp Ramah. — MORTON M. STEINBERG]

60

DAROM • POCONOS • WISCONSIN

ERIC SINGER

Founding President, Camp Ramah Darom

[Interview conducted by Rabbi Mitchell Cohen, National Ramah Director, July 2007.]

Each summer, the National Ramah Commission's Executive Committee (camp presidents and NRC officers) meets at the beginning of July at a Ramah camp to conduct business, share best practices, and get to know the facility, program, and personnel of another local Ramah camp. In 2007, we met at Camp Ramah Darom in Clayton, Georgia, and in addition to the usual meetings, we had the opportunity to meet for a few hours with the Ramah Darom board of directors to share perspectives and to introduce some of the challenges and innovations at Ramah camps throughout North America.

One of the founding members of the Ramah Darom board, and its first president, is Eric Singer, who spent Shabbat at camp with our group. In an hour-long conversation, he shared his story on the founding of Ramah Darom with me — a story that inspired me.

Eric's Ramah roots are deep. He grew up in Columbus, Georgia, in a small Jewish community. In the 1950s, Eric's parents were urged by their congregational rabbi, Kass Abelson, to send his two older sisters, Sharon and Alice, to Ramah camps up north. Alice attended Camp Ramah in Connecticut, and Sharon attended Camp Ramah in the Poconos, where she met her future husband, Neil Norry of Rochester. (Neil and Sharon's children and grandchildren have a long and wonderful legacy of attendance at numerous Ramah camps, as well as generosity toward the building and sustaining of Ramah in many settings.)

Eventually it was Eric's turn to experience Ramah. Together with David Abelson, the rabbi's son, Eric attended Camps Ramah in Wisconsin and the Poconos between 1962 and 1967 and attended the Ramah Israel Seminar in 1968. In 1969, Eric continued his career with Ramah by working on the waterfront at Wisconsin, where he was supervised by the head of swimming, Mort Steinberg, who later became the president of Ramah in Wisconsin and eventually the president of the National Ramah Commission.

Eric describes his years at Ramah as transformative.

> I grew up in a small Jewish community, and for the first time I was exposed to the religiosity of Ramah, w.hich had a huge impact on my life. Our counselors spoke mostly Hebrew to us, and it was great. I learned so much from this experience, which sustained me throughout my life. We learned that it was cool to be Jewish—we could focus not only on sports, but on Jewish life as well, and still have a great time. At Ramah we learned that it was okay to do both.

Eric said that one day at Ramah he had an epiphany.

> I learned to love the outdoors at camp. At the time, I thought I would become a forest ranger, but my passion was to turn on other people to the beauty of experiencing the outdoors. That became a lifetime passion for me. School didn't have a great impact on me, but experiential education, especially at Ramah, made a huge difference in my life in two ways. It helped me develop a strong Jewish identity and instilled within me a deep love for nature and the outdoors.

True to his dream that was born at Ramah, Eric attended the National Outdoor Leadership School (NOLS) and eventually became a NOLS instructor. He moved to Alaska, where he became an outdoors adventure guide, eventually becoming the president of the Alaska Guides Association. Eric got married, and together he and his wife raised three children in Atlanta, all of whom attended Ramah either in New England or at Darom. "Ramah had a wonderful impact on all my kids, but it was nothing like the impact that it had on me, because I came from such a small Jewish community. My kids grew up in Atlanta, where there are many Jewish kids and many Jewish opportunities."

Little did Eric realize, while living in Alaska, that he would later have the opportunity to help realize the dream of creating the same camping experience for thousands of Jewish children in the southeastern United States that was so central to his growth as an outdoor educator and as a Jew. The beginning of his involvement came in 1996, when he received a phone call from Neal Schnall, his old friend from Ramah in the Poconos and Wisconsin. Neal was living in Los Angeles, had been very involved with Camp Ramah in California, and knew the National Ramah Director, Rabbi Shelly Dorph, very well. "He told me about a new venture to create Ramah Darom here in the south, and I knew this had my name written all over it," Eric recalled. Ironically, Eric's father, Sol Singer, had been instrumental in trying to create a Camp Ramah for the South decades earlier. In 1956, as part of a United Synagogue effort, Sol Singer had been involved in conducting a feasibility study to create a Camp Ramah in the region, but it would be decades before this would become a reality.

In 1996 Eric immediately became involved in the efforts to build Ramah Darom, and he recalls a historic meeting in Charlotte, North Carolina, where interested parties from synagogues throughout the South gathered with great enthusiasm for Ramah. Although he describes some political squabbling over potential control of the camp's board, the grassroots enthusiasts from congregations in many southern states wouldn't let the effort be derailed. "The smartest thing the National Ramah Commission did was give us a deadline and a challenge grant," Eric recalls. "They instilled within us the urgency to identify leadership, foster a grassroots movement, and create a structure for local ownership." Eric continued:

> Every project needs a meshuggener and an angel. I guess I became the meshuggener, and Bubba Mitchell became the angel. We also wouldn't have been successful without the incredible efforts of Lynda Walker, our project manager. The three of us working together were the starting point, and then others joined in and helped create Ramah Darom.

After a site was identified, a board was created, and the fund-raising efforts really took off. "By late 1996, we were determined to open this camp in six months for the 1997 summer season, and we had to get everything built in the face of El Niño weather," he recalled. But build it they did, and under the professional leadership of Rabbi Loren Sykes, Camp Ramah Darom opened its inaugural season in 1997. Today it serves over 950 campers and 200 staff members each summer. Additionally, Ramah Darom runs an outstanding retreat program year-round, including a Passover Institute and a conference for Hillel leadership. In recent years, Ramah Darom has pioneered the inspiring Camp Yofi, a family camp program for families with children with autism.

With all the success, Eric hopes that Ramah Darom will grow to even greater heights, particularly with regard to outdoor education and year-round usage.

By all accounts, the first ten years of Ramah Darom have been enormously successful, positively impacting the lives of thousands of young people, giving them the same kinds of experiences that had such a positive impact on Eric during his youth.

> Helping to build this camp is one of the most important experiences of my life. Wherever I go, people express appreciation for this camp, and that is extremely satisfying. How many times do you get a chance to do something like this, to build something that will influence so many people?

As we concluded the interview, we both smiled at the powerful reminiscences and discussed the current efforts underway to build yet another Camp Ramah, this time in the Rocky Mountains of Colorado. Getting to know Eric and his life's story, I can't help but wonder who will emerge as the Eric Singer in Colorado, the meshuggener of the Rockies!

60

BERKSHIRES

RABBI GERALD C. SKOLNIK
The Forest Hills Jewish Center, Forest Hills, New York

Ramah didn't just "change my life" in the colloquial sense. It *really* changed my life in virtually every sense and every way.

My first exposure to Camp Ramah (Berkshires was and is my camp) came in 1971. I had been a very happy camper and staff member at Camp Massad Bet, having grown up in the Orthodox world before it moved so precipitously to the right. As I approached my junior year at Yeshiva University, I was dedicated to the cause of spending my junior year in Israel at the Hebrew University but needed to convince my parents that they could afford it.

My sister, who also had spent years at Massad, had left it for Ramah the year before. She told me about a program that Ramah sponsored in conjunction with the Mercaz Leḥinnuch Yehudi Batefutzot (The Center for Jewish Education in the Diaspora) at the Hebrew University, headed by Dr. Michael Rozenak. If I served as a counselor at Ramah the summers before and after my junior year in Israel and took a few education courses in the Mercaz program, Ramah would pay half my tuition to Hebrew U. (at that time, half my tuition was $500!) and a $300 bonus to my salary when I returned from Israel.

Money was short, and I just wanted to get to Israel. My sister kept telling me what a wonderful place Ramah was so I made the move and signed onto the program.

On my first day at camp, there was a small group session for male counselors only (it was thirty-six years ago!) to discuss davening at camp. The session was led by Dr. Saul Wachs. As if it were yesterday, I can close my eyes and remember the very first words out of his mouth: Who here has ever missed a day of putting on tefillin?

"Oh, my God," I thought to myself. "What is he saying?" In the world that I had grown up in and was still living in, no one—and I mean *no one*—would ever ask that question. It was just assumed that you conformed to the rules and norms of the religious and ritually scrupulous life. No one talked about doubt, or ambivalence, or *keva* and *kavanah,* and the tension between them—not out loud, anyway. I knew he was talking to me. Slowly, inevitably, like a marionette, I felt my hand going up. The first sentence of the first meeting I went to at Ramah hooked me.

The rest is history. All that summer, I developed friendships with Jews the likes of whom I never knew existed—Jews who took their Judaism seriously and struggled with how to integrate it into their lives. They weren't scared to talk about their struggle. Some observed more, some less, but all became my friends. I wound up spending that year in Israel along with many other staff members from Ramah in the Berkshires, and we all returned to camp the following summer, in love with Israel, anxious to spread the feeling, and powerfully bonded to each other.

With us that year in Israel from camp were Rabbi Eliezer Havivi, a future Ramah director, now serving a congregation in Greensboro, North Carolina; Rhonda Kahn, the director of communications for the Women's League for Conservative Judaism; Dr. Barbara Paris, who served as camp doctor at Berkshires for many years; and there were more of us! These people are among my oldest and dearest friends. Many of us, myself included, married men and women with powerful Ramah connections themselves. My wife Robin counts her years as a camper in Palmer in the sixties as among the most important in her life, and she returned with me to work at Berkshires.

Because of Ramah's powerful influence on my life, I couldn't imagine not trying to "spread the magic." When I came to The Forest Hills Jewish Center in 1981, there were two or three Ramah campers from our shul. One of the achievements of my rabbinate that I am most proud of is that for the past few years, ours consistently has been one of the two or three largest feeder congregations to Ramah in the Berkshires. New campers (and staff members, too!) from Forest Hills are discovering Ramah each and every year.

How did Ramah change my life? It's a long and complicated story, but the simple answer is—completely—and very much for the better.

CALIFORNIA

ANDREW I. SPITZER, M.D.
Director, Joint Replacement Program, Cedars-Sinai Orthopaedic Center, Los Angeles, California

My first summer at Camp Ramah in California, *kayitz* 1973, occurred less than a year before my bar mitzvah and barely a year after my parents divorced. I was the only remaining child at home. It was a time of great uncertainty and instability for me, complicated further by the age-related physical, hormonal, and emotional changes raging simultaneously.

Ramah was transformative for me in every way. I was immersed for the first time in the vibrancy of living Judaism, for which I longed throughout the ensuing eleven months. During the following two summers, I was one of a very few two-session (eight-week) campers. I simply could not get enough. Those cherished fifty-seven days at camp were the spiritual nourishment that would sustain me throughout the remainder of the year. After a summer in Israel, I returned for nine years on staff, working my way up the ranks from Mador to *madrich* to music director, until my curriculum in medical school required year-round attendance. After completing my residency and fellowship in orthopedic surgery, I returned as camp physician in 1994. Since then, I have spent one to two months at camp each summer as the chair of our Medical Committee, as the husband of the *mumḥat bishul,* and as the father of four campers. As I now approach my twenty-fifth summer at camp, it is clear that Ramah has provided me the stability, certainty, and purpose that I lacked during that first summer thirty-four years ago.

Ramah has enveloped my life and my family's life. For my wife, too, who jokes that her allegiance to another Southern California Jewish camp was abandoned as part of our prenuptial agreement, Ramah has become a passion. In addition to her work during the last twelve summers in *ḥug bishul,* she recently created a new program, the Legacy/Moreshet Program. By means of this program, eighty bar/bat mitzvah-age Israeli children, who have lost a sibling or parent as a victim of terror or a casualty of war, will be brought to either Ramah in California or the Berkshires this year for a two-week camp experience.

Being a part of the Ramah community has provided great blessings: from lifelong friendships worldwide to perpetual spiritual inspiration and eternal family memories. However, most significant to me is that camp has grounded me with a foundation of Jewish commitment and a recognition that in the seemingly most insignificant gesture or act, lives can be impacted Jewishly forever. Camp taught me that no matter how little time there may be, there is always more time for community involvement, service, and leadership; for volunteerism; for *gemilut ḥasadim*—I learned from camp not to say "I don't have time for that," but rather to say, "I will make time for something so important!"

It is this blessing that has become the most meaningful for me. It is why I return to camp each summer. It is why I am president of my shul, why I go to *minyanim* at *shiv'ah* houses and bar/bat mitzvah celebrations and *beritot,* why I tuck my kids in at night and sometimes even get to wake them up in the morning, and why putting on tefillin is the most peaceful and rewarding moment of my day.

Shehecheyanu, vekiyyemanu, vehiggi'anu lazeman hazeh! Mazal tov to Ramah at 60, and may it continue from strength to strength in its mission of sanctifying time and infusing its campers, staff, and supporters with the love of Judaism, Jewish life, and lifelong commitment to Israel and the Jewish people.

60

WISCONSIN

MAYER STIEBEL
Member, Camp Ramah in Wisconsin Board of Trustees

In 1947 I was a sixteen-year-old in the Machon. My last summer was 1951, when I had the uniquely combined positions of camping and canoeing counselor and third cook. In later years, I was a Ramah Wisconsin vice president and also served on the National Ramah Commission for twenty years.

As we easily drive to Camp Ramah in Wisconsin today, it is difficult to understand how remote and isolated the North Woods, and our camp site, were in 1947. County K, the highway leading from Conover to Buckatabon Road, was gravel; and Buckatabon Road to Bauers' Dam resort and then to camp was merely dirt with ruts wide enough for a vehicle's tires.

Electricity was provided by two old and over-burdened generators; power outages were frequent. The one stove in the dairy kitchen was wood-burning, and the newly built meat kitchen used bottled gas. There was no telephone. One night a week was movie night for the campers, and the movies were brought in by seaplane.

We were only ninety-seven campers in 1947, and there were no new buildings for us to use. But all of us, along with the staff, were able to use the current educational resource center as the *beit am.*

Ramah certainly was the major Jewish influence in my life. The atmosphere and the friends made at camp committed me to a life of Jewish values, education, *tzedakah,* and volunteer work for the Jewish community. This has endured for sixty years and continues to this day.

60

WISCONSIN

RABBI SHELLY SWITKIN (SWITTY)
Community Professor, College of Social Work, The Ohio State University, Columbus, Ohio

In 1947, all Chicago area summer camps began on Monday, June 30, because in those days, the Chicago public schools finished on the last Friday in June. The old Chicago and Northwestern Railway station seemed in utter confusion that morning. Several camp participants, all destined for the Eagle River area, were leaving on the same train. My parents and I pushed through the crowds, anxiously searching for the sign "Camp Ramah." After several minutes, we located the banner and as we approached, we were greeted with a hearty "Shalom." I said my good-byes and at that moment, I began a journey that would not only separate me from my parents for eight weeks, but would become a dominant factor in molding the rest of my life. I had no hint then that June 30, 1947, would become a defining moment in my life.

It all began with a notice from Hebrew school that the Conservative Movement was opening a Hebrew-speaking overnight summer camp in Wisconsin. The announcement made absolutely no impression on me, but I did bring it home, unlike some of my classmates who turned the notices into paper airplanes.

Things then began to happen at a rather hectic pace. My parents became quite excited about the idea of Ramah, an educational camp with Hebrew as the spoken language. They had started me in Hebrew school at the age of seven, in 1944, during the height of World War II, when every day, thousands of Jewish children my age were being murdered by the Nazis. This is a vision that has remained with me all of my life.

I was interviewed at Anshe Emet Synagogue in Chicago, and after replying more or less correctly to a series of questions in Hebrew, I was accepted. My parents were concerned about the tuition—$375—an astronomical figure for a working-class family in 1947. Our synagogue, B'nai Zion in Rogers Park, offered a $100 scholarship, which helped, and my parents put off buying a new car until 1953. I was then officially registered as one of ninety-seven youngsters who could later claim the distinction of being a first camper at the first Ramah.

About that first summer: my counselor was Kass Abelson, a senior in rabbinical school, who was not atypical of the staff that first summer. Many were World War II veterans and in college on the GI Bill. The *edot* were given "creative" names: Edah Aleph, Edah Bet, Edah Gimel. We were, however, one camp; the basic difference was that members of Edah Aleph went to bed a few minutes earlier than Bet or Gimel. We davened together, we ate together, we swam together, and we played together. We knew everyone in camp, and the older campers were our everyday heroes and mentors.

We were asked to memorize Camp Massad's Hebrew dictionary. Hebrew was the language of camp. English was not tolerated and if you wanted to eat, you learned! The site was beautiful, but primitive. Electricity was distributed through a not-always-dependable generator on the camp grounds. A seaplane brought movies weekly, and every light bulb—there was only one in each cabin—had to be shut off while the movie was shown.

Jenson was the first chef, and he was a tuna fish specialist every day for the first week until the kosher meat finally arrived. His helper was known as "Messy Bessy." We survived, and the food actually improved as the summer went on. Two milk machines outside of the *ḥadar ochel* dispensed the richest, best-tasting white and chocolate milk from America's dairy land. No butterfat worries back in 1947! Herman Luttkes, the maintenance man who would work at camp for more than twenty years, was there from the beginning.

There seemed to be a military thread running throughout the camp, or maybe it was Boy Scout style. There was a formal flag-raising ceremony (the old version of "Hatikvah" was sung) and a rigid inspection of the cabin every day except Shabbat. Hospital corners and army surplus blankets were the order of the day! A loudspeaker system (the *ramkol*) played bugle calls for every part of the day, from wake-up to taps, followed by Hebrew messages always beginning with a loud *hakshivu, hakshivu!* Our neighbors around the lake put an end to this tradition with several complaints. They seemed very uneasy about these "strange people who spoke a foreign language and practiced a non-Christian religion."

The list of things to bring to camp included a tennis racquet (the list was copied from Massad), so my uncle and aunt bought me a brand new racquet, which I schlepped up to camp, only to find out like everyone else that there were no tennis courts. Actually, aside from the waterfront, there wasn't much in the way of sports facilities, but we cleared out a pretty decent baseball field and had some great games. Every week we rowed or hiked the three miles to Bauer's Resort where we bought ice cream. Once a summer, there was a trip to Eagle River for those who earned a *resh-mem-heh* by speaking only Hebrew for seven consecutive days for at least three out of six weeks.

Indoor plumbing in each cabin was unknown. Boys and girls, counselors and specialists, all shared two bathrooms, one for males, the other for females. Hot water was unheard of for showers, and toilets were at a premium.

Shabbat eve was special with all of us wearing white. *Tefillot* at the lake were inspirational; the folk dancing after dinner was a time for everyone to participate. Shabbat day was a continuation of Friday night, with services, study, and informal recreation. *Havdalah* was a moving closing ceremony to the twenty-five-hour period that served as the high point of the week.

Tish'ah Be'av was virtually unknown to me before Ramah. I was in awe over the burning of the letters *alef, yud, kaf, hei* on the waterfront and the torches leading to the *beit am*. I recall a camper who was a Holocaust survivor, sitting in sackcloth with ashes on his head and weeping while reciting *Eichah*. Pretty powerful stuff.

It was a fabulous summer for a ten-year-old boy from Chicago. I met incredible people: rabbis who could teach Torah, swimming, and baseball; World War II veterans; and counselors preparing to go to Palestine and fight for the establishment of Eretz Yisra'el. This living laboratory of Judaism hooked me, and I returned as a camper for six consecutive summers, with each summer bringing new challenges and achievements.

The final banquet that first summer was a special moment because Camp Ramah in Wisconsin had survived its birth pangs, and we all vowed to return for the next season. Traditions were created in 1947 that survive to the present day. That evening, professor-to-be Moshe Greenberg spoke his first words of English during the entire eight weeks, as he crooned "Minnie the Moocher."

The next day, I was back in Chicago with my parents, sister, and family, but to this day a part of me always will be at Camp Ramah in Conover, Wisconsin.

CANADA

BILL TAUBENFELD
Ramah Canada parent, New York, New York

[Adapted with the permission of the author from "The Many Levels of Camp Ramah," in *Bulletin of Congregation Habonim* (March 2009): 1–2.]

Growing up, all I wanted to do was play sports in my backyard or at school with friends. So when I was ten years old and my parents told me that I was going to Camp Ramah, two things were on my mind: Would I get my fill of sports, and would I make friends? The answer to these questions was such a resounding "yes" that I ended up spending ten summers at Ramah, seven as a camper and three on staff.

My experiences at Ramah are so much a part of the person that I have become that it is impossible for me to imagine how different my life would be had my parents not made the decision to send me there. The friends that I made during those summers are still my closest friends today at the age of forty-five, and I know that they will be for the rest of my life. At the same time, I can trace so much of my affinity for Jewish traditions and culture to the foundations that were laid during those Ramah summers. A strong, lifetime bond is formed by "Ramahniks."

In addition to the normal experience that a child enjoys at most summer camps, children at Ramah learn about and share their Jewish heritage and culture in a positive way. Under the right circumstances, Jewish camps can instill Jewish values, rituals, and teachings without the feeling that you're being "taught" something, and Ramah has somehow found the perfect formula for achieving this. I played basketball, performed in plays, and hung out with friends but at the same time, I learned Hebrew songs, became comfortable with *tefillah* (prayer) and learned to enjoy and appreciate Shabbat. The informal Jewish education was an organic part of the entire camp atmosphere. The campers in my age group slowly and naturally absorbed these Jewish experiences until they were inside of us, were meaningful to us, and then were part of us. Nothing could have made my father prouder than when I came home from camp knowing the *birkat hamazon* (grace after meals).

I still miss those summers. Fortunately, I now have the opportunity to relive them through my daughter, Hannah. Last year, for the first time, at the age of nine, she went to Camp Ramah and was in the same cabin as the daughters of two of my closest friends, both of whom were in my cabin all those years ago. She had a great summer, made so many new friends, and cannot wait to go back. It made me so happy to see that Ramah is having the same positive effect on Jewish children today as it did on me thirty years ago. When Hannah came home and started reciting the beginning of the *birkat hamazon,* I, like my father, was truly proud and thankful.

60

CALIFORNIA · CANADA

CRAIG TAUBMAN

Musician and composer, Los Angeles, California

It feels like another lifetime since my years at Camp Ramah. Summers spent banging and sometimes even dancing on tabletops to the music. As a songwriter and performer, I strive to recapture those magically simple and awe-inspiring times at camp. When I would dare to go anywhere . . . and try anything, because frankly, I did not know any better.

Ramah was more than a camp experience. It was a life experience.
Ramah was a place where I felt free to explore and experiment.
Ramah was a place where I felt free to challenge old hierarchies.
Ramah was a place where I felt free to challenge my own limitations.
Ramah was a place of firsts.
First kiss.
First song.
First success.
First loss.
First home run.
First ga-ga game.
Ramah was my home.
So, just for a moment, I close my eyes . . .
and wander in wonder.
I close my eyes . . .
and open my heart to the mystery of Ramah.
Before the song is over.

60

NEW ENGLAND

RABBI ANNIE TUCKER

The Jewish Center, Princeton, New Jersey

I can still remember the first time I saw him. The batter stood poised at home plate, his brown hair pulled back in a loose ponytail, and the fringes of his tallit katan *poking out from beneath the tie-dyed fabric of his sweaty Grateful Dead T-shirt.*

I had never before seen anyone wearing tzitzit, *much less anyone this cool. The guy even had an earring!*

The two summers that I spent as Elliot Goldberg's camper profoundly impacted the development of my Jewish identity. The product of an involved yet unobservant family, I had never before been exposed to such institutions as kashruth, daily prayer, and Shabbat, now an integral part of my Camp Ramah routine. I also had never before met Jews like Elliot, the rabbinical student who still went to Phish concerts, whose ability to maintain both a Jewish and a secular identity amazed me. I very much admired Elliot's passion for Judaism and his ability to transmit this passion to others. Even more, however, I was inspired by Elliot's conviction that we, too, were capable of increasing our own level of Jewish commitment.

I wrote the above paragraphs a decade ago as part of my admissions essay for the Rabbinical School at The Jewish Theological Seminary. Although there have been many important influences on my Jewish development, it is hard for me to think of another experience that caused me to grow Jewishly as much as my nine years spent at Camp Ramah in New England.

Summer camp is a magical place where days roll freer, friendships run deeper, and confidence flies higher than in the real world. Many of us know firsthand the tremendous growth that comes from being away from home for the first time, taking risks and embarking on exciting adventures, meeting new friends and role models, and growing into a more rooted sense of self. Many of us also remember the tremendous fun of sleep-away camp—whispered late-night conversations by flashlight, s'mores, scavenger hunts and heated *yom sport* competitions, dances, *etgar* (outdoor adventure programs), and the incredible calm of Shabbat following a week jam-packed with activity. As one of my former bunkmates used to say, "Home is a nice place to be while waiting for camp."

Now a rabbi myself, I have the privilege of visiting our congregation's campers each summer—not at the New England location of my youth but rather at Ramah Poconos, where the same smells of fresh air and shampoo, sounds of Hebrew slang and pop music, tastes of *ḥadar ochel* food, and ice cream from the stand down the road bring me instantly back to the summer joy of my adolescent self.

Home is a nice place to be while waiting for camp, indeed.

BERKSHIRES • CANADA • CONNECTICUT NEW ENGLAND • NYACK • POCONOS

SAUL P. WACHS, PH.D.
Rosalie B. Feinstein Professor of Education and Liturgy and Coordinator, Programs in Jewish Education, Gratz College

I started my twenty-five years at Ramah in the summer of 1951 as a junior counselor at Ramah in the Poconos. My senior counselor was Yochanan Muffs, *z"l.* On the other side of the bunk, the senior counselor was Samuel Schafler, *z"l,* later to become president of Hebrew College. His junior counselor was Joel Kraemer, currently a professor at the University of Chicago. The division heads were people of the quality of Chaim Potok, *z"l,* and Moshe Greenberg. We spoke Hebrew. The model was Camp Massad. Solomon Feffer, *z"l,* was the director.

The internal politics of The Jewish Theological Seminary at that time reflected some ambivalence about Israel and so, along with the American flag, we flew a blue and white flag with the two tablets of stone in place of the Magen David. This so enraged the folks at Massad that some of its staff rented a plane and flew over our camp, dropping leaflets that attacked us as traitors to the Jewish people.

Personally, I was overwhelmed by the combination of traditional observance, commitment to Hebrew language, Jewish study (we studied with Professor Hillel Bavli, *z"l*), and intellectual stimulation. When I returned home, my level of observance was affected.

As the years passed, and I progressed to senior counselor and then *rosh edah,* educational director, and music director, the influence of Louis Newman, *z"l,* became very important in the camp. Character education became a major focus of the program. We were pressed to justify everything that we were doing for and with the campers in educational terms. Sadly, the use of the Hebrew language was weakened beginning in 1964 when the Melton Research Center approach to Bible was introduced at Poconos, and some classes were conducted in English.

Over the years, I also spent summers at Ramah camps in Connecticut, Nyack, Canada, Berkshires, and New England. My late wife Barbara Eidelman Wachs, *z"l,* and my wife Diane Cover also spent several summers at Ramah.

I can honestly say that Ramah changed my life and had a profound influence on my view of education. The models I observed showed me that Jewish education can be a very serious enterprise designed to help people engage in independent thinking about ultimate questions of meaning. Ramah might well be the most successful single contribution of the Conservative Movement to Jewish education.

60

WISCONSIN

PHYLLIS HOFMAN WALDMANN
Member, Camp Ramah in Wisconsin Committee, and
former Administrator and Consultant, National Ramah Commission

I began my career with Ramah when Rabbi Burton Cohen hired me in 1963 to work part-time in the Chicago office of Camp Ramah in Wisconsin. The office was located in the old College of Jewish Studies building at 72 East llth Street. I was Toby Litin's assistant.

The first time I actually went to camp was in the summer of 1965. A few years later, I became the camp business administrator. Part of my job was to meet the administrators from the other Ramah camps. The meetings were held at the National Ramah office in New York, which was then in a brownstone building behind The Jewish Theological Seminary (JTS) on 123rd Street. The building also contained several apartments. Once while we were meeting, we heard screams and what sounded like gun shots. They were gun shots. A domestic argument had erupted in an upper-floor apartment, and someone had been shot. We quickly evacuated the office and continued our meeting at JTS.

In the early 1970s, I assumed the position of the National Ramah business manager. My first task was to move the Ramah office out of its 123rd Street location and into rented space at the Union Theological Seminary at 120th and Broadway. After we settled in, we set up a coffee station, and one of the regulars to join us for coffee was a young history professor named Ismar Schorsch.

As the business manager, I would visit each of the Ramah camps during the summer, some of them more than once. I met hundreds, if not thousands, of campers and staff. No two camps were alike, and yet they were all the same. I knew the routine of each camp and always began my visit with meetings with the business managers and directors, listening to how their summer was going and learning what I could do to help. Of course, they wanted to know how the other camps were doing. In the era before e-mail and the Internet, I was their source!

The saga of opening Ramah Darom is a long one. In the early 1990s, Rabbi Sheldon Dorph, then the director of the National Ramah Commission

(NRC), took it upon himself to work with the committee in Atlanta to make a Ramah in the southern United States a reality. I became one of Shelly's assistants. We attended meetings, went to look at camp sites, and spent hundreds of hours working on the numbers. After the site was purchased and Ramah Darom was ready to open, we were there. The day the campers arrived was like no other day I had ever experienced—but then I wasn't in Conover, Wisconsin, in 1947!

I would not have met all the wonderful people I came to know and love over these past decades—professors-in-residence, directors, business managers, bakers and cooks, bookkeepers, counselors, specialists, *rashei eidot,* and most important—the campers—if I had not accepted that part-time job in Chicago so many years ago. For all my hard work, and at times it was very hard, I have received so much in return. I am so proud of my years with Camp Ramah and so thankful for all the wonderful people who have been part of my life.

60

CALIFORNIA · POCONOS

RABBI STEVEN WERNICK
Executive Vice President and Chief Executive Officer,
United Synagogue for Conservative Judaism

Ramah and United Synagogue Youth (USY) have both played incredibly important roles in shaping my Jewish identity, fostering the development of lifelong friendships, and influencing the core values I cherish as a professional in the Jewish community. I was a camper at Ramah Ojai in the early 1980s and a *rosh edah* in the 1990s. Since arriving in the greater Philadelphia area in 1996 as a congregational rabbi, I have visited or spent part of each summer at Ramah in the Poconos.

My oldest friends to this day are my USY and Ramah friends. And my relationships with many of my closest adult friends were forged at camp. I love the outdoors. I love being away from the phone, cell phone, email, and TV. I love the richness of the Jewish environment. And I love the fact that I am the guy who can teach Talmud and pray enthusiastically wearing tefillin, yet still play basketball with campers and staff alike! That's why my wife Jody (a registered nurse [RN] at camp—more valuable than any rabbi) and I went to camp even before our kids were able to be in a *tzerif.* We wanted to give them the "kibbutz" experience and have it become an integral part of their identities.

My USY and Ramah experiences helped me to grow professionally. My work as a rosh edah at Ramah was probably the best hands-on training I received for my career as a congregational rabbi. I am grateful to Rabbi Ed Feinstein for encouraging me to come to camp in that role. As a rosh edah, one is responsible 24/7 for the physical, spiritual, and educational well-being of a community. I learned how to manage a staff of counselors, motivate a group of campers, resolve conflicts large and small, and work with a team of other dedicated Jewish leaders on the *hanhalah*. The skills and work values I developed at camp remain with me to this day. My USY experiences also played an important role in cultivating my program development and planning skills.

As a congregational rabbi, I have seen firsthand the positive influence of USY and Ramah experiences on the families who send their children to these identity-forming experiences. There is no doubt (as every study shows) that children who attend Jewish summer camps such as Ramah and participate in informal youth groups are more engaged, more educated, and more committed Jews. These kids and their families take on leadership roles, attend *tefillah* more regularly, and support the congregation fully. In this way, I am constantly reminded of the powerful impact that USY and Ramah has had—and continues to have—on the Jewish people.

60

CALIFORNIA

RABBI ROBERT D. WEXLER, PH.D.
President, American Jewish University

As someone who did not grow up spending summers at Camp Ramah in California, it took me a while to understand the deep connection that former campers and staff members feel for this remarkable place. In my generation, we still speak of the "old" Ramah and the "new" one. Of course, at this point, the "new" camp is well over thirty years old. But it was the "old" Ramah that I encountered as a young Hebrew school teacher accompanying his class on a weekend outing. Frankly, I was not too impressed with what I saw at the time. The "old" camp was quite run down, and I was not aware that plans were already in the works to build an entirely new facility.

Soon I was off to New York and three years more of rabbinical school at The Jewish Theological Seminary (JTS), where I learned about the existence of a Ramah movement. I soon came to understand that this confederation of camps was arguably the greatest success of the Conservative Movement and the most powerful and influential camping phenomenon in the country. I started hearing about Ramah venues with exotic names like the Poconos; the Berkshires; Nyack, New York; and Conover, Wisconsin. Many of my fellow JTS students had made the decision to enter rabbinical school or become teachers of Judaica because of experiences at their own Camp Ramah.

When I returned to the University of Judaism (UJ), now the American Jewish University (AJU), in 1977, I became aware of AJU's longstanding connection with Ramah of California. I heard about how the camp came to be founded by the leaders of our university and of the deep emotional connection felt by my colleagues to this special Jewish world in Ojai. During my very first year at UJ, I was sent on a week-long whirlwind tour of four Ramah camps to recruit students for the UJ. With my own eyes, I saw the fabled Ramah camps in the Poconos, in New England, in Canada, and in Wisconsin. These were very lively places with long traditions associated with spending a summer at Camp Ramah.

As our own children grew, they began to spend time at Ramah California whenever I was invited there as a speaker. Our three oldest children all had Ramah experiences of varying types, but it was our youngest, Daniella, who became what I like to call a Ramah "lifer." A Ramah "lifer" is a boy or girl whose entire childhood and connection with Judaism are shaped by Camp Ramah; who considers school just something one does to pass the time between summers at Camp Ramah. With each passing year at Ramah, Daniella's group of Ramah friends grew larger and larger—and so did our telephone bills. But we were thrilled that our daughter was beginning to expand her friendship group to include girls (and the occasional boy) from outside the Los Angeles area. Then came Ramah Seminar in Israel, and the friendship network became truly national in scope.

Since we are in Israel every summer, we saw Daniella a few times while she was on Seminar. We could not have been more impressed by the remarkable planning that goes into this experience. Every activity, every detail of each day, is carefully constructed for maximum impact on the participants. This was, by no means, Daniella's first trip to Israel, but it was certainly the first trip to Israel when "she got it." Thanks to Ramah, she began to comprehend the importance of her connection to the Jewish homeland.

Admittedly, Ramah may not be for everyone. Camp Ramah continues to be serious about its dedication to Jewish ritual, to Jewish culture, and to Jewish education. And precisely for this reason, we may rely on Ramah to continue providing the synagogue community, the Jewish Federations, and a host of other American Jewish organizations with its future leaders and activists. Camp Ramah at sixty remains one of the single most impressive examples of the successful transmission of Jewish values and a commitment to Jewish tradition.

CALIFORNIA NEW ENGLAND · POCONOS

RABBI DAVID WOLPE
Sinai Temple, Los Angeles, California

Camp is a series of snapshots: in the Poconos on the lake, in California on the mountains, at Palmer on the vast green. As a camper I enjoyed Ramah; as a staff member I loved it.

I'm sitting on the porch reading Bertrand Russell, my hero of the moment and the most persuasive atheist I have ever read. Walking by the bunk is Rabbi Michael Brown, who asks what I am reading.

"Bertrand Russell," I answer aggressively, ready for a theological fight.

"David, how old are you?"

"Seventeen," I answer.

"Well, I am glad then that you are reading Bertrand Russell."

I was shocked. "Why?"

"Because," he answered, "I would rather you grow out of him than grow into him."

The prediction came true, and for me that interchange summed up so much of what was wonderful about camp. Beliefs that were open to challenge, friendships leavened with humor and acceptance, the promise—even the certainty—of growth.

Camp memories range from learning Hebrew terms to misbegotten romances to astonishment that campers I knew are now CEOs and parents and rabbis. The magic quality that summer has in one's youth never leaves; everyone who has gone to Ramah, lived there, and learned to love so many things, feels the special glow of foreverness that summer plants in our hearts.

Ramah was instrumental in my Jewish education and in my decision to become a rabbi. Along with so many others, it was at camp as a staff member that I first had the opportunity to turn from a student into a teacher. The campers looked to us as role models, and as a result, we began to become what we were expected to be. Inside ourselves, we found the Jews we spoke about.

"Youth and black hair are fleeting," Ecclesiastes tells us, and so many of us who recall our time at Ramah see it not only as Ramah, but also as a tableau of early life. Its preciousness is that we were lucky enough to spend that early life in a place that was warm, safe, nurturing, and Jewish. *Dayyenu.* For many of us at the beginning of our respective journeys, that was surely enough.

60

BERKSHIRES • NYACK • POCONOS

JONATHAN WOOCHER, PH.D.
Chief Ideas Officer and Director of the Lippman Kanfer Institute, Jewish Education Service of North America, New York, New York

I spent most of my summers during that wonderful decade, the 1960s, at Camp Ramah—or better, Camps Ramah: the Poconos, Nyack, Israel Seminar, back to Poconos for Mador, and then three summers at Ramah in the Berkshires, where I ended my Ramah career as *segan rosh machon.* As for so many others, Ramah was a life-shaping experience for me. Most important, I met my wife there. *Dayyenu.* But all the other clichés were true as well: Ramah sustained me during high school when few of my fellow students shared my interests and concerns. I was fortunate to live in the New York metropolitan area, where I could see my Ramah friends fairly regularly at regional Hebrew high school, Leaders Training Fellowship (LTF), at The Jewish Theological Seminary (JTS), and by hopping the train down to Philly. My Jewish knowledge and skills received a huge boost. And, as I moved from camper to staff member, I had some of my first experiences as a "Jewish educator"—and learned to take that role seriously (thank you, Schwab, Havighurst, et al.).

I left Ramah when I began graduate school and rabbinical school at the Reconstructionist Rabbinical College (why not at JTS is another story), but I've always felt pride in having been part of what I consider to be one of the singular successes of American Jewish education. I display my framed bunk picture from 1961 in my office. And, even though neither of my children really clicked with Ramah, I would recommend it without hesitation to any family that wants to deepen and enrich its Jewish life in manifold ways.

As I look back on my years at Ramah, I do so with more than nostalgia because the longer I have been involved in Jewish education, the more I have come to appreciate what I learned at Ramah about what good Jewish education can and should be. In many ways, just as the people I met at Ramah became a central part of my life, so too the Jewish education that I encountered at Ramah has become a source of inspiration for my professional thinking. As a camper, counselor, and assistant division head, I learned three key lessons that I've carried with me over the course of now nearly forty years of work as an educator.

First, doing is an incredibly powerful way of learning. At Camp Ramah, we had formal classes. Yet, the most important learning took place in the bunks and on the ball fields, celebrating Shabbat, and singing our voices hoarse. Everyone today knows that the power of Jewish camping is due in a large measure to its ability to create a total living environment. Camp is a place brimming with activity. No one can be a spectator at camp. We learn what we live and what we do.

Second, we need to educate the whole person, not just the Jewish part. I remember the late Chaim Potok, my division head one summer, pressing us as we assigned campers to various activity groups to think about what each camper needed in order to develop as an individual and as a member of the camp community. I've come to appreciate his insistence that such decisions were central to our mission and that we not take them lightly. Jewish education is more than mastering texts. It is about all the things that camps teach, the things that make us accomplished, confident, caring, responsible persons.

Third, relationships matter most—relationships with dynamic teachers and with peers. The bottom line is that people are inspired by other people to change and grow. I was privileged to have some great counselors, teachers, and mentors at Ramah—individuals who opened my eyes to understand Jewish tradition, the world, and myself in new, more complex, more challenging ways. They literally helped me grow from a child to an adult.

I have no doubt that my life was changed by my years at Camp Ramah. Ramah is one of the great achievements of successive generations of leaders and of North American Jewry as a whole. May it stay vigorous and continue to grow. *Yom huledet sameaḥ.* Till a hundred and twenty (at least).

CANADA

SHANA ZIONTS

Special Projects Coordinator, National Ramah Commission; master's degree candidate, William Davidson Graduate School of Jewish Education

I am a Pittsburgher, a Brandeisian, and a Ramahnik. As a Pittsburgher, I was privileged to attend a Jewish day school and was an active member of Pittsburgh's vibrant Jewish community. As a Brandeisian, I have been given the opportunity to explore Judaic Studies, both academically and religiously, with insightful teachers. However, it is my identity as a Ramahnik that has given me the foundation for living a Jewish life.

My love for Ramah started when I was ten years old, after spending my first summer at Camp Ramah in Canada. There was something very magical about that place. Maybe it was the friendships that seemed to pick up every summer where they left off the prior year, or the *ruaḥ* that filled the air when 600 Jewish children and teenagers came together for *kabbalat shabbat.* I couldn't put my finger on it, but I knew this place was special.

Now, after spending many summers as a counselor, *rosh edah,* and program director at Camp Ramah in Canada, I can pinpoint what it is that makes Ramah such a special place. It is the fact that it is not, and never has been, "just camp." Rather, it is a Jewish educational institution, one that attempts to instill Jewish values and beliefs in its campers. It is built on the belief that there need not be a *mavdil bein kodesh leḥol,* a separation between the holy and the mundane. Rather, as a paradigm for informal Jewish education, Ramah aims to infuse a bit of *kodesh* into every moment of *ḥol.*

When my counselor sent me a birthday card with a quote from the Talmud on it, that was informal Jewish education. When I spoke to my camper online in transliterated Hebrew, teaching him a new word—that was informal Jewish education. It is happening all the time within the Ramah community, as informal Jewish education fosters a beautiful relationship of Jewish growth in a fun, relaxing environment.

One of my campers, at the age of thirteen, lives by the motto "living ten months waiting for two." This was probably my motto growing up; for ten months I longed to be back at the place that I called home. Now, however, my motto is different. I live ten months inspired by two. The safe, relaxed approach of informal Jewish education gave me the tools to enhance my Jewish lifestyle during the other ten months of the year.

A few summers ago, I was a counselor for the oldest kids in camp, an experience that affirmed my belief that a career in informal Jewish education was the right path for me. Ten days after camp ended, after reading the countless emails from my campers, I wrote in my journal: "I took my love for camp, and turned it into their summer. I want to do this with my life. Taking my love and putting it into something that will become loved. It's the best educational gift." This is what informal Jewish education is all about. I combined my love for Ramah and my love for Judaism and transmitted them to my campers. Two summers later, they returned to camp as counselors, and I was there to watch them transmit their own passions for camp and for Judaism to their campers. It will continue for generations to come, and I intend to continue to be a part of this beautiful tradition. As a result of my Ramah experiences, I am pursuing a master's degree in informal Jewish education at the Davidson Graduate School of Jewish Education of The Jewish Theological Seminary.

I live my life as a product of informal Jewish education. I look forward to passing on these lessons to future generations of Jewish children, in the hope that they, too, will come to understand the beauty of our tradition.

RAMAH CAMPING MOVEMENT

www.campramah.org

OVERNIGHT CAMPS

Camp Ramah in Wisconsin
Conover, WI • Est. 1947
www.ramahwisconsin.com

Camp Ramah in New England
Palmer, MA • Est. 1965
(moved from Connecticut, est. 1953)
www.campramahne.org

Camp Ramah in Canada
Utterson, ON • Est. 1960
www.campramah.com

Camp Ramah Darom
Clayton, GA • Est. 1997
www.ramahdarom.org

Camp Ramah in the Poconos
Lakewood, PA • Est. 1950
www.ramahpoconos.org

Camp Ramah in California
Ojai, CA • Est. 1956
(moved to current site in 1973)
www.ramah.org

Camp Ramah in the Berkshires
Wingdale, NY • Est. 1964
www.ramahberkshires.org

Ramah Outdoor Adventure
Deckers, CO • Est. 2010
www.ramahoutdoors.org

DAY CAMPS

Ramah Day Camp in Nyack
Nyack, NY • Est. 1961 as an overnight camp
(became a day camp in 1966)
www.ramahnyack.org

Ramah Day Camp in Philadelphia
Elkins Park, PA • Est. 1996
www.ramahpoconos.org

Chicagoland Ramah Day Camp
Wheeling, IL • Est. 1999
www.ramahday.com

ISRAEL PROGRAMS

Ramah Programs in Israel
Est. 1962
www.ramah.org.il

FORMER RAMAH OVERNIGHT CAMPS AND PROGRAMS

Camp Ramah in Maine
(operated 1948–49)

American Seminar at Nyack
(operated 1961–71)

Camp Ramah in Connecticut
(operated 1953–64)

Camp Ramah in Glen Spey
(operated 1967–71)

Mador National Counselor Training Program
(operated 1959–80)